China and India in the Age of Globalization

Shalendra D. Sharma
University of San Francisco

CAMBRIDGE UNIVERSITY PRESS
Cambridge, New York, Melbourne, Madrid, Cape Town, Singapore, São Paulo, Delhi

Cambridge University Press
32 Avenue of the Americas, New York, NY 10013-2473, USA

www.cambridge.org
Information on this title: www.cambridge.org/9780521731362

First published 2009

Printed in the United States of America

A catalog record for this publication is available from the British Library.

Library of Congress Cataloging in Publication data

Sharma, Shalendra D., 1958–
China and India in the age of globalization / Shalendra D. Sharma.
    p.   cm.
Includes bibliographical references and index.
ISBN 978-0-521-51571-9 (hardback) – ISBN 978-0-521-73136-2 (pbk.)
1. China – Economic conditions – 1949–   2. China – Economic policy – 1949–
3. Globalization – China.   4. India – Economic conditions – 1947–   5. India –
Economic policy – 1947–   6. Globalization – India.   7. China – Relations –
India.   8. India – Relations – China.   I. Title.
HC427.9.S457   2009
303.48′251 – dc22   2009002792

ISBN   978-0-521-51571-9 hardback
ISBN   978-0-521-73136-2 paperback

CHINA AND INDIA IN THE AGE OF GLOBALIZATION

The rise of China and India is the story of our times. The unprecedented expansion of their economic and power capabilities raises profound questions for scholars and policy makers. What forces propelled these two Asian giants into global pacesetters, and what does their emergence mean for the United States and the world? With intimate detail, Shalendra D. Sharma's *China and India in the Age of Globalization* explores how the interplay of sociohistorical, political, and economic forces has transformed these once poor agrarian societies into economic powerhouses. Yet globalization is hardly a seamless process, because the vagaries and uncertainties of globalization also present risks and challenges. This book examines the challenges both countries face and what each must do to strike the balance between reaping opportunities and mitigating risks. For the United States, assisting a rising China to become a responsible global stakeholder and fostering peace and stability in the volatile subcontinent will be paramount in the coming years.

Shalendra D. Sharma, Ph.D., is professor in the Department of Politics at the University of San Francisco, where he has taught since 1993. He also teaches in the master's program of the Department of Economics. Sharma is the author of multiple books and articles, including *Achieving Economic Development in the Era of Globalization; The Asian Financial Crisis: Meltdown, Reform and Recovery; The Asia-Pacific in the New Millennium;* and *Development and Democracy in India,* which won the *Choice* Outstanding Academic Title Award. Sharma has also served as a consultant to the World Bank and has traveled extensively throughout India and China.

Contents

v

Acknowledgments

This has been a long and at times an all-consuming project spanning many years. Naturally I have incurred enormous debts, both professional and personal, to many colleagues and friends from around the world, debts that are simply too extensive to adequately acknowledge. The extensive bibliography confirms my intellectual debt to a generation of scholars and policy makers. Nonetheless, it is with great pleasure that I extend my appreciation to some of them. The initial writing was done during my sabbatical year at Leiden University in the Netherlands. My time in Leiden was enormously rewarding as I had the good fortune to be around so many distinguished scholars. I am particularly thankful to Rudy Andeweg and Ruud Koole, chairs of the Department of Political Science at Leiden, for creating a collegial and intellectually dynamic environment that facilitated my research and writing. Also at Leiden, I am grateful to Professors Jan Beyers (now at the University of Antwerp), Kees Brants, Oda Crannenburg, Marius de Geus, Jan Erk, Madeleine Hosli, Hans Oversloot, Huib Pellikaan, Richard Sherman, Bal Gopal Shrestha, Maria Spirova, Evangelos Venetis, and Hans Vollaard. The many long conversations over countless pints of good Dutch beer at the "Burcht" stimulated many ideas.

At the University of San Francisco, I thank Jacques Artus, Horacio Camblong, Tony Fels, Hartmut Fischer, Jay Gonzales, Roberta Johnson, Vamsee Juluri, the late Richard Kozicki, Man-Lui Lau, Michael Lehmann, Charles N'Cho, Elliot Neaman, Stanley Nel, John Nelson, Steve Roddy, Rob Toia, John Veitch, Bryan Whaley, Sunny Wong, and Bruce Wydick. Over the years, they have been good friends and wonderful colleagues whose support and good cheer I greatly value. I also want to record my thanks to Deans Michael Bloch and Jennifer Turpin. Special thanks to my outstanding research assistants spanning several semesters – Thomas Curteman, Alyssa V. Ruiz de Esparza, Laura Grace, Jamie Jackson, Bhagman Singh, and Kiran Torani – for their tireless efforts to gather all pertinent material. I gratefully acknowledge Kiran, who helped put together the tables and charts, for her dedication, efficiency, and grace under intense pressure. I would also like to acknowledge Anna Greene, Wilman Stein, Mohammad Sultan, and Crista Yamasaki for their assistance during critical times and for asking probing questions and providing constructive suggestions. For proficient administrative assistance and unwavering support for all things big and small, I thank Cheryl Czekala, Kimberly Garrett, and Spencer Rangitis.

A number of friends and colleagues from around the world have my deepest gratitude for their insightful comments on various themes discussed in the book and for allowing me to air ideas at conferences. These include Professors Robert Scalapino and the late Leo Rose at the University of California – Berkeley, Dr. Andrew Marble at the National Bureau of Asian Research in Seattle, Stephen Johnson from the Union Bank of California, Richard Russack of BNSF (Burlington Northern Santa Fe Railway), Dean and Professor Kalpana Misra at the University of Tulsa, Professors Salim Lakha and Pradeep Taneja at the University of Melbourne (Australia), my good friends Dr. Nadeem Malik and Dr. George Varghese from the University of Melbourne, Mandira Puri and Mr. Harpreet Sawhney in New Delhi, Professor Abdul Matin at Aligarh Muslim University, Professor Ni Shixiong at Fudan University in Shanghai, and Dr. Tak-Wing Ngo at the Sinological Institute at Leiden University. I am also grateful to my good friend Professor Zaheer Baber at the University of Toronto and to former students, Greg Anderson at the University of California – Los Angeles and Martin J. Gilvary. The always good advice I received from Professors Jon S. T. Quah and Stella Quah from the National University of Singapore proved invaluable. Because large portions of the draft manuscript were read by several people, I would like to extend sincere thanks to all for their perceptive critique, suggestions, and encouragement.

Without even the slightest risk of exaggeration, this book would not have been possible without the support and encouragement of Ed Parsons at Cambridge University Press. I will always be indebted to Ed for his interest in this project and for his sound advice and professional guidance. I only hope I have met Ed's high expectations. I would also like to extend my appreciation to Ed's editorial assistant, Jason Przybylski, and Jeanie Lee, editorial assistant to Cambridge's editorial director, Frank Smith. It has been a great pleasure working with both of them. The five anonymous reviewers for Cambridge University Press provided thoughtful, detailed, and trenchant criticisms and suggestions that have significantly improved this book. I have tried to incorporate all their critiques, suggestions, and recommendations in the following pages. However, I take full responsibility for the remaining flaws and omissions. My greatest debt, however, is to my wife Vivian and our son Krishan. They have seen this book's long journey from beginning to end. Despite my frequent travels and many weeks (indeed, months) of absences from home, they never wavered once in their support and let me work on this project. For their unconditional love and support, I humbly dedicate this book to them with gratitude and affection.

San Francisco
November 2008

Acronyms

ACFTA	ASEAN-China Free Trade Area
AMC	asset management companies
ARF	Asian Regional Forum
ASAT	anti-satellite
ASEAN	Association of Southeast Asian Nations
BIS	Bank for International Settlement
BJP	Bharatiya Janata Party
BRIC	Brazil, Russia, India, and China
BSE	Bombay Stock Exchange
CBRC	China Banking Regulatory Commission
CCP	Chinese Communist Party
CDO	collateralized debt obligations
CDPs	Community Development Projects
CENTO	Central Treaty Organization
CIC	China Investment Corporation
CNOOC	Chinese National Offshore Oil Company
CNPC	Chinese National Petroleum Company
CPC	Central Party Committee
CPI-M	Communist Party of India-Marxist
CSRC	China Securities Regulatory Commission
CTBT	Comprehensive Test Ban Treaty
EPZ	export processing zone
ETDZ	economic and technological zone
EU	European Union
FDI	foreign direct investment
FERA	Foreign Exchange Regulation Act
FII	foreign institutional investors
FIPB	Foreign Investment Promotion Board
FRBMA	Fiscal Responsibility and Budget Management Act
FTA	free trade area

FTZ	free trade zone
GATS	General Agreement on Trade in Services
GATT	General Agreement on Tariffs and Trade
GDP	gross domestic product
HYV	high-yielding varieties
IAEA	International Atomic Energy Agency
IAS	Indian Administrative Services
ICICI	Industrial Credit and Investment Corporation of India
IIT	Indian Institutes of Technology
IMF	International Monetary Fund
IOGC	India's Oil and Gas Company
ISI	import-substitution industrialization
ISRO	Indian Space Research Organization
IT	information technology
LAC	Line of Actual Control
LML	Land Management Law
LOC	Line of Control
MFN	most favored nation
MOF	Ministry of Finance
MRTP	Monopolies Restrictive Trade Practices Act
MTCR	Missile Technology Control Regime
NAM	Non-Alignment Movement
NATO	North Atlantic Treaty Organization
NDA	National Democratic Alliance
NEP	New Economic Policy
NGO	nongovernmental organization
NMD	National Missile Defense
NPC	National People's Congress
NPL	nonperforming loan
NPT	Nuclear Non-Proliferation Treaty
NRI	nonresident Indian
NSE	National Stock Exchange of India
NSG	Nuclear Suppliers Group
NSS	National Sample Survey
OECD	Organisation for Economic Co-operation and Development
ONGC	Oil and Natural Gas Corporation
OPEC	Organization of the Petroleum Exporting Counties
PAP	People's Action Party
PBC	People's Bank of China
PDS	public distribution system
PLA	People's Liberation Army
PRC	People's Republic of China
QDII	qualified domestic institutional investors

QFII	qualified foreign institutional investors
R&D	research & development
RBI	Reserve Bank of India
RLCL	Rural Land Contract Law
RMB	renminbi
SAARC	South Asian Association of Regional Cooperation
SAR	special autonomous region
SBI	State Bank of India
SCO	Shanghai Cooperation Organization
SEATO	Southeast Asia Treaty Organization
SEBI	Securities and Exchanges Board of India
SEZ	special economic zone
SMEs	small and medium-sized enterprises
SOE	state-owned enterprise
STP	software technology parks
TRIPS	Trade-Related Aspects of Intellectual Property Rights
TVE	Township and Village Enterprise
UN	United Nations
UPA	United Progressive Alliance
USTR	United States Trade Representative
VAT	value-added tax
WMD	weapons of mass destruction
WTO	World Trade Organization

Map 1. Map of China. *Source:* http://depts.washington.edu/chinaciv/geo/land.htm.

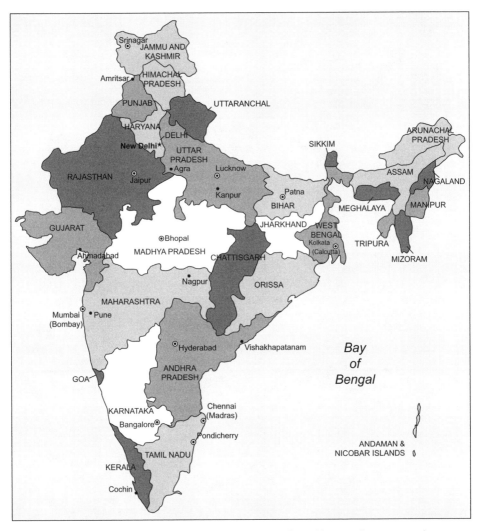

Map 2. Map of India. *Source:* Map Resources. Adapted by CRs (August 2007).

Introduction

China and India in the Age of Globalization

The two Asian giants, the People's Republic of China (PRC) and the Republic of India, are home to some 2.3 billion people or two-fifths of humanity and are currently the world's fastest-growing economies. Over the past three decades, China's move from an autarkic, centrally planned economy toward a socialist market economy underpinned by global economic integration has generated robust economic growth. With a gross domestic product (GDP) growth rate averaging 9.5 percent per year between 1980 and 2004 and 9 percent between 2005 and mid-2007, and endowed with a GDP of US$1.65 trillion, China is now the fourth largest economy in the world in terms of GDP at the current exchange rate. However, when adjustments are made for the differences in domestic purchasing power parity (PPP) of national currencies, China is the world's second largest economy.[1] If China maintains its current level of growth, it could overtake the U.S. economy as early as 2025 (Maddison 1998; Organisation for Economic Co-operation and Development 2005; World Bank

---

[1] GDP is the value of all final goods and services produced in the economy during the course of a year. China now ranks fourth behind the United States, Japan, and Germany. However, in terms of GDP measured by PPP (a metric constructed to permit international comparisons across countries because it adjusts for the relatively low price of services in developing countries), the World Bank ranks China as the world's second largest economy – behind only the United States. The simplest and most popular PPP conversion is *The Economist*'s "Big Mac Index," which compares currencies on the basis of the relative prices for a McDonald's Big Mac in different nations. That is, in PPP terms, China's economy (at almost US$9 trillion) was already much larger than that of Japan (US$4 trillion) and not so far behind the United States (more than US$12 trillion). By the same measure, India's economy (US$3.6 trillion) is almost as big as Japan's. However, it is important to note that there is some debate regarding the accuracy of China's official statistics. According to Rawski (2001), official data greatly exaggerate China's economic performance. Similarly, Young (2000, 2003) argues that Chinese statistics overstate growth. After making adjustments in the GDP, investment, and labor data, he finds a much less striking growth rate in total factor productivity. Others have noted that that the pre- and post-reform differences in growth are more modest when the disastrous Great Leap Forward and Cultural Revolution periods are excluded from the pre-reform period. However, Lardy (2002) claims that the data are basically correct. For a recent overview, see Wu (2007).

Table I.1. *Growth rates in GDP:*
1980–2007 (percent per year)

Period	China	India
1980–92	8.4	5.8
1992–2004	7.1	6.7
1980–2004	7.6	6.3
2003–7	9.5	8.6
2006–7	10.0	9.4

Source: World Bank Development Indicators (various years).

2006). Although the Communist Party still rules China with an iron hand, the regimented Orwellian landscape of austere monotony with men and women in their drab Mao jackets cycling silently by have long melted into obscurity. The streets of China's cities and towns are now congested with BMWs and Mercedes and bustling with people dressed in a kaleidoscope of the latest designer clothing. Even the once "sacred" public spaces reserved for ubiquitous posters displaying defiant socialist iconography have disappeared. As if in a perverse act of desecration, they now avariciously advertise consumer products such as Internet service, cell phones, credit cards, exotic vacations, automobiles, and designer couture, among other symbols of modern affluence.

Although not as spectacular as China's, India's post-1991 economic reforms and global integration have helped the economy grow at more than 6 percent per year (on average) since 1992. This has laid to rest the ghost of the anemic "Hindu rate of growth" of 3.5 percent under which India seemed perennially trapped from the early 1950s to the mid-1980s. India's average annual growth in GDP reached 7.3 percent in 2003 and fluctuated between 8.5 to 9 percent since 2004, placing it among the world's fastest-growing economies. If, as expected, India maintains this growth momentum over the next several years, it will propel the country's US$800 billion economy (the world's tenth largest and third largest in Asia in 2006) into the ranks of the world's five largest economies (Tables I.1, I.2, and Figure I.1)

In both countries, such sustained levels of economic growth have translated into significant increases in per capita GDP. For India, the 1978 per capita GDP of US$1,255 (in PPP terms) increased to US$2,732 in 2003 and US$3,452 in 2005; in China, it skyrocketed from US$1,071 in 1978 to US$4,726 in 2003 and US$6,757 in 2005 (World Bank 2007). The experience of both countries confirms that the most powerful force for the reduction of poverty and improvements in living standards is sustained economic growth. The proportion of Indians living in "extreme poverty" (on $1 a day or less) has fallen from 40 percent in 1990 to about 25 percent in 2007, although the overall population has increased. This means that about 100 million people have been lifted out of extreme poverty. In China, poverty reduction has been simply unprecedented. On the eve of the

Table I.2. *World's ten largest economies: share of world GDP valued at purchasing power parities (in percent)*

	1975	1980	1990	2000	2005
United States	21.8	21.5	21.4	21.2	20.3
China	2.8	3.1	5.5	11.0	14.1
Japan	8.2	8.3	8.8	7.4	6.5
India	3.6	3.4	4.4	5.4	6.3
Germany	5.8	5.6	5.0	4.6	4.0
United Kingdom	4.4	4.1	3.8	3.5	3.2
France	4.2	4.0	3.8	3.4	3.0
Italy	4.0	4.1	3.7	3.2	2.7
Brazil	3.0	3.5	2.9	2.8	2.7
Russian Federation	–	–	4.6	2.3	2.6

Source: Organisation for Economic Co-operation and Development (2007, 28).

reforms, the incidence of poverty in China was among the highest in the world. However, between 1981 and 2001, the proportion of people living in extreme poverty fell from 53 percent to just 8 percent. This means that across China, there were more than 400 million fewer people living in extreme poverty in 2001 than there were twenty years earlier (Gulati and Fan 2007). Few countries have grown so fast over such a prolonged period of time or reduced poverty so sharply (Table I.3).

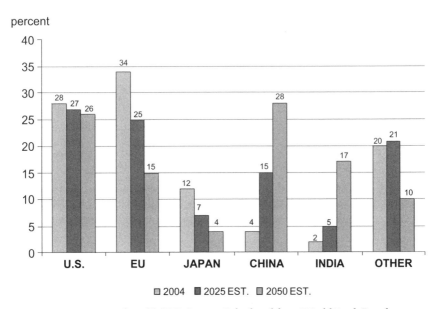

Figure I.1. Percentage of world GDP. *Source:* Calculated from World Bank Development Indicators (various years).

Table I.3. *Basic profiles of the People's Republic of China and India*

		China	India
1.	Annual average GDP growth (%, 1980–2005)	9.6	5.9
2.	Per capita GDP (at constant 2000 US$, 2005)	1,445	586
3.	Per capita GDP (at current US$, 2005)	1,709	705
4.	Share of world GDP at market prices (%, 2005)	5.2	1.8
5.	Share of world trade (%, 2005)	6.8	1.1
6.	International reserves (billion US$, 2006)	1,066	177
7.	Cumulative inward FDI flow (billion US$, 1986–2005)	629	53
8.	Proportion of population below $1 (PPP) per day (%, 2003)	13.4	30.7
9.	Literacy rate, 15–24 years old (%, 2004)	98.9	76.4
10.	Gross primary enrollment ratio (%, 2004)	117.6	116.2
11.	Gross secondary enrollment ratio (%, 2004)	72.5	53.5
12.	Infant mortality rate under age 5 (per 1,000 live births, 2003)	31.0	85.2
13.	Composition of GDP (2005)		
	Agriculture (as % of GDP)	13.1	18.6
	Manufacturing (as % of GDP)	46.2	16.1
	Services (as % of GDP)	40.7	53.8
14.	Fixed line/mobile phone subscriptions per 100 population (2004)	49.7	8.4
15.	Internet users per 100 population (2004)	7.2	3.2

FDI = foreign direct investment; PPP = purchasing power parity.
Sources: Kuroda (2007) and World Bank Development Indicators (various years).

The extraordinary economic transformation of these two Asian giants has captured the imagination of our times, making both countries veritable poster children for globalization. Indeed, the numerous unabashedly celebratory accounts of the symbiotic link between globalization and China and India's economic renaissance that proliferate in the popular media, not to mention the duller renditions in official and scholarly tomes, have made this claim so commonplace that it is hardly contested. The message is powerfully simple and also suggestive: the universalizing impulse of globalization and its inexorable ability to "lift all boats" finally freed China and India – both of which were, not long ago, pejoratively dismissed as either chronic basket cases doomed forever to depend on the generosity of others or as the "sick men of Asia," trapped in an extravagantly wasteful and coercive Oriental despotism of their own making. The implications are also enticingly explicit: current underperformers can learn valuable lessons from these two successful exemplars on how to navigate their way to prosperity in an increasingly enmeshed, integrated, and interconnected world.

No doubt, globalization has been and continues to be the singular powerful engine behind China's and India's spectacular economic rise. The numbers portray a compelling picture. The relative weights of China and India in the global economy have increased substantially. In 1980, China represented only 1 percent of world GDP, and India constituted a mere 0.9 percent. In 2005, these weights increased to 5.2 percent and 1.8 percent, respectively. In the same period, China's share of global trade rose from 0.9 percent to 6.8 percent and India's from 0.6 percent to 1.1 percent. Equally impressive, between 1980 and 2006, China's foreign reserves grew from US$2.5 billion to US$1,066 billion (or just over 1 trillion dollars) and India's from US$6.9 billion to US$177 billion over the same period, and to over US$300 billion in May 2008. China is now the world's leading creditor nation (replacing Japan in 2003) while the United States is the world's largest debtor. In addition, China is the largest foreign holder of U.S. government debt (mostly Treasuries) passing Japan in September 2008. This had made China, in effect, the U.S. government's largest foreign creditor.

Although we know the forces that propelled both countries to embrace globalization in the first place, what is not well understood are their particular approaches or strategies to globalization or how each country has, and is, integrating into the global economy. Just as puzzling, what explains the two countries' successful integration (or at least their ability to derive tangible benefits) from a highly competitive global economy, especially when many other better-placed candidates have not done as well or have faltered? What about the risks and challenges posed by global economic integration and what each country must do to strike the proper balance between the opportunities and the vagaries and uncertainties of globalization. This book fills these gaps by capturing the immutable process of change spanning across time and space, intimately explaining and documenting how the complex interplay of social, political, and economic forces (both global and domestic), including initial conditions and factor endowments, have sometimes worked in tandem to transform these once economically backward societies into global pacesetters. The following pages show a keen appreciation of how both countries, despite their markedly different political inheritances, have successfully ridden the globalization wave. However, contrary to the conventional view, this book also highlights that in both countries, at different times, the power and sway of globalization has ebbed and flowed, sometimes rather unpredictably, making the claim of the seamless link between globalization and each country's miraculous economic transformation far more ambiguous, complex, and multifaceted. Moreover, the following pages discuss both the palpable and the more ostentatious contradictions exemplified by globalization and the various attempts to mitigate its unpredictable effects.

In a rather profound sense, this book evokes memories of another era when scholars and policy makers found comparing China and India irresistible, albeit their reasons and agendas were often different than those of today. More than sixty years ago, the merits and pitfalls of socialism, authoritarianism, democracy, and capitalism were passionately debated when these two Asian behemoths, having overthrown centuries of colonial rule and faced with similarly massive problems of economic backwardness, poverty, illiteracy, and human misery, boldly embarked on diametrically opposed developmental paths for human emancipation. Although in the shrill partisan atmosphere of the 1960s and 1970s, many observers – in particular, the metropolitan left – hastily declared the erstwhile "Chinese model" the winner, the passage of time has revealed a more nuanced reality. With the wisdom of hindsight and, of course, as more evidence became available regarding the callousness and grisly excesses of the Maoist era, there has been grudging recognition that India, the venerable and inchoate democracy, had not done that bad after all, and in some ways may have surpassed its more celebrated northern neighbor.

Today, the stakes are different, but the questions still have a striking resonance with the past and are just as fiercely debated. Observers once again are attempting to come to terms with the sheer scale of change unfolding in both countries and are asking a host of pointed questions, including which country's developmental path is more sustainable and why? Specifically, can the late-starter India overtake its giant northern neighbor? Will India's trajectory prove more enduring, given that its political order respects individual rights and representation in an open market economy based on private property rights? Is the sovereign authority (the state) in both countries up to the task of meeting its instrumental and moral obligations, guiding economic development in a productive and equitable manner, providing security to its citizens, negotiating and accommodating their proliferating expectations, and preserving the nation's far-flung territorial boundaries?

What about each country's towering – indeed, audacious – global ambitions? Will these complement or collide with the status quo? What does the rise of China and India mean for the United States, for the global economy, and for international security and stability? Finally, what lessons do each country's experience and transformation hold for the other, as well as for other developing and transitional economies? The following pages elucidate these deceptively simple, yet profoundly important, questions.

This book is thematically divided into eight chapters. Chapter 1 synthesizes the core ideas, policies, and actors, as well as the interplay of domestic and external events, that influenced and shaped the political economy of pre-reform India (1947–91) and China (1949–78). Specifically, Chapter 1 illustrates both the euphoria and trauma of nation-building during these momentous years and how it profoundly determined the developmental paths and outcomes in each country. The chapter underscores that each country's developmental outcomes were rooted not simply in the differences in their political systems or the decisions made by powerful leaders but were also the result of a zealously state-guided, inward-looking strategy of import-substitution industrialization (ISI) that was not just incidental but an integral part of each country's developmental strategy. Thus, elite politics combined with the pathologies of inward statism is at the heart of understanding both China's and India's miserably poor developmental legacies during the pre-reform period. In the end, it was also the failure – indeed, the rupture – of the eerily similar state-guided or commandist economic models and the sobering realization that statism and its wasteful extravagance had run its course that ultimately convinced the political elites in both countries that economic globalization and the quotidian discipline imposed by market utilitarianism were the wave of the future.

Chapter 2 provides a comparative review of China's and India's approaches to global economic integration – or the "transition to the socialist market economy," as it is officially referred to in China, and more modest "economic liberalization" in India. China's opening to the world, which began in earnest in 1978, has gone through a number of distinct, if not synchronized, phases. Each has been characterized by government policies allowing market forces greater influence over domestic economic activity and deeper global integration through the adoption of particular sets of "open-door" stratagems and policies. If China deftly adapted to the changing global circumstances and seized opportunities as they arose, India's liberalization program or "reforms" were literally forced on the country's political elites by a quickly hemorrhaging economy. Reform was hastily (and hesitatingly) introduced in early 1991. However, after the initial burst, neoliberal or pro-market policies have followed a tortuously meandering path, often losing a sense of direction and urgency – a problem usually attributed to the contingencies of India's democratic politics rather than economic prudence.

Chapter 2 chronicles these shifting priorities through a comprehensive review of the various policies and programs that each country has instituted to integrate itself into the global economy. It explores the politics behind the policy making and how this has influenced and determined the nature, substance, and depth of the various pro-market policies, as well as how policies and programs have evolved and revised to meet the changing domestic and international political and economic circumstances. In addition, the chapter sheds insight on that perennial political-economy puzzle: why, in both countries but particularly China, was a certain approach to global economic integration – namely, "gradualism" – privileged over "shock therapy?"[2] Why, unlike the former USSR and the Soviet Eastern bloc, did market reforms and integration in China not result in economic and political implosion but in political stability and unprecedented levels of economic growth? Equally puzzling, what explains the Indian state's ability to abandon its long commitment to a statist and inward-oriented model for an unprecedented strategy of global economic integration? This despite the fact that a large body of scholarship has long claimed that democratic regimes (especially India's particularly "weak

---

[2] "Shock therapy" refers to implementing bold and decisive market-friendly policies in the expectation that only such aggressive measures can destroy the old command system and replace it with a market economy. "Gradualism" refers to a slow and methodical approach to the implementation of market-friendly policies.

state") lack the requisite capacity and autonomy to make dramatic policy shifts or implement market-friendly public policies, given their potentially negative impact on broad sectors of society?

Chapter 3 assesses the impact, outcomes, and implications of globalization on China's economy, polity, and society. Chapter 4 examines these same issues with reference to India, including why this contemporary era of globalization is qualitatively different from earlier ones and why it has proved to be particularly conducive to India's rise. Drawing on a wide array of data sources (official and academic, as well as from international agencies such as the World Bank and the International Monetary Fund (IMF), Chapters 3 and 4 document and critically appraise the complex and unequivocal patterns of change in each country's macroeconomic structures – agriculture, industry, banking, capital markets, and financial systems, including trade, business, and commerce. Special emphasis is given to explaining China's rise as the world's leading manufacturing hub and India's rise as a premier information-technology service center and outsourcing destination, and the implications of these issues for domestic and global political economies. The discussion underscores that global economic integration is not a linear and seamless process but brings with it new and unintended vulnerabilities and dangers. In both countries, although globalization has served as a catalyst to rapid economic growth, greater exposure to global markets has also made each economy more vulnerable to external market forces, in addition to creating numerous distortions and imbalances, with winners and losers. Both chapters highlight these glaring contradictions and their potential socioeconomic and political implications, as well as assess the efficacy of official policies designed to mitigate the potentially negative, if not malignant, effects of economic globalization – especially unprecedented prosperity amid endemic inequalities. Some of the core political-economic issues addressed in the chapters include how global economic integration has impinged on the ubiquitous powers of the central and subnational (state-level and local) governments and the implications this has for governance, economic growth, and redistribution. Further, why has sustained economic growth in a representative democratic polity like India been far less successful in alleviating socioeconomic inequalities than it has in authoritarian China? What particular challenges do each face in devising and implementing the more exacting "second-generation" reform measures?

Economic linkages and interdependence between China and India have increased exponentially over the past decade, underpinned by expanding investment, commercial, and trade networks. Despite unresolved border disputes and mutual suspicion and animosity rooted in China's seemingly unconditional support of Pakistan, few dispute that Sino-Indian relations have undergone a qualitative transformation since the late 1980s. Chapter 5 traces the evolution of Sino-Indian relations from the heady nostalgic years of the 1950s, characterized by the fortuitous slogan *Chini-Hindi bhai bhai* ("China and India are brothers"); the 1962 border war and India's humiliating defeat; the antagonism and hostility during much of the Cold War; and the gradual "thawing" of hostilities following Indian Prime Minister Rajiv Gandhi's historic visit to China in 1988, Chinese Primer Wen Jinbao's 2005 visit to New Delhi, and the signing of the landmark "strategic and cooperative partnership" between the two countries. Will this improvement in Sino-Indo relations – in particular, the growing economic convergence – further solidify their relations in other areas as well?[3] Chapter 5 highlights that although relations between the two countries will most likely continue to improve, with both cautiously practicing strategies of "flexibility and pragmatism" by deliberately downplaying issues that the other finds objectionable, the current Sino-Indian entente nevertheless remains delicate and fragile and could quickly deteriorate. After all, economic convergence does not necessarily mean cooperation, and it can lead to zero-sum competition and rivalry. Although both countries will try to avoid confrontations and recriminations, given their long history of bitter rivalry, jaundiced perceptions, and mutual suspicion, it seems that China and India are destined to remain strategic competitors. In other words, not fully at ease with each other, they will undoubtedly keep a wary eye on one another as they simultaneously try to improve bilateral relations and jockey for influence in the region and beyond.

A seismic shift in the balance of global economic and political power is currently underway as the rise of China and India has increased not only their regional but also their global influence and leverage. For India, its tireless efforts to overcome its long history of thwarted ambitions and elevate its global power and prestige now seems tantalizingly within reach as it is rapidly acquiring the power capabilities to influence developments both in the South Asian region and throughout the globe. Chapter 6 explores the evolving relationship between the United States, the world's most powerful democracy, and India, the world's largest democracy. It illustrates how, from a rather difficult beginning – indeed, estrangement – during much of the Cold War, Indo-American relations have greatly improved, gravitating somewhat serendipitously toward a more "productive engagement." Indeed, this shift has led some to suggest the flowering of a "beautiful friendship" between the two democracies. Chapter 6 confirms the growing convergence, if not broad congruence, of interests between India and the United States on a number of economic and security matters. Most prominent among these are joint commitment to a global strategic partnership (symbolized by the unprecedented agreement on civilian nuclear cooperation), democracy promotion, and counterterrorism. Relations

---

[3] The view that increased trade can lead to a reduction in conflict goes back to Immanuel Kant. The modern variant, often referred to as "commercial liberalism," suggests that increased economic linkage benefits all parties. It makes states increasingly reluctant to antagonize each other.

between the two countries will most likely expand in the coming years, given both their common interests and their common values.

Nevertheless, Indo-U.S. relations will not be without friction. If U.S. support of India is based on an expectation of automatic reciprocity, this may not always be forthcoming (at least not immediately) because democratic India has to balance other interests and domestic political constraints. Moreover, differences in trade and outsourcing issues, including demands that India further liberalize its trade regime, open up its retail and banking sectors, and make compromises on the Doha Round trade negotiations, not to mention how India resolves the debilitating conflict in Kashmir and joins the Nuclear Non-Proliferation Treaty (NPT) and the Comprehensive Test Ban Treaty (CTBT) will prove to be difficult issues – hardly amenable to quick fixes. Although it may seem axiomatic that Indo-U.S. relations based on a commonality of values and concerns about a rising China provide strong strategic motivations for collaboration, in reality, this may not always be the case.

Today, China's global power and influence rivals only the lone superpower, the United States. China's ambitious military modernization has transformed the country into a formidable power, as well as a genuine strategic competitor to the United States. Yet at the same time, the United States and China are major trading partners with expanding economic ties and interdependence. However, given the profound differences in their political systems, values, and national interests, palpable concerns (and considerable ambiguity) remain on both sides regarding the other's intentions. Beijing fears that the United States may try to preemptively subordinate China's rise; for the United States, there is concern about what future trajectory an ascendant China may choose. Chapter 7 examines the following intriguing questions: what does the rise of China mean for the United States – and indeed, the global community? In particular, will the strategic interests of China be compatible with those of the United States? Can China execute a "peaceful rise" to great-power status and become a "responsible global stakeholder," working constructively with the United States and other nations to accomplish common goals? Or will China, like previous rising hegemons, try to use its growing power and influence to defiantly reorder the rules and institutions of the international system in accordance with its own perceived interests? How best can the United States encourage and engage a rising China to act in a way consistent with U.S. (indeed, Western) interests and international norms?

Drawing on a large body of scholarship and empirical cases, Chapter 7 illustrates that, given the motivations and calculations that drive China's foreign policies, American and Chinese interests will both converge and diverge, making it hard to predict with any degree of certainty China's future behavior or the strategic choices it may make. Nevertheless, China and the United States will not be strategic partners. Rather, they will be strategic competitors engaged in a traditional great-power rivalry for security and influence. Yet at the same time, a conflict-ridden and wrenching global power transition is not inevitable. Constructive and acquiescent Sino-American relations are critical to maintain global economic prosperity and stability. Therefore, it is in the interest of the United States and the international community to facilitate (or at least not obstruct) China's "peaceful rise" and orderly integration in the global order. However, this does not mean that the United States should turn a blind eye to the economic, political, and security challenges that China poses. Rather, it should concentrate on creating and expanding opportunities to build on common interests in the region, including dealing with global challenges such as climate change and terrorism.

Chapter 8 examines the daunting political, economic, and human security (environmental, energy and food supplies, demographic) challenges China and India face and how these challenges may be mitigated. In regard to political change, in the case of China, various scenarios have been proffered. These range from the optimistic, in which China executes a "peaceful rise" to great-power status and transforms into a benevolent and responsible stakeholder and a stable and peaceful constitutional democracy, to the most worst-case scenario, in which the country's "governance deficit" eventually results in disintegration and chaos with the retrenchment of totalitarian dictatorship. Others see a mixed future in which a free and vibrant capitalist market economy operates alongside a closed and secretive Leninist political system. Although China's future trajectory remains uncertain, what is unambiguous, at least to date, is that China's transition toward a market economy and global integration has been accompanied by only limited political reforms. The chapter explores this puzzle: why, contrary to expectations, has China's impressive growth in gross national product (GNP), the rise of its prosperous middle-class, and the opening to the world failed to bring about greater political pluralism and democratization? This does not mean that popular discontent will simply dissipate or that the opaque structures of authoritarianism won't be tested in the coming years. It remains to be seen whether the Chinese state has both the tenacity and the flexibility to manage effectively the profound political and socioeconomic change it is experiencing.

In the case of India, although constitutional democracy is now deeply entrenched, providing "good governance" as well as mitigating the "existential politics" of extremism and exclusivity will remain a continuing challenge. Yet, what explains the broad consensus that these forces will not be strong enough to derail the country's hard-won constitutional practices based on democracy and political pluralism or fundamentally stop its trajectory of economic reform and global integration? Nevertheless, there is also consensus that India must improve the quality of its governance – that is, make its democracy more accountable and responsive to the needs of the majority of its citizens. This is critical to accommodate the wishes of a diverse citizenry and promote economic development that is both sustainable and more equitable. It is argued in Chapter 8 that although India has the requisite political-institutional capital to make these important adaptations, what happens beyond its immediate external environment remains the wildcard. In particular, the continuing militarization and nuclearization of the subcontinent poses a grave threat to peace and stability. Although some maintain that "existential deterrence" based on nuclear weapons will cause caution and inhibit escalation to a full-scale nuclear war, such optimism and restraint are by no means assured. Miscalculation with catastrophic consequences is a real possibility given Pakistan's weak command-and-control arrangements or the possibility of capture of Pakistan's nuclear assets by extremist groups.

In the distant past, both China and India were civilization epicenters. For more than two millennia, their tutelage and influence shaped the destiny of the Asian region and beyond. Yet with the exception of a few fleeting historical interludes, neither were able to translate their enormous socioeconomic, political, and cultural depth into power and greatness – at least into a durable "hard" or instrumental power. As such, they remained, in Karl Wittfogel's evocative phrase, "despotic states" – vulnerable from both within and without. However, the overpowering and irresistible impulses of contemporary globalization is allowing the world's two oldest civilizations to shake off centuries of inertia and the burdens of history and claim their "rightful" place as leaders among the community of nations. The following pages chronicle this remarkable odyssey: how each arrived at this point, the challenges they face in realizing their ambitions, and what their respective rises mean for the world.

1

Prelude to Globalization: China (1949–1978) and India (1947–1991)

When India gained independence in 1947 following more than two centuries of British colonial rule and the Chinese Communist Party took control of the Chinese mainland in 1949 after a protracted civil war, both were among the poorest nations on earth. In 1951, some 85 percent of China's population out of an estimated 540 million was classified as rural, and in India, more than 90 percent of the total population of approximately 360 million lived in the countryside. Moreover, both countries had roughly the same level of GNP per capita income ($50 for China and $60 for India in 1952 U.S. dollars) and had experienced similar slow and stagnant economic growth rates in the previous half century.[1] Basic standard-of-living indicators such as life expectancy (only thirty-two years in India and forty years for China), infant mortality rates, nutritional and consumption patterns, and access to education, health care, and social services were also extremely poor to nonexistent. In such impoverished environments, infectious diseases such as malaria, cholera, smallpox, leprosy, and dysentery were rampant, and frequent epidemics and famine took their deadly toll on weak and vulnerable populations (Maddison 2003; Sachs 2005, chaps. 8–9; Sen 1982; World Bank 1983). In sum, both nations faced formidable challenges to economic development and nation-building. The following sections discuss the paths each country followed to achieve its developmental goals and assesses the outcomes, legacies, and political and socioeconomic implications.

India: Building a Democratic Polity

Although centuries of colonial domination and resistance to it profoundly shaped subsequent political developments in both China and India, the

---

[1] According to Maddison (2003), in 1950, the per capita GDP of China and India (measured in 1990 purchasing power parity) was US$439 and US$619, respectively. For a good overview, see also Naughton (2007, 50), Myers (1980), and Rothermund (1988).

political systems that eventually emerged in each country could not be more different. On Independence Day (15 August 1947), the Indian tricolor was proudly hoisted by Prime Minister Jawaharlal Nehru on top of the historic Red Fort in New Delhi. It marked a triumphant culmination of more than half a century of nationalist struggle against colonial rule. In his address to the nation that evening, Nehru eloquently noted that "the service of India means the service of the millions who suffer . . . it means the ending of poverty, ignorance and disease and inequality of opportunity" by "building the noble mansion of free India where all her children may dwell and prosper" (Nehru 1958). However, Nehru, a cosmopolitan, London-trained barrister remained unequivocal on one core principle: the "noble mansion" could best be built under the legitimacy of a representative democratic polity – or, as Nehru often claimed, a system of government based on representative institutions and the rule of law.

The Constitution of India, adopted in 1950 following three years of spirited debates and discussion in the Constituent Assembly (elected indirectly from the various provinces or state governments in 1946), proclaimed India as a federal democratic republic. The Constitution's 395 articles and 10 appendixes (known as schedules) make it one of the longest and most detailed in the world. Following the British parliamentary tradition, the Indian Constitution embodies the Fundamental Rights, a document similar to the U.S. Bill of Rights (Austin 1966, 2003; Pylee 1992). The Fundamental Rights guarantee basic substantive and procedural protection to all citizens. These civil rights take precedence over any other law of the land and include individual rights common in most liberal democracies, such as equality before the law; freedom of speech; right to assembly, association, and religion; the right to constitutional remedies for the protection of civil rights such as habeas corpus; and the right to private property. In addition, the Constitution outlawed the ancient Indian system of social stratification based on caste and prohibited discrimination on the grounds of religion, language, race, ethnic background, sex, or place of birth. Moreover, the Constitution granted minorities the right to establish and administer their own educational institutions and to converse in the "distinct language, script and culture" of their choice (Basu 1993; Smith 1963).

The Indian Constitution has three interesting features that distinguish it from other constitutions, however. First, is the Directive Principles of State Policy, which delineate the obligations of the state toward its citizenry. These include injunctions, among others, that the state "shall direct its policy towards securing . . . that the ownership and control of the material resources of the community are so distributed to subserve the common good" and that "the state shall promote the interests of the weaker sections of society." The precepts of the Directive Principles are not justiciable, however – that is, they are not enforceable by a court as are the Fundamental Rights. Rather, they are intended to guide the government in framing new legislation. The second feature of the

Constitution is that it can be periodically amended by legislation, and the third is that it allows for temporary suspension of many democratic rights under conditions of "national emergency" or when the country is threatened by "external aggression" or "internal disturbance."[2]

The key institutions of India's national governance are the executive, composed of the president; the Council of Ministers, headed by the prime minister; the Parliament; and the highest judicial system in the land, the Supreme Court. Although under the Indian Constitution executive power is formally vested in the president (who is also the head of the state), the president exercises these powers on the advice of the Council of Ministers, headed by the prime minister.[3] The president "appoints" the prime minister, but in reality, he or she simply confirms the leader of the largest party or coalition for the position. Moreover, the president makes almost all key decisions on the advice of the prime minister, especially if the prime minister has a strong parliamentary majority. Hence, in both theory and practice, power is concentrated in the hands of the prime minister, the de facto head of the Indian executive. Theoretically (and in practice), it is the prime minister who determines the composition of the forty-five-member council of ministers and assigns departmental portfolios to the "inner circle" or the "cabinet," made up of between fifteen to twenty individuals. However, ministers must either be members of Parliament (either house) or become members by nomination or by winning a by-election within six months of their appointment. In India, the nature and composition of the council of ministers and cabinet has varied according to the prime minister in power (Manor 1994; Thakur 1995, 121–36). The prime minister's office is also supported by a "secretariat," a large body (currently more than three hundred strong), headed by a principal secretary, senior bureaucrats, technocrats, politicians, and their legions of assistants.[4]

[2] National emergencies were declared in 1962 and again in 1971 during conflict with China and Pakistan, respectively. However, in 1975, Indira Gandhi used emergency powers to detain her political opposition. To prevent this from happening in the future, the Constitution was amended in 1977, specifying that emergency powers could only be declared in the event of external aggression or armed rebellion.

[3] In the Indian constitutional system, the president of India occupies the same position as the Crown does in the British Constitution. However, unlike the British monarch, the president must be elected by the Lok and Rajya Sabha for a five-year term (although they can stand for reelection). The president is also the military commander-in-chief, appoints state governors and Supreme Court justices, and has the power to dissolve Parliament and call for new elections if the sitting government loses its majority in Parliament. However, the president can be impeached by Parliament for violation of the Constitution. For a comprehensive overview, see Noorani (1990).

[4] Malik (1993, 86) notes that "in some ways the prime minister's secretariat resembles the U.S. president's executive office. It is entrusted not only with preparation of the agenda for cabinet meetings and maintenance of the records of cabinet proceedings but also with coordination of the administration of different departments of the government headed by the members of the council of ministers."

India's Parliament, the supreme legislative body of the country, consists of a bicameral legislature made up of the Lok Sabha (or the House of the People, also known as the lower house) and the Rajya Sabha – the Council of States or the upper house (Kashyap 1989; Morris-Jones 1971). In 2007, the Lok Sabha constitutionally had 545 seats, and all seats (with the exception of two members who are nominated by the president as representatives of the Anglo-Indian community) are popularly elected on the basis of a "first-past-the-post" system, similar to that in the United States.[5] Under the first-past-the-post voting system (also know as the "winner-take-all" and "single-member district plurality" system), the winner is the candidate with the most votes. That is, the winning candidate needs to only secure a simple majority, rather than gain an absolute majority of votes. Therefore, under this system, it is possible that voters in total may have voted for candidates other than the winner.

Seats in the Lok Sabha are allocated among the states on the basis of population, each roughly divided into several electoral districts made up of approximately 1.5 million people. The usual term of service in the Lok Sabha is five years – albeit, as is common in parliamentary systems, the prime minister may choose to call elections earlier. The Lok Sabha must meet at least twice per year with no more than six months between sessions because it is essentially a debating chamber and does not make policy. In contrast, the Rajya Sabha, like the U.S. Senate, is a permanent body and meets in continuous session (Morris-Jones 1971; Thakur 1995). It has a maximum of 250 members, and all but 12 are elected by the state legislative assembly for six-year terms. The members of the Rajya Sabha are elected indirectly, rather than by the citizens at large. As in the United States, the terms in the upper house are staggered so that one-third of the members stand for election every two years. The Rajya Sabha (like the British House of Lords) permits more extended debates. Home to a large number of elder statespeople, it is designed to provide stability and continuity to the legislative process. It is not subject to dissolution as is the Lok Sabha. Nevertheless, because it rests on the confidence of the popular assembly, the authority of the Rajya Sabha in the legislative process is subordinate to that of the Lok Sabha.

Decision making on public policy in India is concentrated at the highest levels of authority with the prime minister, his or her inner cabinet, and high-level officials and bureaucrats through their control of the various ministries of government taking the initiative. The government of the day has the primary responsibility of drafting legislation and introducing bills to either house of

---

[5] Under this system, political parties can gain commanding positions in the Parliament without gaining the support of a majority of the electorate. For example, the Congress Party, which dominated Indian politics until recently, never won a majority of votes in parliamentary elections. The best-ever Congress performance in parliamentary elections was in 1984 when it won 48 percent of the vote but garnered 76 percent of the parliamentary seats. In the 1991 general elections, Congress won 37.6 percent of the vote and 42 percent of the seats.

Parliament, although financial bills for taxing and spending (known as "money bills") can only be introduced in the Lok Sabha. The central government (or the "Center") is aided in its activities by some 17 million central government employees (known as Public Services), of whom some 5,000 are officers of the elite IAS (Indian Administrative Service). Although most of the senior policy makers and bureaucrats who work in the IAS are well educated, professional, and competent, the vast and sprawling underbelly of the Indian bureaucracy is anything but. This explains, in part, the huge gap between well-intentioned policies made at the top of government and the excessive bureaucracy and poor implementation that occurs at lower levels (Misra 1986).

As in other liberal democracies, an independent judiciary is at the heart of India's legal system. As the highest legal tribunal, the Supreme Court is the ultimate interpreter and guardian of the Constitution and the laws of the land.[6] Headed by a chief justice and twenty-five associate justices, the Supreme Court judges cannot be removed from the bench until retirement at age sixty-five. The key political role of the Supreme Court is to ensure that legislation conforms with the intent of the Constitution. Therefore, it is the responsibility of the Supreme Court to oversee that legislation passed by the central and state governments are in conformity with the Constitution and that the constitutionality of any enactment is determined under the power of judicial review by the Supreme Court, which has original as well as appellate jurisdiction.[7] In practice, however, the executive branch of government has often prevailed in limiting the Supreme Court's powers of judicial review. This was especially the case during Indira Gandhi's tenure as prime minister (1966–77; 1980–84) when she appointed a number of pliant judges, including a weak chief justice. During the two years of emergency rule (1975–77), the Supreme Court gave Mrs. Gandhi carte blanche to arrest and detain her political opponents without due process and looked the other way as the political and civil rights of Indian citizens were violated (Baxi 1980; A. Kohli 1988). Although India's Supreme Court is not as independent an institution as the framers of the Constitution intended it to be, neither is it a rubber stamp. The court has effectively adjudicated cases, including sensitive ones dealing with the rights of religious minorities, women, and lower castes. In recent years, it has attempted to assert its authority and function more as a neutral arbiter. The reasons for this, as well as its implications, are discussed in Chapter 8.

[6] Unlike the United States, India has a single or unified judicial system (not a system of dual courts), with the Supreme Court at the head of the judicial hierarchy, the High Courts in each of the states, followed by District Courts. The High Court is subordinate to the Supreme Court. The Supreme Court also covers the disputes arising between the central and the state governments, as well as cases involving two or more states.

[7] Hardgrave and Kochanek (2000, 101) aptly note that although "the scope of judicial review in India is not as wide as in the United States . . . the Court [has nevertheless] held more than 100 Center and state acts invalid, either in whole or in part, and most if its decisions have been unanimous."

Although India's federal system has vested significant powers of legislation in the central government, the Constitution has also provided for enumerated powers divided between the union or central government and the subnational (provincial or state-level) governments.[8] Below the Center are twenty-nine state governments and six union territories with populations ranging from 400,000 for the union territory of Sikkim, to 140 million for the largest and most populous state of Uttar Pradesh. The states do not have their own separate constitutions because they are governed by the provisions of the Constitution of India, which specifies that all the states shall have similar governmental structures and provides for popularly elected bicameral or unicameral legislature in each state and territory to be headed by a chief minister responsible to the assemblies.[9] Elections at the state level are contested by both national and regional (subnational) parties. Each state has a governor who is appointed by the president. Although governors are supposed to serve on the advice of a state's chief minister, governors can (and have) circumvented this rule, especially in states where the central government is at odds with the state government or where state governments are unstable. The central government and the governors can also dismiss or dissolve any elected state government through "President's Rule" if they conclude that the state government is not working in the best interests of its citizenry. Of course, the central government has often used this provision to advance its own political ends (Dua 1979). Once a state government is dissolved, it is governed by the Center until a new state government is elected.

The strength of the central government relative to the states is also apparent in the constitutional provisions (laid down in the Seventh Schedule of the Constitution) for central intervention into state jurisdictions. The Center has exclusive authority over matters of national importance: the ninety-seven items include defense, foreign affairs, interstate trade and commerce, transportation, communications, and finances. In addition, Article 3 of the Constitution authorizes Parliament (by a simple majority vote) to establish or dissolve states and union territories or change their boundaries or names. The Constitution gives the central government considerable powers over the collection and distribution of revenue. The complexities of India's "fiscal federalism" are discussed in the next chapter, but suffice it to note here that a lucrative income – corporate as well as import and export duties – is collected exclusively by the Center. However, the states depend on rural and agricultural income tax, which is extremely difficult to administer and collect (Rao and Singh 2005). Thus, through the financial resources its controls, the Center is

---

[8] The national government is called the Union Government in the Constitution but is popularly known as the Center.

[9] Most states have a unicameral Legislative Assembly (Vidhan Sabha), but five of the larger states also have an upper Legislative Council (Vidhan Parishad). These assemblies consist of between 30 to 425 members (depending on the size of the state) and serve five-year terms.

able to exert considerable control over state governments. According to Hardgrave and Kochanek (2000, 130), the central government "acts as a banker and collecting agent for the state governments," thereby making the states heavily dependent on the Center for financial resources. Again, under the rules of the Constitution, financial resources flow from the Center to the states through a system of discretionary divisible taxes and grants-in-aid, making the states dependent on the Center for their regular budgetary needs, as well as for their capital expenditures.[10] The central government also allocates and distributes substantial "development funds and grants" through its Five-Year Plans. The resources available under the plans are substantial given the Center's exclusive control over taxable income and foreign financial flows.

Although India's federal government exhibits features of a highly institutionalized modern unitary state, appearances can be deceiving. Despite the constitutional powers of the Center, the provincial or state governments are not without significant constitutional powers.[11] In reality, the central and subnational governments share broad areas of ambiguous and overlapping authority. In the words of B. R. Ambedkar, the chairman of the Constitution drafting committee, "the states of the union of India are as sovereign in their field which is left to them by the Constitution as the Center in the field which is assigned to it" (cited in Palmer 1961, 97). Under the Constitution, states have exclusive authority over sixty-six items, including public order, welfare, health, education, local government, industry, agriculture, and land revenue. In regard to the agricultural sector and land revenue, the Constitution, in assigning primary responsibility to the state governments (while placing constitutional and legal limitations on the powers and jurisdiction of the central government), reduced the Center to providing guidelines but leaving the actual task of translating rural development policies into legislation, including their implementation, to the state governments. In other words, the development of the rural sector has depended in large measure on the actions of the state governments. In fact, Paul Appleby (1953), who at the request of the government of India conducted a comprehensive review of the country's administrative system, was astounded to discover how much the Center was dependent on the states for the actual implementation of major national programs and how little real authority it seemed to have in the vital areas of public policy and administration. Appleby (1953, 21) lucidly captured this paradox: "No other large and important government . . . is so dependent as India on theoretically subordinate but actually rather distinct units responsible to a different political control, for so much of the administration of what are recognized as national programs of great importance to the nation."

---

[10] Because states are routinely short of funds, they have to seek central assistance in the form of loans, grants-in-aid, and overdraft facilities to meet their budgetary needs.

[11] Palmer (1961, 94) has argued that the "Indian union is not strictly a federal polity but a quasi-federal polity with some vital and important elements of unitariness."

Below the state governments exists an array of formal and informal governance structures known simply as "local self-government," ordinarily understood as the administration of a locality (a village, town, city, or any other area smaller than a state) by a body representing the local inhabitants. The idea behind these entities, articulated most forcefully by the 1957 Mehta Study Team Report, is that local self-government or "democratic decentralization" could play a vital role in the process of political legitimation and offer a means to develop a sense of participation in the citizenry. The district is the principal formal subdivision within the state governments. In 2000, there were 476 districts in India, varying in size and population – the average ranging from 4,000 square kilometers with average population of approximately 1.8 million. The district collector (a member of the IAS) and the state government-appointed district judge (who is in no way subordinate to the collector) are the most important government officials in district administration. Districts are further subdivided into *taluqs* or *tehsils* comprising anywhere between two hundred to six hundred villages.

Finally, to provide more channels of political and economic participation, Article 40 of the Constitution directs all levels of government to engage in "democratic decentralization of Indian administration" by reviving and creating "traditional village council for self-government" or *panchayati raj* and to "endow them with powers and authority as may be necessary to enable them to function as units of self-government" (Government of India [GOI] 1952, 6–7). Most states now have a fairly institutionalized system of *panchayati raj*, a three-tiered system that has vested extensive responsibilities for community and rural development in three locally elected bodies. At the base of the system is the popularly elected village council or *gram panchayat*. This is followed by the village council chairs, who are elected by members to the village council and who serve as members of the block council or *panchayat samiti*. The third tier, the *zila parishad*, congruent with the district, includes all the *samiti* chairs in the district. The *panchayati raj* received constitutional status with the passage of the 73rd Amendment in 1992. The amendment stipulates that all *panchayat* elections must be held every five years, that individuals must be elected for five-year terms, and that elections must be supervised by the election commission.[12]

However, it is the lively and boisterous practice of democracy by an array of competing and colorful political parties, personalities, and groups in civil society that brings out the real excitement of Indian politics. Since independence,

---

[12] An independent election commission established in accordance with the Constitution is responsible for the conduct of elections to parliament, the state legislatures, and the president. The commission prepares, maintains, and periodically updates the electoral roll (which indicates who is entitled to vote), supervises the nomination of candidates, registers political parties, monitors the election campaign (including the candidates funding), organizes the polling booths, and supervises the counting of votes.

there have been fourteen national elections. In the first in 1952, some 107 million voters out of an estimated 176 million eligible citizens went to the polls, giving the Indian National Congress a resounding victory (Guha 2007). The most recent national election will be held in 2009, and at least one election has been held every five years at the state-level since independence (Suri 2006). Political parties are pivotal actors in this drama, devoting substantial energy to winning elections and forming the government. Since independence, India's party system has evolved from a "one dominant party system," led by the Congress Party (or the Congress), into a competitive, multiparty system with the emergence of two significant national parties, the avowedly Hindu-nationalist Bharatiya Janata Party (BJP) and the Janata Party, as well as several regional parties.[13] The Congress retained its electoral dominance for some four decades from the first national elections in 1952 until 1989 (with a brief interlude from 1977 to 1980), holding a majority share of seats in the Lok Sabha. However, since the 1990s, the party's share of seats has declined, and from 1996 to 2004, it was not even the single largest party in the Lok Sabha. In fact, since the early 1990s, there has been no single majority party.

As a result, before the 1999 national elections, the BJP formed both explicit and tacit alliances with some twenty-four other national and state-based parties. Although the BJP won 182 seats, the BJP-led coalition won 299 of the 537 contested seats. In contrast, the Congress won its lowest ever 114 seats, and the Congress-led alliance won 134 seats. The BJP-led coalition was able to form a relatively stable government at the Center from 1999 to 2004. However, the tables were turned following the 2004 national elections. That year, the Congress won 145 (27 percent) of the 543 parliamentary seats, just ahead of the BJP, which won 138 (25 percent). However, by forming a broad "alliance" with nineteen other parties under the banner of the United Progressive Alliance (UPA), and coalition with the Communist Party of India-Marxist (CPI-M), which agreed to support it "from the outside," the Congress-UPA, with 219 seats (40 percent), was able to form a majority in Parliament. Because the incumbent BJP-National Democratic Alliance (NDA) could not, it was defeated. This trend in Indian politics has led some to suggest that party fragmentation and coalition and minority governments are the wave of the future (Hasan 2002; Sridharan 2005). Chapter 8 explores the political and economic implications of this trend.

Finally, for a country lacking many of the so-called prerequisites of democracy, it is a remarkable achievement that for more than six decades, India has remained a generally vibrant constitutional democracy.[14] Indians are justly proud to be citizens of the world's largest democracy and see it as a precious

---

[13] There is a large volume of literature on the Congress party. For a good overview, see Brass (1966), J. Brown (1985), Frankel (1978), Kochanek (1968), and Weiner (1967).

[14] On the question of prerequisites of democracy, see Lipset and Lakin (2004). With particular reference to India, see Kohli (2001) and Sharma (2002).

national accomplishment. Indeed, democracy has become such an indelible part of the nation's political consciousness that despite cynicism and disillusionment with "politics as usual," Indians continue to maintain a deep philosophical commitment to democracy and embrace the fundamental democratic idea that the state's authority must derive solely from the uncoerced consent of the majority through open competitive elections. Nevertheless, India's democracy faces significant challenges in this era of globalization. The nature of these challenges and the efforts to mitigate them are discussed in Chapter 8.

China: Building a Socialist Nation-State

On 1 October 1949, Chairman Mao Zedong, the enigmatic and undisputed leader of the Chinese Communist Party (CCP), stood atop the fabled Gate of Heavenly Peace in Tiananmen Square and proclaimed the founding of the People's Republic of China (PRC). He proudly announced that the "Chinese people have finally stood up" and were now masters of their own destiny (Bianco 1971). For his part, Mao promised that the CCP's central task would be to overcome the chaos and destruction wrought by decades of civil war, warlordism, and foreign aggression and build a China that was modern, prosperous, democratic, and socialist (Pepper 1978; Rowan 2004; Schram 1969).

However, Mao's conception of democracy was profoundly different from that of Nehru. Drawing on the principles of statecraft developed decades earlier in the USSR by Lenin, Mao and his compatriots, like their Soviet counterparts, saw the Communist Party as the exclusive repository of legitimate political power and the party elite the true bearers of the transcendent truth. [15] Only the Communist Party led by a disciplined revolutionary vanguard was endowed with the visionary foresight to determine the "correct" socioeconomic and political goals for society and best able to represent the interests of the masses by establishing a "people's democratic dictatorship" (Schram 1969; Schwartz 1951). In practice, China's communist party-state not only gave itself exclusive monopoly over political power, it also demanded complete allegiance from all government and institutions – including from the party itself, which had to abide strictly by the organizational rules of "democratic centralism."[16] In practice, this meant that although the party could arrive at all major decisions "democratically" through consultation, deliberation, and discussions with members at all levels of the party's organs, once decisions were reached, they were to be fully supported by all members – including those who may have initially opposed them. However, as Service (2007) in his sobering

---

[15] In the Leninist worldview, the masses generally lack the revolutionary consciousness and are therefore incapable of building socialism.

[16] China's political system is often referred to as the "communist party-state" because the party not only enjoys monopoly on political power but also controls all government and social institutions (Schurmann 1968; Townsend 1967).

Comrades: A History of World Communism notes, the principle of centralism was hardly ever sacrificed to democracy. Important decisions were always made at the very top of the party hierarchy, and these decisions were binding on all party members at all levels of the party hierarchy. In fact, Communist parties explicitly banned the formation of "factions" or any type of "small group activity" within the party – with violators subject to harsh discipline, including long prison sentences and capital punishment. Similarly, all nonparty social and mass organizations had to accept the CCP's exclusive leadership to function openly. Indeed, the CCP perfected "state corporatism" by placing all nonparty organizations under the umbrella of the CCP.

The CCP's Constitution (which is a separate document from the Constitution of the PRC), vests supreme authority in the National Party Congress – making it the party's leading organ. Although the National Party Congress has broad constitutional powers, it is too large and unwieldy (with some two thousand delegates) and meets too infrequently (once every five years) to be truly deliberative to make major political and policy decisions.[17] Lieberthal (1995, 160) likens the National Party Congress to "an American political party convention," noting that "it convenes, hears many speeches, passes resolutions, adopts rules of procedure, and disbands." It is "a vehicle for announcing and legitimating some major decisions rather than for initiating and deciding important policies." The National Party Congress appoints (through carefully orchestrated secret ballot votes) the Central Committee, which in turn "elects" (in fact, appoints) the Political Bureau or "Politburo," the Politburo Standing Committee, and the party's general secretary, all of whom are also members of the Central Committee.[18] The committee, with more than three hundred members, constitutes China's privileged political elite. They have the power to govern the country when the National Party Congress is not in session (which, as noted earlier, is usually the case). However, because in practice the Central Committee convenes only once or twice a year for their plenums (or meetings), it is the inner circle of some two dozen Politburo members, in particular, the four to six members who make up the Politburo Standing Committee and the general secretary (currently Hu Jintao), who are constitutionally responsible for governing when the Central Committee is not in session. Both the Politburo and its Standing Committee wield real power because neither is accountable to the Central Committee. As Service (2007) notes, such extreme concentration of power in the hands of so few is the hallmark of a Leninist political system.

---

[17] The Seventh Party Congress met in 1945, only to meet again in 1956 and 1969. Since then, it has met more regularly: 1973, 1977, 1982, 1987, 1992, 1997, and the most recent (the Sixteenth Party Congress) in 2002.

[18] To do away with the excesses of the Maoist era, in particular, the "cult of personality" and the belief in the infallibility of the all powerful "chairman," the position of party chairman was abolished in 1982. This makes the general secretary the top party leader (Li 2001).

The CCP's organizational structure (like that of the former Communist systems) is extremely hierarchical and bureaucratic with power residing at the national level or the so-called political center in Beijing. From here power percolates downward to both the party organs and the country's political-administrative units. Party organs parallel the administrative units or governments. Below the central government are twenty-two province-level administrative units. The five autonomous regions (Tibet, Xinjiang, Uighur, Ningxia Hui, Guangxi Zhuang, and Inner Mongolia) and large metropolitan cities such as Beijing, Chongqing, Shanghai, and Tianjin are also administered like provinces directly under the central government because of their size.[19] Next are 331 prefecture-level units and large provincial cities, followed by about 2,000 counties (*xian*) or district-level units. At the base are local-level governments, which include some 44,000 townships and 730,000 village-level governments.[20] There are also two special autonomous regions (SARs): Hong Kong (since 1997) and Macau (since 1999). However, unlike India's federal system, China's governmental system is unitary, meaning that the national government possesses ultimate authority over its territorial units and subnational or local governments have limited policy-making autonomy – at least theoretically.[21]

Although the government of the PRC is organizationally distinct from the CCP, it is nevertheless, subordinate to the party. Given its deep links with all government organs, the party wields tremendous control and influence over government personnel and policies (O'Brien 1990). In fact, the vast majority of government officials – most certainly the ones occupying important leadership positions within key institutions – are party members, with a few symbolic exceptions. Similarly, although not all of the estimated 30 to 40 million *cadres* (or bureaucrats) who staff China's gargantuan bureaucracy are party members, the bureaucracy is subordinate to the CCP.

The primary governmental bodies are the National People's Congress (NPC), which serves as China's legislature; the State Council, which exercises executive functions; and the office of the president. Under the PRC's Constitution, the NPC, established in 1954, is the highest organ of government power. It is a large body with some three thousand members and meets annually for about two weeks to review and approve new policy directions and budget and personnel changes, as well as to elect key executive officeholders such as the president, the vice president, and ministers. However, before initiatives are presented to the NPC for consideration by the State Council, it must

[19] The PRC considers Taiwan its twenty-third province.

[20] Communes used to be the lowest level of government. However, after 1982, they were granted the status of an "economic management unit" (Wang 1995.)

[21] Often "subnational" and "local government" is used interchangeably. Both refer to any of the four administrative layers below the central government (province, prefecture/municipality, county/city, and township/district).

first be endorsed by the party's Central Committee. Similar to the National Party Congress, when the NPC is not in session, its permanent organ, the Standing Committee, exercises state power. The NPC is the highest level of a system of People's Congresses that extend in a hierarchically arranged level down through provincial People's Congress all the way down to municipal or county People's Congress and township People's Congress. The structure and functions at each level are similar, although each lower level selects representatives to the next higher level. The State Council is made up of anywhere from thirty to more than one hundred members who are "chosen" by the NPC, but first those selected are screened and approved by the party hierarchy. Led by a prime minister or premier (currently Wen Jiabao), vice premiers, state councilors, and ministers, the State Council functions as the cabinet. The office of the president is largely ceremonial, and the president serves as the formal head of state. To date, the president including the current president, Hu Jintao, who is also the CCP's general secretary, has always been a senior party member.

During the Maoist period, the NPC remained largely moribund, failing to perform any genuinely representative or independent legislative functions. Rather, the NPC was directly under the control of the CCP's leadership and literally functioned as a rubber stamp for the party, becoming notorious for giving unanimous approvals to the "great helmsman's" (i.e., Chairman Mao) every pronouncement. However (as discussed in later chapters), in the post-Mao era, in an effort to reduce party interference and manipulation, curb corruption, and give greater policy autonomy to subnational governments, the NPC has been allowed to take a more active role in drafting legislation, managing budgets, and monitoring policy implementation. The 1982 constitutional revision strengthened the mandate of the NPC and the State Council by opening up the decision-making process, making both more assertive (Goldman and MacFarquhar 1999; MacFarquhar 1997). Nevertheless, compared with parliamentary systems such as India, China's legislature and cabinet still remain institutionally weak and compromised because the CCP's leadership retains veto power over all major legislation and policy decisions.

At first glance, the Constitution of the PRC, first adopted in 1954 and revised successively in 1975, 1978, and 1982, reads rather apocryphally, like the constitutions of liberal democracies. It guarantees the basic rights of its citizens, including the right to vote and stand for election; freedom of speech, assembly, and association; freedom of the press; freedom of religious belief; the right to criticize and make suggestions to any state organ; and due process of law, among other rights. However, whereas in liberal democracies a constitution is considered inviolable with no government or individual above it, in China this is not the case. Rather, the Constitution's preamble boldly states "the leadership role of the Communist Party of China and the guidance of Marxism-Leninism-Mao Zedong Thought" in building a "people's democratic dictatorship" (quote from Lieberthal 1995, 356). Moreover, the power to interpret and apply the

Constitution and subject legal pronouncements to judicial scrutiny is the privilege of the Standing Committee of the NPC, not the courts (Tanner 1999). The revision and adoption of four "different" constitutions reflects the power struggle and the tumultuous political shifts within the high echelons of the party. For example, with the death of Mao in 1975 and the subsequent defeat of the belligerent radical left (the so-called Gang of Four), the Constitution was revised to weaken the radicals decisively. Although the party's central role was upheld, greater separation was put between the CCP and the government. In 1982, when Deng Xiaoping and his followers were firmly in power, they revised the Constitution to align it with the political and ideological changes then under way. Specifically, the Constitution quietly removed the lavish praise for Mao and amended references to the "superiority of state ownership" and "central planning" with terms more in keeping with China's "open-door policy" such as "creating a socialist market economy."

The post-Mao leadership has shown greater commitment to what it calls "socialist legality" in an effort to expunge the legacy of arbitrariness, vigilante justice, and lawlessness unleashed by Mao during the Cultural Revolution (1966–76). Since the Constitution of 1982 recognized the principle of popular sovereignty and the supremacy of the rule of law, a number of statutory and administrative laws have been enacted. The criminal code has been strengthened to provide a much-needed due process, and in 1989, the People's Procuracies were restored to make government officials more accountable by allowing citizens to sue administrative agencies and hold public officials accountable for their actions. Equally significant, the jurisdiction of the courts has been expanded to allow them to settle private litigation, and the availability of legal resources in terms of the number and quality of judges, lawyers, and law schools has increased to facilitate the judicial process (He 2007; Lubman 1999). The greatest priority, however, has been given to promoting legal and procedural standards to advance China's integration in the global economy. In particular, a series of measures have been enacted to end the capricious Soviet-style commercial arbitration rules and practices in favor of those better able to facilitate domestic industrial and commercial development and foster international trade and investment. Such improvements include transparent rules regarding enforcement of contracts and copyright and intellectual property protection (Alford 1995; Lardy 2002).

Nevertheless, although the concept that government itself should be under the law – and not allowed merely to use the law as an instrument of its will – has been strengthened, China still has a long way to go to establish the rule of law (Peerenboom 2002). There is still no independent judiciary to mediate public and private disputes because courts serve as an extension of the state. This reality or contradiction is lucidly highlighted by Trevaskes (2007) with reference to the courts and criminal justice in contemporary China. On one hand, Trevaskes argues that China's legal system is moving toward greater professionalism, independent administration of justice, procedural propriety, and the strict application of law. On the other hand, the resilience of Maoist principles and practices such as the "morally charged and emotive practices of crime control" (p. 12), "an authoritarian style of justice administration manifest in the coercive strategies of crime campaigns" (p. 15), "law as an instrument of social engineering" (p. 32), and the fact that criminal law and the courts are still required by the party-state to "play a coercive role in the domain of social control under the leadership and tight direction of the Party" (p. 41) continues to undermine this effort. Moreover, practical constraints such as the lack of trained personnel and the general unwillingness of local governments to fund the courts have contributed to the court system's difficulty in attaining a degree of professionalism. In the end, however, it is the party's practice of using law as an instrument for political ends – in particular, the regime's obsession with achieving social stability (which it thinks is essential to continued economic growth) – that stands as an obstacle toward legal professionalization and the establishment of genuine rule of law in China.

Finally, although the CCP holds a monopoly on political power through tight vertical control it exercises through an unbroken chain of command over governmental and social institutions, the party has also undergone some significant changes in the Deng era. In 1949, the CCP's membership was estimated at around 4.5 million. The party currently has more than 70 million members. This makes it the largest political party in the world. During the Mao era, the party's base was made up mostly of peasants, workers, and professional revolutionaries. This was because recruitment and promotions within the party were biased toward the "reds," or individuals with proper class and ideological credentials. However, overreliance on revolutionary zeal or "voluntarism" had its limits.[22] The lack of qualified people weakened the party's ability to govern (Harding 1980). In the post-Mao period, the party leadership made a concerted (and successful) drive to broaden the base of the party by including better-educated, professionally and technically qualified "experts." Currently, individuals from all walks of life are members of the party, including middle-class professionals and businesspeople. However, even as the party has become more institutionalized, merit based, and performance oriented, many of the problems such as pervasive bureaucratization, abuse of power, rampant corruption, and eroding legitimacy continue to haunt the CCP.

India: Economic Development

The task of economic development that India faced at the time of independence was daunting. India had inherited an impoverished and stagnant economy. More than two centuries of colonial rule had severely distorted agricultural

---

[22] "Voluntarism" refers to an abiding faith in the masses to overcome any obstacle.

production in favor of commercial and export crops. As a result, food output was not only negligible but declining. Blyn's (1966) exhaustive analysis shows that from 1890 to 1947, the output of staple food grains per head of population declined by roughly 26 percent, despite the relatively low growth of population of 1 percent per year. Under these conditions an Indian, on average, could expect to live for no more than thirty-three years (Balasubramanyam 1984, 6). Further, the near total absence of growth of per capita income, low levels of capital formation in the public sector, a technologically backward industrial sector barely sufficient in the production of basic goods such as cotton textiles, sugar, soap, matches, and salt (with almost nonexistent capacity for the production of basic capital and intermediate goods) stood as a major obstacle to national economic growth and development (Bagchi 1982; Bettelheim 1968, 8–54; Rothermund 1988).

PLANNING FOR INDUSTRIALIZATION

Against this somber backdrop of economic backwardness and faced with the formidable task of economic development, India's political leaders declared that building "national economic self-reliance" was the government's foremost priority. There was a broad consensus among the country's political and economic elites that the quest for national self-reliance could best be achieved through "planned" economic modernization centered on import-substitution industrialization (ISI). The idea of ISI was based on the Keynesian premise of the substitution of domestic products for previously imported ones – hence, the moniker "import substitution." ISI, also known as "inward-looking industrial strategy," was to develop gradually in stages: the first stage would focus on the relatively easy substitution of basic domestically produced consumer goods for previously imported items. The second, and more difficult, stage would involve a shift from "horizontal" to "vertical" ISI with the production of intermediate goods and consumer durables. The third and final stage would include the production of heavy industrial and capital goods.

Prime Minister Nehru, the chief advocate of ISI argued passionately that without such a coherent and bold industrialization strategy, India's economy was doomed to suffer from its peripheral status in the global capitalist economy and remain perpetually poor and underdeveloped.[23] He gave the ISI strategy his imprimatur, arguing that the nation's pursuit of self-reliant development was a carefully thought-out strategic plan designed to make India strong and economically self-reliant but also instructed the National Planning Committee (made up of leading economists and technocrats) to formulate an ISI plan that

[23] In a speech to the special silver jubilee convocation of Lucknow University on 28 January 1949, Nehru (1958, 368), with his characteristic exuberant candor, stated "we are bound to be industrialised, we are trying to be industrialised, we want to be industrialised, we must be industrialized."

was consistent with the government's goal of creating a "socialistic pattern of society."[24] Although Nehru, following his visit to Moscow in 1927 remained deeply impressed by the Soviet model of planned industrialization, the urbane and gentlemanly Nehru was also troubled by the regimentation and totalitarian provenance of the Soviet experiment. Rather, the longtime admirer of the more compassionate, "social democratic" British Fabian socialism, he concluded that an eclectic, it not imaginative, blend of the two models was more appropriate for India (Park and Tinker 1959).

To Nehru, "planned industrialization" was the responsibility of the state. India's democratic state, he presumed, was not only the legitimate custodian of social order and the repository of the public good, it was necessary for the state to assume the role that private capitalists had performed in other settings. Harboring a deep ambivalence, if not suspicion, about India's economic and managerial elites, not to mention his intense distrust of the "predatory" foreign capital, Nehru was adamant that (a) India's private sector had to be guided in the desired direction by the state and (b) foreign economic interests must play, at best, a marginal and subordinate role. Specifically, dependence on foreign capital other than grants and concessional aid was to be kept at a minimum. Rather, the state, through its instrumental ownership and control of the "commanding heights" of the economy, would play the central role in guiding the economy. In practice, this meant direct state control of all key industrial infrastructural facilities such as public utilities, including strict control over the importation of all commodities to exclude those not considered to be central to industrial development (Gupta 1989; Jalan 1992; Sundrum 1987). However, it is important to note that Nehruvian-style centralized planning did not mean suppression of private enterprise. Rather, it meant extensive regulation by the state.

The government's landmark Industrial Policy Resolution of 1948 went to great lengths to outline a blueprint for industrial development, as well as to specify the role of the public and private sector in the planned "mixed economy."[25] The resolution gave the central and state governments a virtual monopoly in railroads and exclusive right to develop mineral resources, including the iron and steel industry, and specified eighteen key industries of "national importance" to be developed under the direct control and regulation of the central government. In March 1950 (shortly after India's Constitution went into effect), a quintessential top-down expert committee called the Planning

---

[24] The antecedent of planning goes back to the colonial period. One of the early champions of planning in India was M. Visvesvaraya (1934). Nehru and the Congress Party recognized the need for economic planning long before independence. The National Planning Committee was established in 1938 under the chairmanship of Nehru. For details, see Chakravarty (1984) and Hanson (1966).

[25] According to the First Five-Year Plan, "in a planned mixed economy, the distinction between the public and the private sector is one of emphasis. The two sectors are and must function as parts of a single organism" (Government of India [GOI] 1952, 9).

Commission was established under the general guidance of the provision in the Constitution. With the indefatigable Nehru as the commission's chairman and his alter ego and confidant the distinguished statistician and professor P. C. Malalanobis as chief advisor, the Planning Commission was entrusted with the explicit task of further articulating and implementing through the Five-Year Plans (the First Five-Year Plan ran from 1951 to 1956) the national government's developmental objectives.[26] Clearly, for a body set up merely as "advisory" and "apolitical," the Planning Commission wielded extraordinary influence over national policy. As Khilnani (1997, 85) aptly notes, "the Planning Commission became the exclusive theatre where economic policy was formulated. The subject was removed from parliament and the cabinet – they were now merely informed of decisions taken by the small cohort of experts."

The Second Five-Year Plan (1956–61), authored by Malalanobis (with Nehru's tacit approval), further bolstered the Indian government's industrialization plan. In particular, the Industrial Policy Resolution of 1948 was amended, and the revised Industrial Policy Resolution of 1956 not only complemented the goals of the Second Plan but also called for an acceleration of industrialization. The Second Five-Year Plan's bias toward rapid industrialization was evident in the budget allocation because industry's share of the total investment was almost tripled (from 7.6 percent to 18 percent out of a total outlay of Rs. 48 billion), whereas agriculture's share was slashed by nearly half that of the First Five-Year Plan (GOI 1956). Also, in an effort to "rationalize" industrial expansion, both the Second Plan and the 1956 Industrial Policy Resolution carefully divided industries into three broad categories or "schedules." Schedule A, consisting of seventeen "key industries" such as rail and air transport, energy and power generation (including atomic energy), telecommunications, steel, mining, petroleum, and heavy machinery, was reserved for development exclusively by the public sector. Schedule B contained a list of twelve industries in which public sector investment would supplement (in the form of equity capital) private sector development. Schedule C, which included industries such as the consumer goods sector, was open to domestic private sector development, albeit the private sector had to conform to plan priorities through quantitative restrictions on private investment, get approvals or "licenses" for imports of all capital inputs and technology, and be subjected to regular governmental oversight.[27] In addition (like pre-reform China), because the state-owned banks controlled some 90 percent of bank deposits, credit was

---

[26] The aim of the Five-Year Plans was to state clearly the government's priorities and objectives for the economy, including setting specific targets for social development. See GOI (1952) and Hanson (1966).

[27] Although the scope of public sector development was expanded, the private sector was not overlooked. In addition to protecting it from foreign competition, private sector facilities were also excluded from expropriation and nationalization, and in some cases, the state even agreed to provide resources for their expansion (GOI 1956).

allocated on the basis of government policy.[28] Similarly, fiscal and monetary policy instruments were deployed to mobilize private financial savings for public investment, and the commercial banks and insurance companies were nationalized so that capital could be allocated to the central government's "priority" sectors (Joshi and Little 1994). The intrinsic logic behind this was that by controlling financial resources, industrial inputs, infrastructure, and production, the state could guide industrial development (both public and private) in an economically and socially desired direction.

The Third Five-Year Plan (1961–66) also made the broadening and deepening of the industrial and manufacturing sectors a top priority (GOI 1961). However, aware that the rural sector starved of resources under the Second Plan was languishing, the Third Plan allocated it more funds in an effort to make the sector self-sufficient (GOI 1959). This proved too little and too late. Nehru's death in May 1964 provided an opportunity for a more critical and objective discussion of the merits of his state-led industrialization strategy, particularly given the fact that his venerable successor, Lal Bahadur Shastri, was never fond of central planning and thus more amenable to limiting state involvement and expanding the scope for private enterprise. However, Shastri's death in January 1966 preempted the potential change in policy direction (Frankel 1978, 246–92; Wadhwa 1977). Rather, the humiliating routing of India's defense forces by the Chinese in the disputed Himalayan territory in 1962 and the second inconclusive war with Pakistan in 1965 were still fresh on the minds of the country's political elites, and Indira Gandhi (Nehru's daughter and now prime minister) was determined to make India a self-reliant industrial power capable of defending its national sovereignty. Despite the fiscal stress (India's foreign exchange reserves became perilously low to pay the import bills) and crisis in the agricultural sector following two successive drought years (1965–67) due to poor monsoons, the government not only doubled the defense budget but reaffirmed its commitment to Nehru's industrialization strategy.

RURAL DEVELOPMENT: AGRARIAN REFORMS TO THE GREEN REVOLUTION

Even as economic development became synonymous with industrialization, Nehru and the Planning Commission recognized that the success of ISI

---

[28] India has a long history of both public and private banking. Modern banking began in the eighteenth century with the founding of the English Agency House in Calcutta and Bombay. In 1935, India's central bank, the Reserve Bank of India (RBI), was established. After independence, it was given broad regulatory authority over commercial banks in India. In 1959, the State Bank of India acquired the state-owned banks of eight former princely states. Thus, by July 1969, approximately 31 percent of scheduled bank branches throughout India were government-controlled as part of the State Bank of India (Banerjee, Cole, and Duflo 2004).

depended on improvements in the agricultural sector. This is because, and despite, the ISI's inherent "urban bias," a vibrant agricultural sector was essential to underwrite industrialization and generate surpluses to avoid shortages of food grains and other basic commodities (Lipton 1977). Because the Congress Party leadership had long argued that the economic backwardness and endemic poverty of the countryside was fundamentally rooted in the highly inequitable patterns of landownership under the feudal *zamindari* system, they made the abolishment of this exploitative system through land and tenure reforms the cornerstone of their strategy for rural and agricultural development (Majumdar 1962; Malaviya 1954; Nehru 1948). It also meant that to provide inexpensive food and basic inputs for industrial development, the government deliberately had to keep farm prices artificially low and agricultural exports curtailed through quantitative restrictions. In time, this would have a negative impact on agricultural production (Srinivasan 1994).

Between 1948 and 1964, after repeated directives, regulations, and decrees from the central government, the state governments promulgated legislation designed to reform agrarian relations in their respective jurisdictions.[29] These reformist measures can be divided into roughly three overlapping phases. During the first phase, from 1949 to 1954, legislation was passed by several state governments to abolish the *zamindari* system or any such system of "parasitic landlordism" that promoted extreme inequalities and exploitation (GOI 1952, 1963). It was widely believed that *zamindari* abolition by itself would significantly ameliorate the problems of agricultural stagnation and rural poverty by breaking up the large "unproductive" estates and redistributing land to the actual cultivators. In the second phase, from 1952 until the end of the decade, emphasis was placed on "tenancy reforms." The aim was to regulate tenancy rights and provide security of tenure to the "actual tillers" – in particular, to help tillers acquire permanent, transferable, and heritable ownership rights to the land they cultivated. In the third phase, from 1956 to the early 1960s, legislation was aimed at placing ceilings or an upper limit on the amount of land an individual or family could own. The aim was to restrict land concentration by distributing "excess" land to the actual tillers and maximize "efficiency of production" by consolidating small and fragmented holdings (GOI 1956, 175–80). Buttressing these measures was the Community Development Projects (CDPs). Launched in 1952 under the joint supervision of the Planning Commission and the newly established Ministry of Community Development, the aim of the CDPs was to stimulate community-centered development projects based on the Gandhian principles of cooperation and self-help. In 1955, the central

---

[29] It is worth reiterating that the central government enjoyed less leverage over events in the agricultural sector than in industry. Because of the constitutional limitations on the power of the Indian state, provincial governments have enjoyed exclusive jurisdiction over the enactment and implementation of rural development policies, including land and tenure reforms.

government established the State Bank of India (SBI) to serve the financial needs of the agricultural sector and the CDPs.

In retrospect, agrarian reforms promised far more than they actually delivered. Although the large estates of the landed gentry was expropriated (albeit with good compensation), the most important feature of land reforms was their nonimplementation, or as Barrington Moore (1966, 395) aptly noted, "Nehru's agrarian program was an out-and-out failure."[30] What explains the discrepancy between the aims and the outcomes? There are a number of explanations. Some attribute the failure to ambiguous or "faulty" legislation with "numerous loopholes," rendering much of the reform ineffective.[31] Others blame administrative and bureaucratic inertia, corruption, and a "lack of political will."[32] Frankel (1978) and A. Kohli (1987) argue that the wide discrepancy between ideals and actual outcomes was due to the constitutional division of power between the Center and the state governments. By assigning significant powers over agriculture to state governments dominated by rural propertied interests, the failure of agrarian reforms was fait accompli. Finally, numerous microlevel studies underscore the role of the dominant rural castes and classes, who, given their traditional authority and hegemonic power in the countryside, were able undermine the reforms at will (Beteille 1974; Herring 1983; Joshi 1975, 1982; Thorner 1976).

Comparative research indicates that successful implementation of reforms in the countryside requires that the state must simultaneously insulate itself from the pressures and demands of the landed classes and effectively penetrate and establish enduring institutional and organizational links between state institutions and rural society. As discussed later, in Maoist China (and in postwar Japan, South Korea, and Taiwan), a strong centralized state with embedded autonomy, applying what Samuel Huntington (1968, 381–96) has termed "concentrated power from above," was able to carry out far-reaching reforms because the state's institutional autonomy enabled it to exclude the landed gentry from the state's institutions and structures. In such settings, the state's policies and goals were often swiftly and effectively implemented by an elaborate and well-organized network made up of dedicated party cadres, a mobilized peasantry, a well-institutionalized bureaucratic apparatus, and a reform-oriented political leadership. However, India's disaggregated polity was ill suited to such a task. Rather, the Congress Party, which had built its rural political and electoral support through local notables, many of whom came from the ranks of the rich and middle peasant castes and upper-caste *zamindar*s, found it extremely difficult to insulate itself from the pressures and demands of these powerful interests. Lacking a firm political-institutional base

---

[30] Also see, Joshi (1975, 1982) and S. C. Jha (1971).

[31] Ladejinsky (1977); Mellor (1976); Singh and Mishra (1965); and Warriner (1969).

[32] See, for example, Malaviya 1954; Myrdal 1968; Jannuzi 1974; Neale 1962; Tai 1974; and Uppal 1983.

in the countryside independent of the rural elites, the Congress leadership did not have many channels open for it to effectively direct and mediate central government policies – in particular, reformist and redistributive ones. As Atul Kohli (1987, 69) succinctly notes, the Congress leadership could not "utilize the party as a tool of direct politicization and social transformation, or use it to goad the governmental and bureaucratic levels below the center to follow through the central directives." Hence, in the absence of such political autonomy and organizational networks, there was no force to counter the hegemonic power of landed interests.

In fact, so limited was the reach of the central government over the countryside that the question of what the leadership could do about the implementation of land reforms was academic. Having abdicated its powers over most aspects of agricultural policy, including those concerning the enactment and implementation of land and tenure reforms (which, as noted, fell within the purview of provincial legislation and administration), the reformers within the central government often found themselves in a frustrating position. For example, even Nehru, lacking the necessary constitutional powers and the support of influential conservative colleagues, including Vallabhbhai Patel and India's first president, Rajendra Prasad (a landlord), could do little but articulate the "broad outlines" of the reform strategy and try to impress upon the provincial political elites the need to carry them out. However, because neither the central nor the state-level political leadership were agreed on the reform strategy and because it was left to each state government to determine the actual policy and the time frame for implementation, the reform policies predictably were left to the pushes and pulls of the political and socioeconomic forces operating within each state. Given that state-level political power was, with few exceptions, closely tied to the hierarchical agrarian power structures, political leaders and functionaries in the states and districts largely composed of and structurally and electorally dependent on the rural propertied classes tended to remain more responsive to the needs of their powerful rural constituency than to the reformers in New Delhi. Thus, irrespective of the numerous policy statements and repeated directives from the central leadership on the need to pursue agrarian reforms consistent with the "directive principles of state policy" as specified in the Constitution, the reformers often had great difficulty even enlisting the support of provincial and district-level politicians and bureaucrats (many of whom were also card-carrying congressmen) for the effective implementation of the provincial governments own "watered down" reformist measures. In fact, when it came down to the actual task of implementing "favorable" (reformist or redistributive) policies and directives, the wily provincial, district, and local level politicos and the sprawling Byzantine-like political-bureaucratic apparatus they controlled built certain defenses against central state penetration and control, often confounding the central planners. To the best of their abilities, these Janus-faced intermediaries actively delayed, distorted, deflected, and destroyed inimical or "intrusive" central policies and directives as often as they faithfully implemented those perceived to be "harm-less" or "beneficial" to their careers and the powerful propertied interests they represented.

By the early 1960s, it was becoming evident that betting exclusively on structural reforms in the countryside to solve the problems in the agricultural sector was misguided. The failure of the reforms was gravely compounded by the ISI strategy, which preempted a lion's share of the government's budget, leaving little for the much-needed investments in rural infrastructure such as irrigation, land reclamation, flood control, and the provision of capital inputs such as fertilizer and machinery to increase farm productivity. This made the countryside extremely vulnerable to the vagaries of the monsoon. The failure of two successive monsoons (1965–67) and the resultant 20 percent decline in food-grain production pushed the economy into an accelerating crisis because even from its peak level of 89 million tons in 1964–65, India was barely able to meet the country's burgeoning food-grain requirements. The decline in food-grain production to 74 million tons in 1966–67 spelled disaster (Mellor 1976). Not only did the per capita availability of food grains for consumption fall drastically to the levels of the mid-1950s, in the face of acute shortages of essential commodities and the spiraling cost of basic food items, the government was forced to institute statutory rationing in several towns and cities as it became confronted with escalating nationwide agitation against food shortages and rising prices.[33] In fact, so severe were the food shortages that only massive grain imports (and food aid under the Public Law 480 agreement with the United States[34]), which saw imports rise sharply from 3.5 million metric tons in 1961 to 10.4 million metric tons in 1965–66, prevented large-scale hunger and famine (Mellor 1976; Paarlberg 1985).

In the midst of the shortages, the Indian government was forced to abandon the Nehruvian strategy of self-reliant rural development based on land and tenure reforms and cooperative reorganization by adopting a strategy empha-sizing technological solutions to the problems of agricultural development. The "Green Revolution," based on reliance on rich farmers (or "bullock capital-ists") using capital inputs (fertilizer, pesticides, and high-yielding variety seeds [HYV]) and modern farming methods, were to be the new saviors in the coun-tryside. India's agricultural performance since the introduction of the Green Revolution strategy has been spectacular, allaying fears about a Malthusian specter of famine. With aggregate food-grain production doubling since the mid-1960s, India achieved food self-sufficiency by the mid-1970s. As noted, in 1965–66 and 1966–67, India's total food-grain output stood at a deficit (in terms of population growth): 72.3 and 74.2 million tons, respectively. However, with the dissemination of technological innovation (improved HYV seeds,

---

[33] According to Biplab Dasgupta (1977, 30), "between 1961–62 and 1966–67 the foodgrain prices registered an increase of 83 percent, which also led to a 28 percent increase in the price of manufactured goods."

[34] In 1956, India signed the agreement of P.L. 480 with the United States to receive food aid.

fertilizer, pesticides, herbicides), increased investment of capital resources, and more efficient and optimal land use and farming techniques, food-grain output increased to 95 million tons in 1968–69 to 108.4 million tons in 1970–71, to 133 million tons in 1981–82, to a record high of 178 million tons in 1990–91. It is important to note that in the pre–Green Revolution period (1947–1966), the increases in agricultural output were almost exclusively due to the expansion of area under cultivation, whereas in the post–Green Revolution period, increases were mainly the result of growth in agricultural production and productivity or yield. Table 1.1 provides a comparative snapshot of the trends in the production and productivity of principal crops (note: the table covers the

Table 1.1. *Production of principal crops: 1969–70 to 1986–87*

Crop	Year	Production	Area	Yield
Rice, wheat, and coarse cereals	1970–71	114.1	102.0	110.4
	1975–76	128.8	104.0	118.8
	1980–81	143.1	104.5	129.3
	1986–87	161.1	104.0	143.5

Source: Government of India (1987, 108–10).

post–Green Revolution period only). Table 1.2 illustrates that the increases in aggregate agricultural production and yield have been accompanied by sustained expansion of the gross cropped area, in particular, by the expansion of wheat and rice under the HYV program and by large-scale use of *bazaar ki khaad* or inorganic chemical-based fertilizers and pesticides.

Table 1.2. *Area under high-yielding varieties (HYV) and use in new inputs in India*

Year	Gross cropped area (millions of hectares)	Area under HYV (millions of hectares)	Fertilizer use (millions of tons)
1950–1951	131.8	–	0.1
1960–1961	152.7	1.9	0.3
1970–1971	165.7	15.4	2.2
1980–1981	173.5	43.1	5.5
1984–1985	177.0	56.0	8.5
1990–1991	180.0	63.9	12.6

Source: Government of India (1992, 42).

POLITICS AND STATIST INDUSTRIALIZATION

India's developmental approach during Indira Gandhi's decade-long tenure (1966–77) as prime minister was marked by abrupt policy shifts – arguably a reflection of the political exigencies than economic logic. Early in her tenure, growing domestic economic pressures, including from the World Bank and the International Monetary Fund, for India to liberalize its economy as a condition for further emergency assistance forced the government to acquiesce to modifications in economic strategy. In particular, this included reducing some government controls, liberalizing investment policies such as reduction in import duties and export subsidies, and, the most controversial, liberalizing foreign exchange controls and devaluing the rupee by more than 40 percent: from 4.7 rupees to 7.5 rupees to the dollar.[35] However, by the late 1960s, there was a sharp shift toward the left in policy orientation. As factional infighting within the top echelons of the Congress intensified between the establishment conservatives or the so-called syndicates and the radicals (an assortment of left-of-center progressives, socialists, and Gandhians) and as Gandhi's own "power was challenged by her senior and more conservative colleagues," the mercurial Gandhi sided with the radicals, effectively "transforming the factional dispute into an ideological crusade" (Hardgrave and Kochanek 2000, 374).

In an effort to consolidate power, Gandhi "began to use economic policy as an active instrument for mustering political support" (Khilnani 1997, 90). To placate and win over the radicals, she not only reaffirmed the government's commitment to Nehruvian central planning (e.g., the Fourth Five-Year Plan [1969–74] gave priority to industrialization) but also promised to reform the economy further by curbing the power of private enterprise and eliminating socioeconomic inequalities through redistribution of wealth to the "weaker sections of society." A plethora of laws, directives, and regulatory measures were introduced to this effect: the Monopolies Restrictive Trade Practices Act (MRTP) was issued to curb the alleged power of large businesses through a highly restrictive licensing policy, and the Foreign Exchange Regulation Act (FERA) was issued to restrict foreign trade and capital. Similarly, the remaining banking, insurance, and mining companies were nationalized between 1969 and 1973. In April 1969, the central government nationalized fourteen of largest private banks with deposits over Rs. 500 million. These banks comprised roughly 54 percent of the bank branches in India.[36] As a result, the public sector banks' share of deposits jumped from 31 percent to 86 percent (Banerjee et al., 2004; GOI 1991). Under the new rules, both the public and the few remaining private banks were required to lend a certain percentage of credit to agriculture and small-scale industry, and the "branch expansion policy" obliged banks to open four branches in "unbanked locations" for every branch opened in a location in which a bank already existed. Although this

---

[35] Political attacks on devaluation cut across ideological lines. Both the right and the left in the political spectrum blamed the government for succumbing to pressure from the rich aid-giving countries, in particular, the United States. For example, the right could find neither "sound economics nor honorable politics" in the devaluation, whereas the left denounced it as "the greatest betrayal of national interest since Independence" (Frankel 1978, 299–300).

[36] The Supreme Court initially declared the nationalization to be invalid. However, Indira Gandhi amended the law and imposed nationalization by an ordinance.

policy increased the scope of banking in India to a scale unique to its level of development (in 2000, India had more than 60,000 bank branches, both public and private, located in almost every district across the country), these policies also made public sector banks attractive targets for political capture because they did not face hard budget constraints nor were they subject to political oversight. In 1980, the center undertook a second wave of bank nationalization by taking control of all banks with deposits greater than Rs. 2 billion. Although these nationalized banks were to function as corporate entities, the banks' boards of directors were replaced by appointees of the central government. Perhaps most unprecedented was the government's implementation of a series of sweeping constitutional amendments that made it easier for the authorities to appropriate industrial assets without due compensation. Under the evocative populist slogan *garibi hatao* ("abolish poverty"), which struck a chord with the masses, Gandhi made generous, indeed extravagant, promises to redistribute wealth and improve the living conditions of the poor. Although these strategies allowed her to reverse the Congress Party's electoral decline and win a landslide victory in 1971, the negative repercussions of populism were soon felt on the economy.

By the end of 1973, the OPEC oil shock, coupled with poor economic policies, pushed the economy into a steep decline, fueling unemployment, soaring inflation (which exceeded 23 percent during 1973–74), widespread shortages of essential commodities, and a thriving black market. The political bickering and ineptitude in New Delhi only made matters worse as agitations, *bandhs* (strikes), riots, and general lawlessness spread throughout the country. For example, massive student-led demonstrations in Gujarat and Bihar forced the government to send 40,000 troops to Bihar. In early 1974, some 700,000 railway workers went on strike, leading the government to arrest most of the union leaders and about 20,000 workers. In the face of eroding popular support, Gandhi resorted to high-handed and coercive measures to undermine her critics (inside both the Congress Party and Parliament). Eventually, when her own power and position were threatened by a court judgment, Gandhi used the pretext of restoring law and order by declaring the "state of national emergency" on June 25, 1975.[37] Under the "emergency law," the fundamental rights and civil liberties of citizens guaranteed in the Constitution was suspended, the collective rights of labor emasculated, the authority of the judiciary and Parliament severely curtailed, the press censored, and more than 150,000

---

[37] In June 1975, the High Court of Allahabad found Gandhi guilty of illegal electoral manipulation and ordered her to vacate her seat. However, President Fakhruddin Ali Ahmed, upon advice from the Prime Minister Gandhi, declared a State of Emergency under Article 352 of the Constitution. This allowed Gandhi to rule by decree. There is a vast literature on the emergency. The best remains Nayar (1977). For a good overview of Gandhi's reasons for the emergency, see Carras (1979), Frank (2002), and Hart (1976).

individuals, including several members of Parliament and prominent journalists, jailed without due process. In mid-January 1977, Gandhi, in a surprise announcement, declared that national elections would be held in mid-March. She expected the elections to legitimize her emergency declaration. When she finally rescinded the emergency on 21 March 1977 (India was not a full democracy for about 21 months) to hold elections, she was summarily defeated at the polls by the Janata Coalition, a rather whimsical alliance of unlikely partners poignantly underscoring the resilience of Indian democracy.[38]

However, the Janata Coalition, a hodgepodge of disparate political-ideological groups, although united against Gandhi's authoritarian rule, had little else in common. It hemorrhaged almost immediately upon taking office. Unable to agree on a common economic policy, the Janata proclaimed support for the Industrial Policy Resolution of 1956. However, it achieved little of substance; the three-year Janata interregnum (1977–80) was characterized by policy ineptitude and political and economic paralysis (Jha 1980). Eventually the unwieldy coalition collapsed, allowing Gandhi's Congress to return to power in the 1980 parliamentary elections. Her tenure was cut short when she was assassinated in 1984 by one of her own Sikh bodyguards, a payback for ordering Indian security forces to dislodge Sikh militants holed up inside the Golden Temple (Sikhism's holiest shrine). Her son, Rajiv Gandhi, a political neophyte, was appointed leader of the Congress. In the wake of a nationwide sympathy, he won a massive electoral victory in the December 1984 parliamentary elections, receiving 48 percent of the popular vote and 77 percent (or 415 of the 545 seats) in the Lok Sabha. Rajiv Gandhi, the scion of the Nehru family, had, at age forty, become India's youngest prime minister.

Rajiv Gandhi's victory brought a renewed sense of hope and optimism. His youth, clean-cut image, zeal for technology and efficiency (he was an accomplished pilot), and pro-Western outlook suggested that India was finally ready to make a break with the failed economic policies of the nationalist generation (Tharoor 1997). Despite Rajiv Gandhi's aggressive push to reform what he often called India's "top-down, over-regulated and shackled economy," in the end he only achieved what A. Kohli (1989, 1990) has illuminating labeled "half-hearted liberalization." Rather, his five-year term (1984–89), characterized by numerous political blunders (largely the result of his overdependence on a small coterie of bungling urbanite "backroom boys"), the Bofors scandal,[39]

---

[38] The Janata Coalition comprised four opposition parties: the Socialists, the Jana Sangh (right-of-center, pro-Hindu party), the Bharatiya Lok Dal (a regional party in North India that had split from the Congress), and the Congress O (which had separated from Gandhi's Congress in 1969).

[39] In 1987, Rajiv Gandhi's government was rocked by charges that the Swedish arms manufacturer Bofors AB had paid illegal commissions to win an artillery contract. The government's stonewalling on a full-scale inquiry and press exposes of illegal transactions involving the prime minister's closest friends, including evidence that came perilously close to directly implicating the prime minister himself, contributed to the government's defeat in 1989.

his widely perceived pro-rich and pro-urban economic liberalization policies (his preference for Gucci loafers and Porsche sunglasses did not help), and his failure to redeem one of his election pledges (to clean up the Congress Party and "return it to the people") saw him squander away the initial advantages he enjoyed as the legitimate inheritor and rejuvenator of the Congress Party. India's ninth general elections (held in 1989), saw the Congress spin into a precipitous political free-fall, dropping from 415 to 197 seats. However, the new minority National Front government, again a coalition of several disparate parties led by V. P. Singh, the iconoclastic former finance minister in Rajiv Gandhi's government (who along with other prominent dissidents were expelled by Gandhi), was overwhelmed by factionalism within its constituent units and irreconcilable policy differences with its main coalition partner, the BJP, collapsed after a little over two years. This was followed by an even shorter-lived Janata (Socialist)-led coalition government. Rajiv Gandhi's assassination by Tamil separatists during the 1991 election campaign decidedly helped tilt the electoral balance in favor of the Congress, now under the leadership of the veteran P. V. Narashima Rao. However, years of economic neglect and mismanagement by both the Congress and non-Congress governments had taken its toll on the economy. As discussed in the next chapter, Rao inherited an economy at the edge of an abyss, and with no way out, his administration was forced to introduce the most far-reaching economic reform measures in post-independent India.

Overall, four decades of central planning and state-led industrialization in India produced contradictory and ultimately disappointing results. Although the strategy provided the Indian economy with a large and diversified industrial base, given the massive volume of public resources put into the effort, the outcomes were hugely disappointing. In fact, India fell far short of achieving the plan's own developmental targets. The GDP growth rate, averaging a listless 3.5 percent a year from 1950 to 1980 (mockingly dubbed the "Hindu rate of growth"), was just above the population growth rate – and dismal compared with the impressive double-digit rates achieved by the high-performing East Asian economies. Not surprisingly, in 1981, out of a group of seventy-seven developing countries, India, with only US$260 in per capita income, ranked sixty-six. India's growth performance was simply not high enough to generate sustained employment opportunities and reduce poverty. Despite its much-touted goal of building a "socialistic pattern of society," access to basic services such as education, health care, and decent living conditions remained out of reach for many. In fact, in 1980, more than 40 percent of India's population or more than 200 million people lived in "absolute poverty," meaning they lacked the income to purchase food to meet their minimum caloric and nutritional needs.

Moreover, India's large and diversified industrial and manufacturing sectors never became internationally competitive in terms of either cost or quality.

Rather, India's export performance eroded over time, and its share of world merchandise exports fell from an already paltry 2.2 percent in 1948 to a stagnant 0.5 percent in 1983 (Srinivasan and Tendulkar 2003, 11). ISI's poor record and the Indian economy's failure to make the transition from ISI to export-led industrialization (as happened in East Asia) was fundamentally due to excessive government and bureaucratic control and regulations (Sharma 1999, 82–91). In particular, Nehru's hostile stance toward foreign trade and the commonly held view that free trade in the unequal and distorted global economy was a "zero-sum game," designed to benefit rich countries at the expense of the poor, evolved into what became known as "export pessimism." In the end, such paranoia prevented India from exploiting its trade and comparative advantage in the international economy (Bhagwati 1993; Waterbury 1993). Similarly, although in theory protectionist measures against foreign goods was seen as a temporary measure designed to build up and insulate India's "infant industries," in practice, these policies did not have a "sunset clause." Instead, conveniently hiding behind growing layers of tariff barriers and a highly protectionist regime of regulations, domestic firms in sheltered industries did not have to make improvements in quality, innovate, or become competitive because they enjoyed monopoly privileges in the closed domestic market. This system also suited the prerogatives of bureaucrats and politicians because business had to beg and bribe public servants to get around the government's elaborate (and cumbersome) rules and regulations controlling private economic activity. Under this arbitrary system, aptly named "permit, license, quota Raj," bureaucrats and state officials treated their positions as personal sinecures, enjoying significant discretion in evaluating applications and granting licenses. Soon malfeasance, corruption, and vice permeated the system as government officials became highly efficient at rent seeking, using their powers for both partisan purposes and personal gain. By the mid-1970s, even as the ISI model was showing signs of exhaustion, the system was too entrenched and difficult to reform.

China: Economic Development

The CCP also inherited a devastated economy. Collapse of both the agricultural and industrial sectors, as well as the country's infrastructure, due to half a century of protracted civil war, brutal foreign occupation, and neglect had left a tragic legacy. Grinding poverty, unemployment, inflation, widespread opium addiction, prostitution, corruption, lawlessness, and criminality were endemic. Mao and the CCP leadership recognized that the very survival of their nascent revolutionary regime depended on how effectively they responded to these pressing problems. After all, Chiang Kai-shek and his Guomindang saw their exile to Taiwan as only a "temporary retreat" and remained committed to taking back the mainland from the Communist usurpers (Barnett 1964;

Fairbank and Goldman 1999), and American intervention on behalf of Chiang remained a real possibility as the Cold War intensified (Christensen 1996; Jian 2001; Hunt 1996; Qing 2007).

GRADUALISM UNDER "NEW DEMOCRACY"

Mao and the CCP leadership were aware that the world's only other Communist state, the Soviet Union, facing similar grave challenges after the Bolsheviks victory in 1917, had initiated the policy of "War Communism."[40] However, the CCP eschewed this radical (and ultimately ruinous) strategy (which among other things included draconian controls over the economy such as immediate and total nationalization of industry, forced appropriations of food and resources from the peasantry, as well as mass arrests, purges, and "liquidation" of perceived "class enemies") for a more a moderate and benign strategy that emphasized building broad-based class coalitions to jump-start the economy – in particular, restoring agricultural and industrial production (Houn 1967; Snow 1961). In practice, this meant that with the exception of assets controlled by the "comprador bourgeoisie" and capitalists who had fled China, the "parasitic" or "evil" gentry, and its Guomindang collaborators, private property rights in land and industry and market-based activity were to be protected.[41] Unlike the USSR, in China, there was no nationwide punitive confiscation of private property, nor were officials and bureaucrats of the *ancien regime* expelled from their positions. Rather, out of both prudence and necessity, the CCP sought the cooperation and support of both private enterprise and the skilled bureaucracy to revitalize the economy quickly and operate the levers of governmental machinery (Harding 1980; Meisner 1986). This spirit of reconciliation and class cooperation received bold expression in the official policy of "New Democracy." Vigorously championed by Mao, "New Democracy" argued that the unique character of the Chinese revolution made the development of capitalism a necessary precondition for building socialism. Hence, Communists and non-Communists, as well as capitalists and the progressive gentry, were to work together with workers and peasants for the common good of the nation.[42]

In the countryside, where the vast majority of the Chinese people lived, the CCP's Land Reform Law of 1950 won it widespread support from the rural populace (Baum 1975; Hinton 1966). Land reforms redistributed some

---

[40] For good overviews of the socialist system, see Kornai (1992) and Tucker (1969).

[41] The "comprador," unlike the "national bourgeoisie," was seen to be inextricably tied to colonialism and thus decadent.

[42] One of the reason for this policy may have had to do with what Meisner (1996, 12) notes was Maoism's insistence "on the necessity of a bourgeois stage of development" and an appreciation of "the historically progressive role of indigenous Chinese capitalism." See also Dirlik (1989), Selden (1971), and Starr (1979).

42 percent of China's arable land on an equitable per capita basis.[43] That is, although land still remained in private hands (actual land titles or ownership deeds were issued to the tillers), ownership became more equitable as millions of the erstwhile landless peasants and tenant farmers became actual small peasant proprietors. In one sweep, the CCP had not only destroyed the political and economic power of the landed gentry (who had remained a ubiquitous feature of the Chinese countryside for more than a millennia) but also lifted millions of the aggrieved peasantry out of bondage and destitution, thereby further reinforcing the legitimacy of the Communist regime.[44] Moreover, land reforms unleashed the latent productive capacity of agriculture as annual crop production increased 70 percent from 113.2 million tons to 192.7 million tons between 1949 and 1956, and total farm income rose by 85 percent during the same period (Gensheng 2001, 3–4; also see Lardy 1983; Walker 1984). Similarly, in the urban areas, industrialists, businesspeople, entrepreneurs, and professionals were encouraged to participate in the reconstruction of the country. Meisner (1996, 29) notes that the "number of privately owned industrial firms actually increased during the early years of Communist rule, accounting for nearly 40 percent of total industrial production in 1953. An even greater percentage of commercial firms remained under private ownership."

INDUSTRIAL AND AGRICULTURAL SOCIALISM

Naughton (2007, 65) notes that "by the end of 1952, economic recovery and rehabilitation had become a resounding success." Equally important, the interlude allowed the CCP to consolidate its power and authority throughout the country. It seems that once these twin challenges were accomplished, Mao turned his attention to his long cherished goal: building genuine socialism in China. Mao found both inspiration and vindication in the only other socialist experiment: the Soviet Union. He saw the Soviet model of "crash" or "big-push industrialization" as an exemplar of economic success and deemed it the only sure way to transform rapidly a backward "semifeudal" order like China into an advanced socialist one (Meisner 1986; Riskin 1987; Schram 1969). To achieve its audacious goal, the Soviet model emphasized near total control

---

[43] Naughton (2007, 65). According to Wang (1995, 21), "land redistribution was completed in 1952, when 113 million acres – plus draft animals and farm implements – were distributed to over 300 million landless peasants." According to recent a Chinese source, land reforms redistributed more than half of China's arable land to some 50 to 60 million poor rural households, making up more than 60 percent of its rural population (China Institute for Reform and Development 1999; also Hsu 1995). Clearly, land reforms were successful in giving land to the tillers.

[44] Of course, the land reform campaigns were not always without violence. Landlords were usually subjected to violent "class struggles," which included public humiliations and "trials" for their past actions (Zhou 1996). The precise number killed during the campaign remains in dispute. According to one oft-cited account, anywhere from 1 to 4 percent of landlord family members were killed during the land reform period from 1949 to 1952 (Stavis 1978, 29–30).

of the economy by the party-state. Specifically, the state's role was not only to control all the levers of economic production such as capital, assets, and land, the central government (or the "central planners") had complete authority to make all key economic decisions, including those pertaining to investment, allocation, production, and distribution. In effect, central planners were to steer, or, more appropriately, "command," the economy from above (hence, the moniker "command economy") – and in the process replace the market as the principal determinant of economic activity.

China's First Five-Year Plan (1953–57), inaugurated with choreographed official fanfare on 1 January 1953, marked a death knell to the pragmatism and openness espoused by the "New Democracy." Mao's ultimately precipitous new "general line" (or deviation to "ultra-leftism") of "rapid transition to socialism" now extolled the virtues of central planning and rapid industrialization. Mao and the CCP leadership urged the country to embrace nationalization of industry and the conversion of peasant farming into agricultural producer cooperatives to fulfill this ambitious goal.[45] This bias toward industry was reflected in the First Five-Year Plan, which allocated roughly 50 percent of its total investment budget to light and heavy industry, whereas agriculture (from which about 90 percent of the population drew a living) was allocated a mere 7.1 percent of the resources. In fact, (similar to India's experience), from the First Five-Year Plan to the Sixth Five-Year Plan (1981–85), industry received some 45 percent of the total investments, whereas the agricultural sector received less than 10 percent (Lin 1994, 26).

Mao's abrupt policy turnaround had immediate consequences.[46] From that point on, every policy had to meet the test of ideological purity rather than economic logic, and the single-minded determination to achieve the end (socialism) was enough to justify any means. By early 1953, economic decision making had become highly bureaucratized and centralized – the exclusive purview of Mao and his close associates. Private commercial and industrial firms faced punitive taxation and confiscation; some were pressured into signing contracts with state-run enterprises, whereas others saw their assets often forcibly expropriated in return for paltry (if not worthless) government bonds. Meisner (1996, 32) notes that by 1956, much private enterprise had been "de facto nationalized"

---

[45] Initially, peasants were encouraged to join cooperatives on a voluntary basis. Until 1955, there were three types of cooperatives: the "mutual aid team" in which four or five households pooled their farm equipment and draft animals and received returns based on the proportion of land and equipment they had pooled. The "elementary cooperative" was made up of twenty to thirty neighboring households that pooled their equipment and labor and were paid on the basis of land, draft animals, and tools owned by each household as well as labor output per worker. In both these systems, land could still be privately bought and sold (Fairbank and Goldman 1999, 352). In "advanced cooperatives," all means of production was collectively owned, and remuneration was based solely on the amount of work each member contributed.

[46] There has been much scholarly speculation as to why Mao abruptly went from being a pragmatist to an obsessed ideologue. For a good overview, see Li (2006) and Starr (1979).

and "the urban bourgeoisie had all but ceased to exist as a social class." Backing the ambitious industrial program were several thousand Soviet advisers who were brought in to help transplant the Soviet industrial model to China. As Naughton (2007, 66), notes, "the very first Five-Year Plan, nominally covering 1953 through 1957, was drawn up "half in Moscow, half in Peking." At the heart of the plan was the construction of 156 large industrial projects, all of them imported from the Soviet Union or from Eastern Europe. Although the USSR provided technical assistance and capital in the form of low-interest loans, the bulk of the capital required for industrial development came in large measure from the Chinese countryside (Lardy 1983; Wang 1995, 22). Specifically, a two-pronged approach that included compulsory agricultural procurement (in which farmers had to sell their crops to the state at government-set prices – i.e., below market prices) to underwrite industrialization and gradual abolishment of private ownership of land was simultaneously carried out.[47] Ironically, to prevent peasants from moving to the cities to buy the lower-priced food products (that were appropriated from the countryside in the first place) created to insulate the urban workforce from price fluctuations, the central government instituted a rigid and draconian urban household registration system (the *hukou*) complete with food-ration cards and residence permits, thereby virtually closing off rural-urban migration.[48]

However, frustrated with what he considered to be an incremental if not, unduly slow, pace of progress toward socialism, especially with the small numbers of the peasantry voluntarily joining agricultural producer cooperatives, Mao upped the ante. In mid-1955, in a much anticipated statement, Mao outlined both his analysis and solution of the problem. He called for a higher and more ambitious (read: "socialist") form of cooperatives in which all members of the rural populace worked for wages regardless of their input of capital, tools, land, and labor. In effect, what Mao had in mind was agricultural collectivization, which he hailed as "the high tide of socialism" (Fairbank and Goldman 1999, 354–7; Meisner 1996, 32). Mao's call served as a rally for many party cadres who earnestly set out in droves all around the countryside to set up "advanced cooperatives" and collectives in conformity with a centrally determined regimen. In the process, they transformed China's agricultural production based on individual small-peasant proprietorships into collectives and communes. As Naughton (2007, 67) notes, "at the end of 1954, only 2% of

---

[47] Kate Zhou (1996, 27) notes that "never before had the state controlled the sale of grain on a nationwide basis. Before the PRC, the government had collected taxes, sometimes years in advance, but the government had never in effect laid claim to the entire crop. With establishment of the procurement system, there were few private grain markets. . . . In twenty-six years, the state's control over grain prices alone extracted 25 billion yuan from farmers." See also Shue (1980), Stavis (1978), and Walker (1984).

[48] As Lin (1994, 30) notes, "the urban residents were entitled to numerous subsidies estimated to be as high as 80 percent of their wage earnings, whereas the rural population had none of those benefits."

farm households had been enrolled in cooperatives or collectives; by 1955, 14%
were enrolled; and by the end of 1956, 98%." The success of collectivization
encouraged the party to make an even bolder move: the establishment of the
"people's commune."[49] In the fall of 1958, communes made up of about 30
collectives of 150 households were introduced. However, "within only three
months, 753,000 collective farms were transformed into 24,000 communes
consisting of 120 million households, over 99 percent of total rural households
in China in 1958" (Lin 1994, 35). Similarly, in the urban and industrial economy what limited private enterprises remained was made into "cooperatives
or else "joint public-private" factories with substantial control exercised by the
state." For all practical purposes, private ownership "was virtually extinguished
during six months in late 1955 and early 1956" (Naughton 2007, 67).

The First Five-Year Plan's success in promoting economic growth proved to
be beyond all expectations. The economy grew by almost 9 percent per year –
a remarkable achievement by any standard. Yet Mao still remained unsatisfied
with the performance of the economy, especially the seemingly slow pace of
change toward socialism. Given Mao's long-held distrust of intellectuals-cum-
"experts," he was not only concerned by what he felt was the party's growing
dependence on experts and the resultant "bourgeois" elitism and bureaucratization it spawned, but also by how their undue caution stifled progress
toward socialism (Starr 1979). Moreover, Mao, who always remained ambivalent toward the Soviet Union, was alarmed by China's increasing dependence
on Soviet technology, personnel, and capital, including the Soviet Union's
growing influence in China's domestic affairs (Bowie and Fairbank 1962; Hunt
1996; Jian 2001; Lee 1996).

Mao's capricious "Anti-Rightist Campaign" in mid-1957 effectively silenced
the intellectuals and other critics inside the party and in the government,[50] and
the ongoing discussions and debates regarding the direction of the Second Five-
Year Plan (1958–62) presented Mao and his confidants with an opportunity to
break away from Soviet dependence and reorient China's developmental trajectory along a supposedly more "self-reliant," "independent," and "socialist"

---

[49] "The average size of a commune was about 5,000 households, with 10,000 laborers and 10,000
acres of cultivated land. Payment in the commune was made partly according to subsistence
needs and partly according to the work performed. Work on private plots (which existed in
the other forms of cooperatives), was prohibited" (Lin 1994, 35).

[50] In mid-1956, Mao decreed that "a hundred flowers should bloom" and "a hundred schools of
thought contend" to encourage citizens to speak their mind about the CCP and its policies.
However, by mid-1957, he initiated the Anti-Rightist Campaign when intellectuals and other
"experts" began to reveal their grievances publicly and speak out against the party. The result
was massive crackdown in which hundreds of thousands of individuals (disproportionately
intellectuals and middle-class professionals) were arrested and subject to "thought reform,"
including consignment to labor camps in remote parts of the country. This betrayal alienated
China's intellectuals and made them extremely wary of engaging in the political process again
(Lieberthal 1995, 101; Meisner 1996).

path. Determined to continue with the heavy-industrialization strategy while at the same time reducing the amount of Soviet capital (which was in the form of loans rather than grants) and expertise China borrowed, Mao came up with a novel (and, in hindsight, a disastrous) plan. China would develop its own unique brand of socialism. The chairman's new plan, enthusiastically hailed as the "Great Leap Forward," was seen as a way to catapult China toward a communist utopia without the assistance of the Soviets and undue reliance on China's haughty "petty bourgeois" experts. Rather, by decentralizing power and relying on the latent energy and creativity of the "masses" and the dedicated party cadres and apparatchiks (the so-called reds), China would overcome daunting resource constraints and achieve rapid economic growth – or, as Mao himself boasted, "achieve the economic levels of the most advanced countries in fifteen years" (Meisner 1996, 42). It seems that Mao, who could never reconcile the divergent goals of economic development and creating a communist utopia, had settled on building a utopia with the commencement of the Great Leap Forward in the spring of 1958 (Bachman 1991; Schram 1969, 1989).

THE GREAT LEAP FORWARD

During the height of the Great Leap Forward (mid-1958), large-scale "people's communes," each initially averaging some 50,000 households, were hastily set up throughout China. Later they were reduced to a more manageable size, combining ten or more villages and township governments. Unlike the cooperatives, communes were to be "self-sufficient" by combining both agricultural and small-scale industrial development. To facilitate this, more than a million "backyard steel furnaces" were set up throughout the country not only to enable each commune to produce industrial inputs for both agriculture and industry but also ostensibly to prove that the masses, with the "correct" guidance, could produce steel in every locality, not just in large steel complexes run by experts in the cities. In each commune, work teams, or "production brigades," were set up to organize and exhort each other to labor long and hard (often the brigades were divided into twenty-four-hour work shifts) to increase production. In return, the communes were to distribute the fruits of labor along "socialist lines" (according to work and need) as well as provide an expanded range of social services, including child care, education, health care, housing, and food supplies, for its members (H. Hinton 1966; W. Hinton 1984).

The unprecedented regimentation of labor, coupled with the frenzied activities in the communes, produced, at least initially, the desired results. The harvest at end of 1958 produced a bumper crop, whereas the backyard furnaces produced more than their quota of industrial output. Mao and top CCP leadership were jubilant. As Lieberthal (1995, 105) notes, "they decided, for example, that in 1959 they would leave roughly one-third of the country's arable land fallow, as otherwise they would have trouble handling all the food produced. The top leaders began to talk confidently of having invented a new strategy for socialist development – a strategy that could work far more successfully than that of the Soviet Union." Sadly, this euphoria was grossly misplaced because the impressive growth rates also masked deep underlying problems. In reality, the crudely built fledgling backyard furnaces had simply produced huge quantities of poor-quality crude iron (rather than steel), squandering precious resources in the process. The much-vaunted steel output had been produced mainly by industrial complexes built by the Soviets from 1953 to 1955, which produced its first output in 1958. In the countryside, the bumper fall harvest was the result not simply of massive labor inputs and more efficient farming practices but also the unusually favorable weather conditions.

Compounding this was the politicization of economic policy making. As the punitive witch-hunts and the vindictive attacks following the Anti-Rightist Campaign had made chillingly clear, Mao and his cohorts, blinded by ideology, hubris, and long-festering feuds and vendettas, were not open to dissenting voices (Teiwes 1979). In this radically charged, poisoned, and unpredictable political environment (in which the slightest hint of questioning official dogma invited being labeled a "rightist" or worse), party bureaucrats watched over by the illiterate and overzealous "reds" deliberately and recklessly falsified production figures by grossly inflating output numbers to tell their higher-ups what they wanted to hear.[51] Even some counties and provinces began to outdo one another in claiming the highest production achievements to show that they were the most loyal to Mao (Yang 1996). However, this is not to say that the truth about the worsening situation on the ground did not reach Mao and the party elite. The solitary few who dared to inform Mao and his inner circle about the worsening situation of hunger and sporadic uprisings in the countryside (these were comrades who knew Mao intimately from the early revolutionary years), including the senior party veteran, "hero of the revolution," and minister of defense, the impeccable Marshal Peng Dehuai, were publicly humiliated and vilified by Mao and ultimately purged for criticizing the Great Leap Forward at a party conference in the summer of 1959 (Lieberthal 1995, 106–7; Meisner 1996, 45).

In similar fashion, reports about sharp declines in farm output and productivity, the growing unrest in the countryside and general unhappiness with the regimentation of rural life, and the intolerable working conditions in the communes were contemptuously dismissed as isolated complaints and pushed aside. Instead, the ever-defiant Mao demanded an intensification of the Great Leap policies (Bachman 1991). The impending disaster was now inevitable. All

---

[51] The political leadership in Beijing deliberately set high output targets, claiming that it was achievable under effective local leadership. Therefore, by implication, failure to reach the set targets was due to poor leadership. Not surprisingly, local leaders compensated local failures by simply falsifying and exaggerating production results. Soon a vicious cycle ensued.

it took was two ill-timed policy decisions in the autumn of 1959 (reduction in the supply of production resources for the agricultural sector and increased compulsory procurement of grain and food products), three continuous years of unusually bad weather conditions (1959–62), and mismanagement and corruption to put the countryside over the edge. In the beginning of 1960, the specter of a full-blown famine gripped rural China. Depleted of food reserves and faced with official, indeed willful, neglect the Chinese countryside was left to its own devices in the bewildering and enervating summer heat of 1960. By the end of 1961, an estimated 25 to 30 million people had starved to death in the worst famine in the twentieth century (Ashton et al. 1984; Becker 1996; Yang 1996).

As the magnitude of the tragedy became evident, Mao grudgingly ordered a retreat from the Great Leap Forward. Although this was too late for the millions who had already perished under the most reckless and unspeakable inhumanity, the retreat did result in the halt to the grotesquely misconceived and destructive policies. Also, Mao (again reluctantly) accepted some responsibility for the failure of the Great Leap and "retreated from the center of the political stage," albeit not without first putting his trusted allies and putative successors Liu Shaoqi and Deng Xiaoping in control (Meisner 1996, 47). Liu was appointed chairman of the People's Republic (a position previously held by Mao), and Deng, who had played an important role as the iron-fisted enforcer in carrying out the Anti-Rightist" purges and was not an entirely unenthusiastic supporter of the Great Leap Forward, was now entrusted to run the day-to-day affairs of government and revive the economy. Showing the pragmatism he would later become famous for, Deng's policies during the years 1961–65 (such as rationing food to ameliorate shortages; restructuring communes into smaller and more efficient household production units; using incentives, including allowing farmers to cultivate private plots[52] and sell the products from these plots, and "expert" management) were successful in restoring order and reviving the economy. By 1965, the worst of the disaster was over (Naughton 2007, 73).

Although Mao conceded – although in his peculiar earthy and crude way – that such policies may have been necessary in the short term, he remained apprehensive that over the long term it would lead to the restoration of capitalism in China. Moreover, Mao smarting from the "rebuke," bitterly complained that he was deliberately marginalized and excluded from major policy decisions by Deng and the other party leaders, often comparing himself to the Buddha – as someone publicly revered, but otherwise ignored and considered irrelevant. In the secretive Byzantine world that Mao inhabited, rumors (both real and

---

[52] Of course, "private plot" does not mean privately owned land, which peasants could purchase, sell, or rent. Rather, it was a small piece of the collective's land allocated to individual households on a per capita basis. The produce of this land could be sold by peasants.

imagined), distrust, and alleged "bourgeois elements" and "counterrevolution-aries" lurked behind every corner waiting for an opportune moment to pounce and subvert the revolution. To Mao, this is precisely what had happened in the Soviet Union following Nikita Khrushchev's denunciation of Stalin after his death in 1953 and subsequent "revisionism" and abandonment of socialism (Lieberthal 1995, 109–11). To preempt a similar outcome in China, Mao, now an increasingly aloof, narcissistic, and paranoid megalomaniac, concluded that Liu Shaoqi and Deng Xiaoping, among other "revisionists" and "capitalist roaders," had to be purged – and quickly. With these paranoiac fears, Mao unleashed the "Great Proletarian Cultural Revolution" in the summer of 1966.

THE CULTURAL REVOLUTION TO DENG XIAOPING

The Cultural Revolution, tragically reflecting the absurdity and Manichaean utopian idealism of Mao's persona, convulsed China for several years, according to some accounts, ending only with Mao's death in 1976. In an environment where political survival was a zero-sum game because party members could be revered at one moment and reviled the next, chaos, fear, servility, uncertainty, despair, and disillusionment characterized this tumultuous period as careers and lives were destroyed, sometimes irretrievably under state-sponsored witch-hunts and guilt by association (Gao 1987; Thurston 1988). During the inquisi-tion's most bizarre and violent phase (1966–69), Mao used his immense prestige and charisma to mobilize the "spontaneous energy of the masses" against per-ceived enemies of the revolution. In fact, no one was safe from Mao's idiosyn-crasies, eccentricities, and lethal wrath. Reminiscent of courtly rituals in which an emperor would pass judgment on his subjects, Mao, both personally and through his obsequious surrogates (including his wife Jiang Qing), duplici-tously cajoled, instigated, and manipulated impressionable youth, especially students, to form groups of Red Guards, sanctioning them to "weed out" and "cleanse" – verbally and physically – the "counterrevolutionary" and "bour-geois" representatives within the party and the state apparatus. This included all intellectuals and high-ranking party leaders – except, of course, the "emperor" Mao (Lieberthal 1995, 112–13). Mao, who believed he could do no wrong, sat on the sidelines vicariously "watching" the torment mete out to his comrades.

In what became a seemingly routine occurrence, the main perpetrators – the unruly Red Guards and their marionettes armed with weapons and the hagio-graphic *Book of Quotations from Chairman Mao Zedong* (also known as "The Little Red Book") – would break into party and government offices, including private homes, and announce that they had found incriminating evidence of counterrevolutionary activity. The "guilty" would than be unceremoniously dragged and paraded in public forums, where they would be subjected to fero-ciously intense "struggle sessions" in which they would be harangued, taunted, ridiculed, forced to give confessions, and sometimes physically assaulted. Once found guilty (and they always were) of some alleged apostasy, the victims were either killed (that is, forced to commit suicide) or sent to purgatory – remote villages and penal labor camps for "reeducation" (Zhou 1996). Even senior party members, including Deng Xiaoping and the octogenarian Liu Shaoqi, were not spared this outrage. Liu died in prison after hours of sustained torture. Deng Xiaoping was publicly humiliated, forced to wear a dunce cap, and placed under house arrest (Evans 1994). He was eventually stripped of all his party posts and sent to work as a field hand in the remote countryside for several years, where he and his wife grew their own food to supplement their meager subsistence existence. Only his resilience and indomitable countenance enabled them to survive those turbulent and treacherous times.

The Cultural Revolution left deep and lasting physical and psychological scars on the Chinese society, polity, and economy, brutally quashing the hopes and aspirations of a generation. The near anarchy, arbitrariness, and double standards traumatized society, forcing the frightened and weary citizens to opt out of the already limited avenues for public life. Richard Pipes (1990) poignant description of the Stalinist "Red Terror" in the 1930s is eerily similar to the Maoist terror. Pipes notes that "the Red Terror gave the population to understand that under a regime that felt no hesitation in executing innocents, innocence was no guarantee of survival. The best hope of surviving lay in making oneself as inconspicuous as possible, which meant abandoning any thought of independent public activity, indeed any concern with public affairs, and withdrawing into one's private world. Once society disintegrated into an agglomeration of human atoms, each fearful of being noticed and concerned exclusively with physical survival, then it ceased to matter what society thought, for the government had the entire sphere of public activity to itself" (p. 838). Of course, in Maoist China, even the party elite and the ranks of the apparatchik, who were the perpetrators (and victims) of the hypocrisy, intrigues, factional power struggles, and witch-hunts, were not safe. As the vicious and belligerent attacks continued unabated and mind-numbing polemics passed for political dialogue in Zhongnanhai (China's White House), and Red Guard factions turned against each other with unrestrained vengeance, society grew more cynical and disillusioned with the political system, the Communist Party, and even Mao himself.[53]

On the economic front many of the controls that had been relaxed by Deng in the early 1960s were reinstated. For example, no market transactions of agricultural products were now allowed outside the procurement system and market exchanges between different production units in the commune system were made illegal. Coupled with years of neglect, corruption and mismanagement (in part, the result of summarily purging numerous qualified "experts" and replacing them with ideologically-motivated, but poorly trained "reds")

---

[53] For a good early appraisal of Mao's legacy, see Wilson (1977).

plunged the just recovering economy into a free-fall as agricultural production and productivity sharply declined (Fan, Zhang, and Zhang 2004). Widespread shortages of basic consumer goods forced the government to set up a strict rationing system for food and other basic necessities. In this environment of economic stagnation, the constant exhortations from the political leadership for even greater sacrifices, thrift and "belt tightening" became a cruel joke as living standards continued to deteriorate – regardless of one's frugality and material sacrifices. Mao's death in September 1976 at the age of 82 marked the end of an era and hope of a fresh beginning. While the old helmsman's radical allies (the so-called "ultra-leftists"), in particular, the notorious "gang of four" led by Mao's wife, Jiang Qing tried to usurp power, their denouement was short as they were ignominiously outmaneuvered and rounded-up and eventually given long prison sentences. Deng Xiaoping who had quietly worked behind the scenes made a triumphant return back to the center of power in Beijing.[54] Although, Deng refused to hold any formal offices in either the party or government, he was reinstated to all his former positions in mid-1977 following the victory of the Dengists at the Third Plenum of the Tenth Party Central Committee. At the conclusion of the Third Plenum of the Eleventh Communist Party Congress in December 1978, the Dengists were firmly in control. Deng Xiaoping was now the undisputed "paramount leader" – the real power behind the throne. He occupied this position until his death in 1997 at the age of ninety-four.

Concluding Reflections

As the preceding discussion has shown, China and India's attempt to lay the foundations of a modern industrial economy produced mixed, if ultimately disappointing, results for both. Their experiences also raise questions regarding the relationship between democratic and authoritarian systems of governance and economic development. The dramatic economic success of East Asian countries (namely, South Korea and Taiwan) under authoritarian regimes led many to conclude that there was an affinity between authoritarianism and development. Yet the experience of China hardly proves the superiority of authoritarianism over democracy in terms of economic development. Clearly, authoritarianism is neither necessary nor sufficient for development. In fact, even when viewed in a purely instrumental manner, democracy has important advantages over nondemocratic forms of government. Democratic India did

---

[54] In 1973, at the behest of his mentor, Premier Zhou Enlai, an ailing Mao called Deng Xiaoping back to Beijing to manage both party and governmental affairs. By 1975, Deng was reinstated to all the party and government posts he had lost during the Cultural Revolution. However, the leftist Gang of Four, who were opposed to Deng, convinced Mao, following Zhou's death in January 1976, to once again purge Deng from his posts. Fearing for his safety, Deng went into hiding in southern China (Baum 1994; Shambaugh 1995).

not succumb to the excesses of totalitarian China, such as Great Leap Forward, which killed millions, or the Cultural Revolution, which destroyed numerous lives. Nobel laureate Amartya Sen (1999, 152) poignantly notes that "no substantial famine has ever occurred in any independent country with a democratic form of government and a relatively free press. Famines have occurred in ancient kingdoms and contemporary authoritarian societies, in tribal communities and in modern technocratic dictatorships, in colonial economies run by imperialists from the north and newly independent countries of the south run by despotic national leaders or by intolerant single parties. But they have never materialized in any country that is independent, that goes to elections regularly, that has opposition parties to voice criticisms, and that permits newspapers to report freely and question the wisdom of governments' policies without extensive censorship."

Of course, democracies are not without problems, although they pale in comparison to nondemocratic systems. India's experience shows that a democratic government does not guarantee sustained levels of economic growth or a pattern of development that effectively combines growth with redistribution. Rather, egregious social inequalities and extensive poverty can coexist alongside democratic governance. Furthermore, democracies are particularly vulnerable to competitive populism (or the short-run pandering and handouts to win elections) and irresponsible nationalist, protectionist, and spendthrift policies. Clearly, the exigencies of electoral politics often make it much harder to make prudent economic decisions, and vested interests can easily undermine well-intentioned plans. However, the Indian experience also shows that democratic governments are more responsive to demands and pressures from the citizenry because their right to rule is derived from popular support manifested in competitive elections. Thus, in open democratic systems characterized by regular elections and political competition, political elites have incentives to furnish public goods and promote more equitable economic development.

2

China and India Embrace Globalization

This chapter provides a broad analysis of how and why China and India opened themselves to the global economy. It provides a comprehensive review of the various policies and programs that were put in place to facilitate each country's integration into the international economic system. The following pages explore not only the politics behind the policy making and how this has influenced and determined the nature, substance, and depth of the various pro-market policies, but also why and how the various policies and programs have evolved or been revised to meet the changing political and economic circumstances. The chapter shows that whereas China – following Deng's famous maxim, "crossing the river by groping for stones" – gradually and sequentially adapted its reform policies to the fast-changing domestic and global political economy and seized opportunities as they arose, India's liberalization program, literally forced on the country's political elites by a fast hemorrhaging economy, was hastily introduced. After the initial burst, pro-market policies have followed a seemingly meandering path – more a reflection of the contingencies of the country's democratic politics than economic prudence.

Moreover, the chapter sheds insight on the perennial political economy question: why was a certain approach to global economic integration – namely, "gradualism" – privileged over "shock therapy"? Why, unlike the former Soviet Union and its Eastern bloc, did market reforms and global economic integration in China not result in economic and political implosion, but rather political stability and unprecedented economic growth? Further, what explains the Indian state's ability to dramatically abandon its long commitment to a statist and inward-oriented model for an unprecedented strategy of global economic integration, despite the fact that a large body of scholarship has long claimed that democratic regimes (especially India's particularly "weak state") lack the requisite capacity and autonomy to implement market-friendly public policies because of, among other things, its potentially negative impact on broad sectors of society and the resultant political backlash it may generate?

The first part of the chapter focuses on the Chinese experience. The second part reviews India's experience.

The Chinese Experience

In 1978, Deng Xiaoping, the sturdy survivor and arch-pragmatist, was firmly at the helm. The Deng Xiaoping era was about to begin. Deng harbored no illusion of just how impoverished China had become under Mao; breaking decisively from the Maoist ideological straitjacket and resolving the destructive socioeconomic and political legacies of Maoism was of utmost importance. As Deng himself often mused, what China needed was a "second revolution" – no doubt, an oblique reference to the need for washing away the detritus of Maoism and starting anew (Deng Xiaoping 1994). Indeed, in his almost twenty-year rule Deng Xiaoping did precisely that. With the "four socialist modernization" (which emphasized the growth of agriculture, industry, military might, and science and technology) as his guiding principle of national development, Deng adroitly and systematically repudiated the main tenets of Maoism by ushering in a series of reforms that profoundly transformed almost every aspect of life in the People's Republic of China (PRC).

However, as a lifelong Marxist, Deng had no intention, at least not initially, to transform completely China's centrally planned economy into a liberal market-based one. Rather, the market was to complement and support state planning, not replace it, as reflected in the oft-quoted phrase, "*jihua wei zhu, shichang wei fu*" (or "planning as a principal part and market as a supplementary part"). In the domestic economy, the goal was to eliminate the pervasive layers of government and bureaucratic red tape and "commands" of Maoist state socialism, while creating incentives for individual initiative and enterprise and expanding the scope of the market. Also, cognizant of the fact that China's "inward-looking economy" was not only stagnating but rapidly falling behind the "outward-oriented" East Asian economies – namely, South Korea and Taiwan – a bold "open-door policy" was adopted to facilitate China's integration into global economy. The Dengists, or "Reformers," believed (in hindsight correctly) that global economic integration not only would allow China to exploit her unique comparative advantage (abundant labor and a huge domestic market) in the emerging global economy, but the flow of Western technology, capital and management practices would also enable China to advance the ambitious goals of socialist modernization more rapidly. Yet the Party also made it clear that socialist modernization had to be carried out incrementally (epitomized in Deng's famous quote, "crossing the river by groping for stones") and within the framework of mandatory central planning and state ownership, which were considered to be inviolable principles of the party-state.

Table 2.1. *Contrasting styles of economic reform*

1980	1990
Introduce markets where feasible: focus on agriculture and industry	Strengthen institutions of market economy: focus on finance and regulation
Dual-track strategy	Market unification, unite dual tracks
Particularistic contracts with powerful incentives	Uniform rules: "level-playing field"
Competition created by entry; no privatization	State-sector downsizing: beginnings of privatization
Decentralize authority and resources	Recentralize resources, macroeconomic control
Inflationary economy with shortages	Price stability, goods in surplus
"Reform without losers"	Reform with losers

Source: Naughton (2007, 91).

By the early 1990s, however, there was growing realization among the Reformers that the "plan-market strategy" (or marketization) had largely run its course – or in Naughton's (1996) evocative phrase, the market had expanded sufficiently, and it was now time for the economy to "grow out of the plan." In the spring of 1992, Deng Xiaoping made his famous "Southern tour" of the special economic zones (SEZs) to mobilize support for deeper reforms. At the Fourteenth Party Congress held in September 1992, the Chinese Communist Party (CCP) after reassessing the plan-market strategy concluded that the time was right for China to adopt a more bold approach, one of building a "socialist market economy with Chinese characteristics." Party secretary Jiang Zemin was given the primary responsibility to work with leading technocrats and prepare the blueprint for the "grand transition." Jiang's landmark report, modestly titled "Decision on Issues Concerning the Establishment of a Socialist Market Economic Structure," became "law" after it was formally adopted by the Third Plenum of the Fourteenth Congress of the CCP in November 1993. Although in the officialese China was making a "transition to a socialist market economy" – or in theory maintaining a proper balance between central planning and the market – for all practical purposes, central planning and state ownership was to be made secondary, if not jettisoned, in favor of the market. Table 2.1 highlights the broad elements of the reform strategy over the two periods, and Table 2.2 provides an overview of the main features of China's reforms from 1978 to 2006.

CHINA'S ECONOMIC REFORMS: RURAL SECTOR REFORMS

During the Mao era, China's agricultural sector was communal with production quotas and prices administered by the party-state. Laborers were

Table 2.2. *Major reform steps in China: 1978–2006*

1978	Communiqué of the Third Central Party Committee (CPC) Plenum of the Eleventh Party Congress initiating "four modernizations"
	Decision to turn collective farms over to households
1979	"Open-door" policy initiated and foreign trade and investment reforms begin; Law on Joint Venture Companies passed
	Limited official encouragement of household responsibility system
	Three specialized banks separated from the People's Bank (the central bank)
1980	First four special economic zones created
	"Eating from separate kitchens" (*fenzao chifan*) reforms in intergovernmental fiscal relations
1984	Individual enterprises or *getihu* with less than 8 employees officially allowed
	Tax for profit reforms of state-owned enterprises (SOEs)
1986	Provisional bankruptcy law passed for SOEs
1987	Contract responsibility system introduced in SOEs
1989	Tiananmen Square events trigger retrenchment policy, halt on reforms
1990	Stock exchange started in Shenzhen, Shanghai
1992	Deng Xiaoping's "Tour through the South" reignites reforms
1993	Decision of the Third Plenum of the Fourteenth Party Congress to establish a "socialist market economy" paving the way for fiscal, financial, and SOE reforms
1994	RMB convertible for current account transactions
	Multiple exchange rates ended
	Tax Sharing System Reforms introduced
	Policy banks established; commercialization of banking system announced
1995	Central Bank Law, Banking Law, and Budget Law enacted
	Shift to contractual terms for SOE staff
1996	Full convertibility for current account transactions
1997	Comprehensive plan to restructure SOEs adopted, "grab the big, let go of the small"
2001	China's accession to World Trade Organization
2003	Third Plenum of the CPC of the Sixteenth Party Congress, decision to "perfect" the socialist market economy
2004	Constitution amended to guarantee private property rights
2005	Construction Bank, Bank of China Initial Public Offerings
2006	Sixth CPC Plenum of the Sixteenth Party Congress establishes the goal of "Harmonious Society"

Source: Compiled from Hofman, Ishihara, and Zhao (2007) and Organisation for Economic Co-operation and Development (2005, 29).

remunerated according to the average production of the commune rather than according to their marginal product. Not only was there little incentive for workers to relocate into other industries in which their marginal productivity may have been higher, the system's intrinsic inefficiencies greatly undermined agricultural production and productivity. To the Reformers, the most prominent (and destructive) symbol of the Maoist approach to development was the "people's commune." They saw the wretchedness of rural life – the grinding poverty, intolerable living conditions, lack of opportunities, and agricultural stagnation (for example, per capita grain output in 1977 was at about the same low level as in 1957) – as a direct result of the "people's commune." The system, by making a virtue of ideological purity at the expense of economic rationality gravely undermined peasant incentives. Regaining the prestige and legitimacy the CCP traditionally enjoyed among China's teeming rural masses meant the government had to revitalize the countryside quickly.

Ironically, China's sprawling and backward agricultural sector proved to be a blessing. Unlike the heavily industrialized Soviet bloc economies, China, on the eve of reforms, was predominantly an agricultural economy employing more than three-quarters of the country's labor force and accounting for a significant portion of its GDP. Consequently, China's core economic sector – the stagnant agricultural economy – was conducive to transition to the market system. This is because the agricultural sector was not only easier to reform through decollectivization and revival of peasant or "family farming," it also involved minimal trade-offs because collectivization was universally hated. Moreover, the sector could be reinvigorated relatively quickly with limited capital inputs, but with increasing returns on investment (Aslund 1989, 1995). However, reforming the industrial sector entailed painful restructuring because state-owned enterprises (SOEs) provided "cradle to grave" protection to workers. As Aslund (1989) and Li (1994) have aptly noted, among transition economies, backwardness can have its advantages.[1]

Almost immediately Deng sanctioned the breakup of the communes and its replacement with the "household responsibility system."[2] Introduced at the beginning of 1979, the household responsibility system created a "two-tier" land tenure arrangement under which land was still owned by the communes, but user rights and production decisions were decentralized from the production teams to individual households. In effect, the household responsibility

---

[1] Aslund (2007, 5) noted that "The economic structures could hardly have been more different in these two countries [the Soviet Union and China]. The Soviet Union was overindustrialized, while three-quarters of the Chinese worked in agriculture. Soviet enterprises were predominantly large-scale and mechanized, whereas China's production was small-scale and manual. Chinese agriculture could easily be reformed through the introduction of quasi-property rights for peasants, which was impossible in the Soviet Union. Soviet industry was too big and distorted to be omitted, but it was also too powerful to be reformed."

[2] It has been suggested that the household responsibility system began in 1978 when peasants in the drought-stricken Fengyang County, Anhui Province, agreed to divide the commune land into separate plots for individual households to cultivate. After fulfilling the procurement quota of grain to the state, the peasants were free to dispose the fruits of their labor as they saw fit because the new system gave them all rights over production – except the right to dispose of the land. Seeing the sharp increases in production, the authorities became enthusiastic converts to the idea, adopting the scheme and extending it to neighboring areas. The success of the new scheme eventually caught the attention of Deng and the party elites, who extended it throughout China (Blecher 1986).

system allowed individual farmers to lease land from the commune in exchange for a fixed production quota. That is, the collectively owned and operated land was "distributed" to peasants on the basis of their family size and the number of family workers.[3] Initially, the previously held collective land was assigned (or leased for three years) to individual households who were now free to make land-use, production, consumption, and marketing decisions. Individual households were also free to sell the fruits of their labor at market-determined prices after meeting their contractual obligations by selling a quota of their output (set at around 15 to 20 percent) to the state at government-fixed procurement rate and paying a modest contract fee to the village, which still technically owned the land (White 1993). Thus, by improving incentives and eliminating the free-rider problems inherent in the commune system, the new arrangement motivated peasants to reduce production costs and increase productivity because their labor was now closely linked to their income. The accompanying increases in procurement prices further stimulated agricultural production. Sicular (1988, 1995) notes that in 1979, the quota prices for rice and wheat was increased by 18 percent to 22 percent, and above-quota prices for grains (which were 30 percent of the quota price until 1978) were increased to 50 percent of the quota rate. Similarly, quota price for oil crops was raised by 26 percent and animal products by 23 percent.

By the end of 1982, more than 80 percent of rural households nationwide had adopted the household responsibility system, and by 1983, decollectivization was virtually complete. The swift dismantling of the people's commune system coupled with the restoration of family farming and the privatization and marketization of agricultural production (and the resultant higher prices) transformed the Chinese countryside, ushering in unprecedented levels of economic dynamism and prosperity. From a stagnant agricultural growth rate from 1957 to 1977, the rate of growth of agricultural output increased to an unprecedented 7.6 per year from 1978 to 1984 (Chen 2005; Lin 1994). Grain output alone "surged to 407 million metric tons, more than one-third higher than in 1978" (Naughton 2007, 89), and "China experienced grain surpluses of 300–350 million tons a year in the early 1980s" (Gulati and Fan 2007, 17). This growth also translated into increases in real per capita rural income by about 15.5 percent per year over the period 1979 to 1984 – from 220 yuan in 1978 to 522 yuan in 1984 (at 1990 prices) – a sharp contrast from the 2.3 percent per annum in the pre-reform period (Fan et al. 2004). In addition, the growth helped to reduce rural poverty dramatically and narrow the rural-urban income gap (Keliang and Prosterman 2007, 4). According to official estimates, rural poverty declined from 33 percent to 15 percent between 1978 and 1984 – or from 260 million people to 128 million people (Gulati and

---

[3] Land was allocated to households mostly in equal per capita shares based on family size (Gensheng 2001).

Fan 2007, 17). To sustain the pace of growth, the government, by the end of 1984, abandoned its compulsory procurement quotas in agriculture with "purchasing contracts" between the state and the peasants, and the land contracts, initially set for three years, were extended to fifteen years to give households greater stability and security in planning their production and investment needs. In 1993, the central government extended farmers land-use rights to continuous thirty-year terms.

THE RISE OF THE TOWNSHIP AND VILLAGE ENTERPRISES

Following the Third Plenum of the Eleventh Party Congress in December 1978 the central government also encouraged local governments, including private citizens to develop new and expand and modernize existing "enterprises" or small businesses outside state tutelage. The growth and accumulation of rural incomes coupled with the reallocation of farm labor to other sectors of the economy (in a sense, an equalization of the marginal productivity of labor across industries) allowed the local and township governments to invest in these new "nonfarm" and "nonstate sector" enterprises.[4] The result was the rise of a dynamic new economic sector – the "township and village enterprises" (TVEs).

In March 1984, the former "commune and brigade enterprises" were renamed TVEs. Although these enterprises took various forms, the moribund industrial units that were established under the people's commune system to serve the collective farms and now rehabilitated as TVEs became most widespread in the countryside.[5] Although technically government enterprises, TVEs were considered to be part of the non–state sector and functioned as private profit-seeking enterprises. Moreover, TVEs were run entirely by local and township governments and were free from central government interference. They were not subject to any planning targets but subject to hard budget constraints and responsible for their own profits and losses. TVEs were also free to encourage overseas Chinese entrepreneurs to invest in local projects and

---

[4] The official definition of the "nonstate sector" is rather broad because it includes all the production units that are not controlled and owned by the state or a government agency. The nonstate sector can be divided into collective enterprises (because they are either owned by workers or group of individuals), private enterprises, and enterprises with various ownership forms.

[5] The origins of the TVEs go back to the Maoist era when they were established as "commune and brigade enterprises" to serve as the industrial arm to the collective farms. On the eve of the Deng reforms, most were moribund and in a state of decay. The Deng reform revitalized and reincarnated them into TVEs. These entrepreneurs can be classified into two types. The first, the collectively owned enterprise (both township- and village-run enterprises), are owned by local governments and operate like a holding company, reinvesting profits in existing or new ventures, including local infrastructure. The second, and more recent, type is much closer to private enterprise in that most are controlled, if not informally owned, by an individual. Nevertheless, both types maintain close fiscal ties to the local and provincial governments.

could buy inputs and sell products freely wherever there was demand, including on the export markets. Remarkably, what began as modest small-scale rural factories producing labor-intensive products quickly became the engine of economic expansion, absorbing millions of surplus agricultural workers in its labor-intensive industries. TVEs grew from 1.52 million enterprises in 1978 to roughly 23 million enterprises in 1996 (Yabuki and Harner 1998, 143–44). By the mid-1990s, TVEs were producing everything from building materials, agricultural machinery, and textiles to garments, processed foods, and beverages, with some even manufacturing high-value electronics and telecom equipment. Equally impressive, from 1985 to 1994, TVEs saw their share in GDP rise from 13 percent to 31 percent. Although initially designed to provide non-farm employment to the surrounding rural workforce, TVEs employed some 100 million people, or roughly 40 percent of China's industrial workforce, by the early 1990s (World Bank 1997). Throughout the 1990s, TVEs continued to be among the most dynamic sectors in the Chinese economy, accounting for a third of total industrial growth, besides creating 130 million jobs over the period 1980 to 1996 (World Bank 1996, 50–51; Yabuki and Harner 1998, 144; Lin, Cai, and Li 1996, 179–81). Indeed, Janos Kornai (1992) notes that the success of China's transition to the market had much to do with the dynamism of its "second economy" (the nonstate sector). In contrast, in the Soviet bloc, where the state sector continued to dominate despite years of reforms, the economy predictably languished.

INDUSTRIAL SECTOR REFORMS

Several analysts have noted that the pre-reform Chinese economy (unlike that of the USSR) was structured in such a way that made it particularly conducive to market reforms (Granick 1990; Qian and Xu 1993; Xu and Zhuang 1998). Specifically, Mao (for strategic reasons) by encouraging local self-sufficiency ended up creating an internally diversified economy.[6] Whereas in the USSR single and highly specialized units supplied the entire market, in China parallel enterprises in different provinces produced similar goods, leading Shue (1988) to describe the economy as "cellular" or characterized by decentralized economic decision-making powers, and Qian and Wu (1993) to compare the Chinese economy to a multidivisional (M-form) organization and the Soviet Union to a unitary (U-form) organization. When markets replaced planning, China's M-form organization had created relatively diversified subnational economies that were far better placed to experiment, innovate, and compete with one another.

---

[6] Naughton (1996) notes that Mao understood the strategic significance of China's "rear areas." He ordered some of China's industrial facilities moved to the interior to serve as a "third-front" during wars.

Thus, on the eve of the reforms in 1978, although virtually all Chinese industry (certainly the largest and those perceived as "strategic") was owned by the state, it was not as rigidly controlled as its Soviet counterpart. Unlike the Soviet Union, China's industries, or SOEs, had multilevel control and ownership. Specifically, many nonstrategic medium and small enterprises were controlled both vertically by the central government and horizontally by different layers of the subnational governments, including the provinces, prefectures, counties, townships, and municipalities. These SOEs had to follow both the central government plan and those drawn up by the various subnational units, although meeting central government targets was less strict than those set by subnational governments. In part, this explains why the Chinese system was less scarcity-prone and more resilient in meeting local needs than its Soviet bloc counterparts.

However, like its Indian and Soviet counterparts, China's SOEs, despite being the beneficiary of state protection and largesse in the form of generous subsidies and tax breaks, remained bloated, inefficient, and uncompetitive and produced shoddy goods. As in agriculture, the Reformers hoped to improve the performance of the SOEs by injecting incentives into the system. Yet the Communist Party elite was cognizant of the fact that reforming the SOEs would be prolonged and had to be carried out delicately to ensure what Lau, Qian, and Roland (2000) have aptly described as "reform without losers." This was because the SOEs were the backbone of the Chinese economy. The more than 300,000 SOEs not only served as the primary job provider to over 100 million workers, they also ensured basic social security by guaranteeing the "iron rice bowl." In other words, besides providing lifetime employment guarantees and a regular paycheck to millions of people, SOEs also took care of the basic needs of their workers, guaranteeing housing, medical expenses, and pensions as well as education for workers' children. Equally important, SOEs monopolized production in all the critical sectors of the economy such as energy, heavy industry, defense, and essential consumer goods. In a scarcity-prone economy, interruptions or decline in production carried the risk of serious political and economic implications. Consequently, reforming the SOEs had to be done with utmost care – it required a smooth landing so as not to break the precarious safety net the "iron rice bowl" provided ordinary people. Unlike, the former Soviet Union and the Eastern bloc's hastily designed privatization of SOEs (in which the state sold off many of its enterprises to private bidders), with its potential job losses and social and economic dislocations, was not seen as a viable option, and bankruptcy was to be used only as a last resort.

Begun concurrently with agricultural sector reforms, the aim of industrial sector reforms was to make the SOEs productive and financially viable. As noted, unlike the former Eastern bloc countries, wholesale privatization was not the preferred choice of China's Reformers. Rather, the government hoped (at least initially) to boost SOEs performance by reforming their internal governance and improving the market environment in which they operated. Thus, saving (if not salvaging) the SOEs through greater competition with each other and the newer private firms and merging ailing and insolvent firms with the more viable ones was seen as a far better option. Such a strategy was initiated in October 1978 by the Sichuan provincial government under future party secretary, Zhao Ziyang. In his attempt to increase economic incentives for SOEs and give their management greater autonomy, Zhao launched a pilot project to expand enterprise autonomy in six selected enterprises. Instead of transferring all profits to Beijing, the enterprises were now allowed to keep a fair percentage of their profits. In addition, incentives such as the various profit-retention schemes under which profit-making SOEs would be allowed to keep a larger share of their profits to be distributed as bonuses to employees was put in place to encourage the recalcitrant and unmotivated enterprise nomenklatura's active cooperation, if not their acquiescence, in the reform process. Similarly, in an effort to reduce central bureaucratic interference in SOE operations and give local managers greater autonomy over production and investment decisions, directives were issued barring government and party officials from running businesses. For example, *chengbao zhi*, the "contract responsibility system," delegated greater decision-making authority to firm managers, including allowing firms to retain a share of the profits, with the precise percentages to be negotiated on an annual basis. By 1987, contracts were extended to three-year terms to give firms greater incentives to boost production and profits.

Zhao's pilot program proved to be such a success that in July 1979, the State Council formally began to encourage local governments to implement similar projects to increase economic incentives for SOEs. By the end of 1979, about 4,200 enterprises nationwide were selected for this new program. In 1980, the experiment expanded to include 6,600 large and medium-sized SOEs, which accounted for 60 percent of the national budgeted industrial output and 70 percent of national industrial profits (Naughton 2007). Also, in February 1985, the central authorities introduced the two or "dual-track" price system (an avowedly intermediate system between a centrally planned and a market system) as a strategy to revitalize the SOEs. Under this system, a fixed price for products allocated by the central government was to coexist with a market-based price for out-of-plan output. After fulfilling their plan-allocated production quota, SOEs were free to sell the rest at a free market price. They were also allowed to purchase inputs in quantities above the plan quota at market rates. As Lau, Qian, and Roland (2000) note, despite limitations, the "dual-track" system contributed to price reform and the development of markets. Specifically, by freeing up prices at the margin, the true domestic market prices for all goods were more or less established by the late 1980s. In contrast, in the former Soviet bloc, although mandatory planning targets were abolished, most prices continued to be "administered" by bureaucrats (Jefferson and Rawski 1994; Perkins 1994). In 1987, the Thirteenth National Party Congress introduced the "manager contract responsibility system" to stimulate SOE managers' interest in profit making by giving them greater autonomy and permission to retain a portion of the profits. Nevertheless, during 1988–92, SOE reforms slowed down markedly because of concerns about the negative social and economic cost of plant closure, including growing unemployment, increases in the cost of living, rising poverty, and civil and political unrest.[7]

FISCAL AND ADMINISTRATIVE DECENTRALIZATION

Before the reforms, China's revenue collection system (modeled after the Soviet Union) was highly centralized; subnational governments remitted most of their taxes and profits to the central government and then received transfers for expenditures from the national budget. However, under the new revenue-sharing arrangement called the "fiscal contracting system" (*caizheng chengbao zhi*), this highly centralized system (under which the central government had a formal monopoly over both revenue and expenditures) was decentralized to the various subnational units, including the provinces, prefectures, counties, townships, municipalities, and villages.[8] As fiscal and administrative authority became more decentralized, the system of intergovernmental revenue sharing was changed from the "unified revenue and unified expenditure" (*tongshou tongzhi*), which meant that all government revenue and expenditures had to go through the central government into a fiscal contracting system nicknamed "cooking in separate kitchens" (*fenzhao chifan*). The new system divided revenue and expenditure responsibilities between the central and the provincial governments, with the latter now allowed to retain a "fairer share" of the revenues after transferring the contracted portion to the central government. While the contractual sharing rates varied from province to province (for example, Guangdong was to pay a fixed amount of 1 billion yuan to the central government and keep the rest, and Fujian would receive a fixed amount of subsidies from Beijing), overall the new "profit-contract system" allowed a significant portion of revenue that was previously appropriated by the central government to go to the provinces, the SOEs, and other subnational units. Although in return for the larger share, subnational governments were now responsible for financing their own expenditures, fiscal decentralization also

---

[7] In the late 1980s, leasing was adopted as the preferred approach to reforming SOEs. The "first significant lease contract involved the Wuhan Motor Engine Factory in 1986, when three people put up 34,000 yuan as collateral to lease the factory. In May 1988 the State Council issued a regulation on the leasing of small SOEs" (Garnaut, Song and Yao 2006, 35).

[8] There are broadly three forms of decentralization: (a) deconcentration, in which some responsibilities are transferred from the central to subnational units; (b) delegation, in which local governments act as agents of the central government; and (c) devolution, in which local governments are given decision-making authority.

created strong incentives for the provincial and other subnational governments to engage in economic activity. By strengthening the link between local revenue and expenditures, the fiscal contracting system gave subnational governments both the authority and incentive to develop their economies because they were now able to retain a significant portion of that revenue. Not surprisingly, by 1985, SOEs controlled by the central government declined to only 20 percent of the total industrial output, whereas provincial and prefectures controlled 45 percent and county governments controlled about 35 percent (Lin 1994).

Because the administrative and fiscal decentralization accompanying SOE reforms led to a strengthening of subnational governments' role in economic management, it has been argued that it was this devolution away from the central to subnational units that has been the engine behind China's economic growth. Montinola, Qian, and Weingast (1995) claim that China's "fiscal federalism" was fundamentally a form of "market-preserving federalism." By devolving regulatory authority from the central to local governments, the interventionist reach of the central government was constrained because it created some checks on central power and authority. This theory provides two possible mechanisms for aligning subnational interest with promoting markets. One is through interjurisdictional competition under factor and goods mobility to discipline the interventionist local units. That is, decentralized control over the economy by subnational governments within a common market prevents the central government from interfering in markets and also reduces their scope for rent seeking. Another is through linking local government expenditure with the revenue generated to ensure that local governments face the financial consequences of their decisions. In addition, intergovernmental competition over mobile sources of revenue serves to constrain individual subnational governments. These served to harden budget constraints on enterprises, thereby forcing them to restructure and become more efficient and competitive.[9]

THE CREATION OF THE SPECIAL ECONOMIC ZONES

In 1978, in keeping with its "open-door policy," China created the SEZs along the coast in Guangdong, Fujian, and Hainan to encourage foreign trade and investment. In 1980, Shenzhen, Zhuhai, and Shantou adjacent to Hong Kong in Guangdong province and Xiamen across the Taiwan straits were established as

[9] A hard budget constraint requires that subnational governments must bear the full financial consequences of their decisions. That is, they will not be bailed out or receive an unlimited supply of loans from the central bank. Thus, runaway spending could mean bankruptcy for the subnational units. In contrast, a soft budget constraint allows subnational government to spend beyond its means. The resultant budget deficits are financed either through central government bailouts or by forgivable loans from a central bank. Therefore, unlike hard budget constraint, the soft budget constraint allows the SOEs suffering from poor performance to ask for and receive preferential treatment such as subsidies and tax breaks from the government, whereas private firms in market economies have no such choice and go bankrupt.

SEZs. Allowing the SEZs to operate with considerable administrative and fiscal autonomy, including lower tax and tariff rates and flexible investment rules, ensured favorable export conditions for both foreign investors and domestic enterprises. In particular, in the SEZs foreign investors were allowed 100 percent ownership, and all exporters were allowed to import intermediate products and capital goods duty free, given generous tax holidays, and assured access to reliable physical infrastructure, often through the provision of land, power, physical security, and transport to the ports. With such incentives, the SEZs became overnight successes, witnessing a massive influx of foreign investment in labor-intensive factories and industries, especially from Taiwan, Hong Kong, and the overseas Chinese communities – an advantage the Soviet bloc did not have.

In short order, this influx created large-scale employment opportunities, in addition to bringing new technologies and managerial know-how. The surge in foreign direct investment (FDI) also resulted in a substantial increase in joint ventures with foreigners and wholly foreign-owned enterprises.[10] Moreover, the SEZs did not remain as enclaves for very long. Rather, they served as a first step to a much wider and deeper opening. In 1984, the Economic and Technological Zones (ETDZs) were set up, followed soon after by the creation of Free Trade Zones (FTZs), established in fourteen coastal cities. This was followed by several more FTZs, "hi-tech development zones," and "border-open cities" in the inland areas, including Dalian, Guangzhou, Zhangjigang, Tianjin, Shenzhen, and Pudong New Area in Shanghai. Overall, Zebregs (2003) estimates that although FDI directly contributed 0.4 percentage points to annual GDP growth during the 1990s, its indirect contribution through long-term TFP (total factor productivity) growth was 2.5 percentage points. In effect, the SEZs served as "laboratories" for experimentation with economic reforms. Here the authorities could introduce more market-oriented modes of production and exchange without exposing the entire economy to the forces of market competition. China not only benefitted from the expertise and technology linked with foreign investment, the SEZs also provided a learning curve for a more gradual liberalization of the Chinese economy.

FOREIGN TRADE, INVESTMENT, AND BANKING SECTOR REFORMS

Given the central government's concerns about the health of the SOEs, it has proceeded rather cautiously with the liberalization of foreign trade and investment regimes by incrementally replacing administrative controls on imports and exports with tariffs and quotas and then gradually reducing tariff

---

[10] If contractual joint ventures were the most important type of FDI in the post-1978 era, since the late 1980s, equity-joint ventures and wholly foreign-owned enterprises became predominant. Each differ from each other in the degree of control exercised by foreign firms and in management structure.

Table 2.3. *Average tariff rates in China (selected years)*

Year	Tariff (%)
1982	55.6
1985	43.3
1992	42.9
1993	39.9
1994	36.3
1996	23.6
1997	17.6
2000	16.4
2001	14.0
2002	12.7

Source: Yang (2006).

rates and abolishing quotas. As discussed in Chapter 3, when China finally entered the World Trade Organization in 2001, the average tariff rate had been reduced to 14 percent – a figure that has continued to decline since that time (see Table 2.3).

Similarly, given the valid concern about the ability of SOEs to compete with foreign companies, the government actively encouraged FDI. As a result, in the 1980s, the bulk of the FDI was in joint ventures with SOEs, and it was only in the 1990s that FDI began to shift toward private companies. FDI increased from US$4.4 billion in 1991 to US$11 billion in 1992 and US$28 billion in 1993. By the late-1990s, China was the largest recipient of FDI in the developing world, accounting for about 30 percent of total FDI flows. To intermediate the massive capital inflows, efforts were made to modernize the banking sector. During the Maoist period, China's financial sector was essentially limited to a Soviet-style monobank. The People's Bank of China (PBC), founded in 1949, was the supreme bank in the country. Although the PBC served as both a central bank and the government treasury (managing foreign exchange reserves, currency issuance, and credit distribution), as well as a commercial bank (receiving deposits from households and enterprises and making loans), in practice the PBC functioned mainly as an accounting body. Its major task was to take in household deposits (which were often the only asset households could hold) and to keep track of financial transactions that corresponded to allocations under the annual plan. In 1983–84, the commercial banking functions of the PBC were split into four "independent" state-owned banks known collectively as the "Big Four": the Bank of China, Industrial and Commercial Bank of China, China Construction Bank, and the Agricultural Bank of China. Table 2.4 shows the structure of post-Mao China's banking system, with the PBC directing and supervising all of China's banking system.

Table 2.4. *Structure of China's banking system*

People's Bank of China (PBC) (*Central Bank*)

1. *Policy Banks*
   (about RMB 1,380 billion in assets at 1999 year-end)
   – State Development Bank of China
   – Export-Import Bank of China
   – Agricultural Development Bank of China
2. *State-owned Commercial Banks*
   (RMB 9,552 billion in assets at 1999 year-end)
   – Industrial and Commercial Bank of China
   – Agricultural Bank of China
   – Bank of China
   – China Construction Bank
3. *"Share-ownership" of Commercial Banks*
   (about RMB 1,680 billion in assets as of 1999 year-end)
   – Bank of Communication
   – CITIC Industrial Bank
   – China Everbright Bank
   – Huaxia Bank
   – Minsheng Bank
   – Guangdong Development Bank
   – Shenzhen Development Bank
   – Shenzhen Merchants Bank
   – Fujian Industrial Bank
   – Pudong Development Bank
   – Hainan Development Bank
   – Yantai Housing Savings Bank
   – Bengbu Housing Savings Bank
   – China Investment Bank
4. *Urban Cooperative Banks*
   (RMB 1,650 billion in assets at 1999 year-end)
   – Roughly 160 urban cooperative banks
5. *Nonbank financial institutions*
   – Includes:
           Financial trust and investment corps
           Finance companies
           Finance leasing companies
           Rural credit cooperatives
           urban credit cooperatives

On 1 January 1984, in an effort to eliminate the PBC's conflict of interest (inherent in its supervisory and commercial roles) and enhancing its ability to independently formulate and conduct monetary policy, the State Council made the PBC the country's central bank. The PBC's central bank status was legally confirmed on 18 March 1995 by the Third Plenum of the Eighth National People's Congress. As a central bank, the PBC enjoys industry-level status. That is, it controls the money supply, determines interest and deposit rates, and handles foreign exchange reserves through its division, the State Administration of Exchange Control. The PBC has the authority in formulating and implementing monetary policy, including issuing renminbi and administering its circulation, regulating interbank lending market and interbank bond market, administering foreign exchange and regulating interbank foreign exchange market, and managing the official foreign exchange and gold reserves. It also oversees bank operations using the credit plan to control overall lending administratively and supervises the People's Insurance Company of China.

In 1986, the State Council approved the establishment of a number of shareholding company-based commercial banks at both national and regional levels, as well as nonbank financial institutions such as credit cooperatives, insurance companies, and international trust and investment corporations (ITICs). These were set up mainly to attract foreign investment, raise funds for local development projects, and make investments on China's stock markets. Apart from the China International Trust and Investment Corporation, all the ITICs are controlled by the provincial and municipal governments. In 1994, the Big Four were reorganized into commercial banks to be operated on a profit-and-loss basis. In addition, three policy banks, China Development Bank, Export-Import Bank of China, and China Agricultural Development Bank, were established to perform policy-lending functions. In 1995, in another dramatic move, the PBC was only allowed to act exclusively as a central bank overseeing China's monetary policy and regulating the financial sector, rather than carrying on commercial banking functions. In 1996, the government permits the establishment of the Minsheng Bank, China's first publicly traded and largely private bank. In 1998, the PBC underwent another major restructuring. Its commercial activities were further devolved and transferred to the more "independent" (yet still state-owned) commercial banks, which took over from the PBC various commercial functions and is now the largest of the four state-owned banks. By the late 1990s, the Big Four state-owned commercial banks accounted for about 75 percent of outstanding loans and had 150,000 branches, employing about 1.7 million people. In 2003, the Standing Committee of the Tenth National People's Congress approved an amendment law to strengthen the role of PBC in the making and implementation of monetary policy and for safeguarding the country's overall financial stability. However, as discussed in Chapter 3, such seemingly prudent restructuring and the separation of powers has not made China's banking system truly "independent." This, of course, has profound implications for the Chinese economy.

FROM PLAN-MARKET TO MARKET

China's reform strategy during its first fifteen years proved to be a remarkable success. Between 1978 and 1993 China's GDP grew at an average annual rate of about 9 percent. Per capita income increased sharply (the total household bank deposits measured against the GDP increased from less than 6 percent in 1978 to more than 40 percent in 1993), and the number of people living in poverty declined substantially (United Nations Development Program 1999). Yet it was also becoming evident that the economy was running out of steam. Part of the problem had to do with the limits of gradual or incremental reform. As Alwyn Young (2000, 1091) has noted, "incremental reform releases segments of the economy from centralized control, while maintaining, for a prolonged period, many of the distortions of the central plan."

Specifically, despite over a decade of reforms, the basic institutional frame-work of central planning remained intact. In addition, although the SOE sector had shrunk in size, it was still burdened with the problem of poor resource allocation, low efficiency, and low profitability – in fact, it was a drag on the rest of the economy. Particularly hard hit was the banking sector because it was saddled with growing volumes of nonperforming loans from unprofitable SOEs. Even most of the nonstate enterprises such as TVEs were mostly controlled by local governments and not truly private entities. In fact, truly private enterprises accounted for less than 15 percent of industrial output by the end of 1993. Nonstate enterprises burdened with ill-defined property rights and increasingly poor corporate governance (many good managers were leaving and joining foreign firms) was hampering TVE expansion and efficiency, whereas competition from the fast-expanding domestic and foreign private firms eroded the profit margins of the TVEs. Finally, the plan-market economy, which Perkins (1994) aptly labels "distorted," spawned rampant corruption and rent-seeking activities. In the absence of rule-based market-supporting institutions, party and government officials used their power and influence for personal gain by granting favors such as land-use rights, tax exemptions, and licenses, besides engaging in the illegal stripping of valuable SOE assets.

As noted earlier, the CCP's historic decision in 1993 to endorse the building of a "socialist market economy with Chinese characteristics" was to speed up the reforms to create the institutional and legal foundations of a modern market economy. Since then, the Chinese government has put in place a number of measures to restructure and reform the government-business relationship. The Fifteenth Party Congress in September 1997 elevated private ownership from a "supplementary component" to an "important component" of the economy, and state ownership was downgraded from a "principal component" to a "pillar" of the economy. Just as significant, the constitution was amended in March 1999 to place private business on an equal footing with public ownership, and in 2004, the constitution was amended to guarantee more secure private property rights. On the macroeconomic front, measures have been adopted to restructure the SOEs; promote more private enterprises; upgrade and modernize the country's financial, monetary, and banking systems; and decisively open the country to world trade. For example, China's foreign exchange markets, which prior to 1994 followed a "dual-track" approach with an official rate and a "swap rate" (or market rate) existing side by side, have been liberalized. Beginning 1 January 1 1994, the plan allocation of foreign exchange was abolished and the dual track merged into a single market system. This unification of the foreign exchange rate, coupled with the decision (in December 1996) to make its currency (the yuan[11]) convertible on the current account, has helped to increase FDI flows into China – in part, because it helped keep the exchange rate relatively stable at 8.7 yuan per US$1 to 8.3 yuan per US$1 between 1994 and 1998.[12]

One of the unintended consequences of fiscal and administrative decentralization was the simultaneous erosion of central government's economic autonomy and the growing power of subnational entities. Local power could now frustrate central reforms by protecting their narrow interests (such as inefficient industries), or advancing their particularistic interests via excessive investments in manufacturing, real estate, service industries and rent-seeking. The broad discretionary powers subnational officials now enjoyed, coupled with the lack of oversight and accountability exacerbated the problems of bureaucratic malfeasance and corruption. Self-serving and recalcitrant officials enriched themselves by thwarting or ignoring central directives. Most troubling, fiscal decentralization encouraged local officials to protect their markets by erecting administrative blockades against competitors. In other words, the growing tendency among subnational governments to engage in local protectionism – thereby creating a "quasi-regionally planned economies" undermined the central government's ability to promote national economic development. Rather, as localities with authority over expenditures were expected to balance their own budgets, over time substantial surpluses accumulated in wealthier provinces, while poorer provinces were in a chronic deficit situation. Not surprisingly, the disparities across the regions widened as wealthier provinces, including the five richest provinces (Shanghai, Beijing, Tianjin, Guangdong, and Zhejiang) made significant economic gains whereas the five poorest provinces (Guizhou, Gansu, Shaanxi, Jiangxi, and Henan) fell further behind. To address this problem, the central authorities were forced to "recentralize" in the mid-1990s – or, in Kelliher's (1986, 480) pithy phrase, "to save decentralization, the reform coalition [had to] recentralize" (also see Naughton 2007, 101; Wedeman 2003). In particular, in an effort to stem central fiscal decline (even as shares of subnational budget revenue continued to rise), the central government introduced major tax and fiscal reforms in 1994.

The new "Tax Sharing System" (*fenshuizhi*) fundamentally changed the way revenue was managed and shared between the central and subnational governments by transferring the role of tax collection back to the central government.

---

[11] The *renminbi* is the name of the Chinese currency, while the *yuan* is one unit of the currency.
[12] However, China did not introduce capital account convertibility and retained capital controls. This help shield the country during the 1997 Asian financial crisis.

This was done through a series of measures such as streamlining China's complicated tax system based on provincial and municipal sales taxes, provincial border taxes, excise duties and levies by imposing a single value-added tax (VAT) on manufactured goods.[13] The new system also clarified fiscal revenues and responsibilities by making changes to the tax administration and establishing a tax-sharing system that separated central and subnational tax collection with each responsible for its own tax collection. The new tax-sharing arrangements allocated certain sources of revenues to the central government (customs duties, consumption tax, sales tax, and profit taxes from centrally controlled enterprises) to the subnational units (taxes on local enterprise income, house and property taxes, profit turnover taxes) and shared according to a predetermined ratio (the VAT, natural resource taxes, stock market trading tax), with the center receiving the bulk of (75 percent) of the VAT. However, even as Beijing devolved responsibility for social welfare programs to the local subnational government, it refused to transfer new funding to them to compensate for their revenue loss under the new tax system. Therefore, the 1994 tax reforms not only enabled the central government to bolster its revenue base by literally redrawing the rules of the game in its favor, it also underscored the central government's overall dominance in central-provincial relations and the subordinate nature of local power. Since the 1994 reform, the central authorities have further attempted to curb local power by curtailing administrative fees and other forms of extra-budgetary revenues. The new Budget Law, introduced in 1995, imposed tough restrictions on both the central and subnational governments spending. The law prohibited the central government from borrowing from the central bank and from deficit financing its current expenditures, and subnational governments at all levels were required to have balanced budgets and restricted from borrowing in the financial markets. Overall, these reforms benefited the center because they now had greater control over more revenues and the regions were more dependent on them for transfers to finance their expenditures.

These shifting relations between the central authorities and subnational governments raise an intriguing political-economy question: did China experience decentralization at the pleasure of the central government, or did decentralization evolve into "market-preserving federalism" independently, under the exigencies of global economic integration. Regardless, it would be simplistic to see the Chinese system as "federal" because the party-state still retains

---

[13] Value-added tax (VAT) was first introduced in China in 1984 but significantly reformed in 1994. VAT is a general consumption tax assessed on the value added to goods and services. VAT applies (at least in principle) to all commercial activities involved in the production and distribution of goods and the provision of services. It is a consumption tax because it is ultimately borne by the consumer. In its collection, VAT is a multipoint tax on each of the entities in the supply chain. VAT is the most important tax collected in China, generating much more revenue than any other tax.

considerable power, including the power to restructure central-provincial fiscal relations in its favor, as the introduction of the 1994 Tax Sharing System illustrates. Indeed, unlike democratic federal systems, China's subnational units do not have enough power to veto the center. Rather, as Y. Huang (1996), Naughton (1996), and others have noted, although decentralization of central-local relations is real (after all, the Li Peng administration failed to recentralize investment and financial powers between 1989 and 1991), the central government is still able to solicit provincial compliance by using an array of economic and political resources (both carrots and sticks) at its disposal. In fact, Huang views the subnational government officials as "agents" of the center with only limited operational autonomy because under China's highly centralized political system, the central authorities can bring local officials into line through both incentives and pressure. However, as is discussed in Chapter 3, this does not mean that local authorities are powerless. Rather, decentralization-recentralization has profound implications for China's political-economy.

POLITICAL REFORMS

If the economic reforms were introduced rather easily, it was a different matter when it came to political reforms. The vast state bureaucracy remained fiercely protective of its vested interests and prerogatives, and Maoism still had its supporters within the party – especially at the middle and local levels of both party and government apparatuses. Moreover, the party leadership was aware that swift replacement of Mao-era institutions or overt criticism of Mao carried its own obvious risks – namely, the masses questioning the very legitimacy of the CCP itself. Consequently, there was consensus that the pace of political reforms had to be incremental and carefully managed, with the party retaining its right to act as the final arbiter. This go-slow and cautious approach was seemingly vindicated and reduced to a crawl after the CCP leadership concluded that Gorbachev's strategy of putting political reforms (*glasnost*) ahead of economic reforms (*perestroika*) was the major reason behind the collapse of the Soviet Union in 1991.

In *The Political Logic of Economic Reform in China*, Susan Shirk argues that, unlike Gorbachev, China's reformers were successful because they were able to develop an effective pro-reform coalition. That is, whereas Gorbachev tried to foster a reform coalition by opening up the hitherto closed political arena in the hopes of developing a counterweight to the antireform Communist Party apparatus, the Dengists opted for another way. While maintaining a firm grip of the central Communist Party state, they simultaneously encouraged and enhanced the power of reform-oriented provincial party and government officials to serve as a political counterweight against the conservatives in the center. Provincial officials had a vested interest in pushing for reforms because economic decentralization, especially the new revenue-sharing contracts, promised by the Dengists would greatly enhance their economic and political power. In the end, Gorbachev's strategy led to the collapse of the Soviet Communist Party (and eventually the Soviet Union itself), whereas Deng's cautious approach achieved market reforms while preserving the CCP.

The slow and cautious approach is particularly evident in the early years. Following the Third Plenum of the Tenth Party Central Committee in 1977, the much-despised Maoist emphasis on "class struggle" was replaced with "socialist modernization" as the guiding principle of Chinese socialism (Misra 1998). In a sense, there was a shift from the Mao-era national emphasis on "politics in command" to the Deng-era "economics in command." Clearly, for the individuals and their families who remained and who had often been arbitrarily trapped and stigmatized into vengeful class categories such as "capitalists," "landlords," and "intellectuals" by the Maoist state and treated accordingly (these "well-to-do classes" were subject to official discrimination when it came to housing allocation or educational access for their children), the changed environment must have been liberating, perhaps giving some a measure of solace. Just as important, the rejection of such class categories and, most famously, Deng's seemingly vicarious exhortation that "getting rich is glorious" was a signal to intellectuals and aspiring entrepreneurs – indeed, to society as a whole – that their talents and skills were now valued and that individuals would be judged on their abilities rather than their alleged class backgrounds.

Also, keeping with Deng Xiaoping's oft-repeated maxim, that "to control things better, one must control it less," the CCP relaxed its hegemonic and draconian control over social and political life, allowing for greater freedom of association by tolerating the rise of various citizens organizations and interest groups. The unprecedented rise of the Democracy Wall on a Beijing street corner in late 1978 (not far from party headquarters), where ordinary citizens, writers, and critics could freely express themselves, dramatically underscored the leaderships' commitment to move beyond the tight control and regimentation of the Maoist era. Yet the wall could just as easily be demolished. When the writings on the Democracy Wall became too discordant and critical of the leadership, especially Deng, the authorities issued a thinly veiled warning against the "subversives" and "disreputable elements." When the "desecration" got out of hand in its satirical lampooning of party leaders, the wall was swiftly closed (painted over) and the "bad elements" and "troublemakers" duly arrested and imprisoned. This Janus-faced approach to political reforms has characterized China's experience since the beginning of the Deng era: a gradual easing of controls followed by a crackdown when civil society attempts to step outside the bounds of what is officially permissible or sanctioned. The brutal crackdown of students and workers in Tiananmen Square in 1989 vividly illustrated the extent to which the party elite were prepared to go to protect their power and authority. Thus, as noted in the previous chapter, the basic ideological and institutional structures of the Maoist-era Leninist political system were preserved under Deng and those who have come after him.

Nevertheless, some important reforms were implemented. In an attempt to make the bureaucratic system more accountable and responsive, a number of organizational reforms were carried out. Most notably, a fixed-tenure system for government officials was implemented, establishing for the first time in the PRC's history mandatory retirement ages at sixty for most men and fifty-five for most women. Between 1982 and 1985, about 1.7 million senior cadres were retired (Gore 1998, 89–90). Moreover, after 1993, civil servants were recruited into the service through open, competitive examinations rather than through labor allocation or connections. Beyond the official measures, administrative and fiscal decentralization also had unintended outcomes. As Minxin Pei (2006, 1994) has argued, the expansion of market forces and simultaneous shrinkage of state control of the Chinese economy has meant that the party's ability to control and regulate the activities of ordinary citizens has decreased. Indeed, the proliferation of private associations and grassroots-based nongovernmental organizations, including religious organizations, underscores the profound changes that have taken place in post-Mao China. Does this mean that China now has a civil society that is independent of the state? This important question, as well as the implications of changes taking place in state-society relations in contemporary China, are examined in Chapter 8.

The Indian Experience

Compared with the GDP growth rate of 3.5 percent a year from 1950 to 1980, the robust 5 percent growth rate in the early 1980s led the Indian government to conclude that the country's economic takeoff was finally at hand. However, such optimism proved premature because the growth was built on weak economic foundations. Srinivasan and Tendulkar (2003) persuasively argue that the "partial liberalization" during the mid-1980s had favorable efficiency effects but that the resulting rise in the growth rate was fragile. Moreover, they show that the increase in India's exports during the 1980s was mainly due to a exchange rate depreciation attributable more to exogenous forces than to explicit policy reforms aimed at reducing the trade barrier. Similarly, Panagariya (2005, 5) finds that "growth during the 1980s was fragile, highly variable from year to year, and unsustainable." He notes that if the exceptionally high growth rate of 7.6 percent in 1988–89 (due to the unsustainable foreign borrowing) is removed from the GDP series, the average growth rate in the 1980s would be significantly lower than in the 1990s.

By the mid-1980s, a number of factors caused the economic situation to deteriorate. The profligate expansionary fiscal policies of the central government (funded in large part by foreign loans) to support growing levels of government expenditures contributed to a sharp increase in the central government's fiscal deficits and a mounting foreign debt burden. The foreign-debt problem was a major concern because the government had borrowed heavily from abroad, both from commercial banks and nonresident Indian (NRI) deposits (much of which was short-term capital inflow at high interest rates), but stagnating exports meant that not enough foreign currency was being earned to service the debts. As a result, in 1984–85, out of US$24.3 billion of public and publicly guaranteed external debt, roughly 20 percent was owed to private creditors. By 1988–89, external debt arrears had more than doubled to US$50.2 billion, of which 40 percent was owed to private creditors. Not only did the debt to private creditors quadruple in less than five years, the debt-service ratio rose from 13.6 percent in 1984–85 to 30.9 percent in 1989–90. Because the borrowing was used to finance both investment and current consumption, the government's deficits increased sharply. By late 1990, the combined gross fiscal deficit of government at all levels had grown to a staggering 10 percent of GDP.

In early 1991, the situation worsened because of a sharp decline in remittances from Indian workers in the Persian Gulf in the wake of the impending Gulf War. Global market concerns also led to massive "capital flight," especially outflows of short-term capital from India putting extreme pressure on the country's foreign exchange reserves. By early June 1991, India's external debt stood at around US$71 billion, and the foreign exchange reserves had declined to about US$975 million – barely sufficient for two weeks of import coverage. Faced with a severe balance of payments crisis and on the verge of defaulting on its foreign debt, the Indian government had to ship part of the country's gold reserves and pledge it as collateral to access the international overnight market and avoid a loan default. Emergency assistance from the International Monetary Fund (IMF; in the form of standby credit of US$2.3 billion over 20 months) came with the usual IMF conditionality. Namely, the beleaguered minority Congress-led government under Prime Minister P. V. Narashima Rao quickly had to implement a wide-ranging economic reform program approved by the IMF. The stoic and unpretentious finance minister, Manmohan Singh, a professional economist and long-time economic-policy administrator in the central government, at first appeared an unlikely candidate to reform an economy of which he had played so much a part in creating. However, given a new set of marching orders, this senior technocrat judiciously devised and implemented an ambitious structural-adjustment program dubbed the New Economic Policy (NEP). The foremost goal of the NEP was to expeditiously convert India from a regulated control-bound, inward-looking economy into a market-friendly, outward-looking one. In effect, the era of economic liberalization had begun – which over the next decade and half would decisively break from some four decades of pervasive government planning and regulation that had earned India the dubious distinction of being the most controlled economy in the non-Communist world.

THE ECONOMIC LIBERALIZATION PROGRAM

Prior to 1991, a complex regime of import licensing requirements, along with other barriers to trade, kept the Indian economy fairly insulated from international market competition. The thrust of the NEP was to open India's closed economy to international market forces. However, following what Rodrik and Subramanian (2005) call an "attitudinal shift in government after 1991," concerted efforts have been made to encourage private investment and participation in the economy such as liberalizing access to foreign capital, cutting tariffs, deregulating the financial sector, and removing quantitative restrictions through industrial and trade liberalization. The NEP also committed to implementing policies conducive to privatization and foreign direct investment, including abolishing state monopoly in all core economic sectors and improving the supervisory and regulatory systems to promote transparency and genuine competition. Like China's "plan-market" system, the NEP also signaled a dramatically changed role for central planning. Although in the officialese, the state and market forces were to work together as "partners in economic development," in practice, private initiative and enterprise was deemed central to economic growth, with the state remaining active only in areas in which the private sector was either unwilling or incapable of acting in the public interest. These included the government's "social justice programs" such as the various "uplift" or poverty alleviation programs, human resource development, and the provision of social services such as basic health care and education.

MACROECONOMIC REFORMS

Because diffusing the balance of payments crisis and restoring macroeconomic stabilization was the government's top priority, measures were quickly put in place to this end, which coincidentally met some of the IMF's conditions. For example, under the highly restrictive pre-1991 trade regime, government authorization (or licenses) was required for the import of virtually all goods, imports of manufactured consumer goods were completely banned, and high tariffs and pervasive import restrictions applied to many others. As a result, the overall ratio of external trade (exports plus imports) to GDP declined from 13 percent in 1950–51 to about 7.3 percent in 1970–71.

The NEP made trade policy reforms a top priority because policy makers recognized that the earlier trade regime had contributed to widespread inefficiencies and corruption and had undermined India's export competitiveness.[14]

---

[14] During 1960–80, the total factor productivity growth (TFPG) in the organized manufacturing sector witnessed a decline of 0.5 percent per annum. However, during the same period, countries such as South Korea and Japan experienced an annual TFPG of between 3.1 to 5.7 percent (Ahluwalia 1998).

Therefore, import control through licensing was quickly and effectively eliminated for raw materials, both intermediate and capital goods, including related
production inputs – although this practice was retained for consumer goods
until the end of the 1990s. Moreover, export incentives were broadened and
simplified, and the trade monopolies of the state trading agencies were eliminated. Similarly, India's traditionally high custom duties were systematically
lowered in each of the four post-1991 budgets. The government was particularly successful in reducing tariffs. Maximum tariff rates that exceeded 300 percent, and the average (import-weighted) tariff rate that stood at 87 percent in
1990–91 (the highest in the world) were sharply lowered, and by 1993, the
average tariff rate stood at 33 percent and in 1997 at 25 percent. The average
tariff rate on imports also declined from 76 percent in 1990–91 to 40 percent
by 1994, and to 29.8 percent in 1999 (OECD 2007, 24). In 2004, the average
tariff rate stood at 18 percent with the peak rate below 30 percent. In addition, steps were taken to end the discretionary aspects of the previous import
regime by reducing nontariff barriers and eliminating quantitative restrictions
(quota and import licensing requirements), particularly on intermediate and
capital goods. For example, before 1991, there were quantitative restrictions on
90 percent of the value added in the manufacturing sector. In April 1992, all
the twenty-six import-licensing lists were eliminated and quantitative import
restrictions on imports of capital and intermediate goods were removed. The
reduction in tariffs and nontariff barriers to trade was also accompanied by a
20 percent devaluation of the Indian rupee against the U.S. dollar in July 1991.
The rupee was further devalued in February 1992, and in March, it was allowed
to float, albeit under a managed floating system. Nevertheless, it gave the market a greater role in influencing the exchange rate. In mid-1993, the exchange
rate system was overhauled from a discretionary basket-pegged system to a
largely market-determined unified exchange rate. Currency convertibility on
the current account was introduced in August 1994 (Srinivasan and Tendulkar
2003).

Tax reform was also an important component of the NEP. Before the reforms,
tax collection authority was broadly demarcated between the central, state and
local governments. The center had the authority to levy taxes on income (except
tax on agricultural income, which was the purview of the state governments),
customs duties, central excise tax, and service tax. The states had the authority
to levy sales tax, state excise tax, land revenue tax, and tax on professions. Local
governments were empowered to levy tax on properties and for utilities such as
water supply and public works. The core aim of the NEP was to (a) rationalize
the tax laws, (b) expand the tax base, (c) reduce rates of direct taxes for both
individuals and corporations, (d) reduce the cascading effect of the central and
state government's indirect taxes, (e) provide tax incentives for infrastructure
and the export-oriented sectors, and (f) simplify taxation procedures and
improve the efficiency of tax administration. However, compared with China,

only modest reforms have been achieved. By 2000, the marginal tax rates for individuals and businesses were reduced, economic distortions stemming from indirect taxes somewhat mitigated by converting excises on manufactured products, and the tax base was widened by the introduction of a service tax. Unlike China, India could not make a switch to a more effective and integrated VAT covering both goods and services given the constitutional division on taxation powers (more on this issue in Chapter 4).

STRUCTURAL REFORMS: FISCAL FEDERALISM

Given the vertical imbalance between the resource-raising powers and expenditure needs of the center and the states, India's federal system provides for a highly complex system of intergovernmental revenue sharing and fiscal transfers between the central and state government.[15] These are carried out on the recommendations of two central bodies – the Finance Commission and the Planning Commission.[16] There are basically three direct channels: statutory transfers (comprising tax and grants-in-aid) through the Finance Commission; plan grants through the Planning Commission; and the so-called discretionary matching grants through central ministries primarily for centrally sponsored schemes such as public works, poverty-alleviation schemes, and child nutrition programs. The Planning Commission's grants are based on the "Gadgil formula," which allocates resources to the states on the basis of population, poverty, revenue mobilization, and economic performance, although fiscal performance weighs just 5 percent in the formula, whereas population weighs

[15] Under the Indian federation, a clear constitutional demarcation has existed between the two levels of government: the Center and the state. Although local structures such as the village *panchayats* and municipalities in urban area had been in existence since the early years following independence, they were not substantially empowered with self-government prerogatives. However, following the 73rd and 74th Amendments to the Constitution in 1992, a third tier of government (the rural and urban local governments) was formally introduced and granted constitutional status. The constitutional amendments were designed to force a minimum level of decentralization across all states. They mandated political decentralization, leaving issues of design and implementation on sectoral, administrative, and fiscal aspects to the state governments.

[16] The Finance Commission was established by the Constitution in 1950. It was created as an independent fiscal agency for the explicit purpose of curbing partisan influence on the sharing of national revenues between the central and state governments. The commission draws its authority directly from the Constitution, not from the governments of the day, whether at the center or in the constituent states. Specifically, the Constitution requires the president to appoint members to the Finance Commission every five years to review and determine the distribution of tax and grant-in-aid revenues both between the central and state governments and across state governments, including how much extra assistance should be diverted to the resource-poor states. The total amounts of transfers to the states the Finance Commission handles are usually smaller than those made by the Planning Commission, which is a federal government body established by parliamentary resolution in 1950 and chaired by the prime minister.

60 percent.[17] There also exist indirect channels such as loans from the central government and the allocation of credit by financial institutions controlled by the Center. However, state governments have wide discretionary power over transfers to local governments. Although the constitutional amendments in 1992 raised the legal status of local governments, they can only exercise taxing and expenditure responsibilities that were devolved for them by their respective state governments.

India's system of fiscal federalism, which Bardhan (2002) has aptly termed "holding-together federalism," has created perverse and conflicting incentives because the central government allocates credit to state governments through a formula that is unrelated to whether state governments put their funds to productive use.[18] This problem is partly rooted in the manner that the Indian Constitution has divided the taxing powers between the Center and the states. Specifically, in an effort to limit intergovernmental jurisdictional disputes, the Constitution separated the taxing authority of the Center and the states without a reasonable degree of overlap. For example, although the states are entitled to levy a broad-based sales tax, this provision is preempted by the authority vested in the Center to impose excises on almost any commodity. Such rules not only have prevented the states from broadening their tax base to meet their growing expenditures, they have also served to undermine cooperative tax harmonization. Rather, the Finance Commission's flawed "gap-filling" approach determines the amount of funds to be awarded to each state on the basis of the "gap" between its revenues and its nonplan expenditures. This provides huge disincentives to the states to exercise fiscal restraint. In

---

[17] The Gadgil formula is named after the deputy chair of the Planning Commission (Professor D. R. Gadgil), who introduced the formula in 1969.

[18] Bardhan (2002) makes a useful distinction between "coming-together federalism" such as that in the United States, in which previously sovereign polities gave up part of their sovereignty for efficiency gains achieved through resource pooling and a common market, and "holding-together federalism" such as the multinational democracies of India, Belgium, and Spain, in which the emphasis is on redistributive or compensating transfers to keep the contending polities together. On a similar note, Weingast (1995) points out that it is not federal structure per se that leads to economically beneficial results but a particular kind he terms "market-preserving federalism." In the case of China, the fact that local governments are equity holders in local SOEs has given them strong incentives to ensure that market conditions are conducive to the rapid growth of at least these firms – and therefore to refrain from confiscatory taxation. According to McKinnon (1998), market-preserving federalism comprises four key components: (1) monetary separation: state governments cannot own or control commercial banks; (2) fiscal separation: state governments do not have access to discretionary or additional central government financing to cover state deficits; (3) freedom of interstate commerce: goods, services, peoples, firms, and capital are allowed to move freely across state lines; and (4) unrestricted public choice: states are allowed to design and deliver alternative bundles of public goods and services and to finance them by alternative means of taxation. Thus, the first two components ensure that there are no bailouts. Although states can still borrow, credit rating agencies are more prudent because they know that states face hard budget constraints. Unrestricted public choice is possible only if the first three are in place.

particular, the states can generate all kinds of expenditures without raising adequate resources to finance them through taxes for recovering costs from users of state-provided goods and services. In turn, central government finances have gone in the red because it has been forced both to raise its tax revenues and to borrow to comply with the Finance Commission's awards.

Unlike China's "market-preserving federalism" in which interjurisdictional competition between governments to attract private economic activity serves to commit them not to bail out failed enterprises, India's system of fiscal federalism has spawned (albeit unintentionally) fiscal indiscipline. Specifically, India's fiscal federalism has encouraged state governments to circumvent hard budget constraints and increase their expenditures. Incumbent government and political parties at the state level, in their eagerness to win elections, openly engage in the free-for-all "competitive populism," making fiscally irresponsible campaign promises and paying for it with funds allocated by the Center. To make matters worse, state governments not only have created large infrastructure and social services programs, they have also recklessly expanded their payrolls to the point that a substantial part of their revenues are spent on wages and salaries alone.[19] The net result has been a systematic diversion of resources meant for investment into current expenditure, not to mention tremendous waste, duplication, and a sharp increase in the fiscal deficit of both the central and state governments. Throughout the 1990s, the combined deficit at the Center and states exceeded a whooping 10 percent of GDP.[20] As a result, general government debt rose to almost 65 percent of GDP. Such a huge fiscal deficit placed tremendous upward pressure on interest rates, besides discouraging private investment. At the same time, the high burden of servicing public debt served to crowd out public investment. Thus, India's fiscal federalism has contributed to both jurisdictional competition between the Center and the states and to centrifugal tensions between them and the have and have-not states. Some states feel that they contribute more in overall resources than they get back, and there is evidence that the Center tends to favor supportive state governments and buy off politically difficult ones.

Efforts to encourage state governments to be fiscally responsible have proved difficult.[21] However, in recent years several state governments have signed memoranda of understanding on fiscal reform programs with the central

---

[19] This problem is compounded by the fact that states have to match any increases, such as recent pay hikes given by the Center to its employees, to prevent massive civil unrest.

[20] The central government deficit rose from 4.2 percent in 1995–96 to some 5.7 percent in 2001–02. This is compounded by the states' fiscal deficits; it is estimated that the combined central and state fiscal deficit was over 10 percent of GDP in 2000–01. See *National Account Statistics 2002*. New Delhi: Central Statistical Organization: 2002.

[21] For example, despite weeks of repeated threats by the central government to dismiss the Bihar state government of Rabri Devi for gross fiscal mismanagement in 1998, nothing much changed in Bihar. Finally the Center imposed President's Rule in Bihar, but the Lok Sahba overturned the rule in short order.

authorities, and steps are being taken to rein in expenditure and improve tax collection. One recent measure was the introduction of the Fiscal Responsibility and Budget Management Bill. This bill aimed to reduce the deficit by at least 0.5 percent per year with a view to reaching a deficit of not more than 2 percent of GDP by 2006 – a goal that has not yet being met. Expenditure reductions are also being pursued, notably through reform of the food subsidy (public distribution system) and administered prices for petroleum. Steps are also being taken to reduce government stakes in state-owned enterprises, which remain a drain on government resources and a cause of inefficiency. To improve the revenue base, attempts are being made to reform the internal tax system. However, as discussed further in Chapter 4, to date, these attempts have met with little success.

INDUSTRIAL POLICY REFORM

During the pre-reform period with import-substituting industrialization, the cornerstone of economic development, the principal instrument of industrial policy was an elaborate industrial licensing framework under the Industries Development and Regulations Act of 1951. The act required a government license for either establishing a new production unit (above a certain defined size) or making substantial expansion to an existing unit, including changing a plant's location. This cumbersome process required applications for an industrial license to be submitted to the government Licensing Committee, which had the authority to either approve or reject each proposal in light of national planning targets for industrial production and investment in the various sectors. On top of this, a long (and ever-growing) list of industries, including iron and steel, heavy machinery, oil and petroleum, air transport, mining, and telecommunications, were reserved solely for the public sector, monitored under the intrusive eye of the Monopolies and Restrictive Trade Practices (MRTP) Act of 1970. The MRTP imposed severe constraints on expansion by large firms by stipulating that all private sector firms with a capital base of over Rs. 20 million were to be classified as MRTP firms and would be allowed to enter only selected industries. This policy not only imposed binding constraints to entry and growth for most firms outside the small-scale sector, it also adversely affected overall industrial performance (Ahluwalia 1985). However, in short order, the heavily protected industrial sector witnessed the virtual abolition of the industrial licensing system and other regulatory impediments. Industrial licensing was abolished for all but fifteen industries, and the MRTP amended to eliminate the need for prior approval for capacity diversification and expansion. Similarly, by the end of the 1990s, a number of sectors previously reserved for the public sector were opened to private investment, including power, mining, telecommunications, ports, transport, and banking. However, relatively little progress was made in reducing the number of industries reserved for small enterprises or "small-scale industries" – only 17 industries were removed from the list, leaving 821 areas still restricted.

REFORMING THE FDI REGIME

In the pre-reform era, restrictions on FDI was so strict that it was reduced to a trickle. This contributed to the almost complete marginalization of the Indian economy from the world economy. The restrictive Foreign Exchange Regulation Act (FERA) of 1973 imposed a ceiling of 40 percent on equity share-holding of foreign companies, required dilution to 40 percent in the existing companies that were not operating in the high-tech and strategic sectors, and imposed limitations on royalty payments. This led a number of major foreign companies such as IBM and Coca-Cola to leave India rather than agree to FERA's unreasonable terms. Srinivasan and Tendulkar (2003) note that as a result, whereas world exports grew at nearly 8 percent per annum from 1951 to 1973, India's export growth rate lagged behind at about 2.6 percent per annum during that period. Moreover, India was able to attract less than 1 percent of all foreign direct investment and less than 3 percent of all portfolio investment received by developing countries. In fact, the average level of equity investment in the period 1973–83 was a miniscule US$10 million per year (Balasubramanyam 1984).

Under the NEP, controls on foreign direct and portfolio investment were significantly relaxed. Along with the abolition of the industrial licensing requirements governing domestic investment, controls over foreign trade and investment were considerably relaxed, including the removal of ceilings on equity ownership by foreign firms. By the end of 1991, the approvals process for FDI was greatly simplified because it became eligible for automatic approval by the country's central bank, the Reserve Bank of India (RBI).[22] That is, the pre-reform policy in which all FDI proposals were considered on a case-by-case basis, with FDI capped at 40 percent of total equity investment, was amended. The NEP allowed majority ownership and automatic approval of foreign investment of up to 51 percent of shareholding for a wide list of industries, a case-by-case consideration of applications for foreign equity ownership of up to 75 percent in sectors related to infrastructure, and a streamlining of procedures relating to approval of investment applications (Bajpai and Sachs 2000).

In September 1992, portfolio investment was allowed for registered foreign institutional investors such as pension funds, mutual funds, and investment trusts. Asset management companies were allowed unrestricted entry (in terms

---

[22] In an attempt to streamline the approval process, the Foreign Investment Promotion Board, the RBI, and the Secretariat for Industrial Assistance now work together to assist investors, including working with state governments to reduce delays.

of volume), in both the primary and secondary markets for corporate securities. In addition, domestic firms with sound financial positions were permitted to raise capital from abroad with fewer restrictions such as by issuing equity in the form of global depository receipts (GDRs), foreign currency convertible bonds (FCCB), and other debt instruments. Reducing these barriers to capital flows lowered the cost of capital and helped Indian businesses benefit from the transfer of skills and technology. The government also created the Foreign Investment Promotion Board (FIPB) as a one-stop "fast-track" shopping arena for foreign investors in obtaining all necessary approvals and to approve foreign direct investment proposals not covered under the automatic approval. By the mid-1990s, the list of industries in which FDI was permitted was further widened. Automatic approval was granted for joint ventures with up to 74 percent foreign equity participation and 100 percent foreign equity and ownership permitted in the export processing zones (EPZs) and units that are 100 percent export-oriented units. These reforms not only forced Indian companies to improve the quality of their products, it also enabled many to restructure their activities through mergers and acquisitions, including technology upgrades.

FINANCIAL SECTOR REFORMS

In the pre-reform era, India's financial sector, especially banking (reminiscent of pre-reform China), was subjected to pervasive financial repression (McKinnon 1973). Following the nationalization of the fourteen largest commercial banks in 1969 (which raised the public sector banks' share of deposits to 86 percent from the 31 percent share represented by the State Bank of India), banks were pressured to lend to government-deemed "priority sectors," such as agriculture, small-scale industry, retail trade, and transport at closely monitored interest rates.[23] By March 1979, the priority sector lending requirements stipulated that 33 percent of each bank's total credit were to be directed to these sectors. In 1980, following the nationalization of six more banks, only about 10 percent of bank branches were left in private hands (Tandon 1989). The state-owned banks now controlled about 92 percent of bank deposits (up from 86 percent in 1973), and priority-sector lending was raised to 40 percent (Government of India [GOI] 1991). In addition, the government determined interest rates and channeled an extremely high proportion of funds to all manner of government-sanctioned projects. In effect, the financial sector served more or less as an extension of the government's fiscal policy (Tannan 2001).

Given that bank-lending rates were tightly regulated through an elaborate system that related charged interest rates to the amount of the loans, it took away funds from more productive opportunities in the private sector. Because

---

[23] In 1980, the nationalization of six more banks raised the public sector banks' share to 92 percent. For further details, see Hanson and Kathuria (1999).

banks were not judged on their profits or on prudential issues such as their ability to evaluate credit risks, exposures, or maturity mismatches but simply by whether loan allocation and interest rate regulations had been met, banks were left with large volumes of nonperforming loans. As a result, Indian banks (like those in the PRC), despite rapid growth of deposits, became progressively unprofitable. Joshi and Little (1996, 110–11) note that by the mid-1980s, the average return on assets was about 0.15 percent, whereas capital and reserves stood at a dismal 1.5 percent of assets.

Finally, in August 1991, as part of the liberalization program, the central government appointed a high-level committee on the "Financial System" (the Narasimham Committee) to review all aspects of the financial system and to make comprehensive recommendations for reform. The committee submitted its report in November 1991, making several recommendations for reforms in the banking sector and the capital markets (GOI 1991). The recommendations included (a) reduction in statutory liquidity requirements (SLR); (b) reduction in the cash reserve requirements (CRR), payment of interest on the CRR, and use of the CRR as a monetary policy instrument; (c) phase out of directed credit, (d) deregulation of interest rates in a phased manner and bringing interest rates on government borrowing in line with market-determined rates; (e) attainment of Bank of International Settlements/Basle norms for capital adequacy within three years; (f) tightening of prudential norms; (g) entry of private banks and easing of restriction on foreign banks; (h) partial privatization of state-owned banks and sale of bank equity to the public; (i) phase-out of development finance institutions' (DFIs) privileged access to funds; (j) increased competition in lending between DFIs and banks and a switch from consortium lending to syndicated lending; and (k) easing of regulations on capital markets, combined with entry of foreign institutional investors (FIIs) and better supervision. The government announced its broad acceptance of the Narasimham Committee recommendations, and the report has served as the basis for subsequent banking sector reforms.

In keeping with these recommendations, the banking sector has been subject to important reforms since the early 1990s. Prudential regulation and supervision of the banking system have been strengthened as the Board for Financial Supervision (BFS) established in 1994 (within the Reserve Bank) has the authority to supervise and inspect banks, financial institutions and other non-bank financial companies. The BFS has been monitoring banks using the CAMELS approach.[24] That is, supervision of banking and nonbank financial companies is based on regular on-site and off-site monitoring. Similarly, a series of measures have been implemented, including allocation of funds for bank recapitalization to reduce the level of nonperforming loans, especially

---

[24] An acronym for "Capital Adequacy, Asset Quality, Management, Earnings, Liquidity and Systems and Controls."

in public sector banks, and overall restructuring of public sector banks. Public sector banks have been given greater independence. Nominee directors from government and the RBI are being gradually phased out with increased emphasis on boards being elected rather than appointed by the government. Furthermore, professional representation on bank boards has increased with the expectation that the boards will have the authority and competence to manage the banks within the broad prudential norms set by the RBI.

Equally important, the RBI, which regulates the banking sector, has also strengthened prudential requirements and introduced a capital risk-asset ratio system as a measure of capital adequacy, raising minimum capital and capital adequacy ratios to conform to international standards. For example, before the reforms, few Indian banks had a capital adequacy ratio meeting the international norm of 8 percent. By 1995, the government set the minimum capital adequacy requirements of 8 percent of risk-weighted assets for Indian banks with foreign branches. In 1998, the standard was raised to 9 percent (effective as of March 2000), with government securities given a 2.5 percent risk weight to begin reflecting interest-rate risk. By the end of 2000, only about two dozen public sector banks fell short of this standard. Competition has also been encouraged by the issuance of licenses to new private banks and by giving more power and flexibility to bank managers, in both directing credit and setting prices. In fact, greater competition in the banking sector (by allowing new private banks, including foreign banks, to enter the market), and improvements in the capital and debt markets have reduced reliance on central bank financing. Banks and financial institutions are now permitted to access the capital market to expand their equity base, and the passage of the Foreign Exchange and Management Bill in 1999 has greatly streamlined foreign exchange regulations.

At the time of independence, India had four functioning stock markets. The Bombay Stock Exchange (BSE), established in 1875, predated the Tokyo Stock Exchange. The stock exchanges enjoyed clearly defined rules governing listing, trading, and settlements and a fairly developed equity culture backed by a banking system with developed lending norms and recovery procedures. However, decades of financial repression after independence stifled the growth of the corporate sector. On the eve of reforms in 1991, India had only one major stock exchange: the BSE. Reduced to a shell of its former self, the BSE was a monopoly of selected brokers, characterized by high entry costs, administrative inefficiencies, high costs of intermediation, and endemic corruption. Soon after the implementation of the economic reforms, four new institutions – the National Stock Exchange of India (NSE), the Securities and Exchanges Board of India (SEBI), the National Securities Clearing Corporation (NSCC), and the National Securities Depository – were created. The NSE, established as a limited liability company owned by public sector financial institutions, now accounts for about two-thirds of the stock trading in India, including virtually all of its derivatives trading, whereas the NSCC is the legal counterpart to net obligations of each brokerage firm. The SEBI was designed to improve corporate governance and enhance investor protection. This was a particularly urgent task because concerns about corporate governance reached a fever pitch following a spate of scandals in the early 1990s (especially the Harshad Mehta stock market scam), including a series of cases in which companies allotted preferential shares to their promoters at deeply discounted prices, or simply disappeared with investors' money. Since its establishment in 1992, SEBI has introduced a rigorous regulatory regime to ensure fairness and transparency. For example, to improve transparency, the SEBI has mandated disclosure of all transactions in which the total quantity of shares is more than 0.5 percent of the equity of the company. In addition, after the execution of a trade, brokers must immediately disclose to the SEBI the name of the client and other trade details, and the SEBI must then disseminate this information to the general public on the same day. Improvements and reforms in corporate governance have made India better equipped to deal with the forces of competition and globalization.

THE OUTCOMES

As Table 2.5 shows, the reforms described here helped the Indian economy recover rather quickly with real GDP growing at an annual average rate of 6.7 percent between 1992–93 and 1996–97 and 5.4 percent between 1997–98 and 2001–02. These rates were not only a significant improvement over the mediocre "Hindu rate of growth," they were second highest in the world, behind only China. However, although India's reforms have been impressive in the economic sectors discussed in the preceding pages, it has been less than satisfactory in many others. In particular, weak measures to reduce the governments' fiscal deficits, coupled with a stagnant and uncompetitive industrial sector burdened with rigid labor laws, have contributed to "jobless growth." Moreover, reforms have generally bypassed the agricultural sector. High levels of tariff as well as export restrictions have remained on agricultural products, and India's domestic support policies for agriculture have remained largely unaffected by the economic reforms of 1991. What explains this? These issues are discussed in detail in Chapter 4.

THE POLITICAL ECONOMY OF INDIA'S ECONOMIC REFORMS

As is well known, building and maintaining political consensus on economic reforms in a democracy, especially a fractious democracy like India, is exceedingly difficult. The task is complicated further when it comes to implementing the reforms because it not only challenges the prerogatives of vested interests, but also because neoliberal or market reforms carry with them attendant short-term pain such as rising unemployment, inflation, higher prices on

Table 2.5. *India's growth performance (percentage per year)*

	Total GDP growth	Sectoral growth of GDP		
		Agriculture	Industry	Services
1970–72 to 1980–81 (average)	3.2	2.0	4.0	7.2
1981–82 to 1990–91 (average)	5.7	3.8	7.0	6.7
1991–92	1.3	−1.1	−1.0	4.8
1992–93	5.1	5.4	4.3	5.4
1993–94	5.9	3.9	5.6	7.7
1994–95	7.3	5.3	10.3	7.1
1995–96	7.3	−0.3	12.3	10.5
1996–97	7.8	8.8	7.7	7.2
1997–98	4.8	−1.5	3.8	9.8
1998–99	6.5	5.9	3.8	8.3
1999–2000	6.1	1.4	5.2	9.5
2000–01	4.0	0.1	6.6	4.8
2001–02	5.4	5.7	3.3	6.5
1992–93 to 1996–97 (average)	6.7	4.6	8.0	7.6
1997–98 to 2001–02 (average)	5.4	2.3	4.5	7.8

Source: Ahluwalia (2002, 68).

state-subsidized goods, falling wages, and other austerity measures. Because governments, especially democratically elected ones, cannot afford such popular backlash, the reforms are usually watered down or altogether abandoned. Indeed, Adam Przeworski (1991), in his important book *Democracy and the Market*, predicted that economic reforms introduced in new democracies would produce populist policies that would undermine both the economy and democracy. Other analysts have highlighted the probable coalitions against reform, arguing that vested rent-seeking beneficiaries of protectionist, state-led development often mobilize through democratic channels to block reforms. However, because the beneficiaries of reform are presumed to be widely dispersed and unorganized, they cannot counter the vested interests. Again, the political implications are that reforms are likely to be unpopular and politically costly, and elected politicians, including well-intentioned democratic governments, would understandably do what is politically expedient but fiscally irresponsible – delaying or altogether scuttling necessary reform measures.

Yet what explains India's relatively successful formulation and implementation of market reforms? A rather novel view of the post-liberalization Indian state and its institutional capacity is presented in Rob Jenkins (1999) in *Democratic Politics and Economic Reform in India*. Jenkins claims that in practice, the Indian state has a far greater degree of autonomy than is assumed by theorists who claim that a democratic state can be easily compromised and captured by particularistic groups, lobbies, dominant-class coalitions, and other vested interests. To the contrary, he argues that India's "real" functioning democratic state (unlike the idealist theoretical conceptions of it) is actually made up of a rather loose, fluid, and frequently changing conglomeration of interest groups. This reality on the ground gives the state much flexibility and autonomy over policy issues. According to Jenkins, nothing underscores this more vividly than the introduction of economic reforms in 1991 and its continued sustainability. He asks why and how India's governing elite, long wedded to a inward-looking statist-cum-protectionist economic program, abandoned this in favor of integrating the country into the global economic system, how it succeeded in "selling the benefits of reform to individual constituencies and the public at large" (p. 3), and how did they go about implementing their ambitious economic reforms agenda?

To Jenkins, the answer to these questions lies in appreciating the mechanisms under which "real democracy" functions in India, – which he argues can best be understood as "incentives," "institutions," and "skills." With regard to incentives, India's mercurial political elites are willing to take risks (i.e., introducing reforms) because they have adroitly calculated that reforms will not endanger their political and electoral survival. They know the rules of the game well enough to develop new and creative avenues for collecting rents, distributing patronage, and, given the highly fluid and fragmented nature of interest groups, creating new coalitions for reform – including dividing and isolating interests opposed to it. Similarly, India's political institutions, both the formal (federal structure) and informal (political party networks), work in ways that help the political elites implement reforms with surprising ease. The federal structure that forces the provincial governments to compete with each other prevents them from uniting against the reforms, not to mention the fact that politically costly reforms are often devolved to these state governments. However, the clientelist and porous nature of India's political parties, in which the boundaries between party and nonparty networks and blurred, allows politicians (away from the glare of publicity) to create multiple channels of influence and patronage, in addition co-opting and accommodating diverse interests. The "skills" include the tactics, if not political machinations, party elites and individual politicians use to "sell" the reforms to their constituencies – indeed, to the general public. More often than not, they "employ political tactics that have little to do with 'transparency' in order to soften the edge of political conflict by promoting change in the guise of continuity" (p. 52), or through "continuity masquerading as change" (p. 194). In other words, the tactics used are often underhanded and deceptive – what Jenkins calls "reform by stealth" – to lull the electorate into accepting the more unpalatable aspects of market reforms. Jenkins' study compellingly shows that democracies can be far more dexterous and capable in formulating and implementing policies than generally thought or given credit for.

Perhaps a more compelling formulation regarding the implementation of India's economic reforms is presented by Varshney (1999). He argues that India's reform dynamics have followed a dual track – what he terms "elite politics" and "mass politics." The "elites" include mainly the English-speaking upper castes and urbanized middle classes, and "elite politics" usually takes place in the upper realms of governmental bureaucracies and business board-rooms. As the major beneficiaries of economic reforms, these elite classes are market reforms' most fervent supporters. However, the vast majority of India's poor and toiling masses, with some justification, feel that the fruits of the reforms have bypassed them and are increasingly resentful of the liberalization program. Because they form an important voting bloc and tend of vote more regularly than the elite classes, both political parties and politicians have proceeded cautiously on the pace and depth of the reforms – especially those that may negatively affect their political fortunes. Specifically, both the federal and the state governments have actively pursued "elite-oriented reforms" such as the deregulation of the stock market and the financial and banking sectors, trade and exchange rate reforms, tax reforms to broaden the tax base and reduce tax evasion, liberalization of investment rules in real estate, and the reduction and unification of tariffs. However, "radical reforms" – or ones that have the potential to cause hardship to the masses such as privatization of public enterprises (with resultant job losses), cuts in agricultural and rural subsidies, or restructuring labor laws that make it easier to lay off and fire workers – have been quietly shelved. To follow Varshney's argument to its logical conclusion, it is clear that India's democratic state (including state governments) are deeply constrained by mass politics and thereby do not have the political will to follow reforms that could potentially have negative consequences on this significant and vocal voting bloc. It also means that the Indian state may not have the requisite autonomy to implement the so-called second-generation reforms.[25] Rather, if the past is any guide, the reforms will move ahead on areas at the elite level but remain decidedly solicitous on policies that may negatively affect the masses, so as not to provoke a punishing verdict from the numerical electorate. Nevertheless, democratic India enjoys an advantage over authoritarian China. Economic globalization increasingly demands free flow of information, a more transparent decision-making process, and freedom of choice for market participants. In its efforts to control and manage the flow of information, the Chinese regime has been inadvertently undermining this critical aspect of a market economy.

[25] Although there is no universally agreed definition of what constitutes second-generation reforms, it is understood that they must include the unfinished business from the first generation and that they must be centered on institution-building to support markets.

3

China

Strategies and Patterns of Global Integration

Over the past three decades, the Chinese economy has gradually but irrevocably moved away from central planning to a greater reliance on markets. Over this period, it has been the fastest growing economy in the world with real gross GDP growth rates averaging 9.5 percent per year during 1980–2004 and over 9 percent since 2005. Endowed with a GDP of $1.65 trillion, China is now the fourth largest economy in the world. If, as expected, China maintains its current growth trajectory it will become the world's largest economy by 2025, if not earlier (Organisation for Economic Co-operation and Development [OECD] 2005). Moreover, as Table 3.1 illustrates, the Chinese economy has undergone significant structural changes. The primary sector (agriculture, forestry, and fishing) has declined as a share of GDP, and the share in GDP of the secondary sector (comprising manufacturing and construction) contracted in the early 1990s as a result of the restructuring of the state-owned enterprises (SOEs) but has since recovered to about the same share in 2005 (47.5 percent) as in 1980 (48.2 percent). The tertiary sector covering service industries has dramatically expanded from 21.9 percent in 1980 to almost 40 percent in 2005.

The aim of this chapter is twofold: first, to elaborate some of the issues discussed in the preceding chapters – namely, how the reforms of the past three decades have affected China's political economy by delineating the outcomes (both the successes as well as the contradictions) and the socioeconomic and political implications of the reforms. The following pages show that although reforms have produced impressive rates of growth in GDP, they have also created new vulnerabilities, while exacerbating existing ones. Second, because the challenge for China is no longer how to achieve economic growth but how to sustain and manage its consequences, this chapter examines what can be done to further advance the gains of the reforms, while mitigating its unintended contradictions. The following pages underscore that despite China's remarkable success in implementing market reforms, the process of transition to a full-fledged market system is far from complete. In part, this is because the first stage of reforms (designed to correct the obvious macroeconomic

Table 3.1. *China's economic structure: 1980–2005*
(as percent of GDP)

Sector	1980	1990	2000	2005
Primary	29.9	26.9	14.8	12.6
Secondary	48.2	41.3	45.9	47.5
Industry	43.9	36.7	40.4	42.0
Construction	4.3	4.6	5.6	5.5
Tertiary	21.9	31.8	39.3	39.9

Source: National Bureau of Statistics of China (2006).

distortions of the past) is usually easier to implement than the second stage, which has to do with the more difficult task of building the institutions of a market economy. Resolving the contradictions inherent in China's hybrid political economy (characterized by a cumbersome mix of private ownership and state control) through institutional reforms that further strengthen and build market-supporting economic and political-legal institutions is essential to sustained and balanced growth.

Patterns of Global Economic Integration

Undoubtedly, China's remarkable economic transformation is the result of favorable initial conditions, including good human capital endowments, a large working-age population, and a large and diversified economic base. However, two factors stand out: China's gradual yet decisive advancement toward a market-based economy and its rapid integration into the global economic system. Specifically, the transition from central planning to a more market-based economy, coupled with global economic integration, has allowed factors of production to move to more productive activities. This is because worker productivity rises when labor moves from low-productivity agriculture to industry in which capital and output per worker are much higher (e.g., in 1978 about 70 percent of labor was employed in primary industries such as agriculture, forestry, fisheries, and mining, but this only accounted for 28 percent of GDP). By 2003, the primary sector share of employment had fallen to 49 percent as there was transfer of labor from agriculture to industry. These changes have led to a more efficient allocation of public resources and contributed to substantial improvements in productivity and overall economic growth (Heytens and Zebregs 2003).

Second, by prudently taking advantage of opportunities afforded by the global economy, China has dramatically expanded its export base. Following in the footsteps of the export-led industrialization strategy used successfully by Japan, South Korea, and Taiwan, China's export growth is driven by its vast labor-intensive manufacturing sector financed by unprecedented volumes of foreign direct investment (FDI). China today is not only the world's largest exporter of manufactured products, it is also a major exporter of agricultural commodities and raw materials. According to Lardy (2005, 123), between 1978 and end-2003 foreign firms invested about US$500 billion in China and accounted for more than one-quarter of China's output of manufactured goods. In 2004, China attracted some US$60.6 billion of FDI.[1] Only the United States, with nearly US$96 billion, and UK, with US$78 billion, received more.

Hence, the oft-mentioned phrase that China has become the "world's factory" is hardly an exaggeration (K. H. Zhang 2006). In fact, China's impact on the world economy has been accentuated by a very high and increasing degree of openness to trade, with the average of imports and exports representing 35 percent of GDP in 2004 (OECD 2005, 30). China's share of merchandise exports increased from about US$10 billion in the late 1970s to US$326 billion in 2002. More precisely, China's total share in world trade expanded from 1 percent in 1980 to about 6 percent in 2004. In 2004, China's merchandise trade with the world totaled around $1.3 trillion, a consequence of annual growth rates above 30 percent in some years. By end-2004, China had become the third-largest trading nation in dollar terms, behind the United States and Germany and just ahead of Japan. Soaring exports have also translated into bulging foreign exchange reserves (US$819 billion) by the end of 2005 and over US$1 trillion in January 2007. China's trade surplus with the United States jumped from US$233 billion in 2006 to US$262 billion in 2007, accounting for almost 30 percent of total U.S. trade deficit of US$763.6 billion (or the gap between what the United States sells abroad and what it imports). This is the largest imbalance the United States has with a single trading partner.[2] However, China's trade surplus with the United States and the European Union (EU) is offset by its trade deficit with its Asian neighbors. In 2006, China's trade deficit with Taiwan, South Korea, Japan, and the Association of Southeast Asian Nations (ASEAN) totaled about US$155 billion (Figure 3.1 and Table 3.2).

Although exports have been the engine behind China's economic resurgence, an important caveat should be noted: this rising export share overstates the contribution of foreign trade to China's overall economic growth. This is because a significant volume of China's foreign trade involves the assembly of imported components and raw materials using designs, engineering, equipment, and technology outsourced by other countries – especially Asian

---

[1] Some claim that China's FDI is inflated by "round-tripping" of domestic investment through Hong Kong SAR (special autonomous regions), whereas others point out that a significant volume of FDI is actually in the non-FDI type of capital inflows, or "hot money." Of course, it is also important to note that FDI inflows also come with production expertise. Significant transfers of technology to foreign-invested enterprises spill over into the general economy and raise total factor productivity.

[2] The United States and China count and compile trade data differently, leading to differing totals. According to the Chinese government, the trade gap with the United States was US$163.3 billion, whereas U.S. customs data put the gap at US$262 billion.

Table 3.2. *China plus Hong Kong SAR
bilateral trade (US$ billions)*

	2000	2004
United States	62	110
EU	20	49
Japan	−14	−40
Rest of Asia*	−65	−143
Others	−3	−41

* Rest of Asia: includes Cambodia, Indonesia, South
Korea, Laos, Malaysia, Myanmar, Philippines, Sin-
gapore, Thailand, Taiwan, and Vietnam.
Source: Prasad (2005, 44).

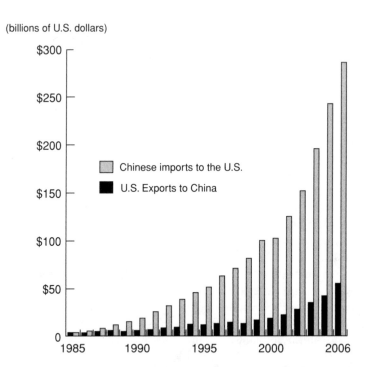

Figure 3.1. U.S.-China Trade, 1985–2006. *Source:* U.S. Census Bureau, Foreign Trade
Statistics.

countries such as South Korea, Japan, and Taiwan, as well as ASEAN, which are linked to China through a complex "regional production network system." This means that countries specialize in particular stages of the production process of various kinds of products, rather than specializing in a small range of goods. In this system of "vertical specialization," China is usually most prominent in the final assembly stages. This also means that more often than not, the value added in China is a small percentage of an exported product's final sale value. Indeed, some analysts believe that China's true ratio of exports to GDP is much smaller because such a large share of the value added to China's foreign trade is sourced in other countries.

Moreover, China is also fast becoming a major importer of goods. China imports raw materials (petroleum, iron ore, agricultural products) as well as industrial inputs such as machinery and unassembled components. In fact, in 2003, China displaced the United States to become the world's leading consumer of most industrial raw materials and surpassed Japan as the world's second-largest oil consumer. Growing demand from China has put tremendous upward pressure on commodity prices, accruing significant gains for resource-rich countries. As discussed in later chapters, China is also becoming increasingly dependent on imported energy and other raw materials to operate its industries. Also, although much emphasis is placed on the U.S. trade deficit with China, as noted earlier, China's trade deficit with other trading partners has risen to offset its rising surplus with the United States. To better manage the diverse and complex challenges of global economic integration is what eventually led China to join the World Trade Organization (WTO) in 2001.

China in the WTO

China was one of the twenty-three original signatories of the General Agreement on Tariffs and Trade (GATT) in 1948. In 1949, the government in Taiwan announced that China was withdrawing from the GATT, although Beijing never recognized this decision. Four decades later (in 1986), China notified the GATT of its wish to resume its status as a GATT contracting party. Following some fifteen years of negotiations, China became a member of WTO (the successor organization of the GATT) on December 11, 2001.[3] The reason it took China several years to join the WTO was because Beijing's demand that China was a "developing country" and thus be permitted to enter the WTO under more lenient terms. The United States, however, insisted that China could only enter the WTO if it substantially liberalized its trade regime. In the end, a compromise was reached that required China to make immediate and

[3] China's WTO membership was formally approved at the WTO Ministerial Conference in Doha, Qatar, on 10 November 2001 (Taiwan's WTO membership was approved the next day). On 11 November 2001, China notified the WTO that it had formally ratified the WTO agreements, and on 11 December 2001, it formally joined the WTO.

extensive reductions in various trade and investment barriers, while allowing it to maintain some level of protection (or a "transitional period of protection") for certain sensitive sectors.

China's decision to join the WTO was hailed as the most significant event in East-West economic relations since Marco Polo's voyages in the thirteenth century. It underscored the Middle Kingdom's desire not only to end its long isolationist tradition but also to expand and consolidate its rapidly growing economic linkages with the rest of the world. Zweig (2002) argues that WTO integration occurred on China's terms because the Communist Party hierarchy, including core members of the bureaucracy, local government, and corporate entities, concluded that such "deep" economic integration could advance their interests. In particular, not only would WTO rules force a much needed discipline on Chinese industries to become more efficient and competitive, but WTO membership would also provide the reformist leadership a much-needed political cover to push for more difficult reforms, including passing the blame on foreigners if things went wrong. Thus, Zweig argues that "internationalization," rather than "globalization" best describes China's economic opening, because globalization implies forces outside government control, whereas internationalization, combines transnational opening with bureaucratic and regulatory controls.

WTO accession allows China such trade-offs. On one hand, it allows China to integrate into the global economy under a rules-based, transparent, and predictable system. WTO accession also grants China "most favored nation" (MFN) status on a permanent basis, reducing the uncertainty over the yearly renewal of this status by the United States and China's other major trading partners.[4] It also means that China's trading partners will have to lift most of their quantitative restrictions on a range of products. For example, quotas on textiles and clothing will be phased out in accordance with the WTO's Agreement on Textiles and Clothing, whereas other quotas will be phased out in accordance with negotiated schedules. Moreover, China can now utilize the WTO dispute settlement mechanism to protect its trade interests. On the other hand, WTO accession requires China to harmonize its regulatory regime over foreign trade and investment with a global framework of rules under WTO auspices. Specifically, the Chinese government has to abide by a set of rules for liberalizing the economy and relaxing state control over foreign trade and investment. This means that China has to standardize its regulatory framework across the country to ensure uniform enforcement of foreign trade and investment policies. Of course, this also means that the Chinese government has to make extensive, far-reaching, often complex reforms at all levels of government. As a WTO member China must provide (and receive) nondiscriminatory treatment to all WTO members and fully adhere to WTO rules. For example, all foreign individuals and enterprises, including those not invested or registered

[4] Prior to WTO accession, MFN status was subject to annual renewal by the U.S. Congress.

in China, must be accorded treatment no less favorable than that accorded to enterprises in China with respect to the right to trade. Also, Chinese exporters can be hit with dumping charges that apply to nonmarket economies because importing countries can use the prices or costs of similar products in third countries (instead of Chinese prices) to determine whether Chinese firms are dumping their products. China (and other members) must, in an effective and uniform manner, revise their existing domestic laws and enact new legislation that are fully in compliance with the WTO agreement. Like other WTO members, China is under the obligation to publish all the laws and regulations on foreign trade and investment in one or more WTO official languages (English, French, and Spanish) and to enforce only those laws and regulations that have been published beforehand. Among specific (and substantial) commitments China made under the WTO were the following:

1. Show transparency and predictability of China's business environment, especially of its trade and investment regimes: to this effect, China agreed to eliminate all prohibited subsidies (including those to state-owned enterprises), liberalize trading rights, and require state trading companies to conduct their operations in a commercial manner.

2. Implement the TRIPS (Trade-Related Aspects of Intellectual Property Rights) Agreement in full from the date of accession.

3. Gradually eliminate trade barriers and expand market access to goods from foreign countries: most tariffs were to be eliminated by 2004, but in no case later than 2010. In agriculture, China pledged to bind all tariffs and reduce them from an average level of 31.5 percent to 17.4 percent. For industrial products, it pledged to phase out quantitative restrictions, cut the average tariff from 24.6 percent to 9.4 percent by 2005, and sign the "Information Technology Agreement" committing Beijing to eliminate in a phased manner all tariffs on telecommunications equipment, semiconductors, computers and computer equipment, and other information technology (IT) products.

4. End quotas on textiles on or before 31 December 2004, albeit with a safeguard mechanism in place until the end of 2008 permitting WTO members to take action to curb imports in case of market disruptions caused by Chinese exports of textile products.[5]

5. Foreign companies were to be permitted to establish joint venture enterprises without quantitative restrictions within five years of China's accession.

6. Under the General Agreement on Trade in Services (GATS) rules governing international trade in financial services, China was obligated upon

[5] Although all quotas on China's textile and clothing exports were to be phased out by 1 January 2005, a special safeguard mechanism was in place until the end of 2008. This mechanism allowed importing countries to restrict imports from China when they result in market disruption.

accession to permit foreign financial institutions to provide services in China without client restrictions for foreign currency business.[6] Local currency business were to be permitted within two years of accession. Within five years of accession, foreign financial institutions were to be permitted to provide services to all Chinese clients, and joint ventures in insurance and telecommunication were to be permitted (with various degrees of foreign ownership allowed).

Since becoming a WTO member, China has taken several, albeit incremental, steps to meet its WTO commitments. For example, on 1 January 2002, China cut import tariffs for more than five thousand goods. The average tariff rate was reduced to 12 percent from a level of 15.3 percent in 2001 and to 9.9 percent in 2005. The rate for manufacturing goods was reduced from 14.7 to 11.3 percent in 2005, for industrial products from 14.8 percent in 2001 to 9 percent in 2005, and for agricultural goods from 18.8 to 15.8 percent during the same period (Pei and Peng 2007). By 1 January 2005, China had also progressively revoked nontariff measures (import quotas, special bidding and licenses) on the import of 424 products and abolished quota and license requirements for a number of other goods. In addition, China has taken significant steps toward opening up its service trade by modifying and enacting a series of laws and regulations for opening up banking, insurance, security, telecommunications, and construction services.

Moreover, China has revised or abolished laws and regulations that are inconsistent with WTO rules. For example, new laws on antidumping and antisubsidy have been put in place. However, fulfilling the entire gamut of WTO commitments will (and has) required China to make profound institutional changes, especially with regard to the relationship between government and industry. Although China has made a concerted effort to meet its obligations under the terms of its accession to the WTO, there are growing concerns about compliance issues. Among these are a lack of transparency in rule making, insufficient notice of new or proposed laws, unfair treatment of foreign firms in certain industries, and inadequate protection of intellectual property rights. The United States Trade Representative (USTR) has long claimed that counterfeiting and piracy infringement of intellectual property remains high in China, causing considerable economic harm to U.S. businesses in virtually every sector of the economy. According to the USTR, China continues to promote industrial policies that restrict market access of products of non-Chinese origin and uses government resources to support domestic industries and their exports. Aggravating these problems is what Lieberthal (1995) has aptly termed "fragmented authoritarianism." That is, the decision-making authority and

---

[6] China must allow foreign financial institutions to provide banking services in accordance with the terms set out in its GATS schedule, which is incorporated by reference into the Protocol on the Accession of the People's Republic of China to the WTO (Accession Protocol).

enforcement capacity in China has become so dispersed and unwieldy that it makes effective coordination among the various government and bureaucratic departments difficult. It also gives the various layers of government tremendous discretion regarding implementation and compliance, including the power to undermine "unfavorable" measures. Finally, the USTR sees China's deliberate currency undervaluation and closed markets (seen as contributing to China's trade surplus) as violation of WTO rules. The implications of these issues on U.S.-China relations and how can China best manage its increasingly sophisticated external economic relations are examined in Chapter 7.

Unshackling the Private Sector

The move from a command to a market system has also meant a simultaneous shrinkage of the state sector and the growth and expansion of the private sector. China's domestic private sector or the "nonstate sector" includes the township and village enterprises (TVEs), small-scale household enterprises or family businesses with fewer than eight employees, private businesses with eight or more employees, state-owned enterprises that have been privatized, publicly listed joint stock companies, and firms owned either exclusively or through joint venture arrangements by investors from Hong Kong, Macau, and Taiwan. Although the precise size of the private sector is unclear, Tsai (2007) estimates that there are more than 29 million private businesses that employ over 200 million people and generate about two-thirds of China's industrial output. According to Li (2006), the share of nonstate enterprises in China's industrial output has risen from 35 percent in 1985 to 67 percent in 2003, while the share of state enterprises fell from 65 percent in 1985 to 33 percent in 2003 (also OECD 2005, 34–36). Arguably, the private sector has become the main avenue of employment in China. Clearly, expanding this sector would help increase job opportunities.

Yet despite its growing importance, the private sector faces constraints. Dickson (2003) shows that during the Jiang Zemin years, the numbers of *hong zibenjia* (or "red capitalists," that is, private entrepreneurs) who were members of the Chinese Communist Party (CCP) grew rapidly, with more than one-third being senior party members.[7] Although the debate regarding what is the appropriate relationship between the CCP and "market socialism with Chinese

[7] On the CCP's eightieth anniversary on 1 July 2001, then General Secretary Jiang Zemin gave a landmark speech viewed as inviting private entrepreneurs to join the party. Zemin's "Theory of the Three Represents" ostensibly designed to integrate "Marxism-Leninism, Mao Zedong Thought, and Deng Xiaoping Theory," recommended that the party should represent "the most advanced forces of production, the most advanced cultural forces, and the interests of the overwhelming majority of people." In practice, this meant that the CCP should not discriminate against private entrepreneurs. No doubt, this was a remarkable shift because it meant that the CCP had to reverse its former ideological depiction of capitalists as exploitative "class enemies."

characteristics" will no doubt continue, it is also clear that this increasingly close relationship between the party and the private sector is not conducive to long-term growth because it is based on personal connections and favoritism rather than individual enterprise and initiative. Moreover, such cronyism fosters corruption. Not surprisingly, according to Transparency International (2007), China now ranks among the "most corrupt" countries in the world in which to do business. Also, as Tsai (2002) points out, in her aptly titled book *Back-Alley Banking,* private entrepreneurs in China have long been denied access to official sources of credit. This is because the legally established state banks' main priority is to serve the state-owned enterprises. In fact, established banks are not allowed to help the private sector, and most private financing remains illegal in China. Under these conditions, private entrepreneurs have developed creative ways to raise capital to fund their businesses, including a variety of informal financing mechanisms such as rotating credit associations, borrowing from family and friends, and creating "backdoor" relations with state banks, the SOEs, and even "disguised" private banks. Of course, such informal systems have inherent limits. China must develop a well-defined system of private property rights and formal economic institutions that serve both public and private interests to maintain sustained growth rates. Expanding the private sector and allowing a larger role for market forces in guiding investment decisions is critical if China is to sustain high growth rates over the next several years.

China's economic growth owes much to the extraordinary share of GDP that is devoted to investment in new capital such as factories, equipment, and buildings. In fact, China's economic growth is so driven by capacity expansion (or fixed-asset investments) that such investments now account for more than 40 percent of GDP in 2005 (see Figure 3.2). This is substantially higher than in developed economies, including most East Asian countries, which have averaged around 25 percent (Dollar and Shang-Jin Wei 2007).

However, the rapid pace of investment growth also raises concerns about whether new capital is being deployed in the most productive ways and whether China is getting a fair return on its investment. For example, from 1990 to 2001, fixed investment as a share of GDP in China averaged about 33 percent and the economy grew at an annual rate of 10 percent. Between 2001 and 2005, fixed investment's share of GDP rose to about 40 percent, but the economy's average growth rate remained about the same, suggesting a lower return on investment (Dollar and Wei 2007). This figure is substantially higher than in developed economies, including other high-performing East Asian countries. In fact, comparisons with other Asian countries such as South Korea and Japan underscore this. In South Korea, the average annual growth was between 9 and 10 percent during 1982–91 and the same for Japan during 1955–70. Yet in both countries, investment's share of GDP was about 30 percent – much lower than China's (World Bank 2006). Moreover, in a number of China's

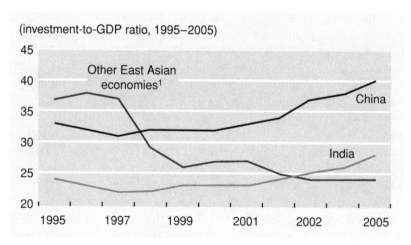

(investment-to-GDP ratio, 1995–2005)

Figure 3.2. China invests a far higher proportion of its GDP than its neighbors. *Source:* International Monetary Fund, Dollar and Wei (2007).
[1] Average for Korea, Thailand, and Singapore.

key industries, heavy investments have continued even with evidence of excess capacity, indicating capital misallocation (Zhengzheng 2006).

This relentless capacity expansion has led to economy-wide overcapacity and declining efficiency of investment (excess capacity in the economy is a sign of inefficient allocation of capital) to such an extent that the profit margins of core industries are becoming squeezed. Martin Wolf (2005) provocatively notes this paradox by observing that the surprising thing about the Chinese economy is not how fast it is growing but rather, given massive injections of investments, how slowly it is growing. Undoubtedly, growth that only translates into ever-declining profitability for firms and decreasing return to their shareholders cannot be sustained forever. The lesson for China is unambiguous: its economy must utilize investments more efficiently through a financial intermediation system that allows for a more efficient allocation of capital. In addition, its economy must graduate up the value chain, from production to also innovation because, as Paul Krugman (1994) has pointed out, growth that is achieved largely as a result of increased inputs and not increased total factor productivity cannot continue in perpetuity.[8] Therefore, improving human capital, upgrading the low quality of institutions, and allowing competitive financial markets to play a much greater role in allocating capital would increase the returns to investment and reduce the risk of financial instability.

---

[8] Total factor productivity (TFP) is the part of non-factor inputs that enables higher growth with lesser application of factor inputs. In other words, TFP implies enhanced output per unit of input. Thus, an increase in TFP means that more output is achieved given the same amount of factors and inputs. TFP broadly encompasses the contribution of technology and managerial aspects to the growth of real output.

Basing investment decisions on market signals also takes better account of the costs of inputs complementary to capital, such as labor (relatively abundant in China) and energy (which is relatively scarce).

Although China's exports have jumped more than tenfold over the past two decades, the composition of its exports has not changed as rapidly as it should have. Although there has been a decline in the share of agriculture and primary manufactures such as textiles and apparel, the share of hard manufactures such as consumer electronics, appliances, machinery, computers, and telecommunications has not grown as fast. In fact, a few years back, Mayer and Wood (2001) pointed out that China's export performance in skill-intensive products was below the level that would be expected on the basis of the country's factor endowments. Their analysis, based on a cross-national benchmark derived from regressing the ratio of skill-intensive to labor-intensive exports on a measure of skill per worker in that country found that China's actual share of skill-intensive exports within manufactures stood at 33 percent compared with a predicted ratio of 40 percent. Clearly, a greater sophistication of its exports, diversification of its product mix, and increased skill content would create much higher-paid jobs and lessen the impact of shocks to specific primary export sectors, which are often vulnerable to downward pressure in terms of export prices. Thus, for the Chinese economy to sustain its growth momentum, it must move up the value chain. Although China is a vital part of the global supply chain as the world's leading producer of manufactured goods, much of its manufacturing base remains concentrated in labor-intensive and basic processing and assembly operations. Also, foreign-controlled companies dominate exports, accounting for more than half of all overseas sales (OECD 2005, 30). It is not sustainable for China to depend so heavily on these low value-added and low-margin businesses. The challenge for China is not just to be a part of the global supply chain but also to move up the value chain in the manufacturing sector and expand into services and knowledge-based industries such as advanced software development and pharmaceuticals.

However, to achieve these ambitious goals, the Chinese government must strengthen and build market-supporting economic and political-legal institutions such as transparent rules regarding property rights and establishing the rule of law; moreover, both the government and Chinese firms must boost investment in research and development (R&D) and upgrade its stock of human capital – in particular, the skills of its workforce. The latter is critical as low cost labor is not a permanent competitive advantage. A better-educated workforce is key to innovation and entrepreneurship. Although China has been producing large numbers of college graduates, the vast majority still lack the skills necessary for the global economy (Farrell and Grant 2005). According to Bergsten and his coauthors (2006, 4), "only about one-tenth of China's scientific graduates can compete internationally," and Prestowitz (2005) notes that only 10 percent of Chinese engineers have the skills required to work in a global economy, while the comparable number for India is 25 percent – although India's capacity to train accredited engineers rose from 60,000 in fiscal 1987–88 to 340,000 in 2003. For IT professionals, it rose from 25,800 to 250,000 over the same period (Winters and Yusuf 2007, 46). More ominous, Wan (2008) notes that because the route to higher incomes (at both the individual and national levels) is access to good education, the huge variation in quality and attainment between regions and provinces will be felt for years to come. However, improving the quality of education does not mean that China should emulate India. The claim that India's concentration of brainpower is the result of disproportionate investment in higher education, especially in the elite Indian Institutes of Technology (IITs), is misleading. In not providing educational opportunities to more than one-third of its population, India is failing to fully utilize its vast reservoir of human capital. In China (and India), strong public support for education and reasonably fair access to educational facilities is an imperative.[9] Otherwise, socioeconomic inequalities can become self-perpetuating if only the privileged can educate their children.

Building a New Socialist Countryside

The importance of the agricultural sector in the overall economy has been shrinking since the reforms began. Agricultural output as a share of GDP declined from 27 percent in 1990 to 11.8 percent in 2006. Similarly, the number of people employed in the agricultural sector has also been declining. In 2005, agricultural employment accounted for 45 percent of China's total employment – down sharply from 62 percent in 1985 as rural residents increasingly look for nonfarming job opportunities both inside and outside rural areas. Nevertheless, the rural sector remains a vital part of the Chinese economy, providing livelihood to millions of people and the country with food supplies and vital raw materials.

Tremendous pressure was lifted from the rural sector in the reform era with the creation of the TVEs and relaxation of labor movement laws. This allowed millions of rural residents to join the exodus either to find employment in the TVEs or become "migrant workers" by leaving the countryside to take up an array of nonagricultural jobs in towns and cities. The estimated 200 million migrant workers and the uncounted millions of "floating laborers" not only have greatly contributed to the prosperity in urban areas but have

---

[9] India spends far more on higher education than on primary education. For example, it spent 86 percent of per capita GDP on each student in tertiary education in 2000 but only 14 percent of per capita GDP per student in primary education. By contrast, China spent 10.7 percent and 12.1 percent, respectively, of per capita GDP per student in tertiary and primary education. In other words, India spent substantially more in purchasing power parity (PPP) adjusted dollars per student in tertiary education than China and even Korea in 2000 (Kochhar 2007).

also generated substantial income for the rural areas. Migrant remittances to their dependents still residing in the countryside – in particular, aging parents and young children – have served to ameliorate hardship at a time when many publicly funded services have ceased to exist. More often than not, migrant workers who have chosen to move back to the countryside to establish new businesses (after accumulating capital, skills, and knowledge derived from their urban jobs) have created employment opportunities in the rural areas. According to official accounts, returning workers have set up about one-fifth of the country's rural enterprises (China National Bureau of Statistics 2004).

However, the lives of the itinerant migrant workers have never been easy. Along with the some 800 million rural residents, they are deprived of the right to settle in cities because they lack the prized household registration permit (*hukou*) that would allow them to live legally in urban areas. As a result, they encounter difficulties working and living in urban centers, including the denial of social services.[10] Wage payment delays, defaults, and unfair and fraudulent deductions by unscrupulous urban employers have been a pervasive problem. Moreover, those working in certain industries such as mining and construction often work under unsafe conditions because they lack both the resources and the legal means to press employers to follow safety guidelines. In his richly detailed study of Guangdong province, Ching Kwan Lee (2007), documents that young migrant workers suffer from not only nonpayment of wages and unattended workplace injuries but also physical and mental abuse. Although such treatment has triggered attempts to use the country's Labor Law to achieve justice, inconsistent state enforcement and discrimination by local authorities remind migrants that they are "second-class citizens, and not even that sometimes, just beasts in the eyes of the police" (p. 198). Because most migrant workers are not eligible to receive social benefits provided by the local and city governments, which are available to documented urban residents, poverty rates are high among these workers. Perhaps the worst off are those

---

[10] Beginning in the 1950s, the CCP introduced a residential permit system (*hukou*) separating urban and rural residents. By specifying where one was entitled to reside and receive benefits, the *hukou* also served to severely restrict people's mobility. Each person was given a registration (*hukou*) in either a rural area or an urban area and could not change it without the permission of the receiving jurisdiction. However, in practice cities usually give registration to skilled people, providing them with an "iron rice bowl" of lifetime employment, as well as health care, housing, and pension benefits. Rural residents were to be provided for their needs by their individual collectives. In the post-Mao period, migrants from the countryside are usually denied urban resident permits despite the fact that they perform the bulk of the unskilled and semiskilled work in the towns and cities. An urban *hukou* is essential for receiving various social benefits provided by the city governments, including such benefits as buying a city bus pass. Stringent restrictions have been in place to prohibit migrants from obtaining urban resident status in the cities even after living and working there for many years. Some 140 million individuals are estimated to live in urban areas without the *hukou* (Wen 2007; Zhang 2001).

migrants whose varied circumstances have made the break with their ancestral villages irrevocable.[11]

In the countryside, official neglect (based on the premise that decollectivization and TVEs would solve the problems), coupled with market-distorting policies, has had a negative effect on rural development. Peasants are subjected to numerous taxes and fees imposed by both the central and subnational governments. According to Aubert and Li (2002), these taxes can be divided into three categories. At the highest administrative level are a plethora of agricultural taxes, followed by the *Tongchou* and *Tiliu* levies, which are de facto taxes collected by the township- and village-level governments, respectively. Cumulatively, taxes constitute some 40 to 50 percent of the total tax receipts of local governments. However, these taxes are a huge burden on peasants, especially poor households, because taxes are determined according to farm output, family head count, or the area of arable land leased to peasants, rather than net income or profits. Aubert and Li note that in 2002, the average tax burden borne by peasants was as much as 225 to 269 yuan per person, or equivalent to 10 to 12 percent of a peasant's average net income. Overall, China's regressive tax system not only has led to distortions for income-producing activities in rural areas, it has also added to the problem of rural unemployment and poverty. As Ravallion and Chen (2004) argue, reducing the explicit and implicit taxes would act as a major antipoverty program in rural China.

Exacerbating the rural-urban divide is the issue of "property rights." Like individuals, who are either registered as urban or rural residents, land in China is also zoned as either rural or urban. However, property rights in land vary widely. In the urban areas, residents can sell their land and buildings or use them as collateral to borrow funds. In contrast, in the rural areas, peasants only have long-term tenure (provided they work the land) but cannot easily mortgage or sell the use rights. In reality, village collectives still own virtually all rural land in China. Although they must contract the land to individual households for a term of thirty years (that is, farmers receive "thirty-year rights" to their contracted land), free from administrative interference, this is hardly the case in practice. Despite the 1998 revisions to the Land Management Law (LML) and the 2002 Rural Land Contract Law (RLCL), which mandate written documentation of land rights, few farmers have official documentation that conforms to the law. Keliang and Prosterman's (2007) exhaustive survey confirms that the land rights of Chinese farmers are still under threat. Many village collectives, despite giving thirty-year land rights to farmers, often illegally readjust or reallocate the contracted land. Moreover, the frequency with

---

[11] Chan and Buckingham (2008, 604) note that "despite a good deal of rhetoric in the press about the recent reforms, the reality is that these initiatives have had only very marginal impact on weakening the foundation of the system. The *hukou* system, directly and indirectly, continues to be a major wall in preventing China's rural population from settling in the city and in maintaining the rural-urban apartheid."

which the government has been taking over farmers' land for nonagricultural use has grown to meet the rapidly expanding urbanization and industrialization demand. Since converting land from rural to urban use requires central government approval, this has predictably resulted in widespread corruption and bureaucratic malfeasance. Peasants rarely receive fair compensation for the agricultural value of the land (as the law requires) and are often cheated by corrupt officials and private interests. Keliang and Prosterman (2007) found that in about one-third of cases in which cash compensation was promised, it was never paid to the dispossessed farmers. Peasants swindled out of their land end up joining the growing ranks of the rural poor. Thomas Bernstein and Xiaobo Lu (2002), in their aptly titled book *Taxation without Representation in Contemporary Rural China,* eloquently document how the rural populace is increasingly at the mercy of self-serving and predatory local officials who impose all manner of fees and informal taxes on the hapless peasantry, including robbing them of their assets through outright illegal confiscation. In fact, over the past decade, the problem has become so severe that it has led to protests, including violent protests between the dispossessed peasants and government officials (So 2007). Moreover, as Keliang and Prosterman (2007) note, insecure land rights reduces this valuable resource into "dead capital," or assets that cannot be held securely and used to their fullest. For example, without secure, long-term land rights, most farmers have little incentive to make necessary investments on their land, such as introducing new crop varieties or installing irrigation and drainage infrastructure, because they have no guarantee that they will be able to recoup the value of their investments and make a profit. Nor can they use their only asset as collateral. Over time, this will also make Chinese farmers less competitive globally.

To mitigate these problems, in 2004, the party and central government issued the so-called No. 1 Document that made increasing rural incomes a top policy priority. Major policy initiatives that came from the document included a phase out of agricultural taxes to grain producers in thirteen of China's thirty-one provinces. In mid-2006, President Hu Jintao, responding to rising rural unrest and stagnating production, announced that it was time to create a "new socialist countryside." Soon after, the central government released the Eleventh Five-Year Plan (2006–10) and formally announced its goal to build "a new socialist countryside" (through massive injections of public investment and agricultural subsidies) to help the 800 million rural residents catch up with city residents. In addition, the central government outlined plans to reduce peasants' tax burden and provide more financial services in the countryside. Rural financial institutions, including, one of the "policy banks," the Agricultural Development Bank of China have been restructured to offer a wider range of financial services to rural households and businesses. Also, to provide protection to migrant workers, the authorities have put in place a wage payment supervision system to monitor wage payments, including requiring employers with a history of payment defaults to deposit sufficient funds into a special account before beginning their projects. Also, to protect migrants' rights in labor disputes and with regard to physical injuries, the government has streamlined legal aid procedures for migrants. Of course, it remains to be seen how effectively these policies are implemented. Unfortunately, what the government has not done is to put in place a market-based (rather than administrative) land conversion system. This would dramatically increase the value of land – the main asset held by rural residents.

Economic Growth, Inequality, and Poverty

China's economic growth has translated into significant increases in the per capita GDP, which jumped from $1,071 in 1978 to more than $5,500 in 2006. In 1999, the World Bank promoted China from a "low-income" to a "lower-middle income" country. The increase in per capita income has greatly improved the living standard of millions of people. The extensive rationing system that determined one's access to basic goods such as grain, salt, cooking oil, sugar, eggs, meat, and even clothing are a thing of the past (Chen and Wang 2001). Ordinary Chinese citizens now take for granted not only the availability of basic consumer goods but also modern conveniences such as TVs, VCRs, washing machines, and refrigerators. The experience of post-Mao China confirms that the most powerful force for the reduction of poverty is economic growth. On the eve of the reforms, the incidence of poverty in China was the highest in the world (Chen and Wang 2001; World Bank 1997). However, between 1981 and 2001, the proportion of population living in poverty in China fell from 53 percent to just 8 percent. This means that across China, there were more than 450 million fewer people living in extreme poverty in 2001 than twenty years earlier.[12]

---

[12] In their study, Ravallion and Chen (2004, 2007) adopted poverty lines of 850 yuan (about $102 at current exchange rates) a year for rural areas and 1,200 yuan ($145) a year for urban areas – both at 2002 prices. They reached the conclusion that poverty levels fell from 53 percent to 8 percent. However, there is an important caveat to these findings. The number of rural poor for each year is also reported in the China Agricultural Development Report, a white paper of the Ministry of Agriculture. According to official data, the proportion of rural poor fell from 33.1 percent in 1978 to 3.7 percent in 1999. Official data defines the poverty line as the level at which income is below subsistence levels for food intake, shelter, and clothing. Using this criterion, the rural poverty line in 1985 was set at 206 yuan in nominal price per person and increased to 625 yuan per person in 2000. The 206 yuan per year poverty line is equivalent to US$0.66 dollar per day measured in 1985 purchasing parity. It is important to note that although there is general agreement that absolute rural poverty has declined in China, there are questions regarding the extent of the decline. This is because the accuracy of China's official poverty measure has been questioned for a number of reasons. For example, the difference in the cost of living among regions or provinces is not taken into account because a single poverty line is used for the whole of the PRC. Moreover, the estimation of the official poverty line is based on income rather than on expenditure data, which has not kept pace with inflation over the years. As a result, the official estimates are seen to be biased because they tend to overstate the decline in poverty (Government of China 2002).

China's record in reducing poverty is simply phenomenal because very few countries have grown so fast over such a prolonged period of time or reduced poverty so sharply. Equally impressive, by 2004, life expectancy at birth in China had reached seventy-one years, the infant mortality rate had fallen to 26 per 1,000 live births, and the literacy rate of those aged fifteen or older had reached 90 percent (World Bank 2006). As a result, China is just one of a handful of countries that is well ahead of the United Nations Millennium Development Goals for cutting poverty in half by 2015.

However, the bulk of this poverty reduction (from 33 percent in 1978 to 11 percent in 2001) was achieved in the early stages of the reform following the breakup of the communes and return to household farming and labor-intensive job creation by the TVEs (World Bank 2000a). However, since the late 1990s, poverty reduction has slowed down markedly and income inequalities have increased sharply, despite the fact that the rates of economic growth have remained high. Thus, China faces a paradoxical problem: although absolute poverty has fallen, income inequality has been rising. Apparently the "trickle-down" theory underlying Deng Xiaoping's policy dictum of "letting some get rich first and the rest will follow" seems only to apply to the rich. China is now one of the most unequal countries in the world, albeit in the Mao era most people were equally poor. In the early 1980s, the richest 10 percent of the population earned less than 20 percent of the national income. By 1995, they earned 33.7 percent, whereas the bottom 10 percent accounted for only 1.8 percent. By 2005, the gap had widened with the top 10 percent earning 45 percent of income, and the bottom 10 percent earning only 1.4 percent. Between 1980 and 2005, the Gini coefficient ratio rose from below 0.2 (considered quite egalitarian) to 0.45 (highly unequal). With an estimated Gini of more than 0.45 in 2007, China was less equal than the United States and Russia. If current trends continue, China could pass Brazil (the most unequal country) in terms of income inequality.

The slowdown in poverty reduction has served to widen the growing economic inequalities between skilled and unskilled workers, male and female workers, the rural and urban areas, and the inland and coastal regions (Wan 2008). In 2003, urban per capita income was more than three times the rural average, up from twice the rural average during the 1980s. Development is so concentrated in the major coastal clusters such as the Pearl River Delta, Shanghai, and Beijing that living standards in these coastal cities are approaching those of middle-income countries like Taiwan, whereas inland cities lag far behind (Figures 3.3 and 3.4). This is clearly reflected in income levels. For example, the difference between the average income for the richest five provinces and that of the poorest five provinces was Yuan 3,719 in 1981. In 1990, it had increased to Yuan 5,622, to Yuan 13,111 in 2000 and Yuan 20,188 in 2004 (Tandon et al. 2006, 57). To date, the central governments' ambitious "develop

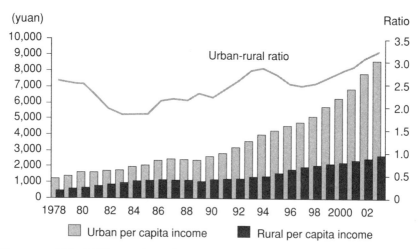

Figure 3.3. China's Urban and Rural per Capita Income, 1978–2003. *Source:* Shane and Gale (2004, 14).

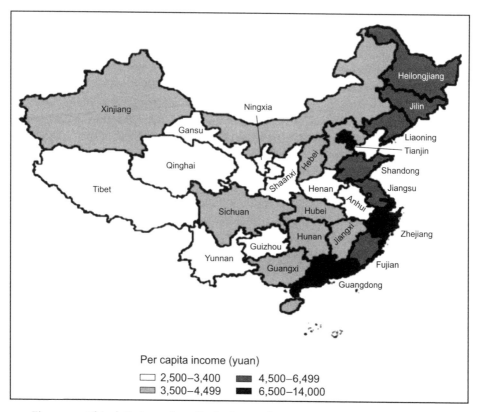

Figure 3.4. China's Estimated per Capita Income by Province, 2003. *Source:* Shane and Gale (2004, 14).

the west" campaign (introduced in 2000) to push both public and private investment into the country's poorer provinces has not been very effective. Regardless, for China, sustaining economic growth while simultaneously uplifting individuals and parts of the country that have shared less fully from the economic boom is an imperative.

Without doubt, amongst China's most daunting and immediate challenge is to deal with the problem of chronic unemployment. Given the sheer size and rapid expansion of China's labor force, the precise extent of unemployment and underemployment is not known. The official urban unemployment rate for 2007 was about 4 to 5 percent. However, actual unemployment is much higher because large numbers of laid-off workers are not counted in the official statistics because they remain on their employers' books despite the fact they draw little or no salary. Also, millions of laid-off workers have been forced into early retirement on minimal pensions or into extremely low-paying jobs. This has overwhelmed the few public assistance programs and exacerbated social tensions. Rural unemployment is a bigger challenge because much of China's rural labor force is underemployed – that is, engaged only in seasonal agricultural work with irregular earnings. According to the Ministry of Agriculture, China has about 2.5 agricultural laborers for every hectare of arable land (China National Bureau of Statistics 2004). This means that rural China has roughly 150 million surplus workers. China now faces the difficult task of simultaneously reducing unemployment while raising incomes. According to official statistics, employment must grow by 2 percent annually just to keep up with growth in the labor force. Nonagricultural job growth will have to be even faster to absorb unemployed and underemployed rural workers. To do this at a time when businesses are under tremendous pressure to raise worker productivity, cut costs, and become efficient to compete both domestically and internationally will not be easy.

Because of the incomplete nature of China's reforms, the citizenry's accessibility to many public goods and social services has not been commensurate with economic growth. For example, basic social services such as the preventive health-care provided by "barefoot doctors" and compulsory primary education have largely disintegrated. Ajay Tandon and his coauthors (2006, 66) note that the drastic cuts in national health spending coupled with the commercialization of health care has only widened both rural-urban and rich-poor health disparities (see also W. Hinton 1991). Wen (2007, 31–32) notes that "from 1980 to 2003, health care costs skyrocketed 15 fold even after inflation was taken into account . . . all clinics and hospitals are increasingly pressured by profit motive." As the government's health care budgets decline, "diseases that once were under control such as tuberculosis and schistosomiasis are making a comeback . . . and new diseases such as HIV/AIDS are spreading rapidly due to illegal blood selling and needle-sharing." Moreover, although literacy rates are high, the reality is that increasing numbers of Chinese do not have access to the high-quality education (again because of rising costs and declining public support), they will need to thrive in a competitive global economy. Pensions now only cover city workers, although Chinese officials acknowledge that most of these pension funds are insolvent. The central and subnational government have pledged to strengthen the social safety-net programs and raise minimum wages to mitigate the negative effect of the market reforms, but given the growing fiscal deficits and China's "fiscal federalism," this is easier said than done.[13] Post-Mao China has one of the most decentralized fiscal systems in the world under which local governments rely primarily on local tax collection to fund basic services such as primary education and health care. However, the fiscal disparities among subnational governments are large and growing with the richest province having more than eight times the per capita public spending than the poorest province. Inequalities in spending are even larger at the sub-provincial level. The richest county (the most important unit for service delivery) has about forty-eight times the level of per capita spending than the poorest county (Ravallion and Chen 2004). As Sicular and his coauthors (2007) note, these differences in public spending translate into differences in social outcomes. Because most counties have limited revenues from taxes, they can barely meet current funding. Therefore, the plethora of new governmental programs designed to fund public services will put additional financial stress on local government finances and may not even materialize. More troubling are potential liabilities, including nonperforming loans held by state banks and unfunded pension liabilities. Fiscal deficits could eventually lead to inflation if the government prints money to pay pensioners or bail out banks, state-owned enterprises, and local governments (Dollar and Wei 2007).

The Contradictions of Quasi-Federalism

Unlike political systems with constitutional federalism, subnational governments in China lack formal political autonomy vis-à-vis the center. Rather, under China's unitary political system, the national government possesses ultimate authority over its territorial units. However, economic reforms have clearly had a decentralizing effect on intergovernmental fiscal relations. Despite "recentralizing" attempts by Beijing, there is no going back to Maoist-type central control. Decentralization or the devolution of authority or responsibility from the center to the lower levels of government is now the predominant feature of China's political and economic landscape, leading many

---

[13] The extent of the central government's fiscal deficit is not known. However, this deficit does not include those incurred by local governments. What is known is that many rural townships and villages are heavily in debt or bankrupt. The extent of local government deficits is also unknown, although press reports often include references to difficulties paying teachers and local government employees.

to describe the nature of central-local relations in contemporary China as "quasi-federal" or federal. This change has had profound policy implications. In particular, contrary to the conventional view of China's one-party state unilaterally imposing its will on all levels of polity and society, the ability of the CCP leadership is actually quite limited. Local authorities can and do frustrate policies they see as inimical to their interests, and even when Beijing makes explicit demands, local compliance is not guaranteed. Some have argued that even if it wants to, Beijing does not always have the ability nor the wherewithal to make good on its commitments – especially those of importance to its trading partners such as intellectual property rights protection, consumer product safety, or environmental and labor protection (Economy 2004).

However, local recalcitrance is not only due to rent-seeking opportunities. The central government, in placing a premium on "economic growth" by granting, for example, promotion of local officials on their ability to generate high growth rates and maintain social harmony has fostered a culture of "growth at any price." More seriously, central policies and mandates such as the recentralization of taxing powers under the 1994 Tax Sharing System has provided incentives for subnational governments to ignore or circumvent central directives. The 1994 reforms greatly increased the amount of revenue that local governments were required to hand over to the center. The central government, by keeping the bulk of tax revenues while at the same time devolving responsibility for social welfare programs to local governments without commensurate increases in funding, has forced local authorities to ignore central mandates on "fiscal responsibility," "burden sharing," and those that may undermine continued growth. As their expenditure requirements have outstripped budgetary allocations, local governments have shifted big chunks of their budgetary revenue into off-budget accounts and other measures to keep a larger portion of the revenues. In response, the central authorities have employed "revenue-grabbing outside the (revenue-sharing) system by changing the scope of central fixed revenues, 'borrowing' etc. and unilaterally resetting contract terms in mid-course" (Wong, Heady, and Woo 1995, 134). In some instances, the central government has simply taken over profitable enterprises from localities and coerced them into purchasing central government bonds. As might be expected, such measures have not only eroded trust between central and local governments, they have greatly hampered policy coordination and implementation. Recent examples of officials not only turning a blind eye, but becoming willing accomplices when gross violations were occurring in the manufacture and distribution of consumer products such as adulterated cooking oil and baby formula, fake medicines, toxic toothpaste, poisonous dog food, and lead-tainted toys, among others, illustrate that resolving the contradiction in center-local relations is essential to more efficacious policy environment.

Restructuring the State-Owned Enterprises

To reiterate, in the pre-reform period, economic activity was dominated by SOEs. The SOEs main task was to gear production to meet plan targets. As a result, they automatically received credit from the banking sector according to a national development plan. Given this close relationship, restructuring the SOEs has proved to be particularly difficult. This is because of the long and close relationship between the government and the state-owned enterprises; and the reality that the SOEs still account for about one-quarter of industrial output. In fact, SOEs remain the backbone of the economy operating in all key sectors – from the production of advanced high-tech industrial products for China's defense industry to the service sectors such as hotel and hospitality, including low-end manufactured goods. Although the SOEs demand a disproportionately large share of the economic resources and represent a big financial burden, they are also a major revenue source for the government. This Janus-faced nature of the SOEs has posed real challenges for the government.

Because China privatized few SOEs before 1992, it was stuck with large numbers of unviable and uncompetitive firms.[14] According to Heytens and Karacadag (2001), SOEs are about 60 percent as efficient (as measured by value added) or profitable (as measured by operating profits to assets) as foreign-funded enterprises. In 1993, losses from the SOEs were estimated to be around 2.4 percent of GDP (Broadman 1999). In 1994, the restructuring of the SMEs (or the small and medium-sized SOEs) was initiated after Zhu Rongji formulated a new strategy for SOE reform described as *zhuada fangxiao* or "grasping the big and letting go of the small."[15] In practice, "grasping the big" meant the government was prepared only to save the large enterprises – in particular, those related to core sectors such as national defense, telecommunications, energy, civil aviation, and infrastructure, while "letting go of the small" implied that the government was willing to relinquish its control of the SMEs. However, this did not mean completely abandoning the SMEs to market forces but carefully restructuring and privatizing (*gaizhi*) them through joint ventures, mergers, acquisitions, public and employee shareholding, and open sales and leasing. That is, although all SOEs were now accountable for their profits and losses, unlike the mass privatization that occurred in Eastern Europe and the former Soviet Union, the Chinese government's gradualist approach to privatization (which really meant an increase in the share of ownership held by private

---

[14] Garnaut, Song, and Yan (2006, 37) note that "private shareholding was first introduced into SOEs in three Guangzhou firms in 1986, when the employees bought 30 per cent of their firms' shares. The first large SOE in which private entities purchased shares was the Shenyang Motor Corporation, which became Shenyang Jinbei Motors when it issued shares to the public in August 1988. The opening of the Shenzhen Stock Exchange in 1990 and the Shanghai Stock Exchange in 1991 enabled a limited number of SOEs to issue shares to the public. Large-scale privatization only started after Deng Xiaoping's famous visit to southern China in 1992."

[15] This policy was formally adopted at the Fifteenth CPC National Congress in 1997.

investors rather that outright and total sales) was designed to make the SMEs efficient, competitive, and innovative and keep them in business.

Nevertheless, Zhu's approach was bold because it would mean "reform with losers," with the closure of thousands of loss-making SOEs (or "zombie firms") and millions of workers made redundant without the SOEs having the responsibility of providing the "iron rice bowl" safety net. In 1995, the central government decided only to retain ownership of between five hundred and one thousand large SOEs and to allow the SMEs to be leased or sold. Although by 1997 about one-quarter of China's eighty-seven thousand industrial SOEs had been restructured, the five hundred largest SOEs still held 37 percent of the state's industrial assets, contributed 46 percent of all tax revenue from the state sector, and generated 63 percent of the state sector's profits (Garnaut, Song, and Yao 2006). In reality, "reform with losers" meant that in the period from 1996 to 1999, an average of 7 million workers were laid off annually, with layoffs exceeding 50 million between 1993 and 2004 (Dong and Xu 2008).

In September 1999, during the Fourteenth Plenary Session of the Fifteenth Congress, the central government decided to go a step further and diversify the SOEs' share ownership system, similar to that of a modern corporate system. The objective of turning around the unprofitable SOEs was largely achieved by end-2000, as the previous loss-makers either began to make a profit or went bankrupt.[16] Moreover, weakening the link between the SOEs and the government reduced SOEs access to government funds. In 2003, the State-owned Assets Supervision and Administration Commission of the State Council (SASAC), which reports to the State Council and to Premier Wen Jiabao, was established to supervise and improve the corporate governance of 196 central SOEs on behalf of the central government, including appointing top executives, approving mergers or sales of stock or assets, and drafting laws related to the SOEs. In December 2006, the SASAC finally specified industrial sectors in which the state economy should have absolute control, be influential, or play a leading role. The SASAC noted that nonperforming SOEs should exit the market, and by 2010, the number of central SOEs should total not more than 80 to 100, of which 30 to 50 should be internationally competitive. Cumulatively these measures – in particular, the hardening of the SOEs' budget constraints – has resulted in a better internal allocation of resources (Naughton 2007).

Yet the SOE process remains incomplete and still work in progress. For example, although the stake the government holds in SOEs has been reduced, the SOEs are still hybrids – publicly traded on the stock exchange but still

---

[16] Chiu and Lewis (2006, 51–2) note that "at the end of 2001, there were a total of 173504 SOEs, a decrease of over 88000 from 262000 in 1997. . . . Of the 173504 SOEs at the end of 2001, 9453 are large while the other 164051 are medium to small."

majority-owned by the government. In 2006, the top ten SOEs were eight times bigger than the top ten private firms. Compounding this, the government's discriminatory regulatory treatment of private or "nonstate entrants" means that the SOEs negatively affect the overall economy through the special treatment they receive and the fact that they use resources more inefficiently, have failed to enhance firm innovation, and, as will be discussed, remain a serious burden for the banking sector. Without meaningful restructuring and reforms – that is, the privatization of the SOEs – problems such as large-scale loss of state assets in the form of price discounts when "selling" state assets and outright "asset stripping" by firm management and public officials will remain. Local governments will continue to give discounts, including land-use rights, to new owners in exchange for bribes and other favors, and party and state officials will continue to use their political and administrative leverage to merge enterprises to create giant monopolies to protect their interests and increase their rent-seeking abilities.[17] In other words, without deep reforms, SOEs will fail to meet the goals of innovation, efficiency, competitiveness, and profitability.

Arguably, the most negative impact of industrial restructuring has been felt by ordinary workers. The government's attempt to mitigate the potentially serious dislocations caused by mass layoffs (some 10 million workers were laid off each year between 1996 and 1998, and from 1998 to 2004, six in ten SOE workers were laid off) has not proved to be effective given the relative lack of safety-net programs and the fact that all levels of government were ill prepared for the challenges.[18] Garnaut, Ligang, and Yao (2006) survey of laid-off workers in eleven cities across China show that although on paper, most workers received a redundancy package equivalent to three years' salary, in reality, the packages were miniscule. Because workers had to contribute to their own pension and insurance schemes, these contributions were deducted from the package. The effect was that workers only received a small percentage of their compensation. Moreover, in enterprises with limited resources or corrupt management, it was

---

[17] Few SOE managers have been punished for corruption – the exception being Chen Shuangquan, the former chairman of the Shaanxi Freeway Construction Group Company, who was sentenced to death in April 2008 for taking bribes totaling some 14.73 million yuan (or US$2.1 million).

[18] For details on worker layoffs, see Qian and Wu (2003, 45). It is important to note that both the central and subnational governments adopted a number of methods to encourage reemployment. For example, before selling off the SOEs, buyers were required to sign contracts guaranteeing the redeployment of employees. Government funds, including the "state asset exit fund" and the "SOE bankruptcy provisional fund," were established to finance compensation packages for laid-off workers. The funding usually came from the transfer of ownership rights or sale or lease of state assets. The government would also offer discounts and, in some cases, the free transfer of ownership rights in return for the new owner's commitment to redeploy more workers. In addition, tax holidays were offered to former SOE employees starting their own business who hired laid-off workers. Yet despite all these preferential policies, new owners often complained that the discounts were insufficient.

not unusual for workers to get no compensation. Many workers were simply cheated or coerced into giving up their jobs for only meager sums of money. Part of the problem has to do with the fact that under China's Labor Law, there is no national standard to determine the exact amount of compensation to which workers are entitled. Therefore, more often than not, what laid-off workers received depended on their bargaining power and the resources available to enterprises and local governments. Although the most intensive phase of SOE reform seems to have passed, reforms designed to improve economic performance continue. In 2006, the State Council's Development and Reform Commission estimated that in the next three years, a further 3.6 million SOE employees could be laid off and another 3 million employees "redeployed" to subsidiary businesses.

Ching Kwan Lee (2007) graphically captures how current and former SOE workers have dealt with the gut-wrenching transition from socialism to capitalism. With elegance and great insight, he argues that the abrogation of the time-honored "socialist social contract" has made SOE workers the clear "losers" in the transition process because they are both "excluded from the market and betrayed by the state" (p. 159). In Liaoning (in northeast China), the radical restructuring of the state and collective enterprise sectors have decimated the industrial heartland into a "rustbelt." Although the former SOE workers remain united in their attempts to overcome their predicaments, the fragmented interests of pensioners, the unemployed, and the laid-off prevent intraclass solidarity and collective action beyond what Lee calls "cellular activism" (p. 111) – that is, the targeting of individual *danwei* (work units) and local state agents. Moreover, the inability and failure of the state to resolve workers' grievances effectively, coupled with potential state repression, has produced a sense of ambivalence and resignation among workers. Cumulatively, these have served to undermine their efforts to make their protests more "revolutionary." Rather, workers "protest" has taken a restorative character, showing nostalgia for an imagined Maoist-moral economy. Nevertheless, Lee warns that the deep financial and emotional trauma left on workers by SOE restructuring can quickly explode into mass protest. In particular, the failure to share the fruits of the economic boom with the workers (the very people who have contributed so much to China's current prosperity but benefited so little), or refusing to mediate and resolve labor grievances fairly can have dire consequences for the Chinese party-state.

Modernizing the Banking and Financial Sectors

In 1949, soon after coming to power, the Communist regime nationalized all banks and assumed responsibility for collecting funds from depositors and directing them to the SOEs through the People's Bank of China (PBC). During the Mao era, the People's Bank functioned as both the central bank and the sole deposit-taking and lending institution. In the Deng era, the PBC became the central bank, whereas the "Big Four" (Bank of China, the Industrial and Commercial Bank of China, China Construction Bank, and the Agricultural Bank of China) became state-owned commercial banks (SOCBs). Today, China's financial system is made up of more than 35,000 financial institutions, including a dozen joint stock commercial banks, more than 100 city commercial banks owned by municipal governments, and more than 30,000 rural and urban cooperatives. The SOCBs dominate the system, accounting for more than half of banking assets, thousands of branches, and hundreds of thousands of employees in every corner of the country. In 2006, the Big Four banks accounted for more than 56 percent of assets. As the state directs the allocation of its credit, the Big Four government-owned banks lend primarily to state-owned enterprises (Goodfriend and Prasad 2006, 17).

Despite financial and banking sector reforms, China's central bank and the Big Four state-owned commercial banks (unlike the U.S. Federal Reserve system) are not independent entities. In fact, the Big Four cannot even be considered "real banks" in the sense of being independent businesses that are, at least in theory, accountable to shareholders for their successes and failures. Rather, even after years of restructuring, they still operate like government units. That is, the banking system still remains subservient to the government. Bank managers are appointed by the central government and have to report directly to the State Council, which ultimately approves policy. As during the Maoist period, the banks' most important responsibility still remains implementing the centrally mandated credit plan – in particular, the "policy lending" mandates. Because China's state-owned banks continue to make loans to money-losing enterprises to maintain employment and social stability, a practice known as "policy lending" (or lending based on political criteria and connections with little regard to creditworthiness and repayment ability), many of these loans have never been paid back. The dependence of China's SOEs on banks for their capital means banks are forced to satisfy conflicting and contradictory objectives: financing employment and social stability while transforming themselves into commercially viable corporate entities. As Goodfriend and Prasad (2006, 32) note, "bank managers cannot be asked to lend prudently, with an expectation that loans be repaid and bank capital preserved, when managers are rewarded by the political system for directing fiscal transfers to state firms, and then largely excused for loan losses in the state sector." Such a paradoxical role has not only resulted in a severe misallocation of investment capital, it has also made the banks portfolios burdened with unsustainable volumes of nonperforming loans (NPLs). Pervasive state control and regulation coupled with lack of skills in the techniques of commercial banking has made China's banks woefully unprepared to perform the functions of modern banking – especially in meeting the needs of a fast-changing and complex global marketplace.

An unintentional outcome of Deng Xiaoping's famous "southern tour" in the spring of 1992, during which he exhorted the need to accelerate economic reforms, was that it made the banking system's problems even worse. In the enthusiasm to speed up growth, the lid literally came off the money supply. This was due in part to the practice in which the PBC continued to allocate the total credit target for each specialized bank and individual targets for their respective branches but left the monitoring to the provincial and local PBC branches. However, horizontal political control over the PBC branches at the provincial, municipal, and county levels gave local officials wide discretion over lending decisions. Given the fact that local government officials have to be consulted before the center appoints a local bank governor (not to mention the fact that the governor's promotion and future prospects is dependent on the local government's evaluation), the various local and regional governments and political bosses predictably were allowed to exert much pressure on the respective branches of the PBC for credit and loans. Compounding this was the "soft budget" constraints faced by the specialized banks (which do not bear the risks of their loan decisions) and the fact that the PBC sets interest rates below market rates. This facilitated the quick issuing of loans and easy credit to support an array of SOEs, both healthy and ailing, not to mention the local and regional government's appetite for speculative investments in real estate and other "lucrative ventures."

Soon it was painfully clear that the central authorities unable to keep the growth of money supply in check or to prevent "soft lending" (loans made without reference to commercial criteria) simply lost control of the money supply. Local banks (which are local branches of the PBC) and the specialized banks under pressure from local governments often exceeded lending limits laid down by the central authorities to subsidize the state enterprises and other pet projects (including illicit ones) in their localities. It was not unusual for the SOEs to roll over due loans automatically or not to repay their loans at all and for banks to finance the deficits of local governments and issue loans to them at below the official interest rates, besides funding the junkets of public officials. As the central bank, unable to impose the necessary hard budget constraints on local banks, passively moved to the sidelines, the regional and local governments and their cronies with explicit and implicit support of the local banks embarked on a nationwide credit and investment binge. Many literally plundered the banks to fuel their self-aggrandizement desires such as building even more skyscrapers and high-tech industrial parks in their towns, not to mention the numerous wasteful and speculative activities. According to Jingping (1995, 20–21):

> As local governments sought accelerated development, the bank was obliged to provide capital indiscriminately.... In one county of Hunan Province, for example, the vice county magistrate ordered the president of the local bank

Table 3.3. *Nonperforming loans (NPLs) in Chinese state-owned commercial banks*

Year	NPLs (US$B)	Total loans (US$B)	Ratio of NPLs to total loans (%)
1997	155	na	25
1998	75	753	10
1999	198	793	25
2000	196	786	25
2001	213	850	25
2002	245	968	25
2003	232	1,139	20

na = not applicable.
Source: Suzuki, Miah, and Yuan (2008, 58).

branch to turn over the bank's seal so the magistrate could issue letters of credit at will. It was common for local officials to force bankers to provide loans to favored projects.

Predictably, the central and subnational governments' pursuit of expansionary monetary policy soon fueled inflation (which jumped to 37 percent in 1987–88) and official corruption and graft, making the NPLs problems in the banking system even worse (Tables 3.3 and 3.4).

On 1 January 1994, Vice Premier and Central Bank Governor (and overall "economic czar") Zhu Rongji stepped in to cool the unsustainable growth. Besides curtailing the runaway local bank loans and commercial credit by squeezing lending and suspending wasteful projects, he announced a series of bank and financial sector reforms. First, in an effort to loosen (if not break) the grip of the local and provincial leaders, all directors of regional branches of the PBC were now to be appointed directly by Beijing. Second, the introduction of the 1995 Central Bank Law gave the central bank the mandate to determine monetary policy independent of subnational governments. Third, all projects

Table 3.4. *Ratio of nonperforming loans (NPLs) in the Big Four banks (December 2003)*

Name	Capital adequacy ratio (%)	Ratio of NPLs (%)
China Construction Bank	6.51	9.12
Industrial & Commercial Bank	5.52	21.24
Bank of China	6.98	16.29
Agricultural Bank of China	na	30.07

na = not applicable.
Source: Suzuki, Miah, and Yuan (2008, 58).

above a certain scale had to be approved by the governor of the PBC in Beijing. Fourth, in an effort to transform the state owned commercial banks into real commercial banks, they were no longer required to carry out policy loans to the SOEs. Rather all bank-financed government investment was now to flow through the three newly created "policy banks": the State Development Bank of China (to provide loans for infrastructure and key industrial development), the Agricultural Development Bank of China (to provide rural infrastructure and finances for crop purchases and food reserves), and the Export-Import Bank of China (to provide trade finance for machinery and electronic export). These three policy banks were made responsible for the provision of preferential loans to projects deemed important by the government.[19] Fifth, the new rules prohibited the PBC from issuing loans to enterprises. Finally, the Central Bank Law and Commercial Bank Law (in March 1995) enhanced the independence of the state-owned commercial banks to function as real commercial banks. Specifically, these banks were made responsible for their profits and losses and were required to maintain an 8 percent capital adequacy ratio (none have met the requirement yet). Moreover, the 1995 Budget Law prohibited the central government from borrowing from the central bank and banned the PBC from financing government budget deficits by printing money (deficits had to be financed by the sale of bonds) and from making loans to the various levels of central and local government agencies. The laws also gave power to the PBC to implement monetary policy and exercise financial supervision over the other financial institutions.

Despite all this, by 1998, the Big Four's NPL ratio was as high as 40 percent. In effect, China's banks were technically insolvent. To pave the way for bank modernization and tackle the serious problem of nonperforming loans in the banking sector, the authorities raised bank reserve requirements and called a moratorium on loans to certain sectors in an attempt to cool down the economy. In 1998, the government issued RMB 270 billion (about US$32.6 billion) in special bonds to recapitalize the Big Four. This was followed by a major loan write-off as well as capital injections. The first write-off mounted to US$170 billion for the Big Four banks, coupled with an injection of about US$35 billion of fresh capital into these capital-depleted banks. In 1999, four asset management companies (AMCs), one for each of the Big Four state-owned commercial banks, was set up to relieve them of some of their NPLs.[20]

[19] It was hoped that the separation of the banks commercial and policy lending functions would prevent the transfer of funds earmarked for state projects to other projects.
[20] The four AMCs, Xinda for the China Construction Bank, Huarong for the Industrial and Commercial Bank of China, Dongfang for the Bank of China, and Changcheng for the Agricultural Bank of China, received a total of ¥400 billion (US$48 billion) in seed capital from the Ministry of Finance (MOF) and issued ¥1 trillion (US$121 billion) worth of MOF-guaranteed bonds. They then used these funds to buy ¥1.4 trillion ($170 billion) in bad loans from the state banks at face value.

Specifically, the AMCs, designed along the lines of the U.S. Resolution Trust Corporation (which was formed in 1989 to clean up the savings and loan mess), were created to deal with the written-off assets from each of the Big Four banks. In mid-1999, NPLs valued at US$168.2 billion were removed from bank balance sheets by transferring them from the banks to the AMCs, which issued bonds guaranteed by the Ministry of Finance to the banks. Upon acquiring the banks' assets, the AMCs assumed the right to dispose of them on a commercial basis.[21]

By 2003, AMCs had purchased some 1.4 trillion yuan of NPLs from the state banks. In addition, the government used US$50 billion from its foreign reserves to recapitalize its two strongest banks and prepare them for stock market listings. In mid-2003, the central authorities established the Central Huijin Investment Company (a wholly owned government investment company) to channel foreign exchange from the State Administration of Foreign Exchange to large state-owned banks. By 2006, Huijin had directly infused capital in the form of foreign exchange (rather than RMB bonds as in previous recapitalizations) to increase bank capital reserves. In exchange, Huijin has taken more than 85 percent of the ownership of CCB and 100 percent of Bank of China. During 2004–5, further capital injections of US$60 billion from foreign exchange reserves helped banks achieve greater stability after writing off the remaining bad loans (for the three nonagricultural banks). Dobson and Kashyap (2006) estimate that the first and second rounds of recapitalization (or, more appropriately, "bailout"), coupled with the unresolved NPLs, implies a total cost to taxpayers of more than US$250 billion. That is, cleaning-up the Big Four's loans can be conservatively estimated as equal to 10.8 percent of China's GDP in 2005.

Perhaps, most dramatically, in 2003 the China Banking Regulatory Commission (CBRC) was established to take over the oversight role formerly performed by the central bank, including the responsibility for regulating all banks and other depository institutions and incorporating international norms for banking supervision to improve risk management. In practice, this has meant to serve as (a) a warning to small retail banks (often controlled by subnational units) about potential closure if they fail to perform satisfactorily; (b) a step to adopt a new accountability measure, in particular, holding each level of managers responsible for violations and malfeasance by those directly below them; and (c) encouragement to Chinese banks, including the Big Four, to form strategic partnerships with foreign banks by permitting foreign entities to buy shares in Chinese banks. Overall, the CBRC has helped to improve the quality of bank supervision by tightening loan-loss provisioning standards and applying a more rigorous asset classification standard to all lending institutions,

---

[21] The AMCs have used several methods to dispose the debts. Although the percentage of original capital they have recovered has typically been only 20 percent or less of the original book value. In addition to Chinese buyers, many leading international banks such as Citibank, UBS, and HSBC have actively acquired assets from the AMCs.

including introducing a clear set of guidelines on market risk management and Internet banking. Moreover, the CBRC has allowed a number of foreign investors and banks to become significant shareholders in Chinese banks.[22] The HSBC holds about 20 percent of the Communication Bank, China's fifth largest bank, and Newbridge Capital, a U.S. venture capital firm, is the controlling shareholder in the Shenzhen Development Bank, a small retail bank.

In 2004, revisions to China's banking laws further separated the PBC and CBRC and allowed the Big Four to carry out commercial banking activities. Specifically, the authorities strengthened the central bank's responsibility for monetary policy (it would no longer regulate financial institutions), while changes to the PRC Commercial Banking Law freed the Big Four from the requirement to provide loans to State Council–approved projects and permitted them to carry out commercial bank activities such as trading government bonds, dealing in foreign exchange, and offering credit card services. Cumulatively, these measures have helped to impose greater market discipline on the bank management – in particular, subjecting bank performance to market appraisals of efficiency and profitability and reducing the subnational governments' influence on monetary policy and credit allocation decisions. This has helped to make the banking system more efficient at financial intermediation. Furthermore, customer services have been upgraded to compete with foreign banks. However, the reforms remain incomplete. Most important, the burden and responsibility of "policy lending" has not been fully lifted from the banks – and will not be as long as the Big Four have government officials as directors and Communist Party appointees among its senior management. Dobson and Kashyap (2006) point out that the indicators of continued government influence on bank operations include unsustainable investment rates accompanied by robust bank lending.

Consequently, in 2005, official estimates put the NPLs at around 25 percent of GDP or US$300 billion. However, it is widely believed that the official number greatly understates the extent of the problem. According to Lardy (2006), NPLs could exceed 50 percent of GDP or more than US$600 billion. To Lardy, banking sector reforms have failed to create a commercial credit culture in China's banking system. In particular, the corporate culture of the Big Four still lacks a profit motive in which lending practices focus on market share rather than profitability. This is because the Big Four's senior management still consists of party and government officials whose loyalties are divided between the government and stockholders. This concern is also underscored by a recent International Monetary Fund study noting that "it is difficult to find solid empirical evidence of a strong shift to commercial orientation by the state-owned commercial banks" (Podpiera 2006). This implies not only that

---

[22] A foreign investor can hold a stake of up to 20 percent in any one bank. However, total foreign ownership of a single bank is capped at 25 percent.

the banks have a substantial bias toward lending to state-owned and politically connected borrowers, but also that they are behind international best practices, especially in regard to governance and accounting standards for bank assets and credit risk when pricing their loans. No doubt, it will take time to build a commercial credit culture because banks are long accustomed to taking direction from influential party members and bureaucrats. Exacerbating this problem is that only limited progress has been made toward commercializing the Big Four banks, which still account for more than 80 percent of total outstanding loans. This means that the potentially promising and profitable private small and medium-sized enterprises find it difficult to borrow from Chinese banks because political pressure to lend to SOEs remain. As long as the Chinese government retains majority ownership of large banks, they are likely to remain inefficient, low-margin, low-growth businesses. Not surprisingly, despite the huge capital infusions, the banking system still remains fragile and vulnerable. Without cleaning up the stock of bad loans and assets (which has to be done simultaneously with SOEs reforms), substantially improving bank governance and risk management, reducing the government's influence over lending, increasing transparency, and enforcing compliance with global lending guidelines, the banking system will remain weak and fragile.[23]

Without meaningful reforms there is concern that much of the loans granted after the capital injections have the potential to go bad. The concern is that two events could trigger a banking crisis: the entry of foreign banks over the next few years under the WTO rules and an economic slowdown, which could lead to a potential recession given the volume of NPLs.[24] No doubt, although most Chinese banks may be near insolvency, they have little competition for domestic household savings – not to mention the inflow of deposits from China's high savings rate has given banks enough liquidity to continue operating. However, as a WTO member, China must continue to open its domestic market to foreign banks. Over time, foreign banks could attract deposits away from the Chinese banks, thereby making many insolvent. This could lead to a major financial crisis. As a precaution, in 2006, the government enacted regulations governing foreign bank operations by requiring them to establish locally incorporated subsidiaries if they wished to offer renminbi retail banking services such as credit cards or accept retail renminbi deposits. Although the large and well-established foreign banks will likely meet the new standards, new foreign bank entrants may find the standards too onerous to compete

---

[23] Of course, given its resources, the government can engage in another bank bailout. Suffice it to note that those funds could be more productively used to fund government programs such as improving rural-urban and regional inequality.

[24] Under WTO accession commitments, foreign banks were allowed to enter China at the end of 2006. Although the degree of penetration by foreign banks is likely to be limited in the near future, China used this date as a deadline for all banks to meet several key objectives, including benchmark capital adequacy ratios and improvements in governance.

effectively in the market. However, the entry of foreign banks may not be as big a problem because they have little interest in battling Chinese banks for the domestic lending market. Arguably, the foreign banks' ultimate goal is independence through full ownership and oversight – in particular, independence from Chinese joint venture partners and freedom from the burden of NPLs and overbearing government influence (Chiu and Lewis 2006).

Dobson and Kashyap (2006) outline two possible strategies for banking reform. The first is to move policy lending to transformed policy banks to eliminate distortions involving management, regulation, and reporting systems. Similar to the "good bank/bad bank" strategy used in Japan after World War II, this solution isolates bad loans into a business within the bank. By giving stature to the "bad bank" and staffing it with management dedicated to resolving NPLs, customers will not receive new loans or special consideration from the "good" side of the original bank. The profit-generating loans would be transferred to the good bank. Remaining staff would need to build management information systems that permit modern credit evaluation and risk management. Freed from the burden of making loans for social stability, the transparency of the remaining operations would be greatly enhanced. The second strategy would be to separate the largest state-owned banks along deposit taking and lending functions and turn them into "narrow banks." This would shift the burden of continuing policy lending to policy banks. Smaller banks and foreign institutions would take over lending functions and the extensive branch networks and staff of these banks would be preserved. Imposing limits on the range of investment options would further increase their attractiveness as organizations for other banks and financial services companies to partner with.

There is also another possibility. Since 11 December 2006, when WTO rules came into effect, foreign banks have been patiently waiting for China to remove all restrictions on foreign ownership and control of banks, including allowing them to compete on an equal footing with domestic banks. To date, however, this has not happened. Although the Chinese government has encouraged collaboration with foreign banks, it has been dragging its feet on fully meeting its commitments in terms of full access. Rather, Beijing has argued that on the basis of its understanding of WTO obligations, China is only required to open its domestic banking market cautiously and up to a point. This means that foreign banks should not expect to receive controlling positions in existing banks or have accessing rights to banking infrastructure and customers through local branches. Although foreign banks and their governments have challenged China's position as restrictive and discriminatory and in violation of its WTO obligations, it is also important to keep in mind the inherent limitations of GATS disciplines. The contradictory interpretations WTO members have in regard their commitments and obligations are common in the WTO. The fact that China and other WTO members have fundamental differences regarding

China's GATS commitments is hardly surprising. In part, this has to do with the sheer complexity of GATS rules, the fact that a significant aspect of the Chinese banking market falls beyond the ambit of GATS rules and commitments, and, as a legal document, the GATS commitments and obligations are open to interpretation. Undoubtedly, the question as to whether the WTOs legal framework supports the case for increased access to China's financial services market consistent with its GATS commitments will remain the subject of ongoing discussion.

The silver lining for China is that it is an attractive market for foreign banks and financial institutions. After all, the savings base of the 1.3 billion people who comprise 20 percent of the potential global consumers is simply too lucrative to ignore. However, until recently, foreign institutions could only bank with foreign customers and Chinese enterprises in major cities. Although foreign financial institutions have increased their market penetration in recent years, at the end of 2006, the total foreign presence amounted to only 2.1 percent of the total assets of banking institutions in China.[25] Undoubtedly, the Chinese banks currently have the banking infrastructure and customers (the four largest state-owned commercial banks have more than 80,000 branches and an established customer base). The fact that foreign banks and financial institutions are eager to access this existing banking infrastructure augurs well for many Chinese banks. Among other things, this will enable them to secure capital infusions from foreign banks to replace government support and allow them to integrate foreign banks' risk assessment and management expertise to deal with the NPL problem.

This seems already to be happening. Since 2005, Chinese banks have benefited from an influx of foreign investment. In 2005, after listing its shares on the stock exchanges in Hong Kong and Shanghai, the Bank of Communications raised US$2 billion, whereas the Bank of China and the China Construction Bank each raised US$9 billion. In June 2005, Bank of America spent US$2.5 billion for a 9 percent holding in China Construction Bank. Since then, a growing number of foreign retail and investment banks have entered partnerships with China's ailing banks. Citigroup recently bought a 5 percent stake in Shanghai Pudong Development Bank. This allowed Citigroup to introduce credit cards to Chinese consumers. Other major investors in China's banking sector include Merrill Lynch, Goldman Sachs, the Royal Bank of Scotland, and the Commonwealth Bank of Australia, among others. Even more remarkable, China's banks are now turning the tables. Flush with cash from these partnerships, not to mention the hundreds of billions of dollars the government has pumped into the Big Four, Chinese banks and financial firms have been on a buying spree around the world. In 2007, the Industrial and Commercial Bank

---

[25] China Banking Regulatory Commission (CBRC), 2006. *Annual Report* available at www.cbrc.gov.cn (accessed 3 October 2007).

of China purchased a majority stake in Bank Halim Indonesia and Macau Seng Hang Bank. In the United States, a plummeting dollar and continuing weakness in American banking stocks in the wake of the subprime crisis has made many U.S. banks and financial institutions great bargains. China Construction Bank, which not long ago sought capital from Bank of America, bought out Bank of America's investments in Hong Kong and Macau in 2007. Also in 2007, China's largest private lender, Minsheng Bank, purchased a 9.9 percent stake in San Francisco–based UCBH Holdings (which serves the Chinese-American community), and China's CITIC Securities agreed to acquire 6 percent of Bear Stearns, the U.S. investment bank, then struggling with the slumping mortgage market.[26] However, to its credit the Chinese government has continued to focus on bank reform. Reported NPL ratios have dropped to historical lows, equity capital has increased, and a number of banks have financially restructured, recapitalized, and been listed on the Hong Kong Stock Exchange.

However, it is important to note that Chinese banks, some of which are large by global standards based on market capitalization and the size of their balance sheets, have only modest international presence. The capital markets are small relative to the size of the domestic economy and China relies heavily on FDI rather than securities investment and other forms of capital flows to access international capital markets. In fact, portfolio flows are still largely channeled through large institutional investors via the QFII (Qualified Foreign Institutional Investors) and QDII (Qualified Domestic Institutional Investors) programs established in 2002. The QFII program is restricted to funds-management and securities companies with at least US$10 billion in assets, including the world's top 100 commercial banks. In addition, securities regulator of the QFII's home country must sign a "Memorandum of Understanding" and have a track-record of good relations with the China Securities Regulatory Commission (CSRC), while the QDII's must have assets of over five billion RMB.[27] This in part, explains Chinese banks' very limited (about US$12 billion) exposure to the U.S. subprime debt. Beijing has also made public that none of its massive US$1.5 trillion foreign reserves (the largest in the world), is invested in the U.S. subprime debt.

Yet despite all these mergers and acquisitions, it is too early to bet on the Chinese banks. Corruption and cronyism still remain a huge problem, and even the best managed of China's banks and brokerages still lack the experience and sophistication of Western banks and lag behind internationally recognized standards of governance. Compounding this, although the ratio of NPLs has been reduced, the conditions that led to its rise are still there as banks are still heavily exposed to government-owned or controlled firms with weak

[26] When Bear Stearns became insolvent in March 2008 and J.P. Morgan stepped in as its acquirer, CITIC Securities cancelled the deal.
[27] The CSRC is the executive arm of the State Council Securities Committee which was established in 1992 to regulate China's securities and futures market.

balance sheets. As China's economy becomes more market based and continues its rapid integration into the global economy, a strong and independent banking system will become increasingly important. To benefit fully from economic globalization, China has to strengthen and develop the institutions that undergirds a modern financial system. These include well-defined property rights, transparent accounting standards, good corporate governance (including civil and criminal penalties for business malfeasance), effective supervisory oversight of banks and markets, the consistent enforcement of contracts, and rules that allow for orderly bankruptcy proceedings for unprofitable firms. In addition, a strong financial market infrastructure, such as a stock and bond market offering a wider range of products to consumers, will greatly relieve pressure on the banking system. On all these fronts, China still has a long way to go.

Sustaining Economic Growth: Short and Long Term

In December 2004, Premier Wen Jiabao proposed the urgent need to adjust the relationship between investment and consumption as sources of economic growth. He pointed out that China's economic growth, long driven by exports and direct investments, now needed a more balanced mix of consumption and investment-led growth. Specifically, China needed to make a transition toward a growth path that relied more on expanding domestic consumption, especially in sectors with excess capacity. This shift was based on the concern that China's growth could slow, possibly abruptly, if continued expansion of capacity eventually led to price declines. This in turn would result in reduced profits, growing loan defaults, and erosion of investor confidence – all with negative repercussions for the Chinese economy. At a time of rising fears about foreign (especially American) protectionism, a more consumption-driven growth strategy was seen as a cushion against an uncertain global environment, as well as a way to help meet the numerous unmet public and private needs in China.

However, as Lardy (2006) notes, this transition has been off to a rather slow start. He points out that in the first half of 2006, investment grew more rapidly than GDP, and China's trade surplus expanded by more than half – implying that net exports as a share of GDP are still rising. As a result, China's external surplus expanded in 2007 and 2008. There are a number of reasons China has thus far failed to make the transition. First, the problem of overinvestment and excess capacity is not amenable to quick fixes. This is because the low cost of capital and inputs (e.g., energy, utilities, land, and labor) continues to allow Chinese companies to receive rising returns on their investment. However, as the Asian financial crisis illustrated, excess capacity can also result in abrupt and sharp declines in profit, making today's investments tomorrow's loan defaults. Second, as Lardy (2006) has noted, the tax burden on rural residents has not declined significantly, and the income taxes paid by urban residents are too modest for cuts to have a perceptible effect on consumption. Third, despite the commitment to increase the provision of social services financed through the budget, there has been little shift in government spending priorities. Therefore, the precautionary demand for savings on the part of China's households persists. No doubt, a reliable pension savings system and health insurance would reduce the need for individuals to put away disproportionate sums from their incomes. As is, even poor households in China try to save because they rightly fear the consequences of serious illness, unemployment, and old age in a country lacking effective government safety nets. Fourth, there has been no real progress toward a more flexible exchange rate and increased independence of monetary policy that would allow higher domestic interest rates. In fact, China's long-maintained undervalued exchange rate has created a widely held expectation among investors that the currency will appreciate only slowly. Thus, investments toward exports are seen as a safe bet. Not surprisingly, although government agencies have issued repeated directives calling for reduced investment in sectors with excess capacity (even after two modest increases in interest rates on loans in 2006), the rates paid by corporate borrowers remain very low in real terms. Fifth, such adjustments are an enormously complicated process. China's financial system would need to undergo a major change to encourage individuals and households to consume more. Among other things, this would require easing access to consumer loans and credit cards, which are rarely issued. Finally, with waning consumer confidence, it seems that China's transition toward more consumption-driven growth is likely to be delayed.

During the Seventeenth Party Congress in October 2007, the Communist Party adopted into the Constitution the "idea of scientific development" to create a "harmonious society." In theory, "scientific development" represents the party-state's commitment to prioritize the quality rather than the speed of development, and "harmonious society" implies a more equitable and sustainable economic development. This shift in official discourse nevertheless leaves unanswered the critical issue of how the public goods and social services associated with "scientific development" for a "harmonious society" will be financed. On 11 November 2008, the Chinese government announced a massive 4 trillion yuan (US$586 billion) stimulus package over two years. Totaling some 14 percent of annual GDP, it is arguably the biggest peacetime stimulus ever, albeit it may include sums already earmarked in the budget. It remains to be seen whether the package can reverse the economic slowdown. After years of double-digit growth, anything less than at least 8 percent a year could lead to further unemployment and resultant social tensions. On one hand, the Chinese government hopes that the new stimulus will generate a much-needed domestic consumption, thereby shifting the economy still skewed toward exports. On the other hand, the package also generously subsidizes exports. Equally perplexing, the package does little to improve the social safety net, which stands at less than 1 percent of GDP. As noted, Chinese citizens are prodigious savers because they are justly concerned about skyrocketing medical and education costs and lack of security when they retire. Unless these concerns are effectively resolved, they will not be spending their rainy-day savings anytime soon. It also means that financial stimulus is one-time shot designed to alleviate immediate problems in the economy by giving it a boost. More sustained growth must come less from capital infusion and more from productivity growth.

Over the long term, to sustain its growth momentum, China must strengthen the core institutional foundations of a market economy: the inviolability of private property. As Nobel laureate Douglass North (2005) has noted, good institutions beget good governance. Institutions matter for both the long and short term because they form the incentive structure of a society and provide the underlying determinants of economic performance. Institutions are composed of both formal (constitutions, laws, and regulations) and informal (e.g., social norms, customs, and traditions) rules that constrain human economic behavior. Specifically, institutions set the framework of rules and incentives that affect how people, organizations, and firms utilize resources in political and economic decision making, or how they "play the game." According to North, when incentives encourage individuals to be productive, economic activity and growth takes place. However, when they encourage unproductive or predatory behavior, economies stagnate. Although informal interpersonal exchanges and social networks can serve the needs of traditional societies, modern economies (given their specialization and complex division of labor) require formalized political, judicial, and economic rules. In providing specific rules of the game, political and economic institutions create the conditions that enable the functioning of a modern economy. That is, formal institutions, by securing property rights, establishing a polity and judicial system, and implementing flexible laws that allow a range of organizational structures, create an economic environment that induces increasing productivity.

North (2005) argues that institutions are "growth enhancing" because they reduce uncertainty and transaction costs. Thus, North's paradigm is often labeled as the "new institutionalism" because it has at its core a set of ideas derived from the analysis of "transaction costs" – that is, costs that result from the imperfect character of real-world institutions and that have to be surmounted for economic activity to occur. Specifically, the institutional framework affects growth because it is integral to the amount spent on both the costs of transactions and the costs of transformation inherent in the production process. Transaction costs are far higher when property rights of the rule of law are absent and not enforced. In such situations, private firms typically operate on a small scale and rely on extra-legal means to function. Conversely, an institutional environment that provides impartial third-party enforcement of agreements promotes exchange and trade because the parties know that a good or service will be delivered after it is paid for. Because institutions and the enforcement of rules largely determine the costs of transacting, good institutions can also minimize transaction costs – or costs incurred in making an economic exchange. Both political and economic institutions are necessary to sufficiently reduce transaction costs to make potential gains from trade realizable. North argues that among the plethora of institutional rules, most critical to economic growth is the protection of private property rights. This is because property rights and contract enforcement are integral to reducing uncertainty in a market because modern economies require property rights and effective, impersonal, contract enforcement. Conversely, personal ties, voluntary constraints, and ostracism are less effective in a large, complex, and impersonal economy.

North's insights shed much light on the problems facing China. Although private property rights have been recognized and protected, they remain poorly defined and insecure.[28] Over two dozen types of ownership systems, including private firms, collective firms, joint stock companies, and foreign-owned enterprises, coexist together – and not always in harmony. For example, it is still unclear as to who owns an SOE. Is it the State Council, some agency, or the local government? Although most of the SOEs have been restructured into stockholding companies, their equity remains in the hands of the state. Under the law, the State Council enforces the ownership of all state assets on behalf of the state, but the central and local authorities "manage" those assets at their various levels. This means that the state as the largest shareholder is an "agent" rather than an owner of state assets. It also means that SOE managers are not fully responsible for SOE performance because managers are selected and appointed by the government. Thus, they are beholden to the government rather than to the interests of the nonstate shareholders. This insecure and obscure nature of property rights invariably results in inefficient use of resources and staggering losses of state assets. Similarly, the state continues to impose strict rules on land ownership. It is still illegal to transfer, mortgage, or lease land. As noted, agricultural land is owned and managed collectively by townships and villages rather than the actual cultivator. This opaque understanding of "property rights" has served to undermine efficient use of agricultural resources because farmers are hesitant to make long-term investments in assets (namely, land) that they do not own. Resolving this contradiction is essential to China's long-term growth.

[28] There was no provision for private property rights in the 1982 Constitution. This right was included under Article 11 in the 1999 Constitution. However, only after the Constitution was amended in 2004 could citizens legally obtain private property and receive protection such as compensation if these rights were violated.

4

India
Strategies and Patterns of Global Integration

It is hard to miss the mood of optimism in contemporary India. Celebrating its sixtieth year of independence, the country's political and business leaders can hardly contain themselves, trumpeting India's economic achievements and its rise to global prominence. If in an earlier time India was patronizingly dismissed as "the country of the future," forever poised for a dramatic takeoff but never quite accomplishing it, today its representatives, like effervescent Commerce and Industry Minister Kamal Nath, confidently proclaim that "we no longer discuss the future of India. The future is India."[1] No doubt, India has shed its image as a land of grinding poverty, starving children, sacred cows, and wandering holy men. Now media stories are about its legions of "techies," savvy entrepreneurs, brand-name multinationals moving or outsourcing their operations to Bangalore, the ever-growing ranks of Indian business tycoons adding to their global portfolios, and the extravagant Bollywood movies. When the Indian industrial conglomerate Tata (with ninety-eight companies spanning a variety of industries) recently took over Corus, a major Belgian steel firm for US$11 billion, and Mittal Steel merged with Arcelor, making Arcelor Mittal the largest steel maker in the world; when the Indian conglomerate Aditya Birla Group purchased the American firm Novelis, the world's leading manufacturer of aluminum products; and, last but not least, when on 26 March 2008, Tata Motors of the Tata Group paid US$2.3 billion for Ford Motor Companies Jaguar and Land Rover brands, they were widely celebrated as conquering heroes – symbols of the "new India" finally taking their rightful place in the world.[2]

Undeniably, India's economic emergence explains this renaissance. It seems that in one broad sweep economic liberalization finally freed pentup entrepreneurial energy, unleashing an economic revitalization and growth

---

[1] Speech by Commerce and Industry Minister Kamal Nath at the thirtieth anniversary of the U.S.-India Business Council in Washington, D.C., June 1, 2005, available at: http://www.indianembassy.org/press_release/2005/June/3.htm.

[2] It is estimated that acquisitions by Indian companies abroad amounted to almost US$35 billion in 2006.

momentum that has literally transformed the Indian economy. Since the inception of the reforms in 1991, India's economic performance has improved appreciably. The Indian economy has continued to expand at a robust pace, with its growth rate averaging an impressive 6 percent throughout much of the 1990s. During 2002–6, the average growth rate increased to 8.75 percent and to an unprecedented 9.7 percent and 9.4 percent, respectively, in the second and third quarters of 2007. In the first two quarters of 2008, India's economy (even amid a global economic slowdown) grew by 8.3 percent. This made India one of the world's fastest-growing economies. These growth rates are a far cry from the lackluster "Hindu rate of growth" of 3.5 percent over three decades from 1950 to 1980. Although poverty is still persistent, economic growth has nevertheless translated into significant increases in per capita GDP – from US$1,255 in 1978, US$2,732 in 2003, and more than US$4,000 in 2007 in purchasing power parity nominal terms.

It is now recognized that economic growth is the result of (a) growth in factor inputs such as labor and capital, (b) a reallocation of misallocated factors of production, and (c) increases in the productivity of labor and capital. India's phenomenal growth has been fueled by a sharp expansion in business and industrial investment and exports as a result of *economic globalization* or global economic integration and (unlike China) in the rise of productivity and growing domestic consumption by the estimated 250 to 300 million "middle-class" households.[3] This also helps explain why, despite rapid integration in global economic system, the Indian economy has shown great resilience in the face of a slowing global economy (in particular, that of the United States) and skyrocketing oil prices.

India and the Globalization of Technology

What is globalization? Although a multifaceted and disparate phenomenon such as "globalization" is hard to define, I use the term broadly as the process through which an ever-expanding free flow of goods, services, capital, peoples, and social customs leads to further integration of economies and societies worldwide.[4] This phenomenon is hardly new as attested by the far-flung trade routes developed under the Romans and trade links forged by Marco Polo and Christopher Columbus – or, as Chanda (2007) colorfully notes, by numerous, "traders, preachers, adventurers and warriors." According to the noted economic historian Angus Maddison (2001), these linkages, or "globalization," played a crucial role in stimulating economic growth. Similarly, Findlay and

---

[3] Bosworth, Collins, and Virmani (2006) calculate that output per worker grew at 1.3 percent annually during 1960–80 and that total factor productivity (TFP) was barely above zero. In contrast, growth in output per worker nearly tripled to 3.8 percent during 1980–2004, whereas TFP increased tenfold to 2 percent.

[4] For a good overview of competing definitions, see Held and McGrew (2000).

O'Rourke (2007) show that it was the "vast web of interrelationships" between Western Europe and other regions that began in the medieval period that set the stage for economic growth and global economic integration (see also W. Bernstein 2008). Broadly, these observers agree that economic advancement across time was sustained by three interactive processes: (a) conquest or settlement of relatively empty regions that had fertile land, new biological resources, or a potential to accommodate transfers of population, crops, and livestock; (b) international trade and capital movement; and (c) technological and institutional innovation.

However, globalization is not a seamless or linear process. Rather, the world has experienced successive waves of globalization. Many view the current phase as the second great wave of globalization of international trade and capital flows. The first occurred from 1870 to 1914 when international trade grew at about 4 percent annually, rising from 10 percent of global output (measured as GDP) in 1870 to more than 20 percent just before the outbreak of the First World War in 1914. The war (1914–18) not only left a massive economic and human devastation in its wake, it also caused an abrupt cessation of trade and capital flow between nations. Rajan and Zingales (2003) have aptly termed the collapse of this phase of globalization as the "Great Reversal," which they argue bred conditions for the Second World War (1939–45).

The creation of the Bretton Woods institutions (the World Bank, the International Monetary Fund [IMF], and the General Agreement on Tariffs and Trade), following WWII laid the foundations for the current era of globalization. This contemporary phase was christened "globalization" in the mid-1980s when it became evident that the unprecedented advances in information technology (IT), coupled with declines in transaction costs and resultant rapid international flows of capital, labor, and technology had made the world a much smaller and qualitatively different place. According to Keohane (2002), Deardorff and Stern (2002), Mishkin (2006), and Sachs (2008), among others, what distinguishes this current phase of globalization from the earlier "partial" ones is rapid technological and economic diffusion. This, in turn, has created strong tendencies toward technological and economic convergence among major regions of the world. This is in sharp contrast to the prewar period, which was characterized by a strong divergence in economic growth – meaning a widening gap in production and income between the richest regions and the rest of the world. The dramatic divergence of per capita output, industrial production, and living standards during the nineteenth century between Western Europe and the United States and the rest of the world underscore this. The postwar era of global convergence is marked by the rapid incorporation of much of developing and post-Communist countries (the so-called new globalizers or emerging market economies) into the global economic system. Scholars agree that the current phase is fundamentally driven by dramatic increases in cross-border trade, capital, and investment flows. International trade has witnessed a sixteen-fold increase over the past fifty years. Specifically, foreign direct investment (FDI) and capital flows that totaled around $160 billion in 1991 soared to over $1.1 trillion in 2000 and skyrocketed to just over $2 trillion in 2005. Similarly, cross-border capital flows, including debt, portfolio equity, and direct investment-based financing topped $6 trillion in 2005 (World Bank 2002, 2006a). These unprecedented volumes of funds can move literally instantaneously across national borders at the touch of a computer keyboard. As a result, almost all national economies have become integrated into a single global marketplace through trade, finance, production networks, and a dense web of international treaties and institutions.

Another unique feature of contemporary globalization is speed – aptly encapsulated in phrases such as "real time" and the "death of distance." Unlike the previous phase, the contemporary phase is unfolding at lighting speed. In the earlier phase, it took massive infrastructure networks – ships, rail, and motor vehicles, along with large support systems such as ports, railways and roads, – to facilitate the cross-border exchange of goods and services. What differentiates the current phase is its dependence on a web of worldwide IT networks that allow for instantaneous cross-border transaction of goods and services at a fraction of the cost. In the case of India, investment expansion and productivity growth has been most pronounced in services, led by the IT sector, which includes computer programming, software development and production, communication networks, call centers, and outsourced business, among others.[5] This sector is at the heart of India's economic renaissance. Arguably, the IT revolution and the resultant globalization of technology ushered in an audacious "new economy," the primary beneficiary of which has been India. This explains India's remarkable economic metamorphosis despite lacking China's more ostentatious advantages (i.e., China's large and dynamic manufacturing sector and relatively efficient and reliable infrastructure). Table 4.1 shows that over the past two decades, the Indian economy has experienced a major structural transformation in terms of the distribution of GDP across sectors, with dramatic growth in the services sector and decline of agriculture and manufacturing.

India's ability to benefit from the "new economy" is by both accident and design. The roots of the Indian software and business-processing services sector go back to the early post-independence period. In 1950, the first Indian Institute of Technology (IIT), modeled after the Massachusetts Institute of Technology, was established at Kharagpur in West Bengal. Six other IITs were

---

[5] Under conventional classification, an economy is divided into three sectors. These include the agricultural (or primary), manufacturing (or secondary), and service (or tertiary) sectors. Services can be broadly divided between the old and the new. Old or the traditional services include trading and hotel services. New services are generally associated with modern communications. Because the latter are tradable internationally, they are also called tradable services.

Table 4.1. *Breakdown of India's GDP by sector*
(in percentages)

	1984	1996	2001	2007
Agriculture	37	28	23.9	19.7
Manufacturing	24	28.1	27.2	26.2
Services	39	43.9	48.9	54.1

Source: Calculated from Organisation for Economic Co-operation and Development (2007).

set up in selected cities across the country after the passage of the Indian Institute of Technology Act in 1956. Winters and Yusuf (2007, 45–6) note that "the seven IITs, with a total enrollment in 2004 approaching 30,000 (17,000 undergraduate and 13,000 graduate students), have provided India with the nucleus of a world-class technological elite. These schools and other training institutions (e.g., the six Indian Institutes of Management and several Indian Institutes of Information Technologies in conjunction with the universities) have provisioned India's labor markets with engineering, management, and IT-relevant skills."

Figuratively, by riding the IT wave, India has fortuitously been able to overcome the once insurmountable constraints of geography and time. Specifically, the global expansion of high-speed Internet and related telecommunications networks that have rendered geography "irrelevant" by creating linkages between countries and businesses that simply did not exist a decade ago has enabled Indian entrepreneurs and the country's large pool of skilled and inexpensive English-speaking "techies" to cash in on the IT revolution. In a relatively short period of time, India has become the location of choice for all sorts of IT-related activities best symbolized in "Electronics City" – the Bangalore main "tech-hub" and the prime stretch on Bannerghatta Road in southern Bangalore housing offices of multinationals such as Oracle, IBM, Accenture, Dell, Hewlett-Packard, PeopleSoft, Honeywell, Intel, Monsanto, American Express, General Motors, and the ubiquitous Microsoft – where everything from advanced software production and programming, data processing, network management and systems integration, multimedia, business outsourcing, and call-center processing are performed.

Today, India's IT services have established a proven track record and a reputation of international renown.[6] Even the solicitous call-center activity has climbed up the value chain, moving from simply filling sales orders and

---

[6] India counts among its populace a third of the world's software engineers. As Khanna and Huang (2003) note, "India has managed to spawn a number of companies that now compete internationally with the best that Europe and the United States have to offer. Moreover, many of these firms are in the most cutting-edge, knowledge-based industries – software giants Infosys and Wipro and pharmaceutical and biotechnology powerhouses Ranbaxy and

performing data entry, payroll processing, and real-time customer support for Western companies to handling medical data transcription and financial analysis for Wall Street firms. Indian accountants and financial analysts are hired not only to prepare tax returns for Americans but also to write brokerage reports for Wall Street. In the past few years the world's leading pharmaceuticals, including Pfizer, AstraZeneca, Bristol-Myers Squibb, GlaxoSmithKline, Novartis, Abbott, Merck, and others, have also established research and manufacturing facilities in India. In fact, anything that can be done digitally (meaning whatever can be done in real time from any location on the globe) has already moved or is in the process of moving, to Bangalore, Chennai, Mumbai, Delhi, and other locations in India because both the low-end and sophisticated IT work can be done at a fraction of the cost compared with North America or Western Europe.[7] Even more impressive, several of India's blue-chip IT giants such as Infosys, Satyam, and Wipro and newer stalwarts such as Tejas Networks and the Mumbai-based Celetronix (all began just a decade ago as modest start-ups) now build, design, and maintain software for nearly three hundred companies in the exclusive Fortune 500 club.[8] With this kind of track record, it is hardly surprising that the IT and related service sector that a decade ago had export sales of US$150 million saw the volume grow to more than US$9.6 billion or 2 percent of GDP in 2001. In 2006–7, export sales reached more than US$24 billion or 4.8 percent of GDP (Ernst and Young 2006, 13). Similarly, the share of IT (mainly software) in total exports increased from 1 percent in 1990 to 18 percent in 2001 (World Bank 2003). This growth, coupled with India's rapidly expanding services sector (which currently accounts for about 54 percent of India's GDP, 25 percent of employment, and 30 percent of export earnings) has provided India with the much-needed growth and stability in the post–September 11 period, which has been characterized by uncertainty, financial market turmoil, and sharp global economic slowdown.

India's services-led strategy fundamentally challenges the long-held assumptions of international economic theory. This theory maintains that technology, capital, and labor are immobile and that low-wage countries receive more benefits by concentrating on labor-intensive production, leaving innovation and

---

Dr. Reddy's Labs, to name just a few. Last year, the Forbes 200, an annual ranking of the world's best small companies, included 13 Indian firms."

[7] India continues to hold on to the top spot as the most attractive location for off-shoring of services such as IT, business processing, and call centers because it continues to remain the best offshore location by a wide margin, even if wage inflation and the emergence of lower-cost countries into the off-shoring market have decreased its overall lead. In regard to China, improved infrastructure and relevant people skills have increased its attractiveness as a low-cost option for servicing Asian markets. However, the gap between India and China, the second-ranked country, is larger than the gap between the next nine countries combined.

[8] Among others, Wipro Technologies helped design MP3 players for a European company and a flat-panel TV for an American company. Such entrepreneurial ventures in the consumer market are not confined to the largest players. Celetronix produces set-top boxes for a U.S.-based satellite TV carrier.

capital-intensive production to the advanced developed economies. However, contemporary globalization makes possible the cross-border exchange of not only tradable manufactured goods but also the once non-tradable services. Therefore, globalization has enabled India to defy earlier assumptions because it has made traditional "non-tradable" service jobs in developed countries into tradeable ones. Moreover, as India races up the value-technology chain, more non-tradable jobs in developed countries can potentially become vulnerable to the vagaries of the competitive forces of international trade and investment. As noted in the previous chapter, if India provides a useful lesson for China, it is that the Chinese economy must graduate up the value chain rather than simply rely on low-end manufacturing and capacity expansion.

Expanding Global Trade and Integration

Because the Indian economy was largely insulated from the global markets before the reforms, foreign trade and investment were just a tiny fraction of the GDP. However, trade liberalization (which saw peak tariff rates on nonagricultural goods fall from 150 percent in 1991–92 to 12.5 percent in 2006) and financial liberalization (with the easing of controls on capital inflows, particularly direct and portfolio investments) has made the Indian economy more open and integrated into the global economy. This integration into the global economy has enabled India also to expand its exports of food and capital goods, including garments, engineering tools, and petroleum products. Cumulatively, this has resulted in a sharp rise in India's trade in goods and services as a proportion of the GDP from 16 percent in 1990–91 to 49 percent in 2006 (Purfield 2006a).

The liberalization of India's FDI regime has seen FDI flow rise from less than $100 million in 1990–91 to $19.5 billion 2006–07. Similarly, portfolio investment rose from $6 million in 1990–91 to over $7 billion in 2006–07, and remittances rose from $2 billion in 1990–91 to $28 billion in 2006–07. Capital inflows have surged since 2006, in part, because capital account liberalization has allowed India to attract large portfolio flows (Chart 4.1). In 2005, net capital inflows amounted to $25 billion. However, in 2006, it jumped to US$46 billion, and by September 2007 it had reached $66 billion. Equally impressive, India's foreign exchange reserves have risen from US$42.3 billion in March 2001 to US$54.1 billion at the end of March 2002, to US$72.4 billion in January 2003, and US$230 billion in 2007. The reserves rose to an unprecedented US$312 billion in May 2008 (Reserve Bank of India 2008). This has helped to make the Indian economy more resilient and attractive to foreign investment.

Moreover, global economic integration has significantly strengthened India's external position. Since the 1991 crisis, the country's balance of payments has remained strong. India's external debt situation has improved significantly as a result of effective external debt management. The external debt-to-GDP ratio

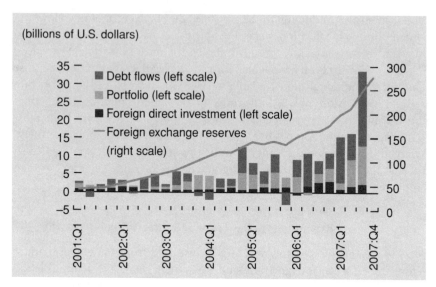

Chart 4.1. Net Capital Flows to India. *Source:* Bloomberg and International Monetary Fund, Finance and Development.

decreased from 28.7 percent at end-March 1991 to 22.3 percent at end-March 2001 and to 20.8 percent in March 2002. The debt service ratio declined from a peak level of 35.3 percent of current receipts in 1990–91 to 16.3 percent in 2000–1. Similarly, the current account deficit as a percentage of GDP declined from 1.1 percent in 1999–2000 to about 0.5 percent in 2000–1 because of strong export performance. Finally, between 1991 and 1993, India moved gradually to full current account convertibility. This means that in the foreign exchange market, dealers are now allowed to buy and sell foreign exchange for current and capital account transactions, and firms earning foreign exchange through exports are allowed to retain a certain proportion of the proceeds, thereby avoiding costs of conversion and reconversion. Also, because the rupee was floated in March 1992, the significant nominal and real devaluation relative to its value prior to 1991 has provided a much-needed impetus to trade flows. The exchange rate of the rupee in terms of the major currencies of the world has remained fairly stable, notwithstanding the occasional fluctuations caused by normal market forces of supply and demand.[9] It is particularly noteworthy that for the first time, the World Bank has classified India as a less-indebted country.

[9] Kohli (2005) notes that the government intervened actively in the foreign exchange market between 1993 and 1999 to arrest the appreciation of the real exchange rate and consequent loss of competitiveness. However, the evidence from 1999 suggests the willingness of the government to tolerate some appreciation of the currency.

The Challenges

Despite India's significant economic achievements in the reform era, global economic integration has also created challenges – some new and others seemingly exacerbated by globalization. Although some claim that this is inherent in the nature of "pro-rich neoliberal globalization," others argue that the challenges are due not to market reforms but rather to the failure to implement effectively the full spectrum of the reform program. This failure, in turn, is often attributed to India's gradualist approach to reform (which has meant a frustratingly slow and haphazard pace of implementation) and the difficulties in implementing the necessary "second-generation reforms" because they require legislative action, which India's fractured coalition governments cannot deliver. The following sections highlight the impact of the reforms, as well as possible strategies to mitigate the present and potential challenges.

RECONCILING GROWTH WITH REDISTRIBUTION

Like the proverbial rising tide that eventually lifts all boats, the fruits of economic growth have benefited (albeit unevenly) all sectors of Indian society. This has made a significant dent in the country's stubborn poverty problem. Reaffirming that the link between economic growth and poverty reduction is unambiguous, the National poverty line estimates show that there has been a marked decrease in poverty incidence from about 45 percent in the early 1980s, to 36 percent in 1993–94, to 27.5 percent in 2004–5 (Government of India [GOI] 2006, 2006a). This translates into a net reduction in poverty of some 100 million people between 1993–94 and 2004–5. In rural India, poverty was down to 27 percent, whereas urban poverty fell by around 8 percent, from 32 percent to 24 percent, by 2005.[10] Other social indicators have shown similar

---

[10] It is important to note that Indian poverty estimates have been the subject of a heated debate – not regarding whether poverty has declined, but by how much. This debate is primarily due to changes in survey methodology in the 1999/2000 "thick" round of India's National Sample Survey (NSS) relative to previous rounds, which has led to difficulties in comparing estimates across rounds. Specifically, in 1950, at the behest of Prime Minister Nehru, the Planning Commission created the National Sample Survey Organization (NSSO) to track through the NSS the performance of the Indian economy by collecting data from a random sample of the population. Over time, this project has compiled a time series of consumption data from thirty-six NSSs spanning 1951–2000. This is one of the longest series of national household surveys suitable for tracking living conditions of the poor. In fact, India has one of the richest sources of data on household-level consumption expenditures across time of any country in the developing world. Specifically, an NSS has been carried out every five years with a sample size of approximately 123,000 households. As a complement to these quinquennial "thick rounds," smaller "thin rounds," with much smaller sample sizes, have also been carried out on an annual basis. The thick rounds of the NSS collect household consumption expenditure data, focusing mainly on food and durable goods but also including data on educational and medical expenditures. Since 1970, large surveys were carried out for years 1973–74, 1977–78, 1983, 1987–88, 1993–94, and 1999–2000. The results from large sample surveys are considered

Table 4.2. *India: Macroeconomic and social trends*

Indicator	1980s	1990s	2000	2005
Poverty incidence* (%)	44.5	36.0	26.1	25
Rural poverty (%)	46	36.8	–	28
Urban poverty (%)	42	32.8	–	25
Infant mortality (per 1000 births)	–	77	–	55
Life expectancy at birth (years)	56	60	61	–
Literacy rate: 7+ years (%)	44	52	65	–
% of net enrollment, grades 1–5	47	51	77	–

*In India, the poverty line is defined as the minimum subsistence income that can support the consumption of 2,400 calories in rural areas and 2,100 calories per person in urban areas. This poverty line was established in 1979 but has been periodically adjusted for inflation.
Source: World Bank (2003, 2–3) and Government of India (2006).

improvements. Over the past two decades, life expectancy has increased from fifty-five to sixty-three years. The total fertility rate for India's large and growing population has been lowered from six children per woman to three since the 1960s. Similarly, since 1950, there was a dramatic reduction in infant mortality from 146 to an average of 55 per 1,000 live births in 2005. The 1990s witnessed important achievements in literacy with enrollment of primary school–aged children rising from 68 percent in 1992–93 to 82 percent at the end of the decade. India currently has 108 million children aged six to ten attending primary school – the world's second largest education system after China. Table 4.2 provides a snapshot of some of these changes.

Yet India's record in reducing poverty pales in comparison with that achieved by China. Although, overall poverty levels have declined, the absolute numbers are still unacceptably high. Not only do significant numbers of Indians still live in abject poverty, an equally large number are negatively affected because of the inadequacy or absence of essential public goods and services such as access to education, health care, housing, clean drinking water, and jobs. Although, both the central and state governments have increased public expenditure in these key sectors, by the government's own admission, given the problems of implementation, outlays do not mean outcomes. For example, although millions of children have access to India's educational system (75 percent of all children attend government schools), chronic underfunding, the lack of proper facilities and high rates of teacher absenteeism (India has the second-highest rate of teacher absenteeism in the world) has failed to capitalize adequately on this "demographic dividend."

more robust and reliable than those from the small sample surveys. The problems with the 1999–2000 round led to conflicting interpretations. Some estimates indicated that the extent of poverty reduction was by 50 percent between 1990 and 1998, whereas others showed a more modest reduction (Sharma 2003a). The latest NSS round (2004–5) shows a poverty rate of 27.8 percent, down from 36 percent in 1993–94.

However, at the heart of India's inability to reduce poverty sharply is the failure of create a wide range of manufacturing jobs, which historically has served as a ladder out of poverty for many countries. In 2007, industry accounted for only 18 percent of employment and 27 percent of GDP, in contrast to China's 24 percent and 48 percent, respectively (World Bank 2007). This failure has meant that India's current elasticity of growth implies that a 5 percent rise in real GDP leads to only a 2.5 percent rise in employment (Purfield and Schiff 2006, 3). As a result, according to an IMF (2007) study, employment in India's organized sector has remained roughly unchanged at about 27 million since the early 1990s, leading some to conclude that India has experienced "jobless growth."[11] As discussed later, this is one major downside of concentration on services at the expense of labor-intensive manufacturing.

Like China, regional economic disparity has widened in India. The phrase "two Indias" illustrates the widening regional differences as growth continues to vary sharply among the twenty-eight states and seven union territories that make up the union (Datt and Ravallion 2002; Purfield 2006). For example, in 2005, the poorest seven states (accounting for 55 percent of the population) had a per capita GDP that was two-thirds the national average, whereas in the richest seven states (33 percent of the population), per capita GDP was nearly double that of the poorest seven states (Devarajan and Nabi 2006). States such as Tamil Nadu, Maharashtra, Andhra Pradesh, the Punjab, Haryana, and Gujarat have surged ahead, whereas others, especially the so-called BIMARU states (Bihar, Madhya Pradesh, Rajasthan, and Uttar Pradesh), have either stagnated or continued to fall behind. For example, in 1997–98, the gross state domestic product (GSDP) per capita ranged from 1,261 rupees per month in Bihar (one of the poorest states with a population of 82 million), to 5,690 rupees per month in Maharashtra (the richest state with a population of 96 million). Similarly, whereas Gujarat achieved growth in state per capita income at 7.8 percent per year from 1992–93 to 1998–99, Bihar experienced a −0.2 percent decline during the same period (Sachs, Bajpai, and Ramiah 2002). The reasons for these sharp interstate variations are complex. Although per capita growth is positively related to the initial levels of income, some relatively poor states such as Kerala, Andhra Pradesh, and Tamil Nadu with better infrastructure and human resource development have been successful in attracting investment in the post-reform period.[12] Even Orissa (traditionally

---

[11] The "organized sector" refers to nongovernment salaried or wage employment in the following sectors: agriculture, hunting, forestry, and fishing; mining and quarrying; manufacturing; utilities; construction; wholesale and retail trade; tourism; transportation, storage, and communications; and various services.

[12] Neoclassical growth theories have long claimed of "convergence," in which poor nations or regions will eventually catch up with richer ones in terms of level of per capita product or income. This is because market reforms facilitate resource flows that tend to equalize factor returns across regions. However, in India, regional inequality has risen in the past two decades. According to recent research, this inequality is attributable primarily to a large rural-urban

one of India's poorest states) has achieved steady growth in the reform period by becoming "an innovator of economic reforms: it was the first state to reform its power sector, it has strongly set out industrial policy promoting private sector investment and offering fiscal and other concessions, and it was the first state to announce new agricultural and tourism policies" (Sachs, Bajpai, and Ramiah 2002, 56). However, laggard states such as Uttar Pradesh and Bihar (which are richly endowed in terms of natural and mineral resources) have fallen behind because of political instability and unpredictable and arbitrary policy regimes that have negatively affected economic growth.

INDUSTRIAL AND MANUFACTURING SECTOR

Although India's industrial sector has become more competitive internationally (Indian manufacturing firms have upgraded technology and adopted more efficient scales of production), manufacturing growth and exports are still quite modest given India's potential and when compared with the growth achieved by China. This discrepancy is due to not only incomplete reforms in this crucial sector but also the higher rates of taxation imposed on manufactured goods in India. Burdened with poor infrastructure (which adds to the already high production and transportation costs), the manufacturing sector remains uncompetitive and inefficient. Underscoring the symbiotic relationship between agricultural and industrial growth, the lack of a dynamic industrial and manufacturing sector has meant that the scope for mobility of low-skilled labor out of the agricultural sector has been limited by the absence of robust and sustained growth in the industrial and manufacturing sectors.

Similarly, the relaxation of FDI controls in manufacturing and improvements in the business environment have been slow and piecemeal. For example, a recent IMF study notes that "to start a business in Korea takes 22 days and in China 41 days. But in India, it takes 89 days" (Purfield and Schiff 2006, 8). The central government still regulates investments by requiring approval or by imposing ownership limits, and India's vast retail sector remains relatively inaccessible to foreign investors. To be fair, although successive Indian governments have reduced the number of activities reserved for the public sector from six to three and the number of sectors reserved for small-scale industry (units whose investment in plant and machinery cannot exceed $250,000) from 821 to 799, the number of these activities is still too high (Figure 4.1). In effect, this "reservation" policy has created protective enclaves within the industrial sector with adverse effect on competitiveness, innovation and job-creation.

income gap and growing inland-coastal disparity. For example, some have found that the differences in per capita income between states can be explained by the literacy and private investment rates across states (Aiyar 2001). Others have argued that a state's proximity to the coast appears to improve its likelihood of being positively affected by the growth impulses of having access to markets. See Sachs, Bajpai, and Ramiah (2002).

Value added per establishment (in U.S. millions dollars)

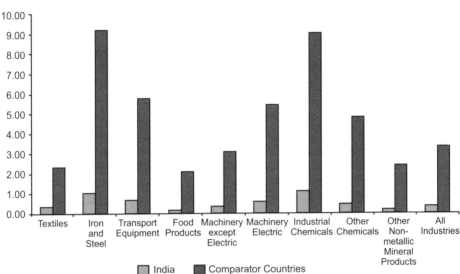

Figure 4.1. Average firm size in India and comparator countries. *Source:* Rajan (2006, 39).

The most dominant characteristic of India's manufacturing sector is the extraordinarily small scale of establishments. With about 87 percent of manufacturing employment in micro-enterprises of fewer than ten employees, small-scale industry reservations continue to preempt the adoption of the optimal scale of production (Organisation for Economic Co-operation and Development [OECD] 2007, 76). For example, the production of goods such as garments, toys, shoes, leather, and textile products continue to be reserved for the small-scale producers, although large firms have a potential comparative advantage. This clearly puts domestic producers at a disadvantage while competing against foreign producers who have no scale restrictions. Nothing underscores this problem better than India's famous textile industry. In 1950, India was the world's leading exporter of cotton textiles. However, currently India's textile industry trails far behind that of China. In 2005, India's "exports of textiles and garments amounted to $9.5 billion and $7.5 billion, respectively, versus China's respective $77 billion and $40 billion" (Winters and Yusuf 2007, 51). India's textile industry, dominated by many small producers, is not only highly regulated, but the average firm in India's formal sector is also constrained from fully exploiting scale economies and new technologies. As a result, little foreign capital has flowed into the sector, and because Indian firms are less well integrated into global production networks than are Chinese firms, they have benefited little from technology transfer. Not surprisingly, the productivity level of India's textiles and clothing sector is only 35 percent that of the

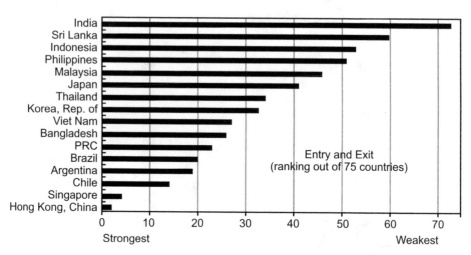

Figure 4.2. Global perspectives on the restrictiveness of hiring and firing. *Source:* Rajan (2006, 46).

United States, while China's is 55 percent (Ananthakrishnan and Jain-Chandra 2005). Most troubling, without reforms, Indian textile producers (unlike their Chinese counterparts) may not be able to take full advantage of the end of the multifiber quotas on textile and apparel exports to OECD countries. This could have serious consequences because India's textiles and clothing sector is the country's second-largest employer with 35 million workers and is responsible for 20 percent of industrial production (Ananthakrishnan and Jain-Chandra 2005).

The Indian government puts restrictions on private enterprise through licensing laws, directed credit, preferences for small-scale industry, and anti-monopoly regulations, and stringent labor laws result in further constraints. Not surprisingly, the World Bank (2006) ranks India very low in comparison to many other developing countries, including China, on the degree of labor market flexibility and general business climate (Figure 4.2). India's labor laws make it very costly to reduce workers in enterprises of more than one hundred workers.[13] The result of this policy is that formal-sector firms (those that are registered and that pay their taxes) loathe taking on new employment. The existence of archaic labor laws is the major reason Bajaj Auto recently opened a new factory that is highly automated. In a labor-abundant country such as India, this was not Bajaj's preferred choice. This also explains why in

[13] The Industrial Disputes Act of 1947 required "large-scale enterprises" to obtain state government approval before firing or laying off workers. "Large-scale" used to refer to firms with more than three hundred employees. An amendment to the act in 1976 made it compulsory for firms with three hundred or more workers to seek permission from the government before dismissing workers. However, in 1982, the ceiling for seeking prior government permission was reduced to one hundred workers.

a country as large as India, fewer than 10 million workers are employed in the formal private sector and why the bulk of India's employment is in the unorganized informal sector, made up of numerous tax-evading, small, and inefficient enterprises. Cumulatively, these restrictions have severely restricted not only export competitiveness but also job creation by forcing businesses to create more capital-intensive manufacturing jobs rather than what India needs: more labor-intensive manufacturing jobs.

Moreover, India's expansive state-owned companies in the small-scale industrial sector remain a drain on government resources. Until recently, the restructuring and privatization program met with limited success because the central government insisted on retaining management control. It seems that the government is more interested in "disinvestment" rather than privatization. Although the government has recently redefined its privatization strategy, committing to privatize all nonstrategic companies including a reduction in its equity to 26 percent (or lower in some cases) in strategic companies such as those involved in the arms and ammunition, defense, and atomic energy, its success in this endeavor has yet to materialize. With roughly two-thirds of industrial output of the organized sector in these enterprises, it will be difficult to stimulate industrial growth without privatization.

Because the services sector overwhelmingly tends to create jobs for the relatively educated urban-based populace, it has had limited impact on income distribution and poverty reduction. Nothing underscores this better than the results from India's 2004 national elections. Basking in the glow of the country's economic renaissance, the ruling national coalition led by the Bharatiya Janata Party (BJP) wistfully settled on the catchy slogan "Shining India" as its campaign theme. Although all the pre-polls predicted the coalition's return to power with a solid majority, the results mocked the pundits as the coalition was unceremoniously ousted from office. How did this happen? Election post mortem revealed that the Shining India mantra did not play well in the countryside or in the sprawling urban *chawls* (slums). In fact, the majority of the rural populace perceived not only that the new affluence had bypassed them but that economic inequalities had sharpened, given their continued destitution despite the growing wealth that was so ostentatiously displayed around them (Suri 2004). The underclass particularly resented the fact that the narcissistic self-serving urban-based nouveaux rich and those with high-level connections had benefitted disproportionately from the reforms. Their vote was a clear remainder that the fruits of the reforms needed to be more evenly distributed. It is sobering to think that India, with a current labor force of an estimated 370 million people, will need to generate in excess of 100 million jobs in the next decade alone simply to keep the unemployment rate from rising.[14]

---

[14] It is estimated that an average of 13 million people are expected to enter India's labor force each year for the next four decades (Rajan 2006).

Clearly, the high-tech and related service-sector jobs by themselves will not be enough. The stark reality is that India cannot grow into a major economy on services alone. Since the industrial revolution, no country has become a major economy without first becoming an industrial power. India will have to improve the competitiveness of its manufacturing base significantly – in particular, the backbone of its industrial manufacturing and employment, the small and medium-sized enterprises (SMEs) – and reform its highly distorted agricultural sector if it is to provide tangible benefits and meet the needs of a growing and expectant population. Thus, the most critical challenge facing India in the next decade is how to develop its manufacturing sector further to create jobs for the more than 100 million people set to join the labor force in the next decade.

Cognizant of the fact that at the center of China's successful manufacturing and export strategy has been its "open-door policy," epitomized in the "special economic zones," India has also established more than two hundred SEZs (modeled, in part, after China's SEZs) to boost manufacturing and create employment. Although India's software technology parks (STPs), created in the early 1990s, have performed quite well (in large measure because they require only basic infrastructure such as broadband satellite communication systems and backup power generation), its several export processing zones (EPZs) have failed to live up to expectations. Whereas the STPs are blessed with tax exemptions, the right to purchase hardware duty free, access to high-speed satellite links, and reliable power and infrastructure support, the EPZs have generally languished for a number of reasons. In part, foreign and domestic investors do not enjoy the kind of incentives offered in China's SEZs. Also, the limited scale and overcrowding of the EPZs in small enclaves, inflexible labor laws, poor infrastructure (especially poor links to ports and airports), cumbersome incentive packages regarding inward investment, and product reservation for small-scale industry have served to undermine the EPZs' potential as dynamic export zones.[15] Perhaps the most controversial aspect of the SEZ policy is the acquisition of land. Indian law grants state governments the power of "eminent domain" with relatively little recourse for the property owner to appeal for fair compensation. In some cases, the land acquired for the SEZs has been appropriated from local farmers under dubious means.[16] This has made SEZs a hot-button issue, eliciting massive opposition from various groups and political parties that have demanded extensive curbs

---

[15] In China, from the very beginning, the major responsibility for the SEZs rested with local and provincial governments. However, in India, until very recently, the EPZs were micromanaged from Delhi. Under these circumstances, many state governments have been averse to the idea of locating EPZs in their state.

[16] Of course, in China, the lack of democratic accountability allows the regime to give generous subsidies and tax breaks to exporters and foreign investors, besides making it easier for real estate speculators acting in tandem with corrupt party bosses to seize agricultural land.

on the SEZ initiative. In 2007, following several violent protests and deaths associated with the establishment of SEZs – the most infamous in Nandigram (West Bengal) – the Indian government decided to put on hold "indefinitely" any further expansion of SEZs.

THE "INFRASTRUCTURE DEFICIT"

Unlike China, which invested great resources to build a world-class infrastructure, India's infrastructure is decrepit, inefficient, and literally overwhelmed. Between 1998 and 2005, India's annual investment in infrastructure averaged between 3.5 to 4 percent of real GDP, compared with 8.5 percent for China (OECD 2007, 56–60). As a result, China has more than 25,000 miles of good expressway. By contrast, India has just 3,700 miles of such highways. Inadequate and inchoate road and rail networks, crippling electric-power deficit, and overcrowded ports and airports where erratic service and long delays are the norm and a drag on economic growth. The two-lane roads still comprise a major portion of India's "highway" network, and pervasive bottlenecks at Indian ports means that, on average, it takes twenty-four days for goods to travel from India to the United States compared with fifteen days from China (Ananthakrishnan and Jain-Chandra 2005). Because poor infrastructure increases costs, manufacturing industries will continue to be uncompetitive in India (even if labor laws are reformed) unless infrastructure improves. Within every major city, an efficient mass-transit system is lacking. Even the high-tech "Silicon Valley City" – Bangalore – has virtually no mass transit system. Indian blue-chip technology firm Infosys Technologies, which is based in Bangalore, spends a reported US$5 million a year on buses, minivans, and taxis to transport its 20,000 employees to and from Electronics City. Also, reliable infrastructure that better links farmers to markets will lead to more jobs, larger incomes, and increases in rural productivity. As is, the impossible traffic jams and bottlenecks caused by the crumbling transport network means that up to 40 percent of farm produce, especially vegetables, fruits, and dairy, is lost because it either rots in the fields or spoils en route to the market, making such goods more costly than they should be.

Compounding this problem is the lack of reliable electricity supply. Because India suffers from chronic electricity shortages, it is widely seen as the country's greatest infrastructure deficit. Electricity distribution and generating capacity is the purview of state electricity boards. In 2005, these boards were able to recover just 68 percent of the costs of supplying power because of government policies that offer low rates to rural customers, and its politicized system for governing electric utilities caps prices, which allows siphoning and widespread theft of power from the grid. With annual losses amounting to 1.4 percent of GDP each year, the electricity boards have been unable to invest in improving the distribution grid, let alone increasing generating capacity. As a result, in every

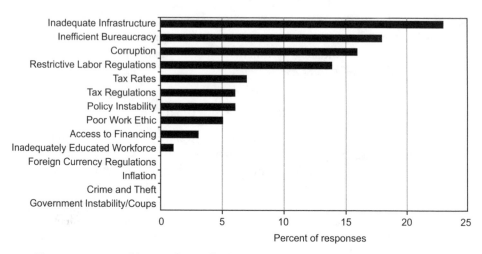

Figure 4.3. Most problematic factors for doing business in India (percent of responses). *Source:* Rajan (2006, 47).

metropolitan city and provincial town, power outages occur fairly regularly. In fact, major cities lose power one day a week to relieve pressure on the grid. In Delhi, a city of more than 15 million people, power is out every Tuesday, forcing businesses and factories to maintain expensive backup generators or simply close for the day. It is estimated that some 61 percent of Indian manufacturing enterprises rely on their own generators for power at a cost of 8 cents per kilowatt-hour, compared with around 5 cents in the United States and 3 cents in China (Mukherji 2006). The lack of an adequate power grid is the main reason no foreign company has built a semiconductor fabrication facility in the country and why Intel Corporation chose Vietnam over India as the site for a new chip assembly plant in 2007 (Figure 4.3). Clearly, India needs to move toward market pricing for energy rather than relying heavily on government subsidies (and the same can be said for China). After all, subsidies have not only accelerated rising energy demand, they have also encouraged inefficient energy use. Increasing the role of market forces in structuring domestic energy markets will also encourage greater private investment in this critical sector.

According to Bhagwati (2004), India's GDP growth would run two percentage points higher if the country had decent roads, railways, and power. Eliminating this "infrastructure deficit" is essential if India is going to be a competitor in manufacturing exports. To its credit the government is finally moving to correct this problem – for example, by working to complete the "Golden Quadrilateral," a US$12 billion initiative spanning more than 3,000 miles of four- and six-lane expressways connecting Mumbai, Delhi, Kolkata, and Chennai, as well as a new subway in New Delhi. However, this is clearly just a beginning. Even by its own estimates, the government will need to raise anywhere between US$350 to US$500 billion over the next ten years to address the country's crumbling infrastructure needs, including highways, power generators, ports, and airports. Yet there is no way the public sector alone can meet this challenge. Financial resources will have to come from the private sector – both internal and foreign. At a minimum, this will require the authorities to provide incentives and the regulatory agencies independent of government to ensure that private investors get a fair return on their investment.

THE RURAL SECTOR

Meaningful reforms (and prosperity) have bypassed India's agricultural sector, which accounts for about 25 percent of GDP and provides the livelihood for roughly 70 percent of the population (or 700 million people). This huge number reflects, in part, the limited availability of manufacturing jobs and high levels of illiteracy and endemic poverty in the countryside. About 60 percent of India's total cropped area is not irrigated, and agriculture still remains heavily dependent on the fortunes of the monsoon.[17] Moreover, with the tapering off of the Green Revolution since the mid-1980s, agriculture is characterized by low productivity with average crop yields well below world levels. Not surprisingly, growth in the agricultural sector has averaged less than 1 percent during the period 2000–6 (Tables 4.3 and 4.4). However, with annual population growth of about 1.9 percent, rural incomes have been stagnating. Cumulatively, this has slowed down both productivity growth and job creation in the rural sector.[18]

Table 4.3. *Agricultural output growth in India (percentages)*

	Food grains	Non-food grains	All
1980s	3.33	3.89	3.45
1990–91 to 2004–05	1.64	2.81	1.90

Source: RBI India Statistical Year Book (various years)

What explains this, and what have authorities done (or not done) to ameliorate this problem? The answer to the first part is a sharp decline of investment in rural infrastructure, severe price distortions in agriculture due, in large part, to the use of subsidies, and a shift by private investors away from agriculture toward more productive sectors (Gulati and Narayanan 2003). Although government spending on agriculture is by no means modest (2.1 percent of GDP in 2006–7), public investment growth has been negative since the mid-1980s

---

[17] It is during the four-month-long monsoon season that about 80 percent of the year's total rainfall occurs.

[18] The share of agriculture in the overall economy has declined from 55 percent in 1950–51, to 38 percent in 1980–81, 31 percent in 1990–91, and about 25 percent in 2000.

Table 4.4. *India: Growth rates of cereal – area, yield, and production (annual growth rate in percentages)*

Commodity	Area	Yield	Production
Wheat			
1970–90	1.7	3.0	4.8
1990–2003	0.6	1.5	2.1
Rice			
1970–90	0.6	2.3	2.9
1990–2003	−0.1	0.9	0.8
Wheat and rice			
1970–90	1.0	2.6	3.6
1990–2003	0.1	1.2	1.4

Source: Computed from *RBI India Statistical Year Book* (various years).

because more than 90 percent of public spending on agriculture is current expenditure, sustaining a wide range of subsidies and price supports. This not only has resulted in the deterioration of the fiscal position of state governments, it has also led to a sharp decline in public investment in areas critical for agricultural growth, such as irrigation, soil conservation, water and flood management, and related infrastructure. Coupled with declining private investment in agriculture, the sector has experienced a deceleration in growth since the second half of the 1990s.[19]

As discussed in Chapter 1, India's agricultural growth since the late 1960s was due to the adoption of the Green Revolution technology. However, even as the Green Revolution contributed to sharp increases in agricultural production and productivity, the strategy also led to increasing reliance on explicit subsidization of inputs such as nonorganic fertilizer and pesticides and implicit subsidization of inputs such as irrigation and power through deliberate underpricing. The subsidies on fertilizer, power, and water have grown about 6 percent annually in real terms since 1990, reaching nearly 500 billion rupees (about US$10 billion) and equivalent to about 11 percent of total agricultural output in 2002–3. Fertilizer subsidies are provided to farmers in the form of reduced prices for domestic and imported fertilizers and to the fertilizer industry in the form of preferential prices to offset their production costs. The central government's fertilizer subsidies amounted to Rs. 110 billion ($2.3 billion) or 0.4 percent of GDP in 2002–3, whereas subsidies on irrigation water were about Rs. 60 billion ($1.2 billion) in 2002–3.

---

[19] Several recent studies have found that TFP in agriculture declined between the 1980s and 1990s. In the Indo-Gangetic plains, the heart of the Green Revolution, TFP growth was 2 percent a year between 1981 and 1990 but negative between 1990 and 1996. For details see, World Bank (2003, 73–75).

The major beneficiaries of this subsidy are the inefficient domestic fertilizer industry and high-income farmers (Gulati and Narayanan 2003). However, fertilizer use needs to be complemented with a regular supply of water. Yet with the irrigation system in disrepair and little capacity for storing water, farmers have turned to pumping groundwater, using heavily subsidized electricity and leading to overexploitation of the country's groundwater. Moreover, heavily subsidized electrical power enables farmers to draw water from irrigation canals or to pump it from deep wells at relatively little cost. The overuse of urea (nitrogenous fertilizers) and water has greatly aggravated the problem of water-logging, topsoil depletion, pollution of groundwater, and a host of related environmental problems. Indeed, there is a growing realization that continued cultivation using intensive inputs cannot be sustained because of rapidly depleting water tables, as well as increasing soil salinity and micronutrient deficiencies caused by overuse of fertilizers and pesticides. Although it is generally agreed that a phased increase in fertilizer prices and imposition of user charges for irrigation and electricity would prevent abuse and raise resources to finance investment in rural infrastructure, the powerful rural interests, given their influence and control over large electoral constituencies, have made this task politically difficult. In fact, successive governments (at both the national and state levels) have generally skirted around the issue, threatening to raise prices and cut subsidies in their budget speeches, only to back down under political pressure.[20]

Further exacerbating agricultural diversification and productivity are outdated laws and regulations. For example, India's private sector as well as foreign investors cannot easily step in to fill the gap left by declining public investment. Foreign investors are prohibited from investing in agriculture, and domestic investors face many bureaucratic and legal hurdles. This is because both federal and state laws control almost every aspect of the agriculture. The federal Essential Commodities Act of 1955 still regulates the production, supply, storage, and distribution of "essential commodities," including all food crops and fiber such as cotton, wool, and jute. The state-level Agricultural Produce Marketing Acts require farmers to sell their agricultural goods in regulated markets. Compounding this, the Factories Act of 1948 restricts the scale of food processing firms, thereby severely limiting development of the industry. Although the Indian government has been trying to remove these restrictions, progress has been slow, because under India's Constitution, agriculture is regulated by the state governments. In practice, this means that the central government can only recommend national agricultural policies. Agriculture is regulated by the state governments because they have the power to ratify and implement legislation pertaining to agriculture. As a result, states

---

[20] Farmers are not the only ones who protest against cuts in subsidies. The urban middle classes are also opposed to cuts in subsidies on food grains, cooking gas, and petrol.

have created their own complex of competing and contradictory legislation. Although the more market-oriented states (e.g., Gujarat and Punjab) have removed restrictions, others such as Bihar enacted restrictive and piecemeal rules that, among other things, have served to discourage private investment. Perhaps the most pernicious are the interstate sales tax and restrictions on interstate and even interdistrict movement of agricultural commodities within a state.

Moreover, the central government's guaranteed price support for food grains – crucial in the 1960s and 1970s to give farmers the incentives to produce more food grains – has long outlived its usefulness.[21] Today, price controls are maintained for staples to ensure remunerative prices for farmers. In fact, support prices have long been fixed higher than market prices, encouraging overproduction. The result has been a substantial increase in stocks to unsustainable levels – over 60 million tons in mid-2002, against a norm of around 17 million tons – considered necessary to ensure food security.[22] Yet, paradoxically, despite these subsidies, market prices for food grains have not kept pace with input costs, resulting in widespread farmer indebtedness. Moreover, the costs associated with maintaining these stocks have been so prohibitive that it is not uncommon to let food grains and other commodities rot in poorly maintained, rat-infested storage facilities.[23] Although short-term measures such as selling excess grain below economic cost are usually undertaken, this is not a viable long-term solution. Both the central and state governments have justified the maintenance of high support prices on the grounds that it allows them to procure and subsidize the sale of certain commodities to low-income families through the public distribution system (PDS), a nationwide network of more than 460,000 "fair price shops," but such claims are not entirely valid. It is well known that the PDS administration is bedeviled by poor administration and corruption, and assistance barely reaches the needy.[24] By the Finance Ministry's own admission, more than one-third of the grain distributed through the PDS system is diverted either by the shopkeepers or through the existence of "ghost

[21] Food-grain production has increased from 50 million tons in 1950 to 152 million tons in 1983–84 to about 188 million tons in 1995.

[22] Nobel laureate Amartya Sen once noted that if all the bags of wheat and rice of the state-owned Food Corporation of India were placed end to end, they would go all the way to the moon and back. However, it should be noted that stocks went down during 2005–8 because of low production and exports.

[23] Also, the lack of cold-storage facilities contributes to substantial losses of perishable vegetables and fruits.

[24] In 1997–98, the Indian government made changes to the PDS in an effort to reduce costs and improve targeting to low-income consumers. The revamped PDS was renamed the targeted public distribution system (TPDS). Specifically, the earlier practice of offering quotas of wheat and rice to all consumers at one subsidized rate through the PDS was replaced by a system with a separate, highly subsidized rate for consumers certified as "below poverty line" and a higher rate for everyone else. Prices for wheat and rice for those below the poverty line were initially set at 33 to 38 percent below those charged under the PDS.

ration cards." The beneficiaries are usually officials in state governments, the Food Corporation of India, and wholesale and retail dealers. Yet procurement by government agencies continues to increase (food subsidies reached Rs. 242 billion (US$5 billion) in 2002–3, or 1 percent of GDP), in large part to maintain the support prices (GOI 2007).

Beyond these constraints the agricultural sector is also shielded through import and export controls, including tariffs and export restrictions. Although India has generally complied with WTO rules and had removed all quantitative barriers to agricultural imports by 2001, as well as voluntarily reduced tariffs below required levels for a number of commodities, it is important to note that it has chosen to liberalize imports for those products for which domestic production is least competitive. As noted, perhaps most pernicious are the states' own legislation and their modification and revision of federal laws to create numerous restrictions on interstate and intrastate trade. Finally, the deterioration of rural cooperative banks and extension services such as crop insurance has had a negative affect on agricultural production. A recent World Bank survey of six thousand rural households found that almost 90 percent of the marginal or landless farmers (the average land holding in India is 0.2 hectares or around half an acre) had no access to formal credit, and 70 percent had no access to a savings account in a formal financial institution (Basu and Srivastava 2005). As a result, many small and marginal cultivators have to turn to private money lenders, who charge usurious rates and provide no extension services. Not surprisingly, rural indebtedness has become a major problem fueling a spate of farmer suicides.[25] It is important to keep in mind that the pervasive fragmentation of landholdings in India is the result of population increase and traditional patterns of inheritance (under which land is divided between sons), as well as the lack of nonagricultural employment opportunities. This has prevented many rural inhabitants, especially young males, to escape the drudgery of farm work and the stifling restrictions of village life by migrating to towns and cities where they can earn supplemental incomes to start new businesses or pool their resources and consolidate family landholdings. The experience of China illustrates that agricultural development can spur growth in rural nonfarm sectors and help to cut down poverty levels. Revitalizing the rural sector will contribute to improvements in real incomes and living standards of the majority of India's population. However, political consensus on necessary agricultural reform remains elusive, in part because of the reform's potential affect on food prices.

[25] It has been estimated that about ten thousand farmers have committed suicide each year over the past decade because of their inability to repay loans taken at usurious rates of interest from moneylenders. To deal with this problem, the government has announced a $15 billion waiver of farmer loans and extended a jobs scheme ensuring one hundred days of work in a year entailing manual labor to every family demanding such work at the official minimum wage.

INDIAN FEDERALISM AND FISCAL PROBLEMS

Economists have long recognized that fiscal discipline is the cornerstone of a sound budget management. Fiscal discipline is important for both maintaining macroeconomic policy credibility and giving policy makers flexibility to manage unexpected shocks to the economy. However, India's fiscal deficit problem, ostensibly the result of an eroding revenue base and mounting spending pressures, remains a major constraint on growth. Although the combined fiscal deficit of the central and state or subnational governments, which peaked at around 10 percent of GDP in 2001 (Kochhar 2006; OECD 2007, 50), has since declined, much more needs to be done if the government is to create jobs and provide the investments needed for sustainable economic growth. The central government's claim that the fiscal deficit has been reduced to around 3.5 percent of GDP in fiscal 2008 is clearly an understatement, if not deliberately misleading, to allow the government to claim that it has met the deficit targets imposed on it by the Fiscal Responsibility and Budget Management Act (FRBMA) of 2003.[26]

However, the federal deficit is only half the story. Most analysts, including those at the International Monetary Fund, feel that the combined states and central deficit is actually around 7.5 percent of GDP, and if one is to include "off-budget" items such as oil and electricity subsidies, it is probably closer to 8.5 percent (there are considerable cross-subsidies in India; these occur in sectors in which the state is a monopoly provider on commodities such as electricity, railway and road transport, and fuel, including kerosene). Similarly, the state governments have also been engaging in creative bookkeeping by excluding electricity subsidies from their deficit estimates. Moreover, the budget figures of the central and state governments give an incomplete account of the liabilities of the public sector. Once the unfunded pension liabilities, various contingent liabilities, and the government-guaranteed debt issued by public enterprises are included, the total contingent guarantees of the state and central governments could be as high as 11 to 12 percent of GDP. Rather than fudging the numbers, the Indian government should take advantage of the strong economic growth in recent years to correct the underlying deficit by building a buffer for down cycles. To date, neither the central nor the subnational governments have been willing to implement reforms to reduce revenue expenditures, which have continued to rise.[27] As Kochhar (2006) notes, this

---

[26] The FRBMA was adopted by Parliament in August 2003 after some three years of discussion. The FRBMA sets a medium-term target of achieving a balance between current revenue and current spending by 2008 (i.e., a zero-sum revenue deficit) and limits the overall fiscal deficit for the central government to 3 percent of GDP.

[27] Accelerating the pace of divestment and privatization of public sector enterprises can help reduce the public sector deficit by raising revenues, increasing the efficiency of resource use, and helping to realign government policy in a way that contributes to faster economic

may be partly due to the fact that India has largely avoided the most negative macroeconomic effects of fiscal imbalances so far. However, this cannot be taken for granted. In this era of globalization, high deficits makes economies particularly vulnerable because it can negatively affect national savings, crowd out private investment, circumscribe the government's ability to deliver much-needed public spending, and ultimately place macroeconomic stability at risk by eroding the economy's competitiveness.

What explains the Indian government's inability to meaningfully rein in the runaway fiscal deficit? Some see it as mainly a "common-pool problem" rooted in the reality that because state governments rely on central government transfers and face no real hard-budget constraints, they have little incentive to practice fiscal restraint because they know that the central government will bail them out if they encounter economic difficulties.[28] Compounding this is India's Constitution, which delegates extensive fiscal responsibilities to the state governments but does not give them the necessary tax-raising authority.[29] The states account for about 60 percent of government spending but raise roughly 40 percent of the needed revenues, and under India's revenue pooling system, they have to share about one-third of any taxes they raise (Purfield and Flanagan 2006). Thus, at the state (and the local) level, the revenue generated falls short of what is needed to meet expenditure responsibilities. As a result, central government transfers account for a significant share of the states' revenue. A prescription that is often recommended is imposing greater fiscal responsibility on the states through borrowing caps, limits on intergovernmental transfers, allowing states to raise more of their own taxes, and the replacement of the old taxation system of interstate sales with a destination-based value-added tax (VAT).[30] In April 2005, most of the state governments finally agreed to replace the sales tax with the VAT. The VAT is to be levied at each stage of manufacture

growth. Divestment proceeds could also assist in retiring domestic debt, thereby alleviating debt-service payments.

[28] In any case, states have been able to get around hard-budget constraints by diverting resources marked for investment to current expenditures.

[29] India's tax system is based on the principle of separation, with categories being assigned exclusively to either the Center or to the states. Most broad-based taxes on income and wealth from nonagricultural sources, including corporate taxes and customs duty, are assigned to the Center. The majority of taxpayers are salaried employees working for either the government or private firms and whose taxes are deducted at the source. Although some streamlining has been carried out through simplification of the tax system and broadening of the tax base, on the whole, progress has been limited.

[30] Since 1951, twelve finance commissions have tried to create a more rational system of Center-state revenue transfers. Appointed once in five years by the president, the Finance Commission makes its recommendations on the basis of an assessment of the financial status of the Center and the states. The Twelfth Finance Commission, headed by C. Rangarajan, in its report to the president in December 2004, proposed a greater role for grants in the overall revenue transfers to ensure better targeting of expenditure in crucial areas such as education and health. The introduction of the VAT in early 2007 will help correct distortions in the domestic internal market.

of a product (albeit at each stage of value addition, the tax levied on the inputs can be claimed back from the tax authorities). If well administered, the VAT will close avenues for tax evasion, besides compelling individuals and businesses to keep proper records of their sales and purchases. Perhaps more important, the VAT, if enforced uniformly, can help with fiscal consolidation by lowering the country's fiscal deficit problem.

However, federal arrangements in India (and elsewhere) are also about political power. Purfield and Flanagan (2006, 112) note that "the split in responsibility for grant allocations between the Finance and the Planning Commission is also unusual, and it leads to coordination problems, creates incentives for states to overstate revenue needs, and allows larger and politically stronger states to bargain for larger transfers." When India was under the Congress, it was easier to sustain centralized federalism. However, in the post-1989 era, characterized by the rise of regional parties and coalition governments, the central government, in its efforts to garner subnational support, has become more willing to negotiate and bargain. In India, it is no secret that the central government's fiscal transfers to the states are more often than not discretionary, based on electoral considerations rather than economic efficiency. At the state level, the political and economic clout of the landed interests have prevented state governments from taxing agricultural land and incomes, and also ignore user charges for public irrigation and electricity. Moreover, the financing of non-developmental or populist programs and overstaffing and increases in salaries and other benefits to staff at both the Center and the states have added to the deficit woes. Finally, a "race to the bottom" that globalization can sometimes trigger is also at play. State governments, in their rush to attract investments, compete with each other by offering generous tax breaks and other fiscally costly subsidies. This in turn has generated adverse socioeconomic and political repercussions. Clearly, India's current federal institutions lag behind the imperatives of globalization.

Some analysts have argued that fiscal indiscipline is the result of the fact that economic liberalization has substantially changed the political economy of federalism in India. As noted in Chapter 2, although the Indian Constitution clearly demarcates specific responsibilities between the central government and the twenty-eight states and seven union territories that make up the Indian union, it gives the central government far greater discretionary authority in political and economic matters over the states (Austin 1966, 2003). However, a growing body of research indicates that economic liberalization and the resultant globalization of India's political economy is dramatically reordering India's "centralized federalism" in terms of both Center-state and state-market relations (Rao and Singh 2005). Specifically, the imperatives of economic liberalization and globalization have forced the Center to relinquish some of its powers over the economy to the subnational governments. Among other issues, this has resulted in the reduction of central control over industrial policy and public sector investments, allowing state governments to become more independent actors, while hard-budget constraints[31] have reduced the central government's role in allocating resources to states.[32] Given the fact that fiscal control at the Center have made state-level expenditures dependent on federal fiscal transfers, greater access to private investment (both domestic and foreign) in the post-liberalization era has given state-level governments greater autonomy vis-à-vis the central government. In fact, state governments are now able to negotiate with multilateral financial institutions and raise investments on their own.

Saez (2002) argues that economic liberalization has permanently transformed federal relations in India by increasing the developmental role of state governments. This in turn has ushered in a level of political and economic decentralization that the earlier, largely political approaches (e.g., the reforms proposed by the 1983 Sarkaria Commission) could not achieve. Saez labels this change in Center-state relations as a shift from "cooperative federalism" to "interjurisdictional competition."[33] The earlier cooperative federalism was premised on the central government's criteria for distributing resources among the state governments. However, economic liberalization policies that relax access to FDI, including portfolio equity investment (or "hot money"), has meant that the state-level governments no longer need to rely exclusively on the central government for their economic and industrial development. In their desire to attract investments, state-level governments engage in intense competition. In the process, this has transformed the original model of "cooperative federalism" based on the idea of intergovernmental cooperation between the central government and the states to interjurisdictional cooperation and competition between the states. Although subnational governments have generally benefited in the process, those that have successfully attracted investments have gained relative to those that have not. Saez shows that states such as Maharashtra and Andhra Pradesh (with relatively better infrastructure and "good governance") have become magnets for investments, whereas laggards such as

---

[31] A hard budget constraint requires subnational governments to bear the full financial consequences of their policies. Unlike soft budget constraints, in which there is a government bailout, under hard budget constraints there are no bailouts, and subnational governments that spend beyond their means risk bankruptcy. For a good overview, see Rodden (2002) and Tanzi (2000).

[32] India's state governments are constitutionally assigned expenditure responsibilities for most local public goods such as in education, health, and infrastructure. However, relative to their expenditure responsibilities, the revenue-gathering ability of state governments are more limited, with high-yielding taxes assigned to the central government. This constitutional assignment was deliberately imbalanced to give the central government greater powers to promote fairer regional redistribution and national unity.

[33] As Saez (2002) notes, although cooperative federalism produces a strong central government, this does not necessarily result in a weak or subservient provincial government. However, interjurisdictional competition is much more contentious for resources among similar tiers of government.

Bihar and Uttar Pradesh have lost out because they not only have failed to attract investment but have suffered due to dwindling central grants. To Saez, interjurisdictional competition has both increased the polarization between states and reduced the Indian state's ability to mediate interjurisdictional competition effectively and address fundamental developmental challenges.

Clearly, fundamental reform in the system of fiscal federalism is needed to instill fiscal discipline. The government's current strategy of cutting fiscal deficits without reducing public sector subsidies is no solution. Similarly, the argument that it is difficult to be fiscally tough in a fractious democracy like India is only partly valid. It is important to keep in mind that other democracies have successfully used fiscal responsibility laws to curb government profligacy; consider New Zealand under the Fiscal Responsibility Act of 1994 and the European Union under the Growth and Stability Pact of 1997. However, in the United States, neither the Gramm-Rudman-Hollings Act during the Reagan era or the Budget Enforcement Act of 1990 has encouraged bipartisan cooperation to balance the budget. Lest it be forgotten: because fiscal profligacy was the major cause of the 1991 crisis in India, the reduction in the fiscal deficit is an urgent priority.[34]

FINANCIAL SECTOR REFORMS

One of the lessons from the Asian financial crises of 1997 is that a strong and well-regulated financial sector can serve as a protective bulwark against global market turmoil. This broadly means three things: that the domestic financial sector reforms are an essential prerequisite for free mobility of capital, an effective prudential and supervisory systems must be in place to ensure financial stability, and authorities must also be able to take swift corrective actions to deal with weak or insolvent financial institutions. Crucial to both India and China's long-term growth is making their financial system more efficient at intermediating resources and directing them to the most productive investments. India has performed better than China on this front.

Over the past decade, India's overregulated financial and banking sector has undergone substantial restructuring and is now better prepared to meet the needs of the country's rapidly growing economy and the challenges imposed by the globalization of financial markets. Although financial sector reforms have included deregulation of interest rates and elimination of credit controls, strengthening regulation and supervision of the domestic banking sector on the lines of Basle Core Principles, and improving transparency and disclosure in accounting practices, policy makers have been cautious with one particular aspect of external liberalization: the liberalization of capital flows. Although

---

[34] A rather puzzling development is that despite the high fiscal deficit, the current account deficit is extraordinarily low at slightly over 1 percent of GDP.

the rationale for capital account liberalization is that it provides increased opportunity for risk diversification and greater efficiency in the allocation of resources, the problem of market failure and financial crisis associated with free capital mobility and as exemplified by the experiences of Latin America in 1980s, Asia in 1997, and Russia and Brazil in 1998 has not been lost on India's policy makers. As a result, India has adopted a gradualist approach to capital account liberalization, guided by the prudent recommendations of the "Report of the Tarapore Committee on Capital Account Convertibility."[35] For example, unlike China, Indian authorities have put in place a set of prudential regulations such as limits on assets in real estate, currencies, and stocks that has served to prevent banks from putting their balance sheets at risk. Moreover, cognizant of the fact that there could be links between the current and capital accounts, procedures have been put in place to avoid capital flows in the guise of current account transactions. Equally important, the extent and timing of capital account liberalization is sequenced with other reforms, such as strengthening of banking systems, fiscal consolidation, and trade liberalization. As R. Kohli (2005, 27) notes, the deregulation of foreign exchange transactions in India "has progressed from outright prohibition to an 'intermediate status' (of prior approval on individual case or automatic basis) to total freeing of the related transaction." Policy makers have also prudently maintained controls regarding who can borrow in foreign currency and in what form (debt vs. equity), including the volume of borrowing and length of maturity. Prudently, corporations, banks, nonbank financial institutions, residents, and nonresidents are treated differently with regard to these issues. The high fiscal deficit and a weak banking system underscores that India's macroeconomic fundamentals are not yet ready for full capital account convertibility.

Similarly, reforms in corporate governance have made India better equipped to deal with global market competition. The Securities and Exchanges Board of India, in creating an environment of improved transparency and better regulation, has allowed the Bombay Stock Exchange (BSE) to become an efficient institution. As a result, the trading of equity and equity derivatives in India has skyrocketed to record levels over the past decade, and the domestic credit markets (characterized by an active corporate and government bond market as well as credit derivative markets) are thriving. India's stock exchanges have been modernized and are now a vital source of funding for enterprises and an alternative savings venue for households. Domestic private banks are also flourishing, in large part because they offer consumers new financial products that the state-owned banks do not. The two largest and most successful of these private banks, the Industrial Credit and Investment Corporation of India Bank (ICICI) and Housing Development Finance Corporation Bank (HDFC), have

---

[35] This committee identified several macroeconomic, institutional, and market preconditions for progress in capital account liberalization in terms of fiscal, financial, and inflation indicators.

increased their market share. However, prudential rules and a bias towards FDI have served to limit Indian banks and financial institutions from investing heavily in assets and derivatives backed by U.S. subprime mortgages. As a result, the Indian financial sector has remained relatively insulated and none of the major Indian banks have much exposure to U.S. subprime debt. The State Bank of India, ICICI Bank (the country's largest private bank), the Bank of Baroda and Bank of India have exposure to international securitized debt in the form of collateralized debt obligations (CDOs) for around US$3 billion. This is tiny in comparison to ICICI's US$100 billion balance sheet. According to the Reserve Bank of India (RBI), the country's central bank, only $1 billion out of India's total banking assets of more than $500 billion was invested in toxic assets or related investments. As in China, the presence of foreign banks has yet to be felt because of government restrictions and the fact that even though the share of private and foreign banks has increased in deposits, public sector banks still dominate. By end-2007, an estimated thirty foreign banks were operating in India but represented only 7 percent of total assets. It remains to be seen how competitive both domestic private and state-owned banks are after foreign ownership rules (regarding how many branches foreign banks can have and how much they can invest in local private banks) are eased in April 2009.[36] Undoubtedly, foreign banks will provide stiff competition because they will be able to take up to 74 percent direct investment in Indian banks.

The Reserve Bank of India (RBI) has moved from a regulatory model of direct interference to governance by "prudential norms." This means that banks now have stronger disclosure norms and are under greater surveillance. The upgrade in transparency through better regulatory and supervisory systems has led to a marked improvement in banks' capital base and asset quality, with a growing number of banks actually showing profitability (Rozhkov 2006). This has helped the Indian banking system (unlike China's) to reduce the volume of nonperforming loans to a much more manageable 3 to 4 percent.[37] Yet despite these achievements, India's banking sector still remains vulnerable. At the heart of the problem (as with China) is that state ownership in the banking sector is

[36] In 2005, the Reserve Bank of India (RBI) announced its policy regarding foreign banks in India. The policy stated that foreign bank expansion would proceed in two phases. In Phase I, the RBI committed to go beyond the existing commitment of twelve new branches for foreign banks in a year and that acquisition of private banks would be permitted only in private sector banks identified for restructuring. The foreign banks could not have a stake of more than 5 percent in a private bank. In Phase II, dated to commence in April 2009 and only after reviewing the experience with Phase I, foreign banks could engage in mergers and acquisitions with private banks subject to a ceiling of 74 percent. Moreover, foreign banks' subsidiaries that had completed a prescribed minimum period of operation would be allowed to list and dilute their stakes so that at least 26 percent of the equity was held by resident Indians.

[37] India has one of the best banking sectors in Asia in terms of the ratio of nonperforming assets. India's nonperforming loan ratio, at around 4 percent of total banking assets, is far below those of China (or Japan) and most other Asian and emerging markets.

high with a few government-owned banks (particularly the State Bank of India, the country's largest commercial bank) accounting for roughly 80 percent of the banking sector. In 2005, public sector banks accounted for 75 percent of banking assets, 78 percent of deposits, and 67 percent of capital (Rozhkov 2006, 104). However, many of these state-run banks are chronically undercapitalized and burdened with substantial volumes of nonperforming loans, high personnel costs, excessive dependence on interest income, and inadequate skills to manage the variety of risks associated with free capital mobility in this era of globalization. Although public ownership of banks has created an aura of invulnerability to shocks, the high level of nonperforming loans needs to be lowered and the insolvent public sector banks restructured or closed. Despite repeated commitments to reduce government ownership from the current 51 percent to 33 percent, political pressure, especially from the powerful public sector unions, has forced the government to back off. Compounding this, although the government has taken steps toward dilution of public ownership, the fact that no individual shareholder is allowed to hold more than 1 percent of shares makes privatization a mockery. Finally, although India's financial system is more effective than China's in allocating capital and India's private sector companies have better access to funds than do those in China, there is much room for improvement. In particular, the RBI's insistence that priority sectors (agriculture and small business) receive at least 40 percent of all loans and advances and that 25 percent of all bank branches serve rural and semiurban areas tends to distort lending decisions, besides never reaching their target groups. Some three-quarters of rural households have no access to formal sources of credit, leaving them vulnerable to informal intermediaries such as moneylenders and predatory loan sharks. It also means that many private businesses, including small and medium-sized enterprises and large corporations, do not get adequate funding

This also explains why private investors are not willing to enter the banking and financial sector as long as they are characterized by weak balance sheets and pervasive government presence. It further explains why the vast majority of ordinary Indians remain wary about the country's banks, parking their savings in gold (in 2005, Indian households purchased more than US$10 billion worth of gold) and in the informal financial sector such as moneylending. Undoubtedly, the government must reduce its shareholding in public sector banks to make them more efficient and attractive. Indeed, as India's rapidly expanding economy puts even bigger capital demands on the banking sector, the banks must become better capitalized to meet domestic funding needs (especially for the majority of rural dwellers who do not have access to finance from a formal source) and to compete globally. If the government is to meet its much-touted objective of making Mumbai a world-class international financial center like Hong Kong and Singapore, India's financial sector needs to be strengthened.

Conclusion

On balance, India has managed the transition from a largely closed economy to a more open economy reasonably well. Although the transition has been slow and incomplete, the cumulative effects of the reforms have nevertheless made India an important player in the global economy. Like China, India's continental size and its huge market, resource base, and human capital give it a comparative advantage in this age of globalization. However, economic globalization also presents new challenges, and sustained benefits will require constant adaptation to the ever-shifting global marketplace. Like China, India, too, has to improve and build market-friendly institutions. Although unlike China, India has an independent judiciary and a relatively well-developed legal system that provides protection for individual and property rights, the legal system is still weak and unreliable in practice. Costly and lengthy legal proceedings, including widespread corruption, especially in the lower ranks of the judiciary, remain a serious obstacle to efficient and fair arbitration. Moreover, complex regulations coupled with poor record keeping regarding land ownership give bureaucrats and politicians excessive discretion in zoning land for various types of use, creating opportunities for rent seeking. Similarly, laws regarding intellectual property rights, especially patent laws, need to be strengthened to encourage more foreign investment. Thus, like China, India must improve its institutional capabilities to implement effectively the second-generation reforms and fully realize the benefits of globalization.

In an influential study, Rodrik and Subramanian (2004) argue that India will not only be able to sustain growth rates of 7 to 8 percent per annum over the next two decades, but will also outperform China. Their upbeat assessment is based on two variables. First, as a functioning democracy, India has much deeper institutional foundations. That is, institutional weaknesses notwithstanding, its foundations are nevertheless tested, resilient, and more transparent and accountable than China's. In such an environment, even modest policy reforms favoring the private sector are often enough to generate economic growth. Second, as faster growth of labor input leads to a faster output growth, India's working-age population, which is expected to grow over the next three decades (while China's workforce will age quite rapidly mainly because of its one-child policy), will position it as one of the world's fastest-growing economies. With between 75 million and 110 million entrants to the labor force over the next decade, India has the potential to raise its economic output dramatically. In contrast, China's declining fertility rates coupled with its "graying" population mean that the costs associated with providing services such as health care and pensions to the elderly (which is expected to account for one-quarter of China's population within the next two decades) will have a major impact on China's economy. Yet these optimistic predictions notwithstanding, India's GDP, lest we forget, is still less than half that of China's. In fact, the value of the annual growth of China's trade exceeds the total annual value of India's trade. Moreover, China's growth is remarkably broad across agriculture, industry, and services, whereas India's growth has been strongest in services; its manufacturing sector remains inefficient and uncompetitive. China will dominate its Asian neighbor for the foreseeable future.

Finally, returning back to the theme noted at the beginning of this chapter, regarding the global rise of India's business class. It is important to reiterate that India's economic renaissance is led by legions of entrepreneurs who have chosen the "exit option" by relying on their own skills and talents and expecting little from the government – in fact, expecting rather that it get out of the way. In other words, India's post-liberalization economic growth is as much about entrepreneurial freedom as it is about reducing the role of the intrusive state in the economy. As state involvement has declined, the private sector has filled the gap, unleashing the country's pent-up entrepreneurial and creative energy. Gurcharan Das (2006, 3) aptly notes, "what is most remarkable is that rather than rising with the help of the state, India is in many ways rising despite the state. The entrepreneur is clearly at the center of India's success story . . . since 1991 especially, the Indian state has been gradually moving out of the way – not graciously, but kicked and dragged into implementing economic reforms." Indeed, over the long-term, economic development that is steered by private enterprise, as is the case in India, is more sustainable and productive than that guided by the state, as in the Chinese case.

5

Sino-Indian Relations

Partners, Friends, or Rivals?

The April 2005 visit by Chinese Prime Minister Wen Jiabao and the November 2006 visit by President Hu Jintao to India, as well as the return visit by Indian Prime Minister Manmohan Singh to China in January 2008, mark an unprecedented level of interaction and dialogue between the leadership of China and India and signal a qualitative transformation in Sino-Indian relations. Following the 1962 border war, relations between the two Asian giants became estranged and increasingly acrimonious, with both sides feeling no compunction about conjuring up rather incongruous images of the other. In the shrill postwar atmosphere, each saw the other as a strategic adversary and used various strategies (e.g., China's unconditional support of Pakistan and India's close alliance with the USSR) to undermine the other's perceived designs (Sidhu and Yuan 2003). However, Prime Minister Rajiv Gandhi's (1984–88) historic visit to Beijing in December 1988 (the first such trip by an Indian leader since Jawaharlal Nehru's in 1954), followed by more high-level visits by both countries over the next several years, set in motion the process of rapprochement, the "thawing of relations," and de-escalation of tensions.[1] In fact, during the signing of the landmark Strategic and Cooperative Partnership for Peace and Prosperity in 2005 both sides effusively described their relations as "warm and friendly."[2]

---

[1] This was followed by Premier Li Peng's visit to India in 1991 and Prime Minister Narasimha Rao to China in September 1993. In November 1996, President Jiang Zemin visited India, followed by Premier Zhu Rongji in 2002. During Prime Minister Atal Behari Vajpayee's visit to China in June 2003, both sides issued a Joint Declaration of Principles proclaiming that "the common interests of the two sides outweigh their differences."

[2] In 2003, China and India signed the joint Declaration on Principles for Relations and Comprehensive Cooperation. This document outlined the principles and goals for bilateral relations – in particular, the pledge that neither country would use or threaten to use force against the other. The 2005 Strategic and Cooperative Partnership for Peace and Prosperity set the guidelines for the first bilateral strategic dialogue between the two countries. 2006 was hailed the "Friendship Year" and marked by numerous political, economic, military, scientific, educational, and cultural exchanges.

The improvement in Sino-Indo relations has also resulted in growing economic linkages between the two countries. In fact, when Prime Minister Singh announced during his China trip that India and China planned to increase their bilateral trade from US$40 billion to US$60 billion by 2010 (the initial $40 billion benchmark set during President Hu Jintao's visit to New Delhi was attained by the end of 2008), it was seen as further evidence of a deepening "economic convergence" between the two countries. It is now commonplace to suggest that the exponential pace of economic integration between the countries – underpinned by expanding investment, production, commercial, and trade networks – is irreversible and augurs well for the future of Sino-Indian relations because it is built on mutual economic interests supported by the forces of the market rather than the whims and predilections of powerful political elites. Indeed, one of India's leading journalists, Jairam Ramesh (2005), even coined a new word, "Chindia," to underscore the profound convergence in Sino-Indian relations.

The following sections illustrate that although intuitively appealing, such claims are also overly optimistic. Although there is no reason to doubt that both countries will continue to nurture and build on their relationship and that the growing economic convergence provides a powerful incentive to set aside political differences and focus on strengthening economic ties, it is nevertheless important to note that the current Sino-Indian entente remains delicate and fragile and could quickly deteriorate. This is because economic convergence and interdependence not only means cooperation, but can also lead to competition and potentially disruptive trade disputes. It is worth noting that although China enjoys robust and growing economic ties with Japan and Taiwan, its interactions with both remain the most unstable and antagonistic of all Beijing's relations. In both cases, nationalistic and political impulses seem to trump economic interdependence. Second, although both China and India will try to avoid the recriminations of the past, their long history of bitter rivalry and the fact that a number of contentious issues that divide them remain unresolved will act as a barrier toward genuine reconciliation. Compounding this is the so-called trust deficit and the lingering jaundiced perceptions and mutual suspicion that each has of the other. Third, unlike democracies with checks and balances against belligerent actions, China's highly centralized, authoritarian political system has only limited internal constraints on the use force. It seems that for the foreseeable future, Sino-Indian relations will be characterized by pragmatic cooperation but not necessarily toward any broad alignment. Rather, China and India will remain strategic competitors engaging in "soft" balancing – that is, each will try to protect and advance its own interests by aligning with the other on an issue-by-issue basis, while maintaining implicit strategic alliances against one another.

Economic Interests: Convergence and Divergence

During his India visit, President Hu Jintao put forward an ambitious Five-Point Proposal to promote closer Chinese-Indian economic cooperation. These included the following: (1) trade diversification to increase bilateral trade between the two countries to US$40 billion by 2010; (2) expand cooperation in key areas such as information technologies, energy, infrastructure, science, and agriculture; (3) improve the trade and investment environment by removing obstacles to trade and investment; (4) strengthen cooperation in the multilateral arenas (in particular, that China and India should work together to strengthen coordination in the World Trade Organization (WTO) and other multilateral economic organizations to uphold jointly the legitimate rights and interests of developing countries); and (5) actively pursue trade liberalization with the goal of establishing a preferential trade agreement and eventually a "free-trade area" between the two countries. In the area of bilateral trade, both countries have already adopted a number of measures to remove impediments to bilateral trade and investment, including the expansion of bilateral trade through preferential tariffs (more preferential than the most favored nation tariffs) on a range of products, including paper, steel, chemicals, and food. The list includes 217 Indian exports and 188 Chinese exports facing lower than average tariffs in each others market.

China and India's bilateral economic ties have greatly expanded. Bilateral trade has grown by an average of 32 percent a year since 1996. From a modest US$332 million in 1992, the two-way trade volume skyrocketed to US$2.91 billion in 2000, to US$20 billion in 2006, to US$38.7 billion by end-2007. China has become India's second largest trade partner and India is China's tenth largest trade partner. In fact, China is poised to replace the United States as India's top trading partner if the slowdown in the U.S. economy continues. Similarly, the volume of investments between the two countries has grown rapidly since 2000. Since 2005, trade in services, particularly in construction, engineering, education, entertainment, financial services, IT services, transport, tourism, and health has seen robust growth. For example, both Chinese and Indian companies have been making significant cross-border investments. In 2006, India's Infosys spent US$65 million to build business development centers in southern China, whereas China's Huawei built a "research and development center" in Bangalore. That fact that both governments have committed themselves to removing administrative barriers and simplifying the regulatory trade and investment regimes will further boost trade in these areas.[3]

No doubt, burgeoning economic ties coupled with the complementary nature of their economies has been the driving force behind the improvements

---

[3] It is assumed that once problems related to standards, certification, regulatory practices, rules, and regulations in terms of national treatment and accessibility are ironed out, trade between the two countries will increase dramatically.

in Chinese-Indian relations. China, with its large and diverse manufacturing base, and India, with its advanced IT industry (what the former premier, Zhu Rongji, once famously called the "hardware and software"), nicely complement what each country currently needs. However, economic complementarity may not last long. Already, wage rates in many of China's export-oriented labor-intensive industries are well above Indian wage rates. This is diverting manufacturing outsourcing of East Asia and (Association of Southeast Asian Nations [ASEAN]) to India. Similarly, China, which has long enjoyed a huge advantage in computer hardware, is losing its edge. India has not only caught up, it is now a real competitor.

During the Doha Round trade negotiations in the WTO, India and China made a common cause and cooperated as members of the group of thirty-three developing countries (G33) to advance the interests of developing countries in the international trading system and have maintained convergent views on a number of issues, especially in regard to the elimination of trade-distorting agricultural subsidies on agriculture. Nonetheless, they also have real differences. Specifically, with China's entry into the WTO (which requires it to reduce tariffs substantially on agricultural and industrial goods in return for permanent most favored nation status with the United States), India is likely to make gains in food grains and light manufacturing and modest growth in other sectors. However, it is also likely to lose export shares to China, especially in textiles and apparel, given India's suboptimal scales of production and labor market rigidities. In fact, the expiration of the thirty-year-old Multifiber Arrangement (MFA) on 1 January 2005, which set export quotas for textile-producing countries, has meant that China, already the world's biggest exporter of textiles, has further enlarged its market share. In India, the textile and clothing sector has long been an important part of its exports. In 2003, the sector contributed 4 percent of GDP and 14 percent to value added in manufacturing; employed 35 million people, or about 10 percent of the workforce; and amounted to $13 billion in exports, or 23 percent of total exports. Thus, any loss of market share in this critical sector will be devastating. The expiry of textiles and clothing quotas has already allowed China to gain substantial market share. During the first five months of 2005, Chinese textile exports to the United States expanded by around 60 percent, with exports in the newly liberalized product lines tripling. Similarly, exports to the European Union (EU) rose by nearly 40 percent. As a result, China now accounts for about 25 percent of both U.S. and EU textile imports, – up from 17 percent from 2004 (International Monetary Fund 2005, 48; Cerra, Rivera, and Saxena 2004).

China's currency misalignment (discussed in Chapter 7) – an issue that bedevils U.S.-China relations, is also becoming a source of contention in India. Both Indian businesses and government have blamed China's fixed exchange rate for unfairly allowing the rupee to gain value against the yuan. According to India's Trade Ministry, this has widened India's trade gap with China from

US$4 billion in 2005 to US$9.6 billion in 2006, to US$10.7 billion in 2007. Although Prime Minister Singh often repeats the mantra that China needs to create a level playing field by addressing such issues as nontariff barriers and market-related exchange rates, Indian manufactures are not so diplomatic, with some demanding that the government impose antidumping duties as high as 35 percent on Chinese imports.

Finally, India and China are currently the world's fastest-growing energy consumers. India imports some 75 percent of its energy requirements, whereas China imports about 35 to 45 percent. Their huge (and seemingly unquenchable) thirst for oil and gas has helped drive up petroleum prices to record highs (India's growing appetite for energy was a factor behind the nuclear deal with the United States, discussed in Chapter 6). It has also forced both nations to aggressively seek and lock down sources of energy around the world, especially in Africa (which holds 10 percent of global energy resources), but also in Russia, Azerbaijan, Kazakhstan, Uzbekistan, Turkmenistan, and the Middle East (Broadman 2007; Taylor 2006). Over the past decade, public sector oil companies from both countries, in particular, the Chinese National Petroleum Company (CNPC), the Chinese National Offshore Oil Company (CNOOC), and Sinopec, as well as India's Oil and Gas Company (IOGC), Oil and Natural Gas Corporation Videsh (OVL), and private sector companies such as Reliance Industries have been making large investments in oil and gas platforms in countries holding significant hydrocarbon reserves (Herberg 2007). For example, China has already concluded long-term deals with a number of countries, including Sudan, Nigeria, Angola, Myanmar, and Russia, among others. Although a bit of a latecomer to this race, India has also embarked on a similar ambitious quest and has already signed agreements with Russia, Kazakhstan, Iran, Sudan, and Libya among other nations, including the US$7 billion Iran-Pakistan-India pipeline envisioned to carry natural gas from Iran's South Pars gas field to western India, a distance of nearly 3,000 kilometers.[4] Another project in the planning stages is the Turkmenistan-Afghanistan-Pakistan-India natural gas pipeline, which envisages a flow of natural gas from the energy-rich Daulatabad fields in Turkmenistan to India.

In fact, India's state-run oil companies, including ONGC (Oil and Natural Gas Corporation) has been emulating their Chinese counterparts by following a strategy of acquiring upstream assets to guarantee energy supplies to domestic markets, besides expanding its refinery capacity. In their quest for "energy security," both China and India have been engaged in fierce competition in acquiring foreign energy assets. India has long been concerned over Chinese assistance in the construction of the massive Gwadar port in southern Pakistan

---

[4] Translating this project into reality remains a logistical nightmare because the Indo-Iran gas pipeline is estimated to cover 1,000 km in Iran, 800 km in Pakistan, and 700 km in India. Securing the pipeline will be difficult. Not surprisingly, Tehran, Islamabad, and New Delhi have only agreed with the project in principle.

and ports and pipelines in Myanmar, which India perceives as an attempt by China to gain permanent access to the Indian Ocean and to "encircle India" strategically. For its part, China views the activities of the so-called quadrilateral grouping of democratic states – the United States, Japan, Australia, and India – as designed to contain its influence in the vital Indian Ocean. In January 2006, both countries signed a landmark energy cooperation deal ostensibly aimed at preventing both from bidding against each other for energy resources, – thereby driving up prices for both. To mark their cooperation, ONGC and CNPC jointly bid for a 38 percent stake in Syria's Al Furat Petroleum, and ONGC and Sinopec combined to buy a 50-percent stake (totaling US$800 million) in Ominex de Colombia. Currently both countries hold shares in Iran's Yadavaran oil and gas field (China 50 percent, India 20 percent) and Sudan's Greater Nile Oil Project (China 40 percent, India 25 percent). However, Sino-Indian cooperation on energy has been limited to these smaller deals. Both remain very competitive in bidding for larger assets. It remains to be seen how long their cooperation lasts.

The Boundary Conundrum

During their historic meeting in 1954, Jawaharlal Nehru and Zhou Enlai reaffirmed the Five Principles of Peaceful Coexistence (or *Panchsheel*) as the foundation of Sino-Indian relations. These principles included mutual respect for each other's territorial integrity and sovereignty, nonaggression, noninterference, mutual equality and benefit, and peaceful coexistence. As a result, throughout much of the 1950s the repository of Sino-Indian relations came to be characterized by the heady nostalgic bonhomie: *Chini-Hindi bhai bhai* ("China and India are brothers"). However, the two nations share a 2,500-mile (4,000 kilometer) common border – one of the longest interstate borders in the world. The China-India boundary, which covers some of the most difficult terrain in the world, remains undefined and undemarcated either on maps or on the ground. This has inevitably led to a long-standing dispute regarding the precise territorial division between the two countries (Garver 2001).

The boundary issue took center stage following China's annexation of Tibet in 1950. India's role in providing sanctuary to the Dalai Lama and his Tibetan government-in-exile in Dharamsala only contributed to the mistrust between the two newly emerging nations. In 1956, when the CCP promulgated its first official map of China, it formally rejected the McMahon Line drawn by the British colonial authorities in 1914 to demarcate the borders between India and China. The map showed large swathes of territory held by India as being within China's borders. The Indian government reacted angrily, accusing the CCP of arbitrarily extending China's borders. In 1959, in his reply to Nehru letter, Zhou Enlai rejected the Indian prime minister's contention that the Chinese-Indian border was based on treaty and custom. Rather, he pointed out that China had never accepted the 550-mile McMahon Line drawn up during the 1914 Simla Convention, which delineated the eastern section of the border between British India and Tibet, a demarcation that Zhou considered part of the strategy of British colonial aggression against China because Tibet, a local government, did not have treaty-making authority. Chastising Nehru for using colonial-era agreement as the basis for its territorial claim, Zhou Enlai made it clear that Tibet as well as parts of China's surrounding border areas held by India was an integral part of China.

Border skirmishes, which had become a regular occurrence by mid-1959, only intensified after an Indian reconnaissance team discovered a completed Chinese road cutting across the Aksai Chin region of the Ladakh district of Jammu and Kashmir. India's ill-timed and provocative unilateral extension of its defense perimeter and "forward policy" of placing military outposts in disputed areas made the situation even worse. By the summer of 1962, India occupied 3,000 square kilometers of land in the western sector by establishing thirty-six new posts – many of them near and sometimes behind Chinese positions (Mullik 1971, 309). Frequent skirmishes, coupled with this provocative action, eventually erupted into full-scale war when the People's Liberation Army launched a preemptive assault on Indian positions on 20 October 1962. Quickly, the woefully inept (poorly trained and equipped) Indian forces suffered a humiliating defeat.[5] The Indian forces were pushed back to within 48 kilometers of the Assam plains in India's eastern sector, while the Chinese forces occupied strategic areas in Ladakh. On 21 November, China declared a unilateral cease-fire and withdrew 20 kilometers behind its new line of control, its unabashedly jingoistic press declaring victory by noting that the effete Indian intruders were taught a good lesson by the valiant People's Army. Unlike the India-Pakistan border dispute in 1947, when a formal peace agreement was signed following the conflict and the cease-fire line was converted into the Line of Control, China and India did not sign a formal peace agreement, and the location of the Line of Actual Control (LAC) remains under dispute today (see Map 5.1). In the aftermath, diplomatic relations were downgraded to a bare minimum, and all manner of formal contact between the two countries was suspended. It also led to the growing enmity between the two countries, before the thawing of relations following Rajiv Gandhi's historic visit to China in 1988.

The improvement in Sino-Indian relations that followed Rajiv Gandhi's visit was largely due to a major Indian "concession." India dropped its decades-long insistence that there could be no real improvement in relations between the two countries until Beijing returned all the territories forcibly taken in the 1962 war. India now tacitly adopted a "broad position," a euphemism that meant India no longer held other areas of interaction hostage to a settlement of the

---

[5] There is a large body of scholarship on this issue, including Garver (2001), Hoffmann (1990), Mansingh (1998), Vertzberger (1984), and Whiting (1975).

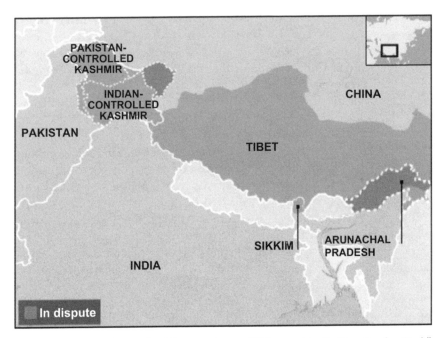

Map 5.1. China–India Border Dispute. *Source:* "China and India Sign Border Deal," BBC News, 11 April 2005 news.bbc.co.uk/2/hi/south_asia/4431299.stm#map (accessed 29 March 2008).

border issue. Finally, in 2005, it seemed that a breakthrough on a number of contentious issues, including the intractable border issue, was in sight. India was ready to address Chinese concerns over Tibet by reiterating its stance that the Tibetan Autonomous Region is part of China and not allowing Tibetans living in India to engage in "anti-China" activities. For its part, China agreed to resolve the Sikkim issue (Sikkim was incorporated into the Indian Union in 1975,[6] drawing sharp condemnation from Beijing, which regarded Sikkim as an independent state), by showing Sikkim as part of India in its official maps and recognizing India's right of access to the trade route through the Nathu La Pass on the China-Sikkim frontier with India.[7] However, rather unexpectedly, China upped the ante by demanding further territorial concessions, and India replied in kind stating that some boundary matters were "nonnegotiable." In effect, border negotiations are now back to square one. The core area of contention remains India's long-standing claim that

[6] Sikkim, formerly an independent kingdom bordering Nepal, Tibet, Bhutan, and India, became India's twenty-second state in 1975 through a popular referendum.

[7] The Nathu La Pass, a key mountain passage on the border between India's Sikkim state and China's Tibet Autonomous Region, is China's only direct trade link with India. It is one of the few areas along the disputed frontier where troops from both sides have remained deployed in close proximity since the 1962 war. In July 2006, the pass was reopened after forty-four years.

China is illegally occupying some 38,000 square kilometers of Indian territory in northwestern Jammu and Kashmir known as Askai Chin (which has been held by China since the 1962 war). Provocatively, this border area, known as the Actual Line of Control, borders the Indian state of Himachal Pradesh, where the Tibetan spiritual leader, the Fourteenth Dalai Lama, has established his government-in-exile in the town of Dharamsala. In addition, India claims 5,180 square kilometers of Jammu and Kashmir ceded to China by Pakistan under a 1963 Sino-Pakistan boundary agreement. The ceded area, known as the Trans-Karakoram Tract, subsequently became part of the land bridge linking Pakistan to China's Xinjiang along the Karakoram Highway. For its part, Beijing claims sovereignty over 90,000 square kilometers of the Sumdorong Chu Valley in India's northeastern state of Arunachal Pradesh, including a nondescript area known as Tawang, which is central to Tibetan Buddhism because it is believed that the sixth Dalai Lama was born there.[8] To make matters even more complicated, New Delhi has obliquely suggested that the area around the sacred Mount Kailash-Mansarovar in Tibet be retuned to India, because it was for centuries a sacrosanct Hindu pilgrimage site.

In May 2007, the passions surrounding the borders were again magnified when a Indian Administrative Service official from the state of Arunachal Pradesh was denied a visa by the Chinese government to attend a mid-career training program that China was hosting on the grounds that he was residing in Chinese territory and did not require a visa. In the tit-for-tat that characterizes the boundary dispute, the Indian government immediately stopped the 107-person official delegation from going to Beijing and in June 2007 extended an invitation to Taiwan's opposition Kuomintang Party presidential candidate Ma Ying-jeou to visit India. Predictably, China voiced its opposition to Ma's visit and called on India to abide by the "One China Policy" (Ganguly 2008). To further show its displeasure, in August 2007, Beijing demanded that the Indian government remove its military bunkers situated in a junction between Sikkim, Bhutan, and Tibet, claiming that these were located on Chinese territory – thereby implicitly retracting its earlier-declared policy of treating Sikkim as part of India.

Eventually, in January 2008, during Manmohan Singh's visit, China recognized "Sikkim State" as part of the "Republic of India" in its official map. The two countries also reached agreement on the "modalities" to implement the confidence-building measures along the LAC by enhancing contacts between

---

[8] During 1986–87, when discussion over the status of the Sumdorong Chu Valley became heated, China threatened to "teach India a lesson," and both sides mobilized several divisions. Eventually, a political compromise was reached, although full withdrawal of forces took place only in August 1995. It should be pointed out that India did show some willingness to give up its claims to the Aksai Chin provided that China give up its claims in Arunachal Pradesh and recognize the McMahon Line, just as Beijing had accepted Tibet's British-drawn boundaries with Afghanistan and Myanmar.

the two militaries, giving advanced information of planned exercises, adding border meeting points along the LAC, and eschewing the use of force in any "face-to-face" encounters. Yet despite some three decades of continuous negotiations, only modest progress has been made. India and China remain as divided as ever on the core territorial issues. Clearly, the border issue will remain a major sticking point in Sino-Indian relations despite their growing economic ties. For two emerging powers like China and India with competing ambitions, dispute about overlapping borders is about more than just land. It is also about power, pride, prestige, and a sense of national honor and propriety. Compounding this is the reality that both countries still harbor deep mistrust and suspicion toward the other's strategic intentions. This is what led to the 1962 war over an uninhabitable piece of ground that is covered year-round by permafrost. Indeed, if the 1962 war holds any lesson, it is that a minor boundary dispute still has the potential to trigger unexpected outcomes. Therefore, the possibility of armed confrontation over borders and territory cannot be ruled out completely.

The Pakistan Factor in Sino-Indian Relations

It is important to note that China has been able to improve its relations with India without compromising its relations with India's neighbor and arch-rival, Pakistan – with whom India has fought four wars: 1948, 1965, 1971 (which led to the creation of Bangladesh), and 1999.[9] As Garver (2005, 222) succinctly notes, "improvement of Sino-Indian relations [has] paralleled continued Chinese assistance to Pakistan's efforts to augment its national capabilities." Malik (2003a, 36), more bluntly notes: "interestingly, China's attempts to improve ties with India since the early 1990s have been accompanied by parallel efforts to bolster the Pakistani military's nuclear and conventional capabilities vis-à-vis India" (also Gill 1992). China and Pakistan, who refer to each other cordially as "all-weather friends," have long-standing political and strategic ties – which, again, both countries refer to as a "special relationship." At least since the mid-1960s, China has been Pakistan's largest defense supplier, transferring equipment and technology to Pakistan's conventional and nuclear weapons and ballistic missile programs. This has served to greatly enhance Pakistan's power and influence in the South Asian strategic balance. India sees China's unconditional support of Pakistan – in particular, Beijing's assistance in helping Pakistan acquire sophisticated nuclear military capabilities – as the

---

[9] India and Pakistan fought for approximately eight weeks in the Kargil sector of the Line of Control in 1999. In addition, India and Pakistan have come close to war on at least two other occasions: in late 1986 during India's military exercise code named "brass tacks" (when the Indian military initiated a massive military exercise involving an estimated 250,000 troops and 1,500 tanks, and concluding with a simulated counteroffensive attack, including Indian Air Force strikes into Pakistan) and then again in 2001–2 after the terrorist attack on India's Parliament on 13 December 2001.

key factor behind Pakistan's intransigence and adventurism, as reflected in its cross-border infiltrations in Kashmir and elsewhere in the region. To New Delhi, by deliberately altering the balance of power on the Indian subcontinent, China is attempting a de facto "encirclement of India" and thereby preventing India from achieving its aspiration in the South Asian region.

No doubt, China recognizes India's dominant role in South Asia and shares Pakistan's deep apprehension and mistrust of India's strategic ambitions. Therefore, part of Beijing's strategy is to ensure that Pakistan remains a strong military counterweight to India. This dynamic in which China views Pakistan as a useful balance to Indian power in the South Asian region has led Stephen Cohen (2001) to conclude that China is pursuing a classic balance-of-power strategy by supporting Pakistan. Predictably, India remains deeply wary of China's long-standing relationship with Pakistan and has repeatedly voiced its concerns regarding Beijing's assistance to Pakistan's conventional and nuclear weapons program and, more recently, its building of military bases throughout the region under the guise of "projects," such as China's role in a project to upgrade the Pakistani deep-sea port at Gwadar. To India, it is the "China connection" in the Pakistani nuclear program that is most troubling. New Delhi has repeatedly pointed out that China, as a nuclear weapon state, despite its commitment to the Nuclear Non-Proliferation Treaty (NPT), has not only turned a blind eye but actively supported the proliferation activities of Pakistani nuclear scientist Dr. Abdul Qadeer Khan. Although Beijing denies this, given Khan's close links with China's nuclear establishment, it seems inconceivable that the Chinese were unaware of Pakistan's clandestine nuclear network and its business activities with North Korea, Iran, and Libya. Indeed, in the face of growing evidence to the contrary, both China and Pakistan have denied any state sponsorship, blaming the proliferation on rogue elements within the Pakistani nuclear establishment (Malik 2003b).

For its part, China has long-rejected what it see as India's "paranoid" concerns about China's intentions. Rather, China maintains that it seeks good "neighborly relations" with all the nations of South Asia as reflected in its official support of the South Asian Association of Regional Cooperation. Beijing maintains that its growing diplomatic and economic activities in South Asia are designed to forge closer relations with all countries in the region and that India's charge of "encirclement" is more a reflection of its own "hegemonism" and the desire to reinforce only an exclusive Indian presence in the subcontinent. In particular, Beijing rejects the claim that its support of Pakistan is unconditional, pointing out that it has made every effort to address New Delhi's concerns over China's defense ties with Pakistan. For example, Beijing has long emphasized the bilateral nature of the Kashmir dispute and the need to settle the dispute peacefully, including its refusal to support or endorse Pakistan's incursions into Kargil in 1999 and reiterating the sanctity of the Line of Control in Kashmir. Much to the chagrin of New Delhi, Beijing has always claimed that the Chinese-Pakistani relationship is not targeted at India. Rather, China is prepared to use its strong ties with Islamabad to facilitate diplomatic reconciliation between Islamabad and New Delhi – provided, of course, that both sides are willing to talk in good faith. As Beijing likes to remind New Delhi, China's neutrality during the 1999 Kargil war demonstrates its "balanced" South Asia policy.

Despite New Delhi's implicit demand, it is clear that China is not prepared to improve its relations with India at the cost of its ally, Pakistan. After all, Pakistan not only provides a significant geostrategic advantage, the alliance with Pakistan also offers other important benefits. Pakistan is vitally important to China's energy security because it provides access to the Persian Gulf region. Moreover, as the world's most populous Muslim nation, Pakistan's often unconditional diplomatic support of China in the Islamic world (and indeed in international forums) gives Beijing "strategic depth" in its relations with the Islamic nations. Finally, there is no evidence that China plans to abandon its national security strategy based on the principle of what Malik (2003b) calls "containment through surrogates." In other words, China will use its well-worn strategy of countervailing its perceived rivals and enemies through proxies.

China-India and the Nuclear Equation

China conducted its first nuclear test in 1964 and is a recognized nuclear weapon state under the NPT. Over the past four decades, it has developed a sophisticated nuclear weapons infrastructure with advanced strategic and tactical nuclear arsenal. It is widely believed that since the mid-1960s, China has been a major supplier of sensitive nuclear and missile weapons technology to several countries despite its commitments to abide by NPT regulations. In particular, Chinese state-owned corporations have continued to engage in illicit nuclear arms transfers to Pakistan, Iran, North Korea, and Libya (before Libya abandoned its quest in 2005; Ganguly and Hagerty 2005; Tellis 2006).

Although India's desire to tap nuclear technology goes back to the nationalist era, it was the United States that helped India develop its nuclear energy capacity under the Atoms for Peace program in the early 1950s. U.S. assistance in terms of technology and nuclear fuel enabled India to build its first advanced nuclear reactor, and financial support allowed Indian scientists to upgrade their skills at U.S. research facilities and nuclear laboratories. However, India's refusal to sign the NPT because of its contention that the treaty was discriminatory effectively ended this cooperation. After India tested its "peaceful nuclear bomb" in 1974 – underscoring that countries could develop nuclear weapons with technology transferred for peaceful purposes – the gulf between the United States and India widened further. The United States, along with other countries – most notably Canada, which had provided technical and financial assistance to India – refused any further cooperation until New Delhi signed the NPT and renounced nuclear weapons. Faced with tough sanctions and denied access to advanced Western technologies such as supercomputers and space and missile technology, India embarked on the ambitious task of building its nuclear program on its own. Over the years, even as it upgraded its nuclear facilities, India chose not to become an overt nuclear weapon state by engaging in weapons testing. Moreover, although not a member of the NPT and related treaties and agreements (most notably, the Comprehensive Test Ban Treaty, or CTBT) that make up the nonproliferation regime, India maintained an exemplary nonproliferation record in preventing the spread of sensitive nuclear materials and technologies to third parties.[10]

Between 11 and 13 May 1998, India ended its quarter-century of self-imposed nuclear abstinence by detonating five nuclear weapon devices. Unlike the 1974 tests, the 1998 tests unambiguously demonstrated India's scientific and technical capability to develop and test the most modern and lethal (thermonuclear, fission, and low-yield) nuclear weapons. To the Indian government, the tests validated that India was now a nuclear weapon state with an operational nuclear deterrent in place. Initially, the official reasons for the tests included that India could no longer keep its "nuclear option" open indefinitely without seriously degrading the technical and material makeup of the prototype weapons and that India had no choice given the failure of the "nuclear-have states" to engage in meaningful disarmament, let alone make nuclear war "obsolete" as agreed under the NPT. However, there were other considerations. In particular, the indefinite extension of the NPT in 1995 and the successful conclusion of the CTBT in 1997 increased, for India, the costs accruing to its traditional posture of ambiguity ("keeping its options open") with regard to nuclear weapons.[11] In addition, the new Hindu-nationalist government (the Bharatiya Janata Party), which had long called for a more muscular foreign policy, used the opportunity afforded by Pakistan's test firing of the Ghauri missile acquired from North Korea (via China) finally to resume nuclear testing.

No doubt, the most pressing factor was the perceived threat from China. In a letter sent by Prime Minister Atal Bihari Vajpayee to President Bill Clinton – which was mysteriously leaked to *The New York Times* – Vajpayee defended the nuclear tests by pointing out that China's rapidly expanding nuclear

---

[10] The CTBT prohibits all explosive tests that lead to a nuclear chain reaction.

[11] In 1995, the Clinton administration managed (admittedly to New Delhi's surprise) to extend indefinitely the NPT. This implied that India would remain forever outside the elite group of treaty-legitimized "nuclear weapon states." Indefinite extension also meant India lost the bargaining power embodied in its covert nuclear weaponry: because all the signatories unanimously agreed to the NPT's indefinite extension in its original form, India could no longer demonstrate its nuclear assets to secure its inclusion among the legitimate nuclear weapon states.

capabilities and its adversarial posture made it a potential apocalyptic threat to Indian security. Vajpayee noted the "deteriorating security environment" in the subcontinent in which India was threatened by "an overt nuclear weapon state on our borders, a state which committed armed aggression against India in 1962. . . . To add to the distress that country has materially helped another neighbour of ours to become a covert nuclear weapon state. At the hands of this bitter neighbour we have suffered three aggressions in the last fifty years." Once this letter became public, it seemed that the diplomatic equipoise on the real reason behind the tests was broken. Indian Defense Minister George Fernandes's inflammatory yet matter-of-fact, remark that China is India's "potential threat number one" and that a strategic review merited India to exercise its nuclear option made matters worse. Similarly, Jaswant Singh (1998, 44), a senior advisor to India's prime minister, wryly noted that "India was left with no option but to go in for overt nuclear weaponization. The Sino-Pakistani nuclear weapons collaboration – a flagrant violation of the NPT – made it obvious that the NPT regime had collapsed in India's neighborhood."

Predictably, the Chinese government reacted with indignation, taking exception to the "outrage" and the "slander" propagated by senior Indian officials and vociferously professing its innocence. China's Foreign Ministry responded by swiftly condemning India's nuclear tests and calling for the international community to adopt a unified stance and demand that India immediately stop both further testing and development of nuclear weapons. The ministry issued a harshly worded statement on 14 May scornfully condemning the tests and noting that "in disregard of the strong opposition of the international community, the Indian government conducted two more nuclear tests. The Chinese government is deeply shocked by this and hereby expresses its strong condemnation. This act of India's is nothing but outrageous contempt for the common will of the international community. . . . It will entail serious consequences to the peace and stability in South Asia and the world at large."[12] China explicitly rejected as "totally unreasonable" India's stated rationale that it needed nuclear capabilities to counter a "Chinese threat." In strong words, China denied Indian allegations that Pakistan had developed nuclear weapons through cooperation with China, noting that Sino-Pakistani cooperation was entirely based on peaceful ends and that "nuclear-cooperation" met with all international accords. Vice Premier Qian Qichen angrily charged: "This gratuitous accusation by India against China is solely for the purpose of finding excuses for the development of its nuclear weapons."[13] Not surprisingly, when Pakistan conducted its own series of nuclear tests two weeks later, China declared that Pakistan's tests were a necessary "reaction" to India's "hegemonic designs" and accused India of exacerbating tensions in South Asia.

[12] "China's Statement on India's Nuclear Tests," *Beijing Review*, June 1–7, 1998, p. 7.
[13] "India's Nuclear Tests Show Fear of China," *Wall Street Journal*, 15 May 1998, p. A13.

China demanded that India apologize for its "slander" and cancelled a top-level Sino-Indian meeting scheduled for November 1998. However, in sharp contrast to the United States and Japan, which led the international community in imposing economic sanctions against India and Pakistan, China did not impose sanctions on either India or Pakistan.

However, by early December 1998, the passions began to cool, and the official acrimony and discord ceased with both China and India trying to soft pedal their differences and renew their "friendly" relations. In April 1999, China and India renewed their top-level "Joint Working Group" meeting for the first time in twenty months. The meeting avoided contentious issues such as the border dispute, India's nuclear tests, and China's nuclear and missile assistance to Pakistan. Instead the meeting focused on strengthening the "friendly, good neighborly relations" between the two countries. Indeed, to show its good neighborly intentions, China not only refrained from overt support for Pakistan but remained neutral during the India and Pakistan conflict in the summer of 1999. Chellaney (1998–99) argues that following India's nuclear tests, both the United States and China began to take India seriously as a "rising power." That is, by showing that it now had a viable nuclear deterrent, India finally laid to rest the reputation of weakness that has long bedeviled it – that is, its glaring structural weaknesses and an inability to project power. With the tests, India served notice that it now possessed the material capabilities to match its bold aspirations.[14]

Arguably, with its advanced nuclear and missile tests, India changed the Sino-Indian military equation in fundamental ways. India's bold nuclear doctrine and its aggressive indigenous development and foreign acquisition of long-range ballistic missile and satellite capabilities presents China with the unwelcome prospect that India now has the capability to militarily retaliate against all of China's major cities and key infrastructure.[15] Against this background and cognizant of the fact that a regional Indo-Pakistani war can unwittingly drag China into the conflict, Beijing's security relationship with

[14] It seems that Chellaney (1998–99) exaggerates somewhat. Tellis (2001), in his exhaustive book, *India's Emerging Nuclear Posture*, demonstrates that India does not currently possess or seek to build a ready nuclear arsenal. Rather, India's objective is to create what he calls a "force in being." This implies a nuclear deterrent that consists of available, but dispersed, components (unassembled nuclear warheads), with their components stored separately under strict civilian control and dedicated delivery systems kept either in storage or in readiness away from their operational areas. However, all can be brought together as rapidly as required to create a usable deterrent force when needed. See also Basrur (2006).

[15] India's nuclear doctrine is based on the principle that it will adhere to a policy of "no nuclear use" against "nonnuclear powers" and "no first use" against nuclear adversaries – albeit India makes exception against biological and chemical weapons. In effect, this implies that nuclear weapons will be used only in response to a nuclear attack on India. India also holds the position of massive retaliation in response to a nuclear attack to inflict "unacceptable damage" to the enemy. Tellis (2001) argues that India's commitment to this policy is not likely to change as long as India maintains conventional military superiority over Pakistan.

Pakistan has become more nuanced, if not cautious. Of course, Beijing's primary (and valid) concern is that given Pakistan's weak command and control structure of its nuclear facilities and its "first-use" doctrine, an inadvertent use of nuclear weapons could result of a deadly escalation engulfing the region and beyond. Although China has not changed its long-held policy vis-à-vis Kashmir (that the 1972 Simla Agreement should remain the framework for resolving the outstanding issue and that the eventual resolution of the conflict should be through dialogue and negotiation), Beijing no longer gives reflexive carte blanche support to Pakistan. Because Beijing remains highly sensitive to any developments in the region that might have serious security implications, the quick Indian-American rapprochement (by mid-2000, the Clinton administration had lifted most of the sanctions on India and moved to build a "strategic partnership," including providing India with spaceflight, satellite, and missile defense technology) was troubling. As is discussed in the next chapter, this was clearly reflected in the recent U.S.-India nuclear accord, which dramatically shifted from a U.S. position of "nuclear rollback" to one of de facto recognition of India as a nuclear state.

China and India in the Asian Region and Beyond

Both China and India have doubled their efforts to engage in diplomacy and trade with countries both within and beyond their traditional strategic domain. As India concentrates on economic development, it has not only sought political reconciliation with Pakistan but also improved relations with its smaller neighbors. To this effect, India has tempered its usual habit of unilateralism when dealing with smaller states with a more conciliatory and multilateral approach. India recognizes this is essential to achieve its stated goal of promoting regional economic integration on the subcontinent into a single ASEAN-style market. Moreover, recognizing the importance of the Indian Ocean littoral (harking back to the vision of Lord Curzon, the British viceroy who called for India's leadership in the region stretching from Aden to Malacca), India has been aggressively expanding its linkages with countries beyond its traditional sphere of influence such as Japan, South Korea, Australia, and Southeast Asian states, raising eyebrows in Beijing.[16] High-level visits and growing economic and defense ties such as the Japan-India Strategic and Global Partnership and rapidly expanding Indian and ASEAN security ties, especially the Indian-Vietnamese defense cooperation, are viewed as potentially impinging on China's territorial interests (China has unresolved border

[16] Because the Indian Ocean affords direct access to the Indian subcontinent, it constitutes an important security area to India. China, and to a lesser extent Pakistan, through their naval bases and relations with the littoral states on India's periphery, represent a consequential challenge to Indian security. Not surprisingly, India maintains a strong naval presence throughout the northern Indian Ocean.

dispute with Vietnam), thereby making a final resolution of the territorial disputes in the South China Sea even more difficult. India has also sought new
ways to improve its relations with the Islamic world beyond Pakistan (even
as it renews its engagement with the once-scorned Israel). India is home to
nearly 150 million Muslims, and Islamic nations have always been an important
factor in its foreign policy. However, if in the past this merely meant supporting the positions of the Arab and the Islamic world in international forums,
today India's relationship with the world of Islam is being deepened on the
basis of economic and commercial cooperation and energy security, including cooperation in combating religious extremism and terrorism. Finally, like
China, India is also making a determined effort to reconnect with its erstwhile
Third World friends – but within a framework that emphasizes economic relations and energy diplomacy rather than the traditional notion of Third World
solidarity through a nonaligned movement.

Not to be outdone, China's more collegial or "proactive" regional posture
is designed to change the perception and image of China from a "revisionist"
power into a "status quo" power – one reflected in virtually all of Beijing's core
policy spheres, expressed politically, multilaterally, economically, and militarily
(Bijian 2005). Politically, China has attempted to improve its bilateral relations
with its neighbors, and today many formerly antagonistic relationships (with
Russia, India, Vietnam, South Korea, and Indonesia) have greatly improved.
For example, since the disintegration of the Soviet Union, China and Russia
have greatly strengthened their relations. During the 1990s, they largely resolved
their boundary disputes and demilitarized their lengthy, 2,640-mile shared border. Following the signing of the 2001 Treaty of Good-Neighborly and Friendly
Cooperation, which affirmed their commitment to enhanced bilateral cooperation, trade between the two countries has flourished, with the Chinese purchasing billions of dollars worth of sophisticated weapons systems from Russia.
Multilaterally, China's "soft power" diplomacy or "constructive engagement"
with ASEAN and the Shanghai Cooperation Organization, designed to settle
long-standing territorial disputes and to demilitarize borders with countries in
Central Asia, has also paid dividends. For example, in the mid-1990s, disputes
over islands in the South China Sea intensified when China built structures on
Mischief Reef, an islet claimed by the Philippines. ASEAN ministers responded
angrily to this provocative move. Realizing the potential dangers of unilateralism, Beijing made a complete about-face in the late 1990s, renouncing
force and worked with ASEAN to establish a universally accepted code of
conduct for the region. China's growing engagement with the Asian region is
most evident in the expanding economic ties. China has repeatedly assured
ASEAN that it is committed to promoting economic prosperity in the region
and, along with Japan and South Korea, has been working with ASEAN in
the ASEAN+3 process. ASEAN+3 finance ministers launched the Chiang Mai
Initiative, a system of bilateral and multilateral currency swap arrangements

designed to provide liquidity in the event of short-term financial crises and the Asian Bond Market Initiative to link the regional economies through the creation of a pan-Asian bond market. In November 2002, China and ASEAN signed the Framework Agreement on Comprehensive Economic Cooperation. Its main stated objectives are the following: economic, trade, and investment cooperation; progressive liberalization of trade in goods and services; creation of a liberal and transparent investment regime; and closer economic integration within the region. Under the agreement, the parties have agreed to work toward the establishment of a free trade area between China and ASEAN within ten years. According to official Chinese customs statistics, trade between China and the rest of Asia topped US$495 billion in 2003, up 36.5 percent over 2002. Today, nearly half of China's total trade volume is intraregional, and unlike China's trade with the United States and Europe, it is relatively balanced (Shambaugh 2005).

In the security sphere, although considerable anxiety remains about the pace and scope of China's military modernization (discussed in Chapter 8), including Beijing's refusal to renounce the use of force against Taiwan, Beijing has nevertheless become much more sensitive to regional concerns and has worked hard to assuage them. Specifically, China has embarked on a series of confidence-building measures of four principal types:

- Bilateral security dialogues have opened with a number of key neighboring countries, including Australia, India, Japan, Mongolia, and South Korea.
- Military-military exchanges such as joint naval exercises with a number of countries, including India, have begun.
- ASEAN and China have signed a declaration on a "code of conduct" to resolve offshore territorial disputes over the Paracel, Spratly, and Senkaku Islands peacefully, based on international law. Even more dramatic, China, under the rubric of the ASEAN Regional Forum (ASEAN's mechanism for security discussion), has participated actively in creating a regional cooperative security community.
- It has increased military transparency, as demonstrated by its publication of several defense "White Papers" and invitations to observe Chinese military exercises.

China's "strings of pearls" strategy to establish naval bases stretching from Southeast Asia to Somalia, including in strategic locations in Myanmar, Bangladesh, the Maldives, and Pakistan, has generated considerable anxiety in India. China's growing links with Myanmar is particularly galling to India, and managing China-India competition in Myanmar will become a bigger challenge in the coming years. Both countries have deep-rooted historical, political, and economic ties to Myanmar. However, in recent years, China has forged far better relations with Myanmar's ruling military junta. Then Burma was the first non-Communist country to recognize the People's Republic in 1949, and China has been a staunch supporter of the military junta, providing it with much-needed military hardware and diplomatic support in international forums, as well as financing massive infrastructure links to facilitate cross-border trade and commerce (both legitimate and illicit). In fact, it is no exaggeration to say that China considers Myanmar to be securely within its sphere of influence and sees India's moves to increase its presence there as a direct challenge. China's strong and expanding presence in Myanmar is a major geostrategic headache for India. The construction of massive Chinese-funded ports and bases around Myanmar only increases India's concerns that China might someday challenge it in the Indian Ocean, which straddles the vital sea lanes linking the Persian Gulf to Asia. Beyond these geostrategic imperatives, Myanmar also offers lucrative commercial opportunities. More than anything else, however, both countries are pushing hard to strengthen their presence in Myanmar (of course, at the exclusion of the other), because of Myanmar's valuable natural resources. With proven natural gas reserves of about 2.50 trillion cubic meters, Myanmar is increasingly at the center of a growing competition between India and China because both seek access to this energy resource to fuel their booming economies. Indeed, as both India and China move to access energy supplies from Myanmar, Iran, and elsewhere, competition between the two to gain preferential access to potential energy resources underscores the potential for conflict.

China on India's United Nations Bid

China is one of the founding members of the United Nations (UN) and a permanent member of the Security Council from its creation in 1945. It is one of the current five veto-yielding permanent Security Council members, along with Russia, the United States, France, and Britain. In 1949, after the Chinese Communist Party seized power, China's seat was taken away but was later given back in 1971. India always maintained that the permanent Security Council seat was rightfully China's, even following the 1962 war. Over the past few years, India has been aggressively seeking a full-fledged permanent membership with veto power in a "revamped" United Nations Security Council. In fact, India, Brazil, Germany, and Japan have formed a unified front to lobby for permanent seats in the United Nations, arguing that the Security Council can gain authority only by being more representative. Although China has repeatedly stated that it wants India to play a "greater role in the United Nations, including the Security Council," to date, it has offered only tepid support for India's bid. In particular, Beijing has declined to clarify whether it is prepared to back a veto-wielding permanent seat for India, claiming that consultations with other permanent members are still ongoing. However, British Prime Minister Gordon Brown has publicly stated that the

Security Council's permanent members need to be increased to include India, Japan, Germany, and Brazil, plus an African country. Under Brown's plans, the new members would not initially have veto powers similar to the existing five. Instead, places on the Security Council would be offered without veto powers during the first (undefined) phase, followed by subsequent changes that would include veto rights. Of course, India is closely following China's position on this vital issue.

China and India: The Challenges Ahead

Although Sino-Indian relations have greatly improved over the past decade, obstacles to future improvements remain. Unresolved territorial disputes, China's relations with Pakistan, and growing competition, if not rivalry, in the areas of energy and regional influence can quickly derail these hard-won gains. In fact, even the occasional ill-timed or provocative statement from either side, such as China's assertion that the entire Arunachal Pradesh state is Chinese territory, can unravel the progress because both sides are extremely sensitive about their respective spheres of influence. Malik (2003, 3) succinctly captures the fragility of Sino-Indian relations by noting that both China and India are "non-*status-quoist* powers: China in terms of *territory*, power and influence; India in terms of *status*, power and influence. The fact that China has advanced further than India in achieving its goals largely explains the competitive relationship between India and China.... The combination of internal uncertainties and external overlapping spheres of influence forestall the chances for a genuine Sino-Indian rapprochement."

Although it is true that both China and India have assuaged each other (as well as many of their neighbors), concerns about their long-term ambitions remain. Despite growing Sino-Indian economic ties, the fact that Indian policy makers talk less and less about the potential "Chinese threat" and the Indian government is accommodating itself to China's rise, India remains deeply wary of China's intentions. Seemingly, their growing ambitions, competing interests, and long history of distrust and suspicion cannot be easily overcome, not even through vigorously growing economic and diplomatic linkages. With the discrediting of the Nehruvian ideas of nonalignment and unconditional cooperation, India's strategic approach to China has become more pragmatic, if not calculated – a trend that will continue for the foreseeable future. It means both a practical engagement with China such as deepening trade relations, government-to-government contacts, confidence-building measures, and even joint military exercises, while also rapidly augmenting its military capabilities to defend its territory against the largest army in the world.[17]

---

[17] In May 2006, China and India signed their first memorandum of understanding on defense cooperation for high-level personnel exchanges, an annual defense dialogue and joint exercises

China, which could once afford to dismiss India as a "third-rate power" cannot be so complacent anymore. Since the late 1990s, China had become deeply concerned by the rise of India and the decisive shift in the regional balance of power in South Asia in favor of India. Although Pakistan, China's "all-weather friend," has progressively become a "failed state" and a hotbed of Islamic extremism and terrorism, India's dramatic rise, not to mention its active courting by other major powers, in particular the United States, is a most unwelcome development for Beijing.[18] The renewed U.S.-India entente or "partnership" that began during the second-term of the Clinton administration and expanded under the Bush administration (and is exemplified by joint military exercises, intelligence sharing, and U.S. sales of military hardware to India, including the recent U.S.-India civil nuclear cooperation) is viewed in Beijing as an attempt by the United States to use its surrogate India to "serve as a counterweight to China" and undermine China's power and influence in the South Asian region and beyond. Suffice it to note that that China will work hard to preempt the development of an anti-PRC coalition. Given these challenges, sustained efforts at the highest political level will be required to maintain friendly bilateral relations and prevent potential conflicts between these two Asian giants.

and training programs. Following small-scale naval exercises, the first significant army counter-terrorism exercise took place in December 2007 in Kunming, China. However, prospects for far-reaching bilateral military exercises are limited.

[18] Following the 11 September 2001 attacks, the United States and Pakistan revived their relations. As a "frontline state" in the coalition against global terrorism, Pakistan became the beneficiary of billions of dollars in aid and debt rescheduling. However, Washington's banking on President Musharraf has not paid the expected dividends. From Beijing's perspective, U.S. support for Pakistan did not result in the anticipated downturn in U.S.-India relations. Rather, U.S.-India relations became stronger.

6

India and the United States
From Estrangement to Engagement

To a generation of India's leaders, their country's economic backwardness and grinding poverty was not only a source of enormous embarrassment, it also stood as an obstacle to the international prestige and respect that they craved and believed was India's natural geopolitical destiny. India's unprecedented economic rise has finally made this dream a possibility. Its leaders realize that after decades of tireless effort to overcome the long history of thwarted ambitions, power and prestige are now tantalizingly within the country's reach. Slowly but surely, India is finally acquiring the capability to influence developments – not only in the South Asian region but throughout the world.

This chapter provides an assessment of the economic and geostrategic implications for the United States of India's rise. It examines the evolving relations between the two countries over the past six decades, highlighting the twists and turns in a complex relationship. In the post–Cold War period, the relations between the world's most powerful democracy and the world's largest democracy have improved dramatically, leading some to conclude that Indo-U.S. relations have finally moved from "estrangement to engagement," and others to suggest blissfully the flowering of a "beautiful friendship" (Ganguly, Shoup, and Scobell 2006; Kux 1992). Yet this chapter argues that although there is currently strong convergence of American and Indian interests on a number of economic and security areas, including the promotion of democracy and countering terrorism and extremism, Indo-U.S. relations will not be without friction. Differences on trade, especially outsourcing and the demand that India liberalize its trade regime, open up its closed economic sectors to American businesses, and make compromises on the Doha Round trade negotiations, will remain contentious issues. Similarly, the position India may take beyond the requirement of protecting its own national security may not always complement that of Washington's. Indeed, India's ambitious national aspirations in a world of shifting geopolitical allegiances and power structures may mean that its geostrategic ambitions do not always parallel that of the United States. Clearly, the United States will closely watch how India deals with the problem of nuclear proliferation, resolves the debilitating conflict in Kashmir, normalizes its relations with Pakistan, and, most importantly, whether New Delhi will side with the United States to "contain" covertly a rising China. Prudence dictates that although the United States should not turn a blind eye to India's ambitions, the countries' common interests provide both with a unique opportunity to expand their cooperative relationship.

Indo-U.S. Relations during the Cold War

During the Nehru years (1947–64), India's foreign policy was based on the principles of nonalignment. Along with leaders of several newly independent countries, including Tito of Yugoslavia, Nasser of Egypt, Sukarno of Indonesia, and Nkrumah of Ghana, Nehru was one of the founding members of the Non-Alignment Movement (NAM) – and also the member who labored indefatigably to create the organization. Calling for a "third way," NAM demanded that all nations should be free to chart their own independent and neutral path in international politics against the prevailing system of alliances and "blocs" that characterized the bipolar world dominated by the United States and the Soviet Union. Although the United States, at least initially, viewed NAM with some bemusement, this did not last long. Even if the United States could tolerate Nehru's imperious manner and obstinacy, as well as his iconoclastic defense minister Krishna Menon's domineering and infuriating negotiating style, it could not tolerate NAM's biases and hypocrisy. In practice, NAM proved to be far from neutral. Its implicit admiration of socialism and support of the USSR (rooted in the exigencies of the Cold War and Moscow's repeated "anticolonial and imperialist" stance), led many – in particular, Nehru – to side repeatedly with the Soviet Union and the Eastern bloc. India's refusal to condemn North Korea's aggression in 1951 and its deafening silence on the Soviet invasion and occupation of Hungary in 1956 profoundly angered the United States (Stein 1969). John Foster Dulles, the U.S. secretary of state under President Dwight Eisenhower (1953–61), was so incensed that he ridiculed nonalignment as an "immoral and shortsighted conception" and NAM's position as fundamentally incompatible with friendship with the United States.[1] Given Dulles's obsession with anti-Communist alliances and "pacts" (hence the term "pactomania"), he found a compliant and strategically placed ally in Pakistan and quickly admitted India's sworn rival into the two anti-Communist military pacts: the Central Treaty Organization (CENTO) and the Southeast Asia Treaty Organization (SEATO). As the political distance between New Delhi and Washington grew, Nehru gravitated even closer to the Soviet Union (Brands 1990). Strobe Talbott (2004, 7), the former deputy secretary of state in the Clinton administration,

---

[1] Dulles made this statement during a speech on 9 June 1955. For details, see Bandyopadhyaya (1970), Gaddis (2005), Kux (1992, pp. 99–180), B. J. Nayar (1976), and Talbott (2004).

succinctly notes that during the Cold War, Indo-U.S. relations were "a victim of incompatible obsessions – India's with Pakistan and America's with the Soviet Union." Both were guilty of being on best terms with "each other's principal enemy."

However, despite what Kux (1992) calls the growing "estrangement" between the two democracies, the United States responded favorably to Nehru's request for "urgent" military support by dispatching two dozen squadrons of B-47 bombers, a dozen squadrons of fighter aircraft, and air defense radars during India's border war with China in 1962 (Maxwell 1970). However, this convergence of strategic interests was short-lived. India's continued commitment to NAM and the United States' continued support for Pakistan, including its widely perceived "pro-Pakistani" position on the emotive Kashmir issue, hindered the further strengthening of ties between the two countries.[2] In his

---

[2] In 1947, Nehru promised to hold a plebiscite in Kashmir to ratify the territory's accession to India. However, the vote was deferred until "normal conditions" could be reestablished in the territory. In 1948 and again in 1949, the United Nations (UN) passed two resolutions granting the people of Kashmir the "right to self-determination." India has long maintained that since the conditions on the ground have never been conducive to hold a "free and fair" election (plebiscite) because of Pakistan's illegal cross-border activities, including terrorism (India has yet to hold the plebiscite), the Kashmir issue was settled in 1954 when the Constituent Assembly of Kashmir, exercising the Kashmiri people's right to self-determination, voted for accession to India. Compounding the problem further is the Simla Agreement. Signed by the leaders of India (Indira Gandhi) and Pakistan (Zulfiqar Ali Bhutto) in July 1972 following Pakistan's defeat in the third Indo-Pak war of 1971, the agreement commits both sides to resolving their dispute through bilateral negotiations. Since then, India had steadfastly maintained that the Simla Agreement supersedes the earlier UN resolutions. However, Pakistan contends that the Simla Agreement in no way supersedes the UN resolutions. Rather, Pakistan maintains that India must conform to the plebiscite as mandated by the UN with the Kashmiris deciding to join either India or Pakistan. Pakistan's assumption is that the predominantly Muslim population of Jammu and Kashmir would vote to join Pakistan. This confidence has led Pakistan to "internationalize" the dispute by asking third parties and the UN to help resolve the dispute. However, the failure to resolve this dispute has made it a touchstone in India-Pakistan relations, with both sides occupying territory the other claims as theirs. Indian-controlled Kashmir consists of three core areas: the Kashmir Valley (or the Vale), Jammu, and Ladakh. The Kashmir Valley is overwhelmingly Muslim, Jammu is mainly Hindu, and Ladakh is mainly Buddhist. The Pakistan-controlled sector is divided into two parts, Azad or "Free Kashmir" and the Northern territories of Gilgit and Hunza. The Chinese control the Aksai Chin region in northeastern Ladakh. India holds the position that the LOC (Line of Control) that separates Indian and Pakistani-controlled Kashmir should be the final border. However, in 2004, President Musharraf seem to move beyond Pakistan's long-held position by offering the demilitarization of all or parts of Kashmir by parceling it into seven geographical regions (five currently under Indian control and two under Pakistan), including the joint control or a UN mandate. The United States was engaged in the Kashmir issue mostly during the Eisenhower and Kennedy administrations. When the Kennedy administration failed even to foster a civil dialogue between India and Pakistan, the United States gave up. As a result, there has since been no significant American initiative on Kashmir. There is a vast literature on this topic. For a good overview, see Behera (2007), Cohen (2001, 2004), Ganguly (1986, 1999, 2001), Kux (1992), Limaye (1992). Paul (2005), Schofeld (2003), and Wirsing (1994), among others.

exhaustive study of U.S. policy toward South Asia across four presidencies from Truman to Johnson, McMahon (1994) concludes that it was America's exaggerated concern about the Soviet threat and its indifference, if not insensitivity, to India's regional imperatives that doomed Indo-U.S. relations during the Cold War.

On the eve of the 1971 Indo-Pakistan war, as the United States "titled" toward Pakistan (President Richard Nixon ordered the aircraft carrier *Enterprise* to the Bay of Bengal), the relations between India and the United States reached its lowest ebb (Chadda 1997; Choudhury 1975; Sisson and Rose 1990). India viewed the American action as an underhanded act of aggression to deter India from ending the bloody civil war and genocide committed by the West Pakistani army in East Pakistan.[3] To preempt a possible U.S.-China-Pakistan "alliance" against India, Prime Minister Indira Gandhi, with a brilliant mix of bluff and bluster, signed the treaty of "peace, friendship and cooperation" with the Soviet Union, a reciprocal agreement under which the two parties promised to aid one another in the event of a military attack for the next twenty-five years (Horn 1982; N. Singh 1986). Indeed, during the three-week war with Pakistan, while the Indian forces were engaged in operations in East Pakistan (which ultimately led to the defeat of the Pakistani army and the creation of Bangladesh), three Soviet vetoes in the UN Security Council prevented the adoption of a resolution calling for a cease-fire and a return to the status-quo ante. Whereas, Gandhi's deft actions and victory earned her the sobriquet "Iron Lady," as Kux (1992) points out, the U.S. action constituted a monumental strategic blunder. He argues that Nixon and Kissinger not only misread the crisis in East Pakistan, their conscious pro-Pakistani bias succeeded in needlessly making a regional conflict into a major global conflagration, besides pushing India decidedly into the Soviet camp. The Indo-Soviet treaty of 1971 further bolstered Indo-Soviet relations. The Soviet Union became India's principal ally and also its major arms supplier, providing India with advanced military hardware under highly favorable terms and supporting Indian positions in the UN Security Council, particularly over Kashmir. In return, India stoically backed the Soviet Union on a variety of controversial international issues, including being the only democracy refraining from criticizing the Soviet invasion of Afghanistan in 1979.

As if Indian-American relations could not get any worse, India's 1974 "peaceful nuclear explosion" made the "relationship" even more testy (A. Kapur 1976). As the United States took on the mantle against nuclear weapons proliferation, India (and later Pakistan) became the centerpiece of its nonproliferation efforts.[4] To India, legislation such as the 1978 Nuclear Non-Proliferation Act, the Pressler Amendment, and the Symington Amendment were discriminatory

---

[3] India's successful creation of Bangladesh (out of East Pakistan) occurred in the face of UN and U.S. opposition.

[4] India is legally considered a "non-nuclear weapon state" because it did not test a nuclear device before 1967 when the Nuclear Non-Proliferation Treaty was being negotiated.

and hypocritical – widely viewed as a surreptitious attempt by Washington to thwart India in defending its national sovereignty.[5] In the 1980s, as the proxy Cold War raged in Afghanistan, Washington's "strategic tilt" once again leaned toward its "front-line" ally, Pakistan – which included the United States' supplying sophisticated weaponry such as the F-16 fighter aircraft – upset the military balance between India and Pakistan, fueling an arms race in the subcontinent. It also heightened India's angst toward the United States. Under these circumstances, the demise of the Soviet Union was seen as a most unfortunate, if not tragic, development in New Delhi. The sobering realization that India was suddenly bereft of Soviet protection and adrift in a "dangerous neighborhood" without a powerful and reliable ally forced India's foreign policy establishment to fundamentally rethink and reassess their options in the emerging post–Cold War world. Leading the charge for a "new realism" in foreign policy was a new generation of defense and security "hawks" (both in the government and in think tanks) who advocated a more vigorous and muscular approach by broadening India's foreign policy options and engaging in diplomacy through strength rather than lofty rhetoric and strategic equivocation. Most important, they demanded that India improve its relations with the world's only superpower: the United States (Mohan 2003).

This new realism was soon reflected in India's post–Cold War policy posture. Indian foreign policy began to shift markedly from trying to be a leader of the "Third World" to the recognition of the potential that India could emerge as a great power in its own right. Although the rhetoric of "anti-imperialism" remained popular, in practice, India's external relations increasingly began to focus on its own national interest. On the diplomatic front, old dogmas and verities were discarded to improve relations with China and the United States. Most emphatically, India now no longer attached preconditions to bilateral negotiations such as demanding that China return territories it occupied following the 1962 war. Rather, diplomacy was to be based on the pursuit of mutually beneficial goals. At the top of the agenda, great urgency was placed on improving relations with the United States. Consequently, the often gratuitous anti-American rhetoric coming from New Delhi sharply diminished (Datta-Ray 2002; J. Singh 2007). Perhaps the most dramatic manifestation was the government's assertive effort to enhance the country's military capabilities.

Since the mid-1990s, India, which has the world's fourth largest standing army, has embarked on an ambitious plan to modernize its Soviet-era armaments. To this effect, New Delhi has upgraded its military hardware by purchasing advanced fighter planes, an aircraft carrier, submarines, missiles, radars, and electronic warfare systems, making it the developing world's biggest

---

[5] In fairness, it should be noted that President George H. W. Bush imposed sanctions against Pakistan under the aegis of the Pressler Amendment in 1990. This was done because the United States suspected that Pakistan had a secret nuclear program and was building nuclear weapons (Hagerty 1998; Moshaver 1991; Perkovich 1999). No sanctions were imposed against India.

arms buyer in 2004–5. In fiscal 2007–8, India raised its defense spending by an unprecedented 8 percent to US$22 billion as New Delhi purchased expensive U.S. military platforms, including the USS *Trenton* and C-130 military transport aircraft. Most dramatically, with calm determination, India upgraded its "nuclear option" by putting in place an operational nuclear deterrent (Chengappa 2000). Cognizant that its actions may well result in international condemnation, India ended its policy of "strategic ambiguity" by conducting five nuclear tests from 11 to 13 May 1998.[6] Clearly, the security imperatives overrode other considerations. This stark choice was candidly noted by then Foreign Minister Jaswant Singh (1998, 41): "while the end of the Cold-War transformed the political landscape of Europe, it did little to ameliorate India's security concerns. The rise of China and continued strains with Pakistan made the 1980s and 1990s a greatly troubling period for India.... Faced with a difficult decision, New Delhi realized that its lone touchstone remained national security."

India and the United in the post–Cold War Era

A confluence of factors has facilitated Indo-U.S. rapprochement. The dissolution of the Indo-Soviet link, the end of the Cold War and the rationale for India's controversial (and contradictory) nonalignment policy, worsening India-Pakistan relations, the rise of cross-border terrorism and Islamic extremism, and finally the challenges posed by a rising China have made the United States more receptive to India's geopolitical and security concerns. Moreover, India's post-1991 economic liberalization and integration in the global economy transformed it into a lucrative market and offered new opportunities to American businesses. The people-to-people contact facilitated by the rapidly growing and influential Indian diaspora in the United States has played a significant role in bridging the gulf between the two countries.[7] Finally, as Strobe Talbott (2004), in his fascinating insider's account *Engaging India*, persuasively argues that the role played by "engaged leadership" has been just as decisive. Talbott notes that the rise of a new generation of leaders in the United States such as William Jefferson Clinton and George W. Bush – men who were not burdened with the Cold War mind-set – is key to understanding why and how America's approach toward India shifted from estrangement to engagement. He notes that from the beginning of his presidency, Clinton made it abundantly clear that he regarded India as a rising power that the United States must "constructively engage."

---

[6] Two weeks later, Pakistan detonated six nuclear devices – five to match India and one in response to India's 1974 peaceful nuclear explosive.

[7] Many Indo-American organizations actively support candidates (either Democrat or Republican) who support strengthening India-U.S. relations.

However, despite good intentions on both sides, U.S.-India engagement proved far more challenging than anticipated. For example, fully aware that President Clinton had invested much "political capital" in the hopes of getting the Nuclear Non-Proliferation Treaty (NPT) extended during the 1995 NPT Review and Extension Conference, India refused to support the NPT because of its long-held view that the NPT and the Comprehensive Test Ban Treaty (CTBT) are discriminatory. Specifically, New Delhi reiterated at the conference what it had steadfastly maintained since 1974: that the goal should be nuclear disarmament as opposed to nuclear nonproliferation. The 1995 NPT Review and Extension Conference had only two objectives: to review the treaty's operation and to decide on its extension. This meant an indefinite and unconditional extension of the NPT without any commitment of disarmament from the "nuclear-have" states (the United States, Russia, the United Kingdom, France, and China) and would only perpetuate the "nuclear apartheid" between the haves and have-nots – with the five "have states" making no commitment to disarmament. Compounding this concern was the upcoming CTBT of 1996 with its controversial "Entry into Force" clause. This clause, inserted primarily at China's insistence, required India to sign the CTBT by September 1999 or face the prospect of UN-imposed trade sanctions. Not surprisingly, New Delhi charged that the CTBT would amount to a permanent division between the nuclear haves and have-nots and denounced it as an "instrument of surrender." Beyond the hype, India's refusal was based on real concerns. As Ollapally (2001, 934) aptly notes, "among the three [nuclear] threshold states, India believed it stood to lose the most, given that both Pakistan and Israel had so-called 'nuclear patrons' – the Chinese and the Americans, respectively – who might be willing to share nuclear test data."

Although the Clinton administration privately acknowledged that New Delhi would not accede to the NPT and the CTBT – at least in its present form – the United States nevertheless exerted substantial diplomatic pressure (both carrots and sticks) on India (and several other nations that were less than enthusiastic about extending the NPT) to come on board. However, if India's "defiance" of the NPT was expected, its May 1998 nuclear tests were clearly not. The Clinton administration reacted almost viscerally to India's seemingly brazen act by immediately slapping punitive sanctions and took the lead in condemning India in the UN Security Council and at the G8 meetings. Led by the United States, the five permanent members of the UN Security Council passed UN Security Council Resolution 1172, calling on both India and Pakistan to stop their nuclear weapon development programs immediately, refrain from weaponization (or from arming missiles with nuclear warheads), cease development of ballistic missiles capable of delivering nuclear weapons, and to become parties to the NPT and the CTBT without any preconditions. Perhaps what the Indians found most insulting and (deeply disconcerting) was when President Clinton, during his June 1998 visit to Beijing, not only condemned India's nuclear tests but also issued a joint statement with the Chinese president that accorded Beijing joint responsibility with Washington for maintaining peace and stability in the Indian subcontinent. However, since India hold's Beijing directly responsible for helping an embittered, failed state like Pakistan acquire nuclear and missile capability (by supplying Islamabad with tested nuclear warheads, including ballistic missile components, fissile material, and the ring magnets for enriching weapons-grade uranium). Clinton's embrace of Beijing only reaffirmed India's gravest doubts about the United States: that it was a shortsighted and selfish power, willing to capitulate to China for the commercial bonanza it promised U.S. business.

Yet as Talbott notes, despite this falling out, President Clinton did not close the door on a "dialogue with India." Rather, what followed behind closed doors was a series of intense and extended discussions on "nuclear matters" between the two counties, with Strobe Talbott meeting with his Indian counterpart, Jaswant Singh, over a period of two years in fourteen sessions in seven countries. According to Talbott (2004, 51), Washington began to come to terms with India's national and global aspirations and its rationale for the nuclear tests, including the stark fact that "India had put on notice that it was now unambiguously, unapologetically and irrevocably, a nuclear armed power." Ironically, it was this realization that ultimately forced the Clinton administration to abandon its declared goal to "cap, rollback, and eliminate" India's nuclear program. Now, in a strange twist, Washington offered India a "grand bargain" under which the United States would withdraw its nuclear-related technology sanctions, provided India met four essential benchmarks: (1) sign the CTBT, (2) negotiate a Fissile Material Cut-off Treaty (FMCT), (3) enforce export controls on nuclear missile technology, and (4) observe a nonthreatening defense posture. However, India's position remained the same: it would voluntary adhere to the main provisions of the treaties without formally acceding to it. Talbott claims that negotiations on these issues would have produced tangible results if time had not run out on the Clinton administration. In any case (as discussed later) the incoming Bush administration successfully picked up where the Clinton administration had left off.

It was the Clinton administration's unanticipated and unequivocal support of India during the 1999 Kargil conflict with Pakistan that convinced New Delhi that the United States was becoming more evenhanded in its dealings with India. In May 1999, Indian intelligence discovered that Pakistani regular forces had blithely breached the Line of Control (LOC) separating the two sides in divided Kashmir and strategically lodged themselves in the Indian sector known as Kargil. From their new positions, the Pakistani army could threaten Indian lines of communication into northern Kashmir. To New Delhi, this "creeping annexation" was simply intolerable. For two months, the Indian military mounted a fierce counteroffensive to repel the intruders. Although the Indian forces carefully stayed on their side of the LOC, Prime Minister Vajpayee informed Clinton that Indian forces might have to fight a "decisive battle" against Pakistan, which meant penetrating deep into Pakistan to dislodge the invaders. American spy satellites indicated that India was preparing a massive offensive into Pakistani territory. Fearing an all-out war between the two nuclear-armed rivals, Clinton, who held Islamabad directly responsible for violating the LOC, placed great pressure on Pakistan to withdraw immediately to its side of the LOC.

As Pakistani Prime Minister Nawaz Sharif was preparing to travel to Washington to meet with President Clinton and ask him to help devise a solution to the conflict, Clinton made it clear that he would not meet with Sharif until all Pakistani forces had retreated to their side of the LOC. Clinton also confirmed that the United States had no intention of actively mediating or "internationalizing" the Kashmir dispute. Rather, the dispute would have to be resolved bilaterally under the terms of the Simla Agreement. In New Delhi, Clinton's stance was taken as an unequivocal endorsement of the Indian position. Clinton also kept New Delhi informed on the progress of his discussions with Sharif. Eventually Sharif agreed to Washington's terms and flew to Washington to meet President Clinton on 4 July 1999. Arguably, Sharif's decision to pull out (which was widely seen as a defeat for Pakistan) is viewed as one of the major reasons behind the coup that overthrew Sharif that October and brought General Pervez Musharaff to power. President Clinton's energetic (and laborious) involvement and his apparent "fairness" won him tremendous goodwill in India and helped to accelerate Indo-U.S. rapprochement. Not surprisingly, when Clinton visited India in March 2000 (the first visit by an American president in twenty-two years), he received a hero's welcome. The fact that Clinton spent five days in India but just five hours in Islamabad – long enough to deliver a somber fifteen-minute televised speech reminding Pakistan of the "dangers of terrorism" seem finally to convince the Indian leadership (and citizenry) that the United States was prepared to treat India with "respect" and "fairness."

Toward the U.S.-Indian Nuclear Deal

In August 1999, India's National Security Advisory Board (NSAB) released its much-awaited formulation on India's nuclear doctrine. It proposed that India needed a credible nuclear deterrent with "effective C412 capacity" (command, control, communication, computer, intelligence, and information), including a triad of delivery systems from land, air, and sea. Although emphatically rejecting the "first use" of nuclear weapons, the report made it clear that "minimum deterrence" must be based on the "maximum credibility" of such deterrent capacity (Basrur 2006). The report admitted that although India had not achieved all the targets, for all practical purposes, it had the minimum "strategic depth" to be able to protect itself from nuclear blackmail and coercion. This objective reality was not lost on the United States.

Even before George W. Bush was elected president, his future national security adviser, Condoleezza Rice, noted that a Bush administration would "pay closer attention to India's role in the regional balance." Criticizing the Clinton administration for connecting "India with Pakistan" and thinking "only of Kashmir or the nuclear competition between the two states," she noted that "India is an element in China's calculation, and it should be in America's too" (Rice 2000, 56). Nicholas Burns, the under-secretary of state for political affairs in the George W. Bush administration notes that like his predecessor, President Bush also "recognized early on the power and importance of India's large and vibrant democracy in global politics.[8] He essentially doubled the United States' strategic bet on India, pursuing an uncommonly ambitious and wide-ranging opening toward it" (N. Burns 2007, 135). New Delhi, of course, was most receptive of President Bush's appreciation of Indian sensitivities. Apparently, like the Bush administration, which sought to distance itself from the liberal internationalism of the Clinton era, the new Bharatiya Janata Party–led Indian government, which had long harbored grave misgivings about the Nehruvian policy of nonalignment and its knee-jerk anti-Americanism in favor of realist-based strategic partnership with the United States, finally had the opening it wanted. Wasting no time, the new Indian government heaped unabashed praise on the new Bush administration and returned the goodwill.

When much of the world was criticizing the Bush administration's controversial initiative on National Missile Defense (NMD; announced on 1 May 2001), India was among a handful of countries to welcome the initiative as a positive effort toward reducing the global stockpile of nuclear weapons. Again, following the September 11 attacks, India was quick to offer the United States its military facilities and unstinting military support in its fight against Al-Qaeda and global terrorism. However, this time New Delhi did not skulk or accuse Washington of shortsightedness when Washington politely declined the offer. Rather, it understood that geographical proximity made Pakistan the logical front-line state. Nevertheless, the realization that it was the Bush administration's ultimatum to Islamabad to support the United States in its fight against terrorism or be treated as an adversary that finally compelled Islamabad to renounce its decades-long support for the Taliban and offer Pakistani bases in support of Operation Enduring Freedom, was not lost on India. As if to placate India, the Bush administration waived the remaining nuclear-related sanctions on India in 2001 and allowed exports to the Indian Space Research Organization to resume. In June 2004, President Bush and Prime Minister Vajpayee signed the Next Step for Strategic Partnership to strengthen further the relations between the two countries.

---

[8] Mohan (2007, 107) notes that "Senior Bush aides have underlined his strong admiration for Indian democracy. As one adviser said, "When I asked . . . Bush in early 1999 about the reasons for his obvious and special interest in India, he immediately responded, 'a billion people in a functioning democracy, isn't that something? Isn't that something?"

The U.S.-India rapprochement reached its zenith on 18 July 2005 (during the U.S.-India Summit) with the issuing of the landmark joint statement in Washington by President Bush and Prime Minister Singh. The statement noted that India was "a responsible state with advanced nuclear technology," and deserved "the same benefits and advantages as other such states," albeit India would have to assume the "same responsibilities and practices" as the recognized nuclear weapons states.[9] In effect, the United States tacitly acknowledged that India was a de facto nuclear state. This was a dramatic shift in U.S. policy because Washington had long insisted that India must first sign the NPT as a precondition for civilian nuclear cooperation. Rather, to accommodate India, the Bush administration conveniently moved the goalpost by replacing the traditional distinction between NPT signatories and nonsignatories with one based on "responsible" and "nonresponsible records." To India, which had never engaged in wanton proliferation of weapons of mass destruction (unlike China and Pakistan), this recognition meant a great deal – as must have the American rejection of Pakistan's demand for similar treatment. Not surprisingly, according to the Pew Global Attitudes Survey, even at the height of anti-Americanism in 2006, six in ten Indians viewed the United States and President Bush favorably (N. Burns 2007, 131).

The details of the agreement, which was finalized at subsequent meetings between the two sides, was made public in March 2006 during President Bush's visit to India. The fine print illustrated the wide-ranging and ambitious nature of the accord. Under the reciprocal agreement, India would "assume the same responsibilities and practices" as the recognized nuclear weapon states. Specifically, New Delhi agreed to separate its civilian and military nuclear reactors and place the former under the International Atomic Energy Agency (IAEA) safeguards. This meant that fourteen of India's twenty-two nuclear power reactors, as well as all future thermal and civilian breeder reactors, would be subject to IAEA inspections. Further, it would negotiate and sign an additional protocol with the IAEA to allow the agency to conduct inspections on India's civilian nuclear facilities without prior notice; permanently shut down the CIRUS reactor in Trombay in 2010; establish a verifiable national export control system; refrain from transferring enrichment and reprocessing technologies to states that did not possess them; and adhere to the Missile Technology Control Regime (MTCR) guidelines. The NPT allows assistance with civilian nuclear programs only to countries that have joined the treaty as non–nuclear powers, and U.S. law and the Nuclear Suppliers Group (NSG, a group of forty-five countries that controls the export and sale of nuclear technology worldwide) rules explicitly forbid the sharing of nuclear fuel and technology to

---

[9] For details, see U.S. Department of State, "Background Briefing by Administration Officials on U.S.-South Asia Relations," 25 March 2005, available at www.state.gov/r/pa/prs/ps/2005/43853.htm.

non-NPT members. Thus, the Bush administration agreed to amend the existing U.S. nonproliferation legislation and to modify restrictions of the NSG to facilitate civilian nuclear transfers to India. As the agreement formally made its way to legislation in the U.S. Congress, a number of modifications were made to it. These included some restraints on India's ability to conduct nuclear tests and reprocess spent fuel, in addition to requiring the U.S. president to issue an annual certification to Congress as to whether India was abiding by the clauses of the agreement. In early December 2006, a strong bipartisan majority in Congress (the House of Representatives by a vote of 330 to 59 and the Senate by "unanimous consent") passed the Hyde Act of 2006, which approved the initiative. On 18 December 2006, President Bush signed the bill, making it a legal instrument. With this in place, American and Indian negotiators began to prepare for a number of additional steps necessary to bring the agreement into reality. In particular, the "123 Agreement" (named after the section of the U.S. Atomic Energy Act) would provide the basis for IAEA and NSC action and a formal legal agreement for the United States to conduct bilateral nuclear collaboration. The drafting of the 123 Agreement was completed in July 2007, after which U.S. Congress had to finalize the requisite changes in U.S. law, and then leaders of both countries would sign the agreement – which, as discussed later – they eventually did.

Although the Bush administration has argued, with some justification, that the nuclear accord would impose a greater degree of transparency on India's nuclear program than had previously existed and that the upgrading of India's civilian nuclear power would help reduce dependence on fossil fuels, arguably more ambitious strategic and economic considerations were behind the U.S.-India nuclear accord.[10] Strategically, to the United States, India represents not only an emerging power but also a potential counterweight to China. Nicholas Burns (2007, 131), the senior American negotiator for the accord, recently noted that the nuclear agreement symbolized "the emergence of India as a great power and the emergence of the strategic relationship between India and the U.S.... [the] rise of a democratic and increasingly powerful India represents a singularly positive opportunity to advance our global interests. There is a tremendous strategic upside to our growing engagement with India. That is why building a close U.S.-India partnership should be one of the United States' highest priorities for the future. It is a unique opportunity with real promise for the global balance of power."

Former Indian diplomat and defense minister Jaswant Singh underscores Burns's view. In his fascinating memoir, *In Service of Emergent India* (2007), Singh notes with great erudition that for decades, among the highest national security objectives for India was finding a way to keep its nuclear weapons while

---

[10] Economically, India represents a lucrative and fast-growing market for American businesses, including producers of dual-use technology (Tellis 2006).

restoring the benefits of international nuclear commerce. However, this goal could not be achieved because the United States demanded strict adherence to the NPT. Therefore, when President Bush offered India the possibility of having both nuclear weapons and access to the global nuclear energy market, New Delhi seized the opportunity. As Singh notes, to India's strategic policy makers, ending this "nuclear apartheid" would not only open up new and important avenues of economic, strategic, and diplomatic cooperation, the American offer of strategic partnership would also encourage China to continue improving its relations with India. Indeed, China recognized the potentially far-reaching impact of the U.S.-India nuclear agreement on the strategic balance of power in Asia. Throughout the long process, China did not obstruct the agreement. Rather, Beijing diplomatically maintained that it would carefully study the India-specific IAEA safeguards agreement before rendering its decision. As a member of both the IAEA and the NSG, Beijing's approval is essential to take the Indo-U.S. nuclear deal forward; after receiving approval from IAEA, India would have to obtain a waiver by consensus from the NSG to allow nuclear commerce with the international community. Although Beijing's official reaction has been measured, unofficially its disapproval of Washington's double standard in its nonproliferation policy (e.g., punishing Iran and North Korea for their nuclear programs while facilitating a deal for a non-NPT signatory) was duly noted.[11]

Despite strong support by both governments, the nuclear accord was still not a done deal by September 2008 (with just months remaining for the Bush administration), and many felt the deal would remain unfinished business. In India, the accord was vociferously opposed from its inception by the Left Front coalition (made up of four Marxist parties). The coalition's support in Parliament was crucial for the ruling minority coalition government led by the Congress Party. Predictably, the Left Front argued that the nuclear deal would make India a junior partner in an American imperial endeavor and repeatedly threatened to withdraw its support if the government went ahead with the accord. Beyond this, a number of issues still needed to be concluded before the deal could come into effect. First, India had to sign a nuclear safeguards agreement with the IAEA. Second, the United States had to persuade the NSG to waive existing sanctions against India. Third, the U.S. Congress had to approve the already-negotiated agreement, after which the Indian and American

---

[11] China is not the only critic of the agreement. Other countries have also claimed that the agreement undermines the NPT by rewarding countries such as India that have chosen not to be a party to the NPT. The critics note that India proved to be the winner because it had to make only minimal concessions. The deal does not require India to cease fissile material production, nor does it prevent it from testing nuclear weapons (not entirely true), and thus it will enable India to expand its nuclear arsenal. To the political left in India (who are coalition partners in the current government), the agreement (at least in its current form) has the potential to make Indian interests subservient to those of the United States.

governments both had to sign it. Predictably, with time of the essence, the Bush administration wanted all this to happen as soon as possible, recognizing that the U.S. presidential campaign could make further discussions difficult. Nevertheless, the Bush administration remained convinced that the agreement would eventually be passed because it was the cornerstone of India's new security strategy and important to the United States in its efforts to balance a rising China. To underscore its commitment to the accord, the Indian government, in quick order, worked out the text of a safeguards agreement with the IAEA, despite concerns that signing would precipitate its ouster by the Left Front. In fact, influential factions within the ruling Congress Party openly called for the signing of the agreement anyway, risking an ouster and a general election on the issue. Under the Indian Constitution, an ousted government would continue as a caretaker government until the next election. Aware of this, the Bush administration announced that it was prepared to sign the deal with any constituted government, including a caretaker one. In other words, the nuclear deal could be completed even if the Left Front toppled the government. With such determination on both sides it seemed that it was just was a matter of time before the nuclear accord would become a reality.[12]

On 9 July 2008, the ruling coalition government's Communist allies finally carried out their threat to bring the government down unless it shelved the nuclear agreement. In reply, the prime minister called for a "confidence vote" in Parliament to thwart them. On 22 July, following a rancorous two-day debate, India's coalition government won a parliamentary vote of confidence. Although this did not ensure the survival of the agreement, the fact that the governing coalition won by an unexpectedly "large margin" (275 votes to 256 with ten abstentions) saved the deal from certain death. Internationally, the agreement also faced a number of hurdles, although it overcame a significant one when, on 1 August 2008, the IAEA's thirty-five-member board of governors unanimously approved the agreement without objections. The agreement now had to secure the backing of the forty-five-member NSG, which would have to waive its rules on nuclear trading with India. Specifically, because India is not a signatory of either the NPT or the CTBT, all NSG member countries (including China) must agree to exempt India from rules prohibiting nuclear sales to countries that do not accept the full-scope safeguards agreements on all of their nuclear facilities. On 21 August, the NSG finally reviewed the U.S. draft proposal on the civil nuclear cooperation with India. Their two-day meeting ended without reaching an agreement on lifting the thirty-four-year-old embargo on nuclear trade with India. It seemed that at least some members of the highly secretive NSG expressed reservations about the agreement because they opposed, in principle, supplying nuclear technology to countries outside

---

[12] On 10 July 2008, India submitted to the IAEA a key document (the Draft Nuclear Safeguards Accord) required to finalize a civil nuclear deal with the United States.

the NPT and because of India's failure to accede to the long-stalled CTBT. Some members even proposed setting conditions before giving their approval. For its part, India made it clear that it would not accept any new conditions to win approval from the NSG. However, the NSG must vote unanimously for lifting export restrictions against India for the treaty to progress.

Finally, on 6 September 2008, the NSG lifted the ban on nuclear trade with India following three days of acrimonious talks in Vienna, overcoming opposition from countries fearful that the NSG's decision could set a dangerous precedent. Now all that remained to be accomplished was final approval from the U.S. Congress. Although both parties recognized that this might not be possible given that Congress was expected to recess later in September so members could campaign for the November elections, not to mention that the Bush administration's term would end in January 2009, Secretary Rice publicly assured that the administration would try to get the agreement through Congress. For their part, both U.S. presidential candidates, Senator John McCain and Senator Barack Obama, praised the NSG for allowing its members to engage in nuclear cooperation with India, and both candidates urged the U.S. Congress to quickly pass the U.S.-India Agreement for Civil Nuclear Cooperation. This concerted effort paid off: on 2 October 2008, the India-U.S. nuclear deal secured the approval of the U.S. Senate, which voted overwhelmingly in favor of the accord (eighty-six vs. thirteen votes). All three senators directly involved in the presidential race – Barack Obama, Joe Biden (Obama's vice presidential running mate), and John McCain – voted for the bill. The legislation, which had already been cleared by the House of Representatives, now headed to the White House for President Bush to sign into law, which he did on 8 October, effectively ending a three-decade ban on U.S. nuclear trade with New Delhi.

The unprecedented U.S.-India nuclear accord has generated heated debates among the accord's supporters and opponents. The critics claim that it weakens the global nonproliferation regime by rewarding countries like India that are not signatories to the NPT, have never accepted IAEA safeguards, and have ambitious nuclear weapon programs in place. Second, they point out that the idea of separating "civilian" and "military" nuclear facilities is a canard because nuclear activities cannot be fully separated. Third, they contend that the accord sets a bad precedent because it has the potential to encourage other states to demand similar deals. The fact that Pakistan's demand for equal treatment was rejected by the Bush administration because of the proliferation activities of Pakistani nuclear scientist A. Q. Khan is hardly a reason to celebrate; Pakistan could seek a similar agreement with China. Fourth, allowing India access to more fissionable materials will enable it to produce more nuclear weapons. This, coupled with the fact that although India has declared it seeks only "minimal" credible deterrence, it has never specified what level of nuclear armament level this might entail, carries the risk of further intensifying the two-way nuclear arms race on the subcontinent between India and Pakistan and India and China. More broadly, opponents of the accord worry that the weakening of the NPT is virtually a green light to some supplier countries to provide nuclear technologies and materials to any country with the requisite technical capabilities to develop nuclear weapons, including potential proliferators. Most troubling, they argue, countries such as North Korea and Iran may become even more emboldened to challenge the NPT regime – with serious implications for global stability.

In contrast, proponents of the accord argue that it actually strengthens nuclear nonproliferation goals because it brings India into the nonproliferation regime. They point out that India's willingness to subject its civilian nuclear facilities (which represent about 65 percent of its nuclear power capacity) to IAEA inspections, despite India's status as a non-NPT signatory, is a significant step toward meeting nonproliferation objectives. Second, they reject the claim that the accord weakens the NPT by arguing, for example, that North Korea's and Iran's nuclear weapon programs have nothing to do with the accord because both were already underway long before the U.S.-India accord was under discussion. Rather, the cases of North Korea and Iran illustrate that the reasons to pursue nuclear programs are based fundamentally on each country's strategic considerations. Third, in regard to the potential expansion of India's nuclear arsenal, the accord's proponents argue that the global fissile material treaty would keep close tabs on India's weapons program and prevent potential expansion or proliferation. This is because the fissile material cutoff treaty would halt India's accumulation of plutonium for military purposes by preventing the use of both weapons-grade and reactor-grade plutonium for nuclear weapons. Fourth, because the accord requires India to place a moratorium on nuclear testing, New Delhi cannot engage in further testing of thermonuclear devices. Fifth, India has been a reluctant nuclear power, forced to develop weapons because of legitimate security needs. Sixth, unlike active proliferators such as Pakistan (and NPT signatories such as North Korea and Iran), India's record has been exemplary when it comes to nonproliferation. Seventh, India is a "responsible" global actor; its "no first-use" nuclear doctrine and the defensive and deterrent nature of its weapons program do not pose a threat to other countries. Finally, the expansion and modernization of India's aging civilian nuclear power reactors would help the country meet its burgeoning energy needs, in addition to reducing its growing dependence on polluting hydrocarbons. Supporters of the accord point out that nuclear power remains underutilized because it provides only about 3 percent of India's electrical power. In contrast, coal and fossil fuel, which generate the bulk of the country's energy, emit large amounts of greenhouse gases. Because nuclear power emits almost none of these gases, upgrading and expanding India's civilian nuclear program will have a positive environmental impact.

On Democracy Promotion

"Democracy promotion" has a long and distinguished history in U.S. foreign policy going back at least to the presidency of Woodrow Wilson (1913–21). In 2000, the Clinton administration launched the Community of Democracies, ostensibly to support democracies worldwide. In the post-9/11 period, the idea of democracy promotion was boldly resurrected by the Bush administration, which saw it as critical to secure American strategic interests, to stay true to American ideals, and to keep America safe in a volatile world. With India as the world's largest democracy and the United States as the most powerful, President Bush assumed a natural affinity and convergence of interests when he noted that "India and the United States share a commitment to freedom and a belief that democracy provides the best path to a more hopeful future for all people. Because of our shared values, the relationship between our two countries has never been stronger." In July 2005, the United States and India jointly launched a global democracy initiative to counter the existential threat of terrorism by promoting democracy and economic development. Each country agreed to dedicate US$10 million a year and to work closely with each other to advance conflict-resolution and democratic capacity building in troubled nations and regions throughout the world.

Yet beyond the rhetorical flourishes of solidarity and symbolic gestures, India has only recently made democracy promotion a priority in its foreign policy. Mohan (2007, 99) points out that "New Delhi's conspicuous lack of emphasis on democracy in its engagement with the world is largely a consequence of the Cold War's impact on South Asia and India's nonaligned impulses in the early years of its independence. It attached more weight to solidarity with fellow developing countries and the defense of its own national security interests without a reference to ideology at the operational level." Today, however, a more confident and assertive India, which views itself as a rising power commanding a global stage, unabashedly claims that democracy promotion is both a natural component and an obligation the world's largest democracy and inheritor of the Gandhian principles of nonviolence owes to the rest of the world (Singh 2007). Yet despite the hubris and bravado, India remains deeply wary of the U.S. mission of democracy promotion. This is in large measure because in this era of neo-Wilsonian internationalism, the United States is keenly aware of the strategic value of Indian democracy and its tradition of political pluralism and liberal propriety. India fears the United States may use this to serve its own imperial ends (Mohan 2007).

The rather sanguine assumption that democratic governments share principles that allow them to also harmonize their foreign policies is problematic. History shows that it would be grossly misleading to assume that common systems of politics and governance automatically translate into shared foreign policy goals or the convergence of strategic interests. Despite broad support for American-led democracy promotion, India has cautioned that democracy promotion must be made less "America-centric" – that is, it must be a broad-based global effort rather than a unilateral American mission. Again, beyond symbolic gestures, India has distanced itself from democracy promotion that is contingent upon U.S.-led military interventions, forcible regime change, or policies that could compromise its relations with China. However, New Delhi is amenable to the idea of a "concert of democracies," that is, coordinating its foreign and security policies, especially those that strengthen security cooperation. Yet India is generally reticent in promoting democracy beyond its borders, and like the United States, which applies far more pressure on nondemocratic countries that represent no economic or security interests (such as Burma and Zimbabwe, compared with China or Russia), India does the same – vociferously calling for an immediate restoration of democracy and civil liberties in Pakistan and Bangladesh but conveniently turning a blind eye to its main oil suppliers, Iran, Burma, and the Central Asian republics.

Indeed, India increasingly views Iran as serving as the fulcrum of its "Near Eastern policy" by providing petroleum as well as land transit routes to Afghanistan and Central Asia. India and Iran also share the desire to contain Sunni militancy, including the Taliban and Al-Qaeda; both supported the Northern Alliance against the Taliban and now support the Karzai government in Afghanistan. With the signing of the 2003 New Delhi Declaration outlining an India-Iran "strategic partnership," the relations between the two countries have never been better. As a result, New Delhi has refrained from criticizing Teheran on the controversial nuclear issue, steadfastly defending Iran's right to use nuclear energy for "peaceful purposes." It was only after intense U.S. pressure that India reluctantly voted with the United States and the EU-3 (European Union-3: Britain, France, and Germany) in September 2005 to support the UN resolution demanding that Iran abide by the NPT rules.[13] However, India has made it clear that it will not support or participate in any economic sanctions or military action to stop Iran's nuclear program. Moreover, within the subcontinent and its immediate environs, which India's considers to be its sphere of influence, New Delhi has not hesitated to support both democratic and nondemocratic regimes and movements or occasionally use military force beyond its borders to defend it interests under the guise of humanitarian intervention.[14] As a rising power with great-power ambitions,

[13] Of course, the Indian government tried its best to assure Tehran privately that its vote should not be interpreted as "anti-Iran." This was not entirely successful because it followed on the heels of U.S. Ambassador David Mulford's ill-timed remark that if India did not support the United States with regard to Iran's nuclear program, the Indo-U.S. nuclear agreement could be in jeopardy.

[14] The most obvious examples include successful intervention in East Pakistan in 1971 and the unsuccessful actions in Sri Lanka in the late 1980s – ostensibly to defend the territorial integrity of Sri Lanka and to protect the rights of the Tamil minority.

India unambiguously puts its own interests first. These interests may not always be consistent with spreading democracy abroad; more often than not, political expediency and national interests will win over morality or any commitment to the inviolability of sovereignty. Arguably, New Delhi would be more interested in being a member of a "concert of great powers" (the United States, the EU, Japan, Russia, and China) than in a concert of democracies.

U.S.-India Economic Issues

TRADE

Since the 1990s, economic ties between India and the United States have experienced a phenomenal growth. From a modest US$5.6 billion in 1990, bilateral trade in merchandise goods increased to US$41.6 billion in 2007, representing an impressive 743 percent growth in less than two decades. India's merchandise exports to the U.S. increased from US$21.83 billion in 2006 to US$24 billion in 2007, and U.S. merchandise exports to India increased from US$10 billion in 2006 to US$17.5 billion in 2007.[15] The growth in U.S. foreign direct investment in India parallels the growth in bilateral trade. Between 1990 and 2000, U.S. investments in India rose from US$372 million to US$2.4 billion and to just over US$8.5 billion in 2005 (Martin and Kronstadt 2007, 39). Of course, these figures are small when compared with the U.S. investments in China.

However, faced with record trade deficits and intense competition from rapidly growing economies such as China and India (the U.S. trade deficit with India has grown steadily, reaching $12.6 billion in 2006), the Bush administration's trade policies came under sharp criticism at home. Specifically, "mercantilist" or "unfair" trade practices of emerging economies such as China and India is widely viewed as the major reason behind burgeoning U.S. trade deficit and job losses because American workers are alleged to face unfair competition from low-wage countries. In turn, the Bush administration intensified its demand that China and India, along with other large developing countries, reduce their trade barriers and open their markets to American goods and businesses.

As discussed earlier, until the early 1990s, India was a closed economy: average tariffs exceeded 200 percent, quantitative restrictions on imports were extensive, and there were stringent restrictions on foreign investment. Beginning in 1991, India began cautiously to reform its economy, liberalizing some sectors only under conditions of extreme necessity. Agriculture, which is an important part of the Indian economy, has generally bypassed the reforms. Although the contribution of agriculture to the country's GDP has decreased from 35 percent to 20 percent over the past two decades, more than 70 percent

---

[15] *Source:* http://www.indianembassy.org/newsite/indoustrade.asp (accessed 4 April 2008).

of India's workforce still depends (both directly and indirectly) on agriculture for its livelihood. To achieve self-sufficiency in food and fiber, India's inward-looking trade policy regime insulated the country from the global agricultural markets through a wide range of restrictions and prohibitions on both the imports and exports of agricultural goods. The government's food procurement operations and the Public Distribution System kept food prices relatively low, and farmers were supported through subsidized inputs (fertilizers, pesticides, seeds, irrigation, and power) and credit. Given the importance of and the massive state intervention in the agricultural sector, it is not surprising that the Indian government has remained deeply protective of the sector, introducing only minimalist reforms. More important, it has entered negotiations on agricultural trade liberalization in the World Trade Organization (WTO) with deep trepidation (Hoda and Gulati 2007, 41–43).

Yet India is not alone in protecting its agricultural sector. In fact, agricultural trade is globally among the most distorted of all sectors. It is characterized by high tariffs and high levels of government support to primary producers. For example, average tariffs for agricultural goods are more than three times higher than for nonagricultural goods, with some agricultural tariffs running as high as 800 percent. In no other area does domestic support distort international markets to the extent it does in agriculture, with more than US$300 billion in 2007 provided in support and protection for agriculture by rich countries. Indeed, export subsidies (the most trade-distorting form of subsidies) are tolerated in the agricultural sector, in contrast to other sectors, such as manufacturing, where they have long since been prohibited (Sharma 2007). Although India has lowered import tariffs on most industrial goods to around 12.5 percent (from about 150 percent in 1991), it still maintains high agricultural tariffs of approximately 40 percent. This has placed India and the United States on opposing sides on the current discussions in the Doha Development Round of trade negotiations in the WTO. As a key player of the G20 group of developing nations, India has refused to negotiate tariff cuts (as has the G20 as a whole) without rich nations' first making deep cuts in their trade-distorting domestic subsidies and offering greater market access for the developing world's agriculture products. However, the United States, the EU, and other Organisation for Economic Co-operation and Development (OECD) countries argue that for Doha to be a success, all major trading nations need to make strong market access commitments in agriculture, manufacturing, and services, including financial services. In particular, the United States has made it clear that large developing countries such as India, China, and Brazil bear a special responsibility as major players in the world economy. That is, they need to substantially cut their applied tariffs on agricultural and manufactured goods. With particular reference to India, the United States pointed out (with some justification) that it continues to limit market access in various sectors through high taxes and tariffs, nontransparent procedures, discriminatory treatment of imports, and nontariff barriers. The United States has appropriately demanded that India must enforce intellectual property rights laws as well as expeditiously improve the investment climate and eliminate glaring regulatory hurdles. Clearly, the volume of bilateral trade between the United States and India is not consistent with the size and potential of both economies. If trade is to grow between the two countries, the resolution of these difficult and contentious issues will require concessions by both sides in bilateral negotiations as well as through multilateral channels such as the WTO.

OUTSOURCING

Today, the main bilateral source of friction between the United States and India relates to the outsourcing and off-shoring of jobs, which involves moving jobs to people rather than people to jobs.[16] A significant effect of contemporary globalization on labor markets is reflected in the technologically-assisted outsourcing of jobs to lower-wage countries like India and China. From a purely economic perspective, outsourcing and offshoring is ultimately a matter of cost savings for businesses because it enables them to take advantage of cheaper labor by substituting foreign workers for domestic (American) workers. According to economic trade theory, other nations and the United States ought to benefit from such open trade, whether in goods or labor. Nations with lower labor costs gain jobs and entrepreneurial opportunities, and U.S. consumers gain from lower prices. As long as the United States continues to climb up the technological ladder and build on its comparative advantage in high-value products and services, offshoring is a win-win situation for all. Yet as Alan Blinder (2006) (former vice chair of the Board of Governors of the Federal Reserve) reminds us, this current phase of globalization, or what he calls the "Third Industrial Revolution," is profoundly different from earlier phases in that jobs that were once considered nontradable and safe (such as white-collar jobs) have become tradable as a result of rapid advances in technology and transportation.

   The outsourcing of traditionally white-collar activities has been driven by several factors, the most important of which are improvements in international communications, computerization and digitization of many business services, and the availability of educated English-speaking workers abroad who can perform similar services for far less pay. Comparative wage data for 2003 shows that average wages for software developers was $6 per hour in India compared with $60 per hour in the United States (Farrell 2005; McKinsey Global Institute 2003). Similarly, average wages for call-center operators was estimated to be less

---

[16] Offshoring refers to the relocation of jobs and production to a foreign country. In contrast, outsourcing does not necessarily imply that jobs and production are relocated to another country.

than $1 per hour in India compared with about $12.50 per hour in the United States (A. Bardhan and Kroll 2003). In 2004, a junior accountant at a large U.S. firm with less than three years experience would earn between $39,000 and $50,250 per year, whereas in India, a junior accountant would earn less than $10,000 per year. More astounding, in 2002, the average salary for an MBA from India's prestigious Institutes of Management was around $13,000, compared with more than $60,000 in the United States. Despite this wide disparity, both providers and receivers of outsourced services have benefitted. According to Mann (2003), outsourcing has reduced prices of computer hardware by 10 to 30 percent, boosting the diffusion of information technology throughout the U.S. economy and raising both productivity and growth by a significant amount – 0.3 percentage point per year. Similarly, the McKinsey Global Institute (2003) estimates that every dollar of activity outsourced to India results in a global gain of $1.47 – that is, a net gain of 47 cents. The United States captures $1.14 and the remaining 33 cents accrues to India. Of the $1.14 collected by the United States, 47 cents go to the "re-employed" workers, whereas American shareholders and consumers gain 62 cents. Undoubtedly, according to this study, shareholders and consumers gain at the expense of workers.

Although outsourcing and offshoring are not entirely new economic phenomenon, in this era of globalization, marked by economic interdependence and convergence, the pace of outsourcing and offshoring has been exponential because many economic activities previously considered immune to foreign competition can now be outsourced. Technology has not only reduced time and distance, it has also allowed production processes to become geographically fragmented. Rather than producing goods in a single process or at a single location, firms are increasingly breaking the process into discrete steps and moving or outsourcing the various steps to whatever location allows them to minimize costs. For example, computer chip producers may do most of their research and development in the United States (in California's Silicon Valley), but some may occur in India and the EU as well. In contrast, hardware production can be performed in any number of locations, spread across the globe. As increasing numbers of potentially offshorable jobs have exposed new groups of workers to international competition, it has invariably led to growing concern regarding large-scale "export" of American jobs to countries such as India.

Although there are few empirical studies on the scale of job losses in the United States due to outsourcing, Goldman-Sachs (2003) has estimated that U.S producers shifted anywhere between 300,000 and 500,000 jobs abroad during 2000–3, or an average of between 100,000 and 167,000 jobs per year since 2000. This estimate includes jobs in both manufacturing and in the services sector. A more recent study by Van Welsum and Vickery (2005) estimates that in 2003, about 20 percent of total employment in the EU, Australia, Canada, and the United States were potentially affected by offshoring of services enabled by information and communications technology. Regarding future trends, Bardhan and Kroll (2003) estimate that the number of jobs that could be offshored over the next few years is 14 million; using a measurement of the proximity of service workers to their customers as a proxy, Jensen and Kletzer (2005) estimate that roughly 70 percent of professional and business services employment in the United States could be offshored. In 2006 Blinder claimed that up to 40 million U.S. jobs were at risk over the next ten to twenty years because of outsourcing. If outsourcing proves to be inexorable and accelerates with newer technologies and as enterprises seek to drive down their costs, the challenge for American (and OECD) policy makers will be how best to benefit from outsourcing, while mitigating its negative impact.

Studies also show, however, that outsourcing and offshoring of most high-value work may prove to be uneconomical in the long run because it requires creative interaction and a highly educated and skilled workforce. Moreover, a rather understated fact is that in contrast to its trade deficit in goods, the United States runs a significant trade surplus in services. This is because it continues to be the leader in providing many high-value services abroad, including financial, legal, engineering, architectural, and software development services, whereas many of the services imported by U.S. companies are less sophisticated and hence of lower cost. It seems that which activities become tradable or offshorable will also depend on whether India (and China, as well as other developing countries) can take on the new and sophisticated activities from the developed economies. This will not be easy for some high-value goods. In India, it will require as a precondition drastic improvements in the power supply and infrastructure; in China, it will require improvements in human capital such as English-language skills, as well as laws that provide protection of intellectual property. Perhaps most critically, it will depend on wage developments for the relatively small numbers of highly skilled workers in these countries. There are already signs of rising real wages of skilled workers in India, although these have been partially offset by rising productivity. Nevertheless, the recent decision by Apple Computers to shut down its Bangalore center and Intel's plan to lay off workers from its Indian operations have sparked fears that rising cost may have already started threatening India's attraction as an IT offshoring destination. India is already facing increasing competition from China, Brazil, Mexico, the Czech Republic, Hungary, Poland, and Russia for the IT offshoring market.

No doubt, outsourcing and offshoring will remain hot-button issues for Indian and American policy makers for the foreseeable future because it involves significant trade-offs regarding employment, including income distribution, especially real wages of workers. For example, trade between two countries – say, one relatively abundant in skilled labor (the United States) and another relatively abundant in unskilled labor (India) – may increase the real income of U.S. skilled labor and lower that of U.S. unskilled labor. This usually means that unskilled workers may lose their jobs or be rehired at a lower wage. Thus, real wages of low-skilled domestic workers can decline with trade. In fact, the real wages of low-skilled U.S. workers have fallen since the late 1970s, and the gap between wages of high-skilled and low-skilled workers has widened. Second, although the "benefits of free trade are widespread, costs tend to be concentrated." U.S. producers may lose out to lower-cost import competition, and "U.S. workers may face downward wage pressure or lose their jobs" because of relocation of production overseas. At the same time, however, American consumers benefit from low-cost imports from developing countries, such as India and China; U.S. firms that import cheaper intermediate inputs may become more efficient and globally competitive as well (Kletzer 2001, 1). Third, given the astonishing pace of technological advancements, a wide array of jobs and services will become offshorable – not only low-skill services such as keyboarding and data entry, transcription, and telemarketing but also high-skill services such as radiology, architecture, and engineering. How large will this be? Although no one knows for sure, many people could potentially lose their jobs. Given this possibility, elected officials in the United States will continue to put tremendous pressure on American companies to keep jobs in the United States. They may do this by giving U.S. companies tax incentive to stay, by closing tax loopholes, making it harder for U.S. employers to move jobs overseas, or by demanding that countries such as India meet more stringent environmental and labor standards before jobs can be moved there; the last alternative is the most politically convenient.[17] Indeed, in 2004, several U.S. state and local governments were already debating various laws forbidding the offshoring of government-related services. Unlike the relocation of manufacturing jobs overseas, which mostly affected blue-collar workers, service offshoring involves displacing white-collar, college-educated workers. These more politically savvy workers will not sit idly by and see their jobs and livelihood shipped-off to distance shores, but demand action by elected officials, including the erection of protectionist measures to protect their jobs.

Future Directions

Indo-American relations have now reached a level of maturity and sophistication that makes it virtually certain that both countries will be able to tolerate

---

[17] Interestingly, Blinder (2006) notes that the traditional remedy for coping with offshoring has been "more education and a general 'upskilling' of the work force" because the United States' comparative advantage is seen increasingly in services requiring highly skilled workers. Yet Blinder argues that the jobs threatened by offshoring today cannot be divided conventionally between those that require high levels of education and jobs that do not. As a result, upskilling the workforce will not necessarily slow the movement of jobs overseas. Instead, the key determinant of a job's offshoring vulnerability is whether it is impersonal or personal, not low or high-end. For example, factor workers, accountants, and computer programmers are vulnerable to offshoring, but taxi drivers, construction workers, teachers, and nurses are likely not.

differences, while cementing their bonds. The accelerating economic interdependence and security convergence of the two nations are bound to strengthen in the coming years, as are the manifold ties wrought by the influential Indian-American community, an elite diaspora with high-level connections in both countries that, through its campaign contributions and lobbying efforts, has already changed U.S. perceptions about India and Indian perceptions about the United States. Just as propitious, Pakistan, formerly the biggest obstacle to improved Indo-U.S. relations, no longer looms as large in Indian-American relations. The traditional U.S. practice of treating India and Pakistan with equivalence has been quietly abandoned. The "decoupling" of India from Pakistan in U.S. strategic calculus confirms that the United States now places a much higher priority on improving its relations with India because the U.S. now sees India as the undisputed "regional hegemon" – meaning Washington recognizes that India enjoys a disproportionate economic, demographic, and military superiority over its regional neighbors. It also underscores Washington's growing frustration with its "front-line ally" given Pakistan's lackluster (and expedient) efforts to combat the Taliban and Al-Qaeda, including the Pakistani army and paramilitary forces covert undermining of U.S. counterterrorism and counterinsurgency efforts, despite billions of dollars of American military and economic aid to Islamabad. Without doubt, the nightmare scenario for both Washington and New Delhi would be if Pakistan unravels from within because both have an interest in the stability of Pakistan. Today, the Pakistani state is besieged by unprecedented levels of political, ethnic, and sectarian violence and faces a deeply uncertain future. If Pakistan deteriorates further into a failed, an extremist, or a radicalized state with uncertainty regarding control and command of its nuclear arsenal, the entire region could become destabilized with prohibitively negative repercussions. Thus, despite the history of antipathy between the two nuclear-armed neighbors, Pakistan's internal stability is in India's national interest (more on this in Chapter 8).

As Indo-U.S. relations evolve and mature, the United States will expect much more from India. New Delhi is cognizant of the fact that it sacrificed relatively little for the nuclear accord, but this may not be the case in the future. Indeed, many U.S. policy makers already feel that Washington has given India enough without asking for reciprocation. When this eventually happens, it will mean New Delhi will have to make some difficult choices. In July 2007, in an unprecedented move, the Indian government permitted the U.S. nuclear-powered aircraft carrier USS *Nimitz* to dock off Chennai. Yet such gestures are relatively easy fist steps. On significant economic and security issues such as outsourcing, trade, global warming, and the NPT, its relations with Iran, or greater burden sharing in Iraq or Afghanistan, New Delhi has either sidestepped them or used self-serving rhetoric. Yet as ties with the United States deepen and New Delhi's power grows, India will no longer be granted a "free ride" but will have to take positions on these and other major regional and international issues. Of course, if the United States expects automatic reciprocity for its support, it may not always be forthcoming – at least not right away. For example, given India's large Muslim minority (about 150 million strong), New Delhi cannot be expected to back Washington at every turn on issues that affect the Islamic world. Moreover, New Delhi will face increasing pressure, just as Beijing does now, to become a major stakeholder in the international system, with responsibilities and obligations. How India will balance its "national interest" with that of global "collective interest" remains to be seen.

What is certain, however, is that as India's power grows, it will emerge as an important player in the game of great-power politics. This reality is not lost to either Washington or Beijing. India's economic growth has allowed it to increase its defense budget sharply (an 8 percent increase in 2007) and dramatically upgrade its indigenous weapons production capabilities. These include advanced weapons systems. For example, on 27 November 2006, India successfully carried out its first missile interception test when its Prithvi surface-to-surface ballistic missile shot down a similar missile off India's east coast, demonstrating local capability to develop an antimissile shield. This was followed by the successful test of the 3,500-kilometer-range nuclear-capable Agni III missile in April 2007; in June 2007, the Indian army formally inducted into service the BrahMos supersonic cruise missile. Given these developments, will India be able to hold on to its much vaunted policy of "nonalignment" and "independence" in foreign policy amid potential U.S.-China competition and rivalry? If history is any guide, India (like other major powers such Russia and Japan) will be compelled to make choices – often difficult ones. India has historically eschewed formal military alliances, but the imperatives of great-power rivalry will demand that India can no longer sit on the sidelines. After all, it is the rise of China that has provided the strong strategic motivations for renewed Indo-U.S. collaboration. Although India will do its best to avoid becoming a pawn in U.S. efforts to contain China, if push comes to shove, it will decisively "tilt" toward the United States. However, if the new Obama administration returns to the Bush senior and Clinton-era policies of "putting China first" in its approach toward Asia, it will greatly weaken, but not eliminate, the strategic convergence of Indo-American relations.

7

The Rise of China and Its Implications for the United States

Throughout much of her long history, China was the dominant power in Asia to which surrounding states paid homage and tribute. The Middle Kingdom saw itself as the center of progress, propriety, and righteousness – a bulwark against the uncivilized barbarity on its periphery. The collapse of the Soviet Union eliminated the major land-based threat to China, and its economic rise has enabled it once again to regain its earlier power and glory. Today, China's global influence and leverage rivals only the lone superpower – the United States. For the international community, and especially China's neighbors, the rise of a potentially Sinocentric world has prompted them to rethink and readjust their relations with Beijing by taking into account its interests and concerns in their foreign policies and diplomacy. Although some hope that China will play a greater role in world affairs (at least to balance the American "hyperpower"), most remain ambivalent – uncertain as to what China's emergence means to them and its implications for global stability and security.

Arguably, nowhere is this ambivalence more pronounced than in the United States. Although the United States remains the world's most powerful state, it also knows that its power and influence are neither limitless nor uncontested. To the United States, if there is a "peer competitor" on the horizon, it is China. Indeed, China's ambitious military modernization is fast transforming the country into a formidable power and a genuine strategic competitor to the United States. Yet at the same time, the United States and China are major trading partners with expanding economic ties and growing economic interdependence. Nevertheless, given their profound differences in values, political systems, and national interests, palpable concerns remain about the possible future trajectory an ascendant China may choose. Can China execute a "peaceful rise" to great-power status? In other words, will China be a "responsible stakeholder," working constructively with the United States and other nations to accomplish common goals, or will it behave like previous rising hegemons and use its growing power and influence to reorder the rules and institutions of the international system in accordance with its own interests? The following pages will show that given the motivations and calculations that drive China's foreign policies, American and Chinese interests will both converge and diverge, – making it difficult to predict with any degree of certainty China's future behavior or the strategic choices it may make. As former Secretary of State Condoleezza Rice (2008, 3) recently noted, "By necessity, our relationships with Russia and China have been rooted more in common interests than common values." Given the ever-expanding common interests of the United States and China, a conflict-ridden and wrenching global power transition is not inevitable; constructive Sino-American relations is critical to maintain global economic prosperity and stability. Arguably, it is in the interest of the United States and the international community to facilitate China's "peaceful rise" (or "peaceful development," according to Chinese leaders) and orderly integration in the global system.

China's Foreign Policy from Mao to Deng

On its founding, the People's Republic of China (PRC) announced that its foreign policy would be guided by the rules and norms of "peaceful coexistence." In practice, this meant that China's diplomatic ties would be based on "the principles of equality, mutual advantage, and reciprocal respect for territorial sovereignty," including noninterference in the internal affairs of other states (Hunt 1996, 176). However, these lofty ideals were often subordinated to the myopic exigencies of the Cold War and China's national interests. The outbreak of the Korean War in June 1950 – the first major test for the new Chinese state – proved to be a victory for Mao and the Chinese Communist Party (CCP). China's ability to fight U.S.-led United Nations (UN) forces to a stalemate greatly enhanced its stature, especially among the formerly colonized and now newly independent countries. Following the bitter Sino-Soviet split in the late 1950s, Chinese foreign policy devoted much energy in actively promoting and supporting revolutionary insurgencies throughout the world, including rallying the "Third World" in opposing Soviet and American imperialism (Jian 2001; Mansingh 1998; Meisner 1986). However, Mao's perception that the Soviet Union was a greater imperialist threat than the United States (a view shared by the United States) helped to reduce tensions and eventually led President Richard Nixon to visit China in February 1972 (Macmillan 2007). With the signing of the landmark Shanghai Communique and adoption of the "one China" policy, the resultant Sino-American détente marked the end to over two decades of antagonism between the United States and the People's Republic.[1]

[1] U.S. policy toward Taiwan is articulated in the "Three Communiques," which establish U.S. support for a "one China" policy. "One China" has been defined differently by various

After 1978, with Deng Xiaoping firmly in control, China's domestic and external policies came to reflect Deng's policy of pragmatism and reform as articulated in his twenty-four-character strategy of *taoguang yanghui*: "Observe calmly; secure our position; cope with affairs calmly; hide our capacities and bide our time; be good at maintaining a low profile; and never claim leadership" (Deng Xiaoping 1994). Under Deng and his successors, the Maoist era emphasis on ideological solidarity and material support for revolutionary and "anti-imperialist forces" were subordinated and ultimately abandoned in favor of the singular pursuit of national development. Chinese foreign relations became less confrontational and belligerent, the rhetorical excesses scrupulously turned down as China turned its energies toward improving diplomatic and cultural ties and expanding economic relations with nations around the world. Yet the prudent post–Deng era leaders, cognizant of the fact that they could not forever "hide China's capacities" and "not claim leadership" gradually began to balance the imperatives of national economic development with the responsibilities that came with China's status as a rising power. Moreover, the collapse of the Soviet Union and the rise of the United States as the sole superpower had a decisive impact on China's strategic thinkers. Initially, these cold and calculating realists believed that the shift toward multipolarity was imminent, but they soon came to terms with the possibility that U.S. unipolarity and a U.S.-dominated world could endure for a long time. Chinese policy elites, such as former vice president of the CCP Central Party School Zheng Bijian (2005), who see the contemporary global power configuration as characterized by "one superpower" (the United States) and many "great powers" (France, England, Japan, China, and Russia), see China's central task as protecting its national interests under the constraints of an emboldened American hegemony – the central goal of which is to contain China.

CHINA'S GRAND STRATEGY: THEORY AND PRACTICE

Avery Goldstein (2005), in his book *Rising to the Challenge: China's Grand Strategy and International Security*, provides a panoramic look at China's contemporary worldview. He persuasively argues that the key to understanding the implications of China's increasing economic and military capabilities and the motivations guiding its diplomatic and foreign policy and how the world – especially the United States – should respond to this emerging giant lies in

U.S. administrations. However, at a minimum, it includes three core elements: (1) The PRC is the sole legitimate government of China, and the United States does not maintain official relations with Taiwan; (2) the United States does not support Taiwan independence nor its membership in international organizations whose members are sovereign states; and (3) the United States does not challenge China's position that Taiwan is part of China and would accept unification as long as it occurred peacefully (Vogel, Ming, and Akihiro 2002).

understanding China's "grand strategy."[2] According to Goldstein, the various elements of China's grand strategy coalesced in the mid-1990s as China's leaders, conscious not only of their nation's growing power but also its continued weakness, adjusted to the realities of the post–Cold War world. Most fundamentally, they came to appreciate the unexpectedly stiff international challenges they faced in pursuing their central foreign policy goal: to facilitate China's rise as a true great power in the twenty-first century. From Beijing's perspective, China faces broadly four major constraints, which Goldstein argues explain why Beijing embraced its current foreign policy approach or "grand strategy" in the mid-1990s.

The *first* constraint is the unprecedented nature of American power. Goldstein points out that by the mid-1990s, Chinese leadership finally came to terms with the reality that, contrary to their earlier assumptions, the global balance of power was not moving toward multipolarity – at least not anytime soon. Rather, unipolarity could last for several decades, with the United States remaining the world's uncontested superpower. To Beijing, this meant that, for the foreseeable future, China would have to operate in a world where the United States has the ability to frustrate China's ambitions to become a great power. It also meant that engaging in an arms race with the United States was not prudent, because, like the former Soviet Union, it could led to "overstretch" and even economic collapse. *Second,* China's risk-averse leaders recognized that although their country's economic and military capabilities had greatly improved in the post-reform period, it was still a "developing country" and lagged far behind the technological and economic superiority of the world's leading capitalist states, especially the United States. Goldstein argues that the spectacular display of U.S. military firepower during Operation Desert Storm in 1991 convinced Beijing just how far they had to go before their armed forces were in the same league technologically with those of the United States and its allies.

Third, Beijing began to better appreciate that China's growing economic and military capabilities were a source of concern and alarm to other nations and, if left unchecked, could provoke a potential backlash and efforts to "contain China." Specifically, China's dramatic rise both economically and militarily was generating a palpable sense of resentment and trepidation, especially among China's neighbors. In Southeast Asia, there was growing concern about China's highly assertive posture toward maritime and territorial disputes, leading Association of Southeast Asian Nations (ASEAN) to ask publicly what this might portend with an even more powerful China. Similar concerns were raised by Japan, South Korea, and India. Even in the United States, there was high-level

---

[2] Goldstein (2005) notes that unlike the U.S. grand strategy, China's grand strategy is not announced with a formal declaration. Rather, it remains implicit and is best discerned through observing China's practice of international relations.

discussion and debate about a looming "China threat" and what could be done to forestall it. Beijing was particularly alarmed by Washington's efforts in the mid-1990s to revive its Cold War era alliances with Australia and Japan, as well as expanding U.S. military cooperation with the nations in Southeast Asia. To China's leaders, this signaled the beginnings of an American-led regional effort to form new balancing coalitions against China with the ultimate goal of "containing China." *Fourth*, China recognized that the Taiwan problem could easily escalate, drawing China into a ruinous conflict with the United States. This danger was underscored in 1995–96 when Beijing used military exercises by deploying ground, air, and naval forces and conducting missile tests in the Taiwan straits (about 100 nautical miles separate Taiwan from the mainland) to threaten Taiwan's leaders about the risks of pursuing independence.[3] More ominously, Beijing issued a thinly veiled threat about the risk of nuclear escalation should the United States become directly involved in any cross-straits confrontation. Apparently the bluff did not work. The United States responded by directing the Seventh Fleet battle carriers to the region, signaling continued American support for Taiwan's security. To Beijing, this was not only another example of the United States frustrating China's rise, the prospect of a prohibitively costly war in the Taiwan Strait with the United States was not in China's interests – at least not at a time when China lacked the military wherewithal to challenge the world's only superpower.

Arguably, China's leaders have been working diligently (and clandestinely) to translate these "four realities" or "strategic logic" into policy outcome. To this effect, they have actively embraced policies designed to reassure China's neighbors (and the international community) of China's "friendly intentions" and to enhance the perception that the PRC is a felicitous and responsible global stakeholder, committed to cooperative and peaceful resolution of contentious bilateral and multilateral issues. Besides the standard formulaic incantations that China was never a hegemon, will never practice power politics, and will never pose a threat to its neighbors or to world peace, Beijing, by demonstrating remarkable restraint during the Asian financial crisis, hoped to underscore that it took its responsibilities and obligations seriously.[4] Following Goldstein's logic, one can conclude that China's recent efforts to convey a kinder, gentler face abroad – the so-called charm offensive – nicely suits the needs of its current grand strategy. As Goldstein notes, by cultivating and expanding partnerships,

---

[3] Taiwan's independence movement gained momentum in 1995 when Washington allowed Taiwan's president, Lee Teng-hui, to visit the United States. Before this, it had banned visits by Taiwanese leaders in deference to Beijing. During his visit, Lee publicly championed Taiwan's independence.

[4] During the Asian financial crisis, Beijing announced that it would not devalue its own currency because this would have forced further devaluations across Asia and created more problems for Thailand and other countries caught in the crisis. Although the United States, Japan, and the International Monetary Fund eventually provided aid, many Thais remember only China's gesture (Kurlantzick 2007).

Beijing seeks to increase the benefits countries see in working with China as well as the costs of working against it. These partnerships are expected to establish a simple linkage: if countries chose to press Beijing on matters important enough to sour relations, they will jeopardize important benefits such as economic opportunities for trade and investment as well as cooperation on pressing security matters such as weapons proliferation and terrorism.

Although China's grand strategy is not without trade-offs, as noted in Chapter 5, China's policy shift toward fostering bilateral and multilateral relations is more than just perfunctory. Rather, it marks a significant departure from only a few years ago when Beijing tended to view all manner of multilateral organizations and forums with suspicion – as fronts for imperialist powers. However, over the past few years, China has embarked on an aggressive activist agenda to improve its image abroad. These include, for example, Beijing's increased participation in UN peacekeeping operations in East Timor, Congo, and elsewhere. This is a milestone because Beijing has been a one of the world's strongest defenders of the principle of nonintervention in the domestic affairs of sovereign states. Medeiros (2007) persuasively shows that China's arms control and nonproliferation policies have undergone significant changes since the 1980s. Beijing has not only come to accept international nonproliferation norms and principles, it has also become an active participant in international efforts to stop the proliferation of weapons of mass destruction to both state and nonstate actors. Specifically, Beijing has abandoned its earlier "reluctant" approach toward global arms control and nonproliferation by ratifying several important arms control and nonproliferation accords, including the Nuclear Non-Proliferation Treaty (NPT; in 1992) and the Chemical Weapons Convention. In 1996, China signed the Comprehensive Nuclear Test Ban Treaty and independently announced a moratorium on nuclear testing (despite the fact that modernization of its nuclear warheads required ongoing testing) and agreed to abide to the basic tenets of the Missile Technology Control Regime (MTCR). In fact, by end-2005, Beijing had signed or joined all major international nonproliferation agreements and regimes. What explains that China, once a harsh critic of the global nonproliferation regime, is now one of its supporters? Provocatively, Medeiros claims that American diplomacy has been instrumental in affecting and shaping China's nonproliferation policies and practices for the better by getting Beijing to recognize the dangers of proliferation.

Equally significant, since the mid-1990s, China's leaders have been engaged (both bilaterally and multilaterally) in a concerted effort to improve relations with the United States, the European Union (EU), and other major powers to preempt the likelihood that they will unite against and try to "contain China." In fact, Beijing has worked particularly hard to reassure Washington that it has neither the intention nor the capability to challenge American leadership in Asia – even as it privately seeks to promote a regional environment where

American political-military presence will gradually recede. For example, China has actively encouraged the development of new multilateral security-related arrangements as an alternative to the currently dominant U.S.-led bilateral alliance structures in Asia. In the aftermath of the September 11 attacks, China has used the global "War on Terrorism" to position itself as a "partner" of the United States in its struggle against global terrorism.

Closer to home, and as if to reassure its emergence as a "peaceful rise," Beijing has actively embraced multilateralism and open dialogue with its neighbors by embarking on a series of confidence-building measures (Bijian 2005). China has made a decisive shift away from a passive observer to active participant – indeed, it was the chief mediator in the six-party talks to find a peaceful resolution of the nuclear crisis on the Korean peninsula and, from China's perspective, to prevent another fratricidal war on the Korean peninsula. Such actions have won numerous plaudits. Indeed, Beijing's role was central in bringing the United States and North Korea to the negotiating table following the unraveling of the "Agreed Framework" (a bilateral accord signed by Washington and Pyongyang in October 1994) to prevent North Korea from developing nuclear weapons in 2001. On a brief visit to Beijing in November 2005, President Bush publicly thanked China for "taking the lead" in the negotiations with North Korea (Kahn and Sanger 2005).

Also, as noted in Chapter 5, many of China's formerly antagonistic relations (with Russia, India, Vietnam, South Korea, and Indonesia) have greatly improved. The six-nation Shanghai Cooperation Organization (SCO) is a Beijing-led regional multilateral forum. It is successor to the Shanghai-Five grouping put together in 1996 to resolve China's border disputes with former Soviet Central Asian republics. The SCO has already helped settle China's long-standing territorial disputes with Kazakhstan, Kyrgyzstan, Laos, Russia, Tajikistan, and Vietnam – and not always in terms favorable to Beijing.[5] Since 2001, the SCO has actively cooperated on a range of issues, including counterterrorism, energy, economic linkages, and defense. To Beijing, the SCO is an important regional alliance. After all, the organization has allowed China not only to secure its borders but also to further Chinese trade in the region – in particular, giving China access to the regions rich raw materials, besides curbing U.S. influence in Central Asia. Arguably, the SCO has helped Beijing's fill the void left by the decline of Moscow's influence in the region. Not surprisingly, the SCO summit meetings routinely endorse Beijing's foreign policy agenda. In 2005, the SCO became the first regional organization to oppose the proposal by the Group of Four (Japan, Brazil, Germany, and India) to expand the UN Security Council's permanent membership, besides calling for an end to U.S. military presence in Central Asia. Given the fact that SCO member-states have

[5] Fravel (2005) argues that China has offered substantial compromises in most of these settlements, usually receiving less than 50 percent of the contested territory.

conducted regular military exercises since 2005, some have concluded that the organization's long-term goal is to become the "NATO of the East."

Similarly, China's "soft power" diplomacy or constructive engagement with ASEAN has assuaged the organization's concerns regarding the territorial disputes over the Paracel, Spratly, and Senkaku Islands. Since 1994, the focal point of China's security relations with South and East Asia has been the Asian Regional Forum (ARF). Made-up of twenty-three countries from both sides of the Pacific, ARF seeks to promote dialogue on contentious issues, rather than pursuing a unilateral solution. In 1997, Beijing advocated the "new security concept" to resolve disputes peacefully and within the framework of international law. China's embrace of multilateral diplomacy reached its high point in 2000, when it proposed the establishment of the ASEAN-China Free Trade Area (ACFTA).

Perhaps most important, considerable anxiety remains regarding Beijing's refusal to renounce the use of force against Taiwan. In March 2005, China's legislature, the National People's Congress, passed the Anti-Secession Law, which codified Beijing's threat to go to war if Taiwan declared independence. On the other hand, the PRC has also emphasized that the best way to prevent the Island's de jure or formal independence is through economic interdependence and "peaceful unification" – seemingly rejecting the earlier policy of "liberating Taiwan" through force and coercive diplomacy.[6] To Beijing's relief, internationally there is also growing appreciation that Taiwan is a "special case." The global community generally shares the view that Taiwan is an integral part of China, and China's neighbors, especially ASEAN, have implicitly noted that Taiwan's challenge of the "one China" policy (the view that Taiwan is a part of China), in demanding the right to self-determination, is unduly provocative and unacceptable.[7] No doubt, the loss of Taiwan would not only deal a severe blow to China's prestige, it would also establish a dangerous precedent for other potentially secession-prone areas of the mainland, including Tibet, Xinjiang, and Inner Mongolia (Wachman 2007). Not surprisingly, China has made it clear that although it will not renounce its right to use force, there are also other options – it recognizes that China and Taiwan are parts of a single shared sovereignty and that the "one China principle" remains a precondition to any

---

[6] Of course, this does not mean that Beijing will not do everything in its power to reduce Taiwan's influence. To this effect, it has pursued a policy that uses all manner of economic and diplomatic tools to reward countries that are willing to isolate Taiwan. This extends beyond pushing nations to adhere to the "one China" policy and includes trying to keep Taiwanese officials from participating in bilateral, regional, and international forums, as well as punishing businesses for links to Taiwan.

[7] Bush and O'Hanlon (2007) concur that Taiwan represents a potential flash point by noting that "regaining the island is the brass ring of Chinese politics; to somehow 'lose' Taiwan can be the kiss of death." However, they warn that Taiwan does not always fully grasp the danger of pursuing "independence" vis-à-vis China and that economic interdependence and geopolitical rivalry are two different things.

peaceful political negotiation with Taiwan. Again, although most analysts agree that the use of force by Beijing would occur only if the prospect of permanent Taiwanese separation from the mainland appeared imminent, miscalculation on either side could exacerbate the problem.

China's "Charm Offensive"

Is China's current emphasis on peaceful rise merely a transient and tactical necessity, or does it in fact represent an enduring strategic shift in China's international orientation? A large body of research argues that China's "charm offensive" has not only worked, it has also convinced many of Beijing's sincerity about being a responsible global stakeholder. For example, in his provocative book *Rising Star: China's New Security Diplomacy*, Bates Gill (2007) claims that China's new security diplomacy is designed to alleviate external tensions to address challenges at home, reassure her neighbors about China's peaceful intentions, and win acceptance and respect as a major global power. Gill is convinced that China has fundamentally changed its global and regional security strategies for the better. He maintains that the Chinese leadership has, for all practical purposes, abandoned revolution and ideology in an effort to gain acceptance as a responsible player in the international system. To Gill, China's efforts to assuage the concerns of its neighbors and work diligently in numerous bilateral and multilateral forums, including contributing to the UN peacekeeping missions, are concrete examples of its constructive intentions. He argues that Chinese foreign policy, in both words and actions, is increasingly consistent with international norms and reflects a "more proactive, practical, and constructive" approach to regional and global security affairs.

Similarly Joshua Kurlantzick's *Charm Offensive: How China's Soft Power Is Transforming the World* (2007) reveals how Beijing has been successfully exploiting its "soft power" (diplomacy; trade promotion; and cultural, educational, and sports exchange) to project a benign national and international image. He argues that China's leaders have been generally successful in transforming the negative image of their country as a "revisionist" and menacing power prone to bullying its neighbors into passivity and submission into one that is a team player committed to global peace and stability:[8] "as Beijing has looked outside its borders, it has altered its image across much of the globe, from threat to opportunity, from danger to benefactor."

How has Beijing managed such a remarkable shift? Kurlantzick notes that this began during the Asian financial crisis. While Washington remained initially indifferent and then asked the International Monetary Fund to deal with

---

[8] "Revisionist" broadly implies that China still harbors resentment and humiliation about some chapters of its history – especially foreign domination – and will use nationalism to correct the perceived injustices committed against it.

the crisis, Beijing won praise by refusing to devalue its currency, thereby helping to speed the regional recovery. Moreover, in recent years, Beijing has deployed a new generation of sophisticated and well-trained diplomats who have conscientiously promoted China's interests abroad. In addition to promoting the study of its language and culture by setting up numerous "Confucius Institutes" (*Kongzi Xueyuan*), China has also opened its universities to foreign students and cultivated better relations with the large ethnic Chinese diaspora, especially business elites across Southeast Asia and beyond (see Shambaugh 2005). In 2004, China established the Leading Small Group for Foreign Chinese Language Education under the State Council. The objective was to establish one hundred Confucius Institutes around the world. Since the establishment of the first one in South Korea in 2004, roughly 140 institutes have been set up worldwide. Finally, besides shrewdly using "tools of culture," Beijing has also prudently used "tools of business" to forge new alliances and exploit new opportunities for political and economic influence. Developing nations that are eager to trade their natural resources (minerals, food, and raw materials) in return for inexpensive Chinese consumer goods welcome Chinese investment in their industries and infrastructure, not to mention Chinese official aid that comes with the irresistible no "good-governance" strings attached.

To what extent is China's "charm offensive" a deliberate and calculated strategy? How well is it working? What are the implications for the United States? Does the embrace and practice of soft power mean that China is also unwittingly being transformed into a responsible status quo power? Kurlantzick wrestles head-on with all of these questions, but suffice it to note here that given ambiguities in the evidence and uncertainties about the future, his answers remain tentative. Nevertheless, he notes that China's "new diplomacy" is clearly part of a larger and deliberate government-directed campaign to reassure and gain influence. In regard as to whether China's charm offensive has been effective, he cites opinion polls from around the world that show China's popularity has been rising, even as American popularity has declined. He admits that China is in a "honeymoon period," but, how long this will last is uncertain. Overall, Kurlantzick feels that Beijing is wielding its soft power responsibly, citing China's constructive role in the North Korean nuclear standoff as an example. He feels that China's positive role in helping to resolve international disputes and embrace multilateral institutions are signs of its growing maturity and responsibility.

However, to the cynics, China's current grand strategy is a "strategy of convenience" – a disingenuous ploy designed for this current transition phase before China actually rises. Critics claim that once China has amassed the requisite capabilities, it will demand changes in the international order that signal its arrival as a "disruptive, revisionist power" determined to alter the international system to its advantage. Bernstein and Munro (1997, 19), argued more than a decade ago that "China is seeking to replace the United States as the dominant power in Asia" and is just biding its time. Others also see China as a fundamentally revisionist power whose goal is to correct both the real and imagined historical wrongs done to it. The argument is that to many Chinese leaders (and the Chinese public), the seminal event in China's recent past is the "century of humiliation" that began with the Opium Wars of the 1840s and ended only with the expulsion of foreign powers from the mainland after the revolution. This has made China's leaders acutely sensitive to perceived slights (both real and imagined) to national honor and prestige, leading some to argue that China is likely to behave assertively, even at the risk of conflict with others to correct historical wrongs (Swaine and Tellis 2000). Drawing on the lessons of great-power politics, the dean of American realism, John Mearsheimer (2001), in his majestic *The Tragedy of Great Power Politics*, insists that a more powerful China will inevitably behave like rising powers of the past, posing a threat to international peace and stability. Mearsheimer notes that as long as China's power continues to grow, "China, like all previous potential hegemons, [will] be strongly inclined to become a real hegemon" (p. 400). He warns that China's rapid acquisition of advanced military capabilities is a portent of things to come – namely, that it will allow China eventually to contest America's long-standing global preponderance. Mearsheimer chillingly notes, "If China continues its impressive economic growth over the next few decades, the United States and China are likely to engage in an intense security competition with considerable potential for war." Many others who do not fully agree with Mearsheimer nevertheless see possible future trends in Beijing's current behavior. They cite three core areas in which Beijing's behavior has not changed: unrestrained military buildup, its "new dictatorship diplomacy," and its self-serving mercantilist economic policies. The following sections elaborate on each.

China's Defense Spending

Since the reform era, China's military has experienced both a quantitative expansion and qualitative improvement in personnel and capabilities. Recently this led U.S. Secretary of State Condoleezza Rice to observe that because no nation threatens China, "its military build-up looks outsized for their regional concerns" and inconsistent with Beijing's stated goal of a "peaceful rise."[9] Although precise figures on China's military expenditures are hard to come by, there is consensus that Chinese military spending has witnessed a phenomenal rise over the past two decades.[10] In 2007, the publicly disclosed defense budget

---

[9] Condoleezza Rice talks with CBS News, 12 September 2005. http://www.state.gov/secretary/rm/2005/53033.htm.

[10] Until 1998, when China released its first "White Paper" on defense spending, little was known about the People's Liberation Army budget, save for a single aggregate line item in the annual central government budget. Since then, White Papers have been published every other year.

rose to RMB350 billion. This was up from RMB280 billion in 2006, marking the sixteenth successive year that the official budget had grown by more than 10 percent. After adjustment for inflation, the official budget has increased by 127 percent since 2000 and more than four-fold since 1995 (IISS Strategic Comments 2007) In March 2008, China announced its largest-ever annual increase in military spending – 17.8 percent. This raised defense spending to about US$45 billion, and there is suspicion that the "announced" budget is only a fraction of what the government actually spends each year. This is because China's official defense budget is divided into three categories: personnel, operations, and equipment; it omits several relevant categories such as weapons purchases, military research, development expenditures, and the People's Liberation Army's (PLA) earnings from its numerous business and commercial ventures (including revenue-sharing agreements with the central government from arms exports), a variety of personnel and other costs, not to mention the opaque accounting and auditing procedures. This makes it relatively easy for the PLA to hide its assets and has inevitably generated suspicion that China's military spending is two or three times higher than official figures. The Pentagon's annual report to Congress in 2007 concluded that Beijing's real military spending was at least US$70 billion – and could be as much as US$105 billion. Not surprisingly, the United States 2006 Quadrennial Defense Review Report (U.S. Department of Defense 2006) notes that China poses a major long-term military challenge to the United States.

Regardless of the precise figures on defense spending, it is clear that the PLA is in the midst of an ambitious upgrading (both quantitatively and qualitatively) of its offensive military capabilities. In other words, China has been actively engaged in a determined effort to transform its military from an army based on Mao Zedong's principles of mass-oriented, infantry-heavy "People's War" into a modern and agile force capable of projecting power throughout the Asia-Pacific and beyond. To this effect, Beijing has invested heavily in the blue-water navy, acquisitions of advanced fighter aircraft, submarines, in-flight refueling, miniaturized multiple nuclear warheads, and tactical nuclear weapons. Predictably, such an ambitious and comprehensive "revolution in military affairs" has alarmed China's neighbors and the United States. Related to China's military buildup is concern regarding its weapons proliferation activities, given China's role in selling arms, including ballistic missiles, to disreputable third parties. In fact, Washington has long been concerned about Beijing's weak compliance with the MTCR and in 2001 imposed sanctions on Beijing for its alleged violation of a November 2000 understanding in which

However, the budget details remain sparse, containing a simple breakdown of the official budget into the three broad spending categories: Personnel, Training and Maintenance, and Equipment (Blasko 2006).

China had promised to suspend further transfers of missile technology to Iran, Pakistan, and North Korea and to provide a complete list of missile parts and equipment that it would bar from export. Moreover, on more than one occasion the United States has appropriately accused China of violating the NPT by transferring nuclear equipment and dual-use technologies to countries such as Iran, Pakistan, and North Korea. The United States is not entirely convinced that Beijing has done enough to pressure North Korea to be fully transparent regarding its nuclear weapons program, arguing (with some justification) that Beijing seems to have been more intent on protecting an ally than forcing it to give up its nuclear weapons. On 12 January 2007, China's stunning test of its antisatellite weapons capabilities, despite its long-standing opposition to the "weaponization of space," has served only to renew concerns about China's military ambitions.

Yet despite such concerns, the United States must keep a balanced perspective regarding China's military modernization. Specifically, it will need to recognize "generic modernization" of the PLA's defense needs, in which China has been modernizing its weapons systems and upgrades its personnel commensurate to its economic expansion. This trend will undoubtedly continue. The United States must avoid perceiving normal upgrades or precautionary or defensively motivated policies and measures as offensive threats. However, the United States must remain alert to the potentially destabilizing weapons modernization aimed at the acquisition of capabilities that specifically target or threaten Taiwan, exacerbate the "security dilemma" in East Asia, or raise doubts about Beijing's intentions. On these issues, the United States and its allies must press Beijing and work with the international community to lower tension in the region, especially the volatile Taiwan Strait.

Chinese Support of Dictatorial and Rogue Regimes

Beijing's apparent "no-strings attached" collaborationist relations with governments that are in gross violation of international conventions on issues such as human rights, political repression, and other violations, together with its seemingly unconditional support for dictatorial and rogue regimes – especially Sudan, Myanmar, Zimbabwe, North Korea, Syria, and Iran – is seen by many to belie its commitment to act as a responsible international stakeholder. Over the past two decades, China has developed significant energy interests in Sudan. Beijing has invested heavily in Sudan's oil infrastructure, constructing numerous pipelines and refineries, and the state-owned China National Petroleum Corporation is the majority owner (40 percent) of the Greater Nile Petroleum Oil Company – the largest oil company operating in Sudan. In addition, China is Sudan's major arms supplier. It is also the major arms supplier to the Mugabe regime in Zimbabwe and trains the "internal security" personnel in both these countries.[11] Thus, Beijing's failure to use its leverage over Sudan to persuade President Omar al-Bashir to permit UN peacekeepers to enter into the Darfur region, including threatening to use its UN Security Council veto in September 2004 power to block further sanctions on the Sudanese regime, have reinforced the view that China's interests and motivations are narrow and self-serving.[12] In similar fashion, when the Iranian nuclear crisis began to escalate in August of 2004, China made it clear that the matter was inappropriate for the Security Council. China's failure to put pressure on Sudan to stop the genocide and bring peace to the Darfur region or demand that the junta ruling Myanmar stop its brutal suppression of Buddhist monks only seem to confirm that Beijing puts narrow interests above the common good. As Kleine-Ahlbrandt and Small (2008, 50) note, "three days after China vetoed the punitive Security Council resolution last January [2006], the Burmese government granted a Chinese company a major oil and gas exploration contract, even though it had been outbid by an Indian competitor." In January 2007, China, together with Russia, was one of only two governments that cast vetoes in the Security Council against a U.S.-sponsored resolution censuring Myanmar's brutal military regime.

Although China has recently supported UN-backed measures against Iran (to compel it to abandon its alleged nuclear weapons program), Beijing has opposed more punitive sanctions against Teheran and continues to advocate for Iran's right to peaceful nuclear power, despite Iran's violation of the NPT. Given China's strong ties to the Islamic Republic and the fact that Iran is a key source of energy for China, it is unlikely that Beijing will agree to measures that would seriously threaten its lucrative economic interests in Iran.[13] The United States has long expressed deep concerns about Chinese firms aiding the development of Iran's ballistic missile capability, especially the 2,000-kilometer range Shahab-3. In 2007, the Pentagon officially designated China as a principal supplier of nuclear technology to Iran. Perhaps more than anything, China's heavy-handed crackdown in Tibet in March-April 2008 and its outright refusal to engage with Tibet's exiled spiritual leader, the Dalai Lama, has reignited fears about Chinese belligerence, particularly because the Dalai Lama (unlike some of his followers) is willing to forgo full independence for Tibet for the sake of genuine autonomy. China's refusal to even have a dialogue with the Dalai Lama, who is widely seen to represent the best hope of a peaceful settlement,

---

[11] Kleine-Ahlbrandt and Small (2008, 52) note that "in 2006 a UN panel of experts found that shell casings collected from various sites in Darfur suggest that most ammunition currently used by parties to the conflict in Darfur is manufactured either in the Sudan or in China."

[12] Only recently, after years of unequivocal support of the Khartoum regime, did China endorse the UN Security Council resolution authorizing the deployment of a mixed UN-African Union peacekeeping force in Darfur.

[13] In 2004, China and Iran signed two accords estimated to be worth some US$100 billion over the coming twenty-five years, granting Chinese firms extensive rights to develop Iranian oil and natural gas reserves.

has convinced many of China's bullheadedness and lack of commitment to political dialogue and compromise.

Is China Mercantilist?

In his best seller *Three Billion New Capitalists*, distinguished trade analyst Clyde Prestowitz warns that the postwar era of U.S.-led globalization is giving way to a global order headed by China and India. However, what Prestowitz finds different about the current phase of globalization is that these nations are not simply integrating into the "Western-created world economy," they are also changing and transforming its "battered and strained" foundations because they are playing by different rules. Although Prestowitz blames the United States for many of its domestic economic woes (especially America's failure to deal with its unsustainable trade deficits and allowing "dangerous" buildup of massive dollar reserves with Japan and China), he also sees the "sudden entrance of 2.5 billion people in India and China" into the world's skilled job market as a profound challenge – one that the United States is simply too ill prepared to confront. To Prestowitz, the United States must rethink its "laissez-faire economic ideology" and hubris in its technological supremacy because it has prevented it from fully grasping the magnitude of the problem and devising a programmatic national response. Specifically, Prestowitz calls for broad changes in U.S. policies – in particular, a reduction in the dollar's role as the world's key currency, because it has allowed the United States to live well beyond its means. Although not advocating protectionism, Prestowitz argues that the United States needs an active mercantilist "competition policy" because the free trade model of globalization has proved to be harmful to America's long-term economic and security interests.

Although Prestowitz's prescriptions are long term, of immediate concern to the United States is China's allegedly mercantilist economic policies, which are largely seen in the United States as responsible for its massive trade deficit with China. The American contention regarding Chinese mercantile behavior is rather straightforward: China engages in gratuitously unfair trade practices through protectionism, violation of intellectual property rights, and deliberate manipulation of its currency. More specifically, for several years, the United States has experienced a large and growing deficit in its current account – which is the broadest measure of a country's trade with the rest of the world. In 1991, the current account was roughly in balance; by mid-2007, it had reached just over US$1 trillion, or a deficit of 7 percent of GDP. To finance both the current account deficit and its own sizable foreign investments, the United States must import an estimated US$1 trillion of foreign capital every year, or more than US$4 billion every working day. This deficit means that the United States is buying more goods (and services) from abroad than it is selling. The main source of financing for the difference in the balance of imports and exports

Table 7.1. *U.S. merchandise trade with China: 1980–2007 (US$ billions)*

Year	U.S. exports	U.S. imports	U.S. trade balance
1980	3.8	1.1	2.7
1985	3.9	3.9	0
1990	4.8	15.2	−10.4
1995	11.7	45.6	−33.8
2000	16.3	100.1	−83.8
2001	19.2	102.3	−83.1
2002	22.1	125.2	−103.1
2003	28.4	152.4	−124.0
2004	34.7	196.7	−162.0
2005	41.8	243.5	−201.6
2006	55.2	287.8	−232.5
2007	65.2	321.5	−256.3

Source: U.S. Congressional Research Service (2008, 2).

is the flow of foreign funds into the United States. This can take the form of foreigners purchasing U.S. Treasuries and bonds and shares in companies or property.[14] Over time, the level of U.S. net foreign liabilities relative to GDP has risen substantially.[15]

However, China's foreign exchange reserves reached an unprecedented US$1.8 trillion in mid-2008, whereas its current-account surplus (the sum of its trade surplus and net receipts from foreign assets and foreign remittances) totaled US$300 billion in 2007. This is roughly equivalent to about 10 percent of its GDP. Two-thirds of this amount (US$200 billion) represents a bilateral surplus with the United States, keeping in mind that the U.S. global current-account deficit was about $800 billion or nearly 6 percent of GDP in 2007. Thus, China's bilateral current-account surplus with the United States equaled one-quarter of the global U.S. deficit (see Tables 7.1 and 7.2).

American manufacturers with the backing of lawmakers in Congress have long argued that the artificially low yuan has placed American companies at a huge competitive disadvantage contributing to the bankruptcy of U.S. companies and the loss of tens of thousands of jobs in the United States.[16] The

[14] Treasury securities are the debt financing instruments of the U.S. Federal government. They are often referred to as Treasuries. There are four types of marketable treasury securities: Treasury bills, Treasury notes, Treasury bonds, and Treasury Inflation Protected Securities (TIPS).

[15] U.S. Department of the Treasury (2005, May), "Report to Congress on International Economic and Exchange Rate Policies"; Office of the U.S. Trade Representative (2005, July 11), "The U.S.-China Joint Commission on Commerce and Trade (JCCT): Outcomes on Major U.S. Trade Concerns."

[16] From its peak in early 1998, the United States has lost over 3.3 million manufacturing jobs. While not all of the job loss can be attributed to China, the U.S. manufacturing sector, despite significant productivity growth could not overcome the huge trade advantage China

Table 7.2. *U.S. merchandise trade balances with major trading partners: 2007 (US$ billions)*

Country/trading group	U.S. trade balance
World	−791.0
China	−256.3
European Union (EU27)	−107.4
Organization of Petroleum Exporting Countries (OPEC)	−127.4
Japan	−82.8
Canada	−64.7
Mexico	−74.3
Association of Southeast Asian Nations (ASEAN)	−50.6

Source: U.S. Congressional Research Service (2008, 2).

contention is that the yuan is so undervalued (by some accounts as much as 40 percent) that it amounts to an unfair trade subsidy. This unfair advantage permits a flood of cheap Chinese-made goods into the United States, but makes American products expensive in China.[17] Thus, it is claimed that if the yuan was traded at its true market worth the bilateral imbalance between the two countries would be substantially reduced, if not altogether eliminated. This is because China's exports to the United States would become more expensive in dollars and would therefore decrease, while China's imports from the U.S. would become less expensive in yuan and therefore increase. To critics, making matters worse, China's unwillingness to allow the yuan to appreciate has, in turn, made other Asian Pacific Rim countries reluctant to allow their currencies to appreciate because of their fear of losing further export sales to China.[18] As U.S. trade deficit with China soared to record level in first-quarter 2005, the Bush administration came under intense pressure to take unilateral action to address the problems associated with the artificial undervaluation of the yuan. While the former U.S. Treasury Secretary John Snow called for an immediate

gained by having an undervalued currency. The decline in manufacturing employment has led both Democratic and Republican senators to threaten the Chinese with substantial tariffs on Chinese imports to offset the Chinese currency advantage (Hufbauer and Wong 2004).

[17] Some economists claim that the yuan is anywhere from 15 percent to 40 percent undervalued against the dollar, making Chinese exports to the United States cheaper and contributing to China's trade surplus with the United States (Lardy 2005). Of course, no one really knows the true extent of the undervaluation. This is because in not letting the market decide a currency's value means the nominal exchange rate – literally the number of units of one currency you can get for one unit of another – is essentially made up. It is whatever the government chooses it to be, so long as the regime can be feasibly maintained.

[18] Indeed, following the Chinese revaluation, Malaysia responded by shifting its own currency regime from a dollar peg to a basket peg. However, given the very small initial change in the yuan's value, most countries in the region seems to be waiting for a more substantial yuan revaluation before taking action.

Chinese exchange rate adjustment, many other lawmakers called for punitive tariffs (i.e., taxes) on cheaply priced Chinese imports unless China sharply revalued its currency.

China sought to placate critics by taking a number of measures to reduce its trade surplus with the United States. For example, China reduced the export rebate from 15 percent to 11 percent for textiles, clothing, shoes, and toys. Controls on foreign currency holdings for individuals traveling abroad were relaxed and regulations on foreign currency retention by exporters were revised. Most notably, the Chinese government sharply increased its purchase of U.S. Treasury Bonds, besides placing well-publicized huge orders for U.S. made goods.[19] However, these failed to impress the critics. In early May 2005, the U.S. Senate by a margin of 67 to 33 voted to consider a proposal to impose a 27.5 percent tariff on all imports from China unless Beijing stopped inflating its currency. In May 2005, the United States decided to reimpose quotas on seven categories of clothing imports from China limiting their growth to no more than 7.5 percent over a 12-month period. On June 23, 2005, the Bush administration, which until then had insisted that diplomacy was working in getting China to allow the yuan's value to be set by currency markets rather than controlled by the government, finally warned China that it could be cited as a "currency manipulator" and face economic sanctions unless it switched to a flexible exchange system. Labeling China's currency policies "highly distortionary," the Bush administration warned that it was going to closely monitor China's progress towards adopting a flexible exchange system.

It seems that the mounting pressure worked. On 21 July 2005, Beijing made its biggest monetary shift in more than a decade by revaluing the yuan and dropping the currency's peg to the U.S. dollar.[20] In 1994, the value of the renminbi was pegged to the U.S. dollar at a rate determined by the People's Bank of China. Since 2000, the yuan had been trading within the range of 8.27 to 8.28 to the dollar. This nominal rate approximated an equilibrium market rate or the rate at which the market demand for the yuan was equal to the market supply. However, in recent years as the demand for yuan at this fixed price greatly exceeded the supply the Chinese central bank finally decided to intervene to meet the excess demand for the yuan. Beijing abandoned the peg and moved to a system that now linked the yuan to a basket of currencies effectively raising the yuan's value by 2.1 percent.[21] This means that prior to

[19] U.S. Treasury Bills are short-term debt instruments (issued in 3, 6, and 12 month maturities) of the U.S. government to finance the federal government. They pay a set amount at maturity and have no interest payments. However, they effectively pay interest by initially selling at a discount – that is at a price lower than the set amount paid at maturity.

[20] Revaluation is the resetting of the fixed value of a currency at a higher level.

[21] Both flexible and floating exchange rates have distinct advantages – albeit, no single exchange rate regime is appropriate for all countries in all circumstances. A fixed exchange rate that pegs the value of a currency to a stronger foreign currency like the U.S. dollar or the euro has advantages for developing countries seeking to build confidence in their economic policies.

balance (U.S. billion dollars)

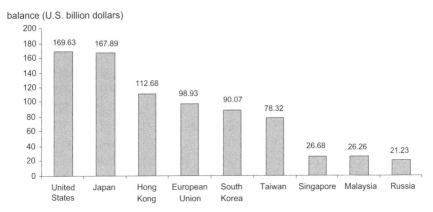

Figure 7.1. China's Top Trade Partners in 2004. *Source:* The World Bank (2005).

the revaluation US$1 bought 8.28 yuan, following revaluation US$1 would buy roughly 8.11 yuan. Beijing made it clear that it set tight parameters on how much the yuan could rise. Clearly, the aim was to make sure that the yuan did not float by a big margin, but appreciate[22] by a modest 2 percent by moving within a tight range of 0.3 percent band against a group of foreign currencies that make up China's top trading partners (see Figure 7.1).

Under this "managed float," the People's Bank of China (PBC) hopes to keep exchange values, especially the dollar/yuan rate, from experiencing big shifts in either direction by resetting the value of the yuan at the end of each trading day.[23] That is, the PCB will adjust the RMB exchange rate band when necessary, based on market conditions with reference to a basket of currencies.[24] Initially, no one knew for certain what was in the PBC's basket of currencies, albeit the guess was that it likely included the dollar, euro, yen, and possibly money of

On the other hand, countries with fixed exchange rates are seemingly more vulnerable to currency crises. As economies mature and become more closely aligned with the international financial markets, exchange rate flexibility seems more advantageous.

[22] When a currency increases in value, it experiences appreciation. When it falls in value and is worth fewer U.S. dollars, it undergoes depreciation. Thus, when a country's currency appreciates (rises in value relative to other currencies), the country's goods abroad become more expensive and foreign goods in that country becomes cheaper. Conversely, when a country's currency depreciates, its goods abroad become cheaper and foreign goods in that country become more expensive.

[23] China calls its new system a "managed floating exchange rate regime." While it is a form of managed float, some aspects of it, such as allowing the currency to move 0.3 per cent per day against the dollar, have some similarity to a crawling peg. Also, to reiterate, the renminbi (RMB) is the name of the Chinese currency. The yuan is one unit of the currency.

[24] Specifically, each day the PBC will announce its target for the following working day on the basis of that day's renminbi closing price in terms of a "central parity." For example, the target may be expressed in terms of the value of the renminbi against the dollar. The following day, the renminbi exchange rate will be allowed to fluctuate against the dollar within a band of plus or minus 0.3 percent around the announced central parity.

China's dozen or so top trading partners. Those currencies will now fluctuate in value against the yuan, but, as one appreciates, others might fall, balancing out the overall effect on Chinese trade. From July 2005 until the end of May 2008, the RMB appreciated by 14.4 percent in terms of the U.S. dollar – but much less in real terms (because most other major currencies have appreciated against the dollar) despite China's large and growing trade surpluses.

Although the PBC did not disclose the currencies in the basket or how much weight each would carry, it did announce that it would choose one currency from the basket to be the reference currency; yet it did not say which one. In not disclosing the basket's composition, the PBC could play with the exchange rate by changing the mix, giving dollars more or less weight as needed to keep rates from shifting too dramatically. However, on 10 August 2005, Beijing made good on the promise to disclose more details regarding the basket of currencies, noting that the basket would depend on the amount of foreign trade that China conducted. Because the United States, euro zone, Japan, and South Korea are China's biggest trading partners, their currencies are naturally the main ones in the basket. Other currencies holding a lesser weight include the Singapore dollar, British pound, Malaysian ringgit, Australian dollar, Russian ruble, Thai baht, and Canadian dollar. Although the exact percentage weightings were not disclosed, the Chinese authorities did note that the weights would be based on how much trade each country did with China, as well as how much debt China owed to each country. China has refrained from disclosing the basket weightings because it would provide too much information for currency speculators. Finally, both the central bank governor Zhou Xiaochuan and Premier Wen Jiabao have noted that the revaluation should be viewed as the first in what is expected to be a series of steps over years to shift the yuan toward even greater flexibility as China increases its participation in the world trading system.[25]

WHY DID CHINA REVALUE THE YUAN?

Despite years of intense pressure from the United States, Japan, and the EU, China has been reluctant to revalue the yuan because of the concern that a currency appreciation could slow export growth, increase unemployment, and lead to a decline in foreign direct investment.[26] This is hardly surprising;

---

[25] People's Bank of China (2005, July 21), "Public Announcement of the People's Bank of China on Reforming the RMB Exchange Rate Regime"; People's Bank of China (2005, August 10), "Speech of Governor Zhou Xiaochuan at the Inauguration Ceremony of the People's Bank of China Shanghai Head Office," available at http://www.pbc.gov.cn/english/detail.asp?col=6500&id=82.

[26] To Chinese authorities, concerns about the domestic consequences of large or rapid revaluation are paramount, especially the potentially disruptive adjustment for exporters of labor-intensive goods.

China has kept the value of its currency artificially cheap because it implicitly subsidizes its exports and taxes its imports. Arguably, during 2003–5, China's macroeconomic situation became more conducive to the yuan's revaluation. First, the growth rate of GDP, which averaged between 7.1 percent and 8.8 percent from 1997 to 2002, accelerated to more than 9 percent during 2003–5. Second, the undervalued renminbi contributed to excessive credit growth and overheating because it attracted large capital inflows motivated by expectations of a yuan appreciation. In fact, tens of billions of dollars of "hot money" had poured into the economy by speculators and China's trading partners in the expectation of an imminent rise of the yuan. The PBC viewed these developments as inflationary, with the real threat being a "hard landing" or recession. Having suffered through two painful hard landings (1985–89 and 1992–94) when growth dropped sharply, the PBC hoped that an appreciation would slow down the growth rate and help the economy achieve the desired soft landing.

Although in theory, revaluation ought to make Chinese exports more expensive (thereby increasing imports and slowing down GDP growth), the Chinese policy makers were aware that this may not happen – at least not right away, given the modest scale of the revaluation. Nevertheless, the PCB felt that a more flexible yuan would ease the real problem: the flood of hot money into China's money markets and real estate.[27] In the past, this flow, as well as the export earnings that needed to be recycled back into yuan, placed huge strains on the PBC. To defend the fixed currency peg between the yuan and dollar, the central bank had to buy (or sell) foreign currency in exchange for yuan.[28] In other words, to maintain the peg, the PBC had to intervene by selling domestic currency in exchange for foreign reserves.[29] As a result, the volume of foreign reserves jumped to more than $100 billion in 2004, placing tremendous inflationary pressures on the economy.

The PBC managed to offset much of this pressure through sterilization policies that soaked up the excess liquidity associated with money inflows. Specifically, when too much yuan circulated around the money system, the PBC withdrew the extra cash through what money traders call "sterilization" – issuing notes and bonds.[30] However, it is not clear that sterilization will be effective over the long term because China's domestic bond and capital markets

---

[27] Portfolio investment refers to paper securities such as stocks, bonds, and T-bills.

[28] Under a fixed exchange rate regime, the central bank buys and sells its own currencies to keep its exchange rates fixed at a certain level.

[29] This is because maintaining the dollar peg required China to buy foreign exchange at the official rate – that is, to supply yuan in exchange for dollars or other reserve currencies to meet any excess demand for yuan. In the absence of these official transactions, market forces would have caused the yuan's value to appreciate.

[30] A bond is a debt security that promises to make payments periodically for a specified period of time.

are relatively shallow.[31] Of course, if sterilization fails to soak up the extra cash, the money supply can expand dramatically, igniting inflation and encouraging banks to lend recklessly because they have more yuan than they can effectively circulate. Although this could be less of a problem now, China is still not out of the woods. The reality is that the extent of the revaluation is too modest and the yuan is still undervalued. Naturally, speculators will see a managed float as an invitation to pump in more money into China and pull it out at a more favorable time. However, the People's Bank has enough reserves to intervene in the markets and sterilize the speculative flows.

The revaluation underscores the PBC's stated long-term goal to build a managed floating exchange rate mechanism based on market supply and demand and to maintain the yuan's basic stability at a reasonable equilibrium. Moreover, Beijing hopes that revaluation will better align China's economy with the rest of the world, as well as head off rising U.S. discontent at the growing bilateral trade deficit. Some view the new managed float against a narrow basket of currencies as the first step in a larger effort that will result in the value of the yuan being completely determined by market forces; however, the current revaluation, is nevertheless likely to fuel a drive to increased flexibility in exchange rates. Overall, this is a positive development because it means that China will be less able to manipulate rates for trade advantages. As is well known, pegging to a basket of currencies has the advantage of reducing the transmission of external shocks to the domestic economy and tempering the exchange rate's exposure to the potentially erratic movements of a single currency. Greater flexibility in its exchange rate would give China a more independent monetary policy, as well as allow the exchange rate to play a positive role in correcting external imbalances.

PLACATING AMERICA? BE CAREFUL WHAT YOU WISH FOR

To many U.S. policy makers and businesses, a further revaluation of the yuan is urgently needed to correct the large U.S. trade imbalance and prevent manufacturing job losses. However, some economists have their doubts that this is the cure (Hale and Hale 2008; Mann 2005). They challenge the claim that the U.S. trade deficit is the result of China's currency policies. Rather, in recent years, U.S. bilateral trade deficits have been increasing not only with China but with other trading partners as well. Although the imbalance with China is large, it still accounts for less than one-quarter of the total. Thus, the overall U.S. imbalance cannot be blamed entirely on China, nor is it realistic to assume that an exchange rate adjustment will altogether eliminate or significantly rein in the large U.S. trade deficit. In fact, Chinese authorities have long pointed out

---

[31] Capital markets are where longer-term debt (often with original maturity of greater than one year) and equity investments are traded.

that balancing China's trade will not by itself resolve the problem of the U.S. current account deficit because the U.S. deficit reflects a fundamental savings-investment imbalance. Mann (2005) also points out that the official purchases of U.S. dollar assets by China and other U.S. trading partners have allowed for the continued high levels of U.S. domestic spending and kept interest rates low. With international banks, investment funds, and multinational firms increasingly reluctant to hold working capital in dollar-denominated assets, China invests a lion's share of its foreign exchange reserves in U.S. Treasury securities. This has helped to keep interest rates down in the United States despite large and chronic budget deficits and weak domestic savings. Finally, although revaluation could help some U.S. manufacturers by making Chinese goods more expensive, it could be costly for others who do business in China. That is, even if Chinese exports become more costly due to revaluation, it will still be cheaper to produce most of these goods in China than in the United States. It is more likely that the benefit of an increased cost of Chinese production will be felt by other Asian countries.[32]

China, in contrast, has long claimed that the relatively low prices of its goods are because of its low labor costs, from which the American economy derives great benefits because lower prices allows it to maintain low inflation and robust household consumption.[33] Moreover, trade restrictions against Chinese imports are hardly a solution because the United States would not only be forgoing the benefits of inexpensive imports, such policies would not help America's low-skilled workers. On the contrary, low-priced Chinese imports help low-income working families; instead of blaming China, the United States can better help its low-skilled workers by improving their skills. The implication is clear: a more expensive yuan not only means higher prices for Chinese goods, it could also put pressure on U.S. domestic inflation. Finally, there is the view that revaluation will not fundamentally change the makeup of China's huge foreign currency reserves, 70 percent of which are in dollar assets like the U.S. Treasuries.[34] That is, to maintain a fixed exchange rate with the dollar, China's central bank has been forced to purchase U.S. dollar assets that, in turn, help finance the huge U.S. trade deficit and help prevent further falls in the dollar (in other words, China has kept the yuan from strengthening by plowing part of its trade surplus with the United States back into

[32] China's increase in market share has largely come at the expense of middle-income countries, rather than low-income countries. This, in part, is because importers have been maintaining diverse low-cost suppliers in case the United States or the European Union imposes bilateral quotas on China. Thus, textile exports of Bangladesh, Cambodia, and Vietnam to the United States have increased since 2000.

[33] See People's Daily (2005). "Trade Surplus with the U.S. Viewed from Another Angle." Available at http://english1.people.com.cn/200508/12/eng20050812_202051.1html.

[34] To maintain its currency against the dollar, China has become a big investor in U.S. securities. China is the second-largest foreign holder of U.S. Treasury securities with US$243 billion in Treasuries in 2006 (J. Wong 2006).

U.S. Treasuries). Although, there is always the possibility that China might sell off some of those reserves and buy yen and euros, the PBC will still need lots of U.S. dollars – the world's most liquid currency. However, on one hand, revaluation may force China to cut its investment in U.S. Treasuries and shift investments to government bonds in Europe and Japan (thereby contributing to higher U.S. interest rates[35]); on the other, it is unlikely that the PBC will orchestrate a precipitously destabilizing sell off of its U.S. Treasury holdings because it could harm its biggest export market, besides sharply reducing the value of the assets Beijing holds.

Since the revaluation, the RMB exchange rate has been moving in both directions against the U.S. dollar, displaying a larger flexibility based on market supply and demand. By 31 March 2006, the RMB had appreciated by 3.20 percent against the dollar. To critics, this was not good enough. They urged the Bush administration to continue to pressure China on its exchange rate policy. With some justification, they argued that given the modest revaluation, the renminbi is still technically pegged to the dollar with little de facto flexibility. Some have argued that China's maintenance of a fixed exchange rate is part of its larger mercantilist strategy to promote export-led growth. In April 2006, the U.S. Treasury Department announced it might officially label China a "currency manipulator." This label would provide a basis for trade and economic sanctions against China. On their part, Chinese officials continue to maintain that the yuan will be adjusted at China's pace. Although former Treasury Secretary John W. Snow noted that the administration was extremely dissatisfied with the slow pace of reform of the Chinese exchange rate regime, he also cautioned that imposing trade sanctions against China over this matter would invite protectionist policies in other parts of the world. Senators Charles Schumer (D) and Lindsey Graham (R), who in mid-2005 were on the verge of sponsoring legislation that would impose high tariffs on China if Beijing failed to adjust its currency, agreed to delay pushing the bill until the end of September 2006; both publicly stated, however, that they were ready to move forward if China fails to make significant progress on the issue.

Chinese leaders have pledged to reduce the growing trade surplus and reiterated Beijing's commitment to make the yuan more flexible. However, while every other major currency has appreciated against the dollar since April 2006, the yuan is only 0.2 percent stronger against the dollar. Clearly, this issue is

---

[35] Revaluation could affect interest rates by reducing China's appetite for U.S. Treasury bonds. Specifically, if the Chinese government reduces the amount of dollars that it holds in reserve or slows the pace at which it buys dollars, the revaluation could put upward pressure on U.S. interest rates. China uses U.S. government bonds as a way to hold dollar reserves. Holding fewer dollars would mean fewer bonds. If the demand in the bond market that is attributable to China were to be reduced, bond prices might fall, and yields, which move in the opposite direction, might rise.

hardly settled. The depreciation of the U.S. dollar relative to the euro and the Canadian dollar has only further redirected U.S. import demand toward China. As Chinese auto parts began entering the U.S. market in large quantities (not to mention Chinese-made vehicles in early 2007), protectionist voices in the United States have grown louder. Beijing has attempted to placate, if not implicitly warn, these voices by reiterating that China's economy today serves as an engine of global growth because it is also importing vast quantities of goods. Chinese leaders are quick to point out that in 1995, China was the thirteenth leading export market for U.S. goods, but in 2006, it was the fourth leading export market. Again, the implication is a wealthier China is a strong market for U.S. goods and services, especially agricultural and high-tech goods. As if to underscore this, President Jintao, during his visit to Washington in April 2006, announced that China would buy US$16.2 billion worth of Boeing jets and medical equipment.

Beyond such gestures, it would be prudent for China to adopt a more flexible exchange rate. China's emphasis on exchange rate stability in the face of rising current account surpluses has generated intense protectionist pressures in the United States and elsewhere. For example, a study by R. E. Scott (2007) of the Economic Policy Institute claimed that between 1997 and 2006, the United States lost 2,763,400 jobs as a direct result of the bilateral trade deficit with China; from these data, Senators Max Baucus (D), Charles Grassley (R), Charles Schumer (D), and Lindsey Graham (R), on 14 June 2007, introduced legislation to "punish China" if it did not change its policy of intervening in currency markets to keep the exchange value of the yuan low. Moreover, the current policy has also forced China's central bank to accumulate massive foreign exchange reserves with negative domestic consequences. By keeping the yuan from rising against the U.S. dollar, China's central bank has to print more money to keep interest rates low; in addition, such a strategy can also exacerbate the problem of inflation if more money ends up chasing too few goods. It also means that China is exposed to large capital losses on its foreign reserve holdings (which are largely held in U.S. dollars) as the renminbi appreciates. Moreover, an appreciation of the exchange rate would also boost domestic consumption – and this is something China needs.

In late 2008, China maintained the world's largest cash reserves of roughly $2 trillion. This made China the world's leading creditor nation and the United States is the world's largest debtor. Beijing is the largest foreign holder of U.S. government debt – passing Japan in (September 2008) to become, in effect, the U.S. government's largest foreign creditor. China's investment in Treasury bonds totaled some $585 billion in September 2008, compared to Japan, which held $573.2 billion worth – albeit, most analyst estimate China's holdings to be over $800 billion as China also purchases U.S. debt through third countries which are not recorded by the Treasury as being held by China.

To some this is an ominous development because America's growing dependence and Beijing's growing financial leverage as a creditor grants it extraordinary influence over the U.S. economy. If for economic or strategic reasons Beijing decided to move out of U.S. government bonds it would force other investors to do the same, and in the process drive up the cost of U.S. borrowing and undermine Washington's ability to manage the economy. Similarly, if China stopped buying or, worse, began selling U.S. debt, it would sharply raise interest rates on a variety of loans in the United States. However, not everyone shares these pessimistic outcomes. The conventional view (as discussed earlier) is that Beijing depends on a strong dollar to keep its export engines humming. That is why it purchases U.S. bonds (which are denominated in dollars) to make the dollar stronger against the Chinese yuan as an artificially weak yuan helps to boost Chinese exports, in addition to making Chinese exports cheaper relative to U.S. exports. In effect, Beijing has also put itself in the unenviable position where it has to literally defend the dollar's value.

Moreover, reminiscent of Japan, which also had the bulk of its foreign assets denominated in U.S. dollars rather than yen, and them saw the value of those assets drop when the U.S. dollar depreciated sharply following the Plaza Accords in 1985, China today face the same risks – and more. China is often referred to as an "immature creditor" because it does not lend in its own currency, but in the currency issued by borrower (the loans China makes are denominated in U.S. dollars), it is exposed to exchange rate risks as the value of the debt fluctuates with the dollar's rise and fall. Since an unprecedented volume of China's reserves are estimated to be in dollars, even a modest depreciation of the dollar will translate into significant losses for Beijing. As a result, China has much incentive to defend the U.S. dollar – and the fastest and easiest way to do this is to buy even more Treasury bonds. This also means that the oft-mentioned claim that if Beijing were to dump its holdings of Treasury debt, the resulting market disruption would likely lead to higher U.S. interest rates and a collapse of the dollar on foreign exchange markets is exaggerated. This is because even the largest foreign holdings of U.S. government debt are smaller than the daily volume of trade in Treasury securities. If, say, the Chinese did employ such a strategy, the resulting decline in the value of U.S. Treasury securities would generate substantial losses to all debt holders, including those attempting to use their debt holdings as leverage.

Of course, all this could change if the unfolding global financial crisis deepens and the U.S. budget deficits expand because this could drive down the dollar and the value of China's investments, especially Treasuries. This could push Beijing to liquidate some of its U.S. Treasury bonds. Contrary, to conventional belief, it would not be as difficult as one thinks. After all, not only is China's foreign assets held as "official" foreign exchange reserves, the Chinese party-state via its control of the banking sector has a pervasive command over the economy. It can act quickly and decisively. Finally, in contrast to Japan,

China does not have to be deferential to the United States. Despite being a creditor, Japan, a member of the western alliance and beneficiary of the American security umbrella, was "indebted" to its major debtor. China, on the other hand, a competitor to American power and whose relations with its major debtor is best described as a "marriage of convenience," has the potential to utilize its economic influence as a tool of foreign policy.

The Security Challenge: How to Deal with an Emergent China?

THE REALISTS

To realists like Mearsheimer (2001), the "iron laws" of international relations point to an inevitable collision between China and the United States. It is useful to reiterate briefly the basic premise of political realism that informs Mearsheimer's pessimistic worldview. In the realist perspective, the international system has several defining features. First, the main actors are nation-states that operate in an environment of anarchy. Second, conflict is an enduring feature of the international system. Third, great powers have offensive military capability. This means they have the capacity to commit violence against each other. Fourth, no state can know the future intentions of other states with certainty. The best way to survive in such an anarchic system is to be as powerful as possible – at least relative to potential rivals. This is because the more powerful a state is, the less likely that another will try to coerce or attack it.

Mearsheimer draws on these ideas with elegance and insight to articulate his own theory of international relations, which he labels "offensive realism" and claims has greater explanatory power regarding the causes of war and peace in contemporary times. In a nutshell, offensive realism rests on the assumption that great powers "are always searching for opportunities to gain power over their rivals, with hegemony as their final goal" (p. 29). This view contrasts with "defensive realism," which posits that states seek security rather than power, making the international system less conflict-prone. Also, unlike "classical realists" who see the "urge to dominate" and aggression as intrinsic to states, offensive realists attribute this tendency to the elusive quest for security in a world of uncertainty and the constantly shifting balance of power. In the pervasive logic of offensive realism, great powers invariably seek to gain power at each other's expense and to establish themselves as the dominant state. To Mearsheimer, this constitutes the iron laws of international relations; he notes that if history has taught us anything, it is that powerful states attempt to establish hegemony in their own region while making sure that no rival power dominates another region. Although the ultimate goal of every great power is to dominate the global system, this is almost impossible in the modern era given the prohibitive costs associated with projecting and sustaining power around the globe. Thus, under these conditions, even the United States is a regional, rather than a global, hegemon. According to Mearsheimer, once a state gains regional hegemony, it will prevent others from gaining a foothold because "regional hegemons" abhor peer competitors. Therefore, an increasingly powerful China is also likely to try to push the United States out of Asia – much the way the United States pushed the European powers out of the Western Hemisphere. Moreover, gaining regional hegemony is probably the only way that China will restore Taiwan to mainland control and satisfy its other irredentist claims (also see Bernstein and Munro 1997; Betts 1993; Chang 2001; Friedberg 1993–94). Once China establishes its regional hegemony, it will be in the position to dictate the boundaries of acceptable behavior to neighboring countries, much the same way the United States does in the Americas. Given this reality, Mearsheimer concludes that China cannot rise peacefully because "like all previous potential hegemons, [it will] be strongly inclined to become a real hegemon" (p. 400). Thus, in the coming decades, the United States and China are likely to engage in an intense security competition with considerable potential for war. Because China's neighbors will feel the brunt of its aggressive hegemony, Mearsheimer claims that countries such as India, Japan, Singapore, South Korea, Russia, and Vietnam are likely join with the United States to contain Chinese power. Given this possibility, Mearsheimer offers a concise missive: prudence requires the United States should not invest too much in the strategy of "engagement" because it is doomed to fail. Rather, it must "prepare for the worst" by taking a hard line against China while it is still relatively weak and vulnerable.

Predictably, Mearsheimer's claims generated a heated debate, with critics noting a number of flaws in his arguments. First is the charge that Mearsheimer's claims are mechanistic because how great powers behave is not predetermined. For example, although Schweller (1999) agrees that rising powers tend to be dissatisfied with the status quo, this does not necessarily mean that China will behave in a particularly hostile manner. This is because rising powers can differ in the extent of their dissatisfaction with the status quo – and therefore in the scope of their ambitions. Although some rising powers do have radical objectives in that they seek to overthrow the established system of international rules, norms, and institutions, others have more modest or limited aims because they seek only minor adjustments to the status quo. Schweller argues that in sharp contrast to the Maoist era, China today is hardly a "revolutionary power." Rather, it has long abandoned its goal of spreading Communism. Instead, what Beijing seeks are some basic changes to the status quo that are limited to the reintegration of Taiwan with the mainland and a number of border disputes that can be resolved peacefully. Fravel (2005) underscores this by arguing that China has hardly become more assertive in its territorial dispute as its relative power has grown in the past two decades. To the contrary, it has been not only conciliatory but quite willing to offer territorial concessions. Thus, the claim that China harbors aggressive irredentist claims and that its growing power will allow it to pursue these ambitions are disingenuous.

Second, a number of analysts have noted that the assumption that China can easily push the United States out of Asia or out of Japan is not only simplistic, it is not in China's interests to do so. Given Japan's resources, it could quickly develop a significant nuclear deterrent. China's unapologetic, intense dislike and distrust of the Japanese some six decades after World War II cannot be overstated (Pyle 2007; Samuels 2007). To the Chinese, who with some justification point out that Japan has never demonstrated genuine contrition for its brutal occupation of China, a militarily powerful, nationalistic, and nuclear-armed Japan would be an unacceptable and intolerable breach.[36] Therefore, China is prepared to accept America as "Asia's pacifier" because U.S. disengagement could lead to a dangerous rivalry or "power balancing" in the region (Lieber 2007). Third, a policy of containment is self-defeating because the economic costs would be exceedingly high. Fourth, unlike the broad consensus on the necessity of containment against the former Soviet Union, there is little appetite for a similar strategy against China. This is because China is not an immediate threat but a rising power, and there are no guarantees that it will one day be a threatening great power. Fifth, unlike during the Cold War when the United States and the USSR had minimal exchanges, China and the United states have developed an extensive web of commercial, cultural, and human relationships. This will militate against knee-jerk impulse to contain China. Sixth, contrary to realist assumptions, the disagreements between the United States and China (including the difficult question of Taiwan) are not intractable problems but can be managed and resolved through dialogue and diplomacy. The U.S. policy of strategic ambiguity toward Taiwan has not only helped to reduce open conflict between China and Taiwan but can also aid in promoting dialogue and reconciliation between the two adversaries. Seventh, a containment strategy would by callous and undermine long-term American interests as China would reciprocate American hostility.

The perennial case for "engagement with China" has long centered around economic issues. The core claim is that economic development and increased connection with the outside world would unequivocally spur the development of a Chinese middle class, which, in turn, would press for capitalism,

---

[36] Most famously, during their November 1998 summit in Tokyo, Japanese Prime Minister Keizo Obuchi refused to offer an apology to President Jiang Zemin for Japan's brutal occupation of China. Compounding this, Japan's blatant revision of history textbooks for public schools to downplay (and glorify) its imperial past and its refusal to satisfactorily acknowledge the crimes committed by Japanese militarism has greatly angered the Chinese. China's anti-Japanese passions and rhetoric reached its zenith following the visit by former Japanese Prime Minister Junichiro Koizumi to the Yasukuni Shrine in Tokyo, which honors the Japanese war dead, including "spirits" of the convicted "fourteen Class A war criminals" from the Second World War. Of course, Koizumi is the latest Japanese leader to make this pilgrimage. In 1996, Prime Minister Ryutaro Hashimoto also visited the shrine despite loud Chinese protests.

democracy, and peace. However, this conventional view has come under increasing criticism in recent years. Recently, James Mann (2007), in his pugnacious *The China Fantasy: How Our Leaders Explain Away Chinese Repression,* laments that a loose alliance of American leaders, academics (especially sinologists), and business interests have allegedly foisted this "fantasy" of a "progressing China" on a gullible American public and Congress.[37] Mann argues that the pervasive assumption that "China's economic development will lead inexorably to an opening of China's political system" is false. This flawed reasoning is due to an honest misinterpretation of developments such as the organization of village elections and recent moves to strengthen the rule of law, but also, to Mann's stinging consternation, to a "lie" peddled by "American China-watchers" (i.e., academics) to advance their own interests and agendas. Mann notes that far from being genuine reforms, these measures are actually designed to shore up the regime because they "create the appearance of change, while leaving the fundamentals of China's political system undisturbed" (p. 144). Mann argues that there is no compelling evidence to show that market reforms in China are leading to greater political openness. Contrary to expectations, China's emerging middle class is more interested in holding onto its perks and prerogatives than to push for potentially disruptive political reforms (more on this issue in the next chapter).

Mann warns that over the next two to three decades, China could be much wealthier and "fully integrated into the world's economy" while remaining "entirely undemocratic" and belligerent. Thus, the assertion that reform is inevitable and that it will be the direct result of economic growth is profoundly misguided. Rather, if China continues on its current path, it will not only be richer but also more autocratic and aggressive than it is today. Given this possibility, Mann argues that the United States must remain vigilant and pursue a strategy that mixes engagement with intensified efforts to maintain a favorable balance of power with China. Specifically, Washington needs to reinvigorate its presence in the region by continuing with its existing alliances, especially with the region's democracies. More audaciously, Mann proposes that the United States needs to develop, deploy, and maintain forces that are capable of deterring and, if necessary, defeating China's growing "anti-access" capabilities because these are designed to push the U.S. military out from the region. The United States must do this even as it continues to wage a prolonged war against

---

[37] Mann states boldly, if without subtlety, that "most of the China scholars at American universities and think tanks also strongly support the idea of engagement, as do the chairmen and chief executives of most Fortune 500 companies.... The proclivity of American elites to refrain from public criticism of China's repressive system is reinforced all the more by the influence of money." That is, the "think tanks" get funding from companies doing business in China. High-ranking politicians and government officials know that if they work on China issues and "don't become identified as critics of the regime," they can move on to lucrative careers as advisers and consultants to those same corporations. Even academic China specialists can make money on the side by playing similar roles.

Islamist terrorism and rogue states. Mann concludes that while maintaining the right mix of "engagement and balancing" will not be easy and is fraught with peril, failure to do so to avoid being "provocative" or creating "self-fulfilling prophecies" will be worse.

Mann's thesis has been criticized for being unduly linear, ahistorical, deterministic, and alarmist. Some not only reject the emergence of a *Pax Sinica* anytime soon, but predict China's imminent collapse (Chang 2001). To most analysts, however, China's rise does not necessarily mean that it will be able to challenge American power effectively (Lampton 2001; Menon 2007; Shambaugh 2005). The argument is that even under the best of conditions, China has a long way to go before it catches up with the United States. Drawing on the conventional measures of power such as GDP, China's GDP, rendered in current exchange rates, was $2.5 trillion in 2007 or less than one-fifth of America's $13.2 trillion. The same huge disparity is evident in military power. The United States defense budget in 2006 was estimated at $520 billion, or roughly 43 percent of global military spending and equal to those of the next forty-seven countries combined. By contrast, China's was under $100 billion. Even assuming, as noted earlier, that Chinese spending is grossly understated, the American military budget is still larger. Complementing this is the American "revolution" in military hardware. Cordesman and Kleiber (2007) argue that China's military lags far behind its American counterparts in advanced weapons system and training (also Shambaugh 2002). In fact, the PLA still relies heavily on armaments that are from the 1950s and 1960s and simply no match for their American equivalents in speed, accuracy, and lethality. Cordesman and Kleiber conclude that in terms of advanced military hardware such as aircraft, missiles, naval carriers ships, and electronic and information warfare, China is decades behind the United States. Given this, some have argued that Mann is simply hoisting a straw man.

A more nuanced realist perspective regarding how best to deal with an emergent China centers around the idea of "offshore balancing" (Layne 2006). Offshore balancing is predicated on a number of assumptions: first, that any attempt to perpetuate U.S. hegemony is self-defeating because the United States cannot prevent the rise of new great powers and such an attempt will provoke other states to coalesce in opposition to it. Second, the United States should deploy its power abroad with great prudence, or only when there are direct threats to vital American interests in areas of the globe of strategic importance to the United States. Third, to prevent rival powers from threatening these areas of strategic importance, the United States should rely primarily on regional powers to stabilize the regional balance of power. The United States would intervene only when regional powers are unable to uphold the balance of power on their own. Thus, to its proponents, offshore balancing would not only relieve the United States of the huge burden of managing the security affairs of turbulent regions such as the Persian Gulf, the Middle East, and parts of Asia; by "burden shifting" (rather than "burden sharing"), the United State would be able to transfer to others the task of maintaining regional power balances. It forces other states to become responsible for their own security and for the security of their regions, rather than looking to United States to bail them out.

With respect to China, offshore balancing would require the United States to embrace a new set of policies in the economic and security arenas. For example, in the economic realm, a policy of "strategic trade" would replace the current practice of "free trade." The United States would intervene economically and through legal instruments to force "closed" foreign markets like China (and others who trade "unfairly" by subsidizing their exports or dumping them in the U.S. market) to open, curtail the flow of high technology and "strategic" goods, and reduce the bilateral trade deficit with China. In the security realm, the powder keg of Taiwan needs to be diffused. Specifically, the United States should extricate itself from the unfinished business of the Chinese civil war. This is because it is not in the United States' interest to go to war with China to prevent it from using force to achieve reunification with Taiwan (or in response to a unilateral declaration of independence by Taipei). This means that the United States should recognize that the Taiwan issue is an internal Chinese matter. In similar vein, it should mute its criticism of China's human rights policies and disengage in efforts to bring democracy to China because these are generally politically expedient rhetoric. The reality is that Washington not only lacks the leverage to transform China into a liberal democracy, "democracy promotion" is also an unreasonable (and costly) goal of foreign policy. Moreover, such gratuitous pressure only tends to exacerbate Sino-American relations. Finally, because China's immediate neighbors, including Japan, India, and Russia, have a much more immediate interest in "containing China" than does the United States (separated as it is by a vast expanse of water), they should assume more of the risks and costs of dealing with China. Thus, instead of keeping active forces in the region, the United States, given its long-range strike capabilities, should keep its forces in an "over-the-horizon" posture and intervene only in the unlikely case that the regional balance of power falters.

THE LIBERAL INTERNATIONALISTS

Goldstein (2005) points out that one simply cannot be sure how a more powerful China will behave in the international system. He suggests that the United States use this "period of strategic opportunity" to devise a set of strategies to deal with China. Because both countries' interests converge in a number of areas, including fighting terrorism, preventing proliferation of weapons of mass destruction, and coping with the challenges posed by global warming, there are strong incentives for Beijing and Washington to cooperate. Such cooperation, which could possibly last a couple of decades, would give the United States a better sense as to whether a longer-term modus vivendi with China is possible. Bates Gill (2007) also proposes active U.S. engagement with China. He argues that China is genuinely open to diplomacy and that the U.S. must seize the moment because there is a wide range of international security issues in which the two countries can effectively cooperate.

Susan Shirk (2007), a former deputy assistant secretary of state responsible for U.S. relations with China, provides a nuanced set of reasons why the United States must peacefully engage China. In her *China: Fragile Superpower*, Shirk argues that despite the appearance of the Chinese government as strong and monolithic (a view fostered by the Chinese government itself), it is anything but. Rather, following the 1989 Tiananmen Square violence, the CCP suffers from a growing lack of legitimacy and is deeply worried about the loyalty of its own citizens. It is this weakness and insecurity at the highest levels of the party that often force China's leaders and their backers to act in a bellicose and belligerent manner to all sorts of "foreign provocations" – both real and imagined. Lacking the prestige of the old revolutionaries like Mao and Deng, the new leadership of the CCP has deliberately whipped up a virulent nationalism to shore up its flagging legitimacy.[38] However, in poking this unpredictable hornet's nest, both the leadership and the party now finds itself in a bind because its responses to international events, especially those relating to Taiwan, Japan, and Tibet, have become unduly constrained. To be seen as "soft" on Japan, Taiwan reunification, and the United States, one runs the risk of being vilified as a traitor and a counterrevolutionary (punishable by death). However, taking a hard line is not only "safe" but guarantees the label "patriotic." Not surprisingly, leaders and senior party officials try to outdo each other as to who is most patriotic. In the process, they make statements that can sometimes exacerbate foreign relations. Shirk points out that attitudes toward Taiwan have hardened considerably over the past decade – from persuading the Taiwanese government to negotiate in the 1990s to the now-unconditional demand that Taiwan accept its status as a province under control of the mainland. According to Shirk, leaders such as Jiang Zemin have exacerbated the problems with Taiwan with their knee-jerk and jingoistic overreactions to Taiwanese statements, not to mention his highly emotional outburst to Japanese Prime Minister Junichiro Koizumi's visit to the Yasukuni shrine. In fact, the nationalist passions got out of hand in April 2005 when anti-Japanese demonstrations stoked by the government resulted in large-scale rioting and significant economic damage.

---

[38] See also Gries (2004). In the mid-1990s, Nathan and Ross (1997) described China as a "Great Wall, Empty Fortress," implying that China was a weak and defensive power and posed no threat to regional or international stability.

Given such events, the United States must engage with the Chinese leaders with calm and cool-headed tact, thereby preventing China from "losing face" and doing something irrational and dangerous.

A strong case for broad engagement with China is also made by Ikenberry (2008). He notes that as China's rise eventually brings the United States' "unipolar moment" to an end, the key question will be this: "Will China overthrow the existing order or become a part of it? And what, if anything, can the United States do to maintain its position as China rises?" (p. 23). To Ikenberry, this transition does not necessarily have to be a wrenching power struggle, nor does it mean China will overthrow the Western system. Rather, the postwar international political and economic order so assiduously created by the United States and its allies can remain dominant even while integrating a powerful China. This is because China faces not only an American system but also a resilient and expansive "Western-centered system" that is based on universal membership, consensual institutions, and shared decision making, underpinned by the rule of law. Because it encourages engagement, integration, restraint, and accommodation, the Bretton Woods system, built around rules and norms to facilitate free trade, provides all nations, including rising powers like China, opportunities to advance their economic interests and resolve their collective problems. Indeed, China's very economic success is a testament that all countries can "gain full access to and thrive within this system." Ikenberry aptly notes that "today's Western order, in short, is hard to overturn and easy to join." Nevertheless, the United States can help by facilitating China's full transition into the liberal order. He states, "Washington must work to strengthen the rules and institutions that underpin that order – making it even easier to join and harder to overturn. . . . It must sink the roots of this order as deeply as possible, giving China greater incentives for integration than for opposition and increasing the chances that the system will survive even after U.S. relative power has declined" (pp. 24–25).

Thus, Ikenberry challenges Mearsheimer's thesis by noting that not all power transitions lead to war or an outright rejection of the old order. He states: "clearly, there are different types of power transitions. Some states have seen their economic and geopolitical power grow dramatically and have still accommodated themselves to the existing order. Others have risen up and sought to change it. Some power transitions have led to the breakdown of the old order and the establishment of a new international hierarchy. Others have brought about only limited adjustments in the regional and global system" (p. 27). Given that the postwar Western order is historically unique in the sense that "it has been more liberal than imperial – and so unusually accessible, legitimate, and durable . . . with a wide and widening array of participants and stakeholders. It is capable of generating tremendous economic growth and power while also signaling restraint – all of which make it hard to overturn and easy to join" (p. 28). Although the postwar global order has already helped facilitate

China's global integration and its economic interests are now quite congruent with the current global economic order, Ikenberry argues that more can be done to help this process. In particular, to give China a real stake in the global system, the United States and its allies must allow a bigger role and greater voice for rising powers, especially the so-called BRIC countries (Brazil, Russia, India, and China), in global governance institutions. Most important, to show that the West is serious about incorporating China into the inner circle of core economic governance institutions such as the International Monetary Fund (IMF), the World Bank, and the World Trade Organization (WTO), China must be given greater avenues for voice and representation. In similar fashion, the West must strike a "strategic bargain" with China by offering it status and position within regional and global arrangements in return for Beijing's accepting and accommodating the West's core strategic interests. This, Ikenberry argues, will help further strengthen the global order and gradually transform China into a team player. Of course, what is ostensibly missing from Ikenberry's "primacy of economics" argument is how contentious issues regarding territory and sovereignty (i.e., Taiwan) will be resolved.

Finally, Ann Kent's (2007) innovative study, *Beyond Compliance: China, International Organizations and Global Security,* provides a nuanced perspective as to whether China is a responsible international stakeholder by empirically examining its participation across a number of cases. These include China's participation in the UN Conference on Disarmament, the World Bank and IMF, the UN Environment Program, the International Labor Organization, the UN Committee against Torture, and surveys of the WTO and World Health Organization. Predictably, Kent finds wide variation on China's compliance. Beijing has been least cooperative with organizations concerned with human rights issues (the International Labor Organization and Committee against Torture) and most cooperative with organizations that provide tangible financial assistance (the World Bank and IMF) and promote global trade (the WTO). Beijing is only partially compliant with the UN Environment Program – that is, it is more compliant on ozone protection than amelioration of climate change. However, its participation in security regimes such as the Conference on Disarmament has been the most remarkable, especially China's support for agreements and treaties dealing with nuclear nonproliferation and verification procedures. Clearly, China is no longer an uncompromising and strident critic of the international order. As Kent compelling illustrates, since the Deng era, Beijing has exhibited a steady deepening of its involvement in global organizations, moving beyond membership accession and "procedural compliance" to what she describes as "substantive compliance" with the norms, principles, and rules of multilateral organizations. Overall, China's record of compliance varies by issue. Kent points out that Beijing's participation in international organizations and support for and compliance with global accords and treaties has been quite positive – and in some cases, exemplary. She notes that "its acceptance of, and integration into, the international system have been nothing short of extraordinary" (p. 222). Kent's study provides empirical backing that China has been a constructive player in multilateral diplomacy and that continued engagement with China is necessary for its further integration and socialization in the international system.

Concluding Reflections

No one knows for sure whether and when a "changing of the guard" will occur with China displacing the United States as the great power. Yet even under the most favorable conditions, China has a long way to go before it catches up with the United States. As noted, in every critical measure of power – economic, military, and technological – China lags far behind the United States; by some accounts, given the formidable challenges Beijing faces, China may fall even further behind in the coming decades (Brooks and Wohlforth 2008). Likewise, it is impossible to know with certainty from Beijing's current behavior or official statements whether China will remain a responsible global stakeholder or turn revisionist as its power grows. Just as uncertain is the future trajectory of U.S.-China relations. Although growing bilateral economic relations between the United States and China provide both nations with a strong incentive to avoid conflict and China's expanding participation in global institutions and the benefits of membership encourage Beijing not to threaten the status quo, the potential for conflict cannot be ruled out. It would be naïve to assume that China's interests and priorities will not change as its power grows. After all, the international norms and institutions that liberal internationalists claim will help "domesticate" or "tame" China are mostly products of the West, not necessarily universal, and definitely not Chinese. Consequently, there is no reason to assume that China will not break with precedent and try to promulgate its worldview, charting its own course in world affairs. As the power transition theory has long informed us, there is an incongruity between a rising power's growing capabilities and its continued subordinate status in the international system. China is a rising power, and historically the emergence of new powers in the international system has been geopolitically destabilizing. How both sides approach the inevitable collision between the expanding interests and imperatives of an intransigent rising power and those of the American status quo will determine the future contours of Sino-U.S. relations.

Of course, China's behavior will depend much on how the United States defines its future strategic calculus and behavior, especially in East Asia. If the United States continues to pursue the George W. Bush administration's clumsy policies of unilateralism and preemption and seeks unchallenged global supremacy by dissuading others from becoming peer competitors, it will inevitably perceive China's rise as a threat to the United States, regardless of

Beijing's conduct. In such an environment, a destabilizing power competition becomes almost inevitable and conflict a self-fulfilling prophecy. If, however, the United States defines its international role more moderately and cultivates balanced cooperative relations with the global community, Washington may be able to maximize leverage while minimizing conflict in its relations with China. Lest we forget, at the end of World War II, the United States responded to its new role as leader of the free world by adopting multilateralist policies and creating a host of international organizations, including the United Nations and the Bretton Woods organizations. Although the multilateral principles were not always fully respected, the fact that an immensely powerful nation was willing to play by the rules it asked others to accept brought the United States international respect and prestige. Moreover, the nation prospered under multilateralism: "self-binding" helped to enhance and legitimize American power, not diminish it.

For good or ill, America's most important bilateral international relationship over the course of the next few decades will be the People's Republic of China. The United States, although powerful, is not omnipotent. It will need to work closely with China (and other nations) if it is to manage and solve the many pressing foreign policy challenges it now faces, as well as those it will undoubtedly confront in the future. Despite differences in values and political systems, the United States and China share common interests. In addition to fighting terrorism and the proliferation of weapons of mass destruction, they share mutual interest in maintaining global economic growth and stability and combating climate change and environmental degradation. Indeed, it is in the strategic interest of the United States to help foster political liberalization in China by integrating it into the international economy and embedding it in the complex web of international institutional arrangements. Can the countries work together to accomplish common goals? Only time will tell.

8

China and India
Future Challenges and Opportunities

In April 2008, the World Bank issued a public statement warning that skyrocketing food and fuel prices were threatening recent hard-won gains in overcoming poverty and malnutrition throughout the world. More ominously, it warned that the sharp increases in global prices (overall global food prices increased by 83 percent over the 36 months leading up to February 2008) are expected to remain high throughout 2008–9, and likely remain well above the 2004 levels through 2015, for most food crops. While China and India have not experienced the large-scale and often violent protest and riots over rising food prices that have hit several countries, including Bangladesh, Mexico, Zimbabwe, Egypt, Haiti, Indonesia, Cameroon, Peru, Somalia, Guinea, Mauritania, Morocco, Senegal, Uzbekistan, Yemen, and Argentina, there is palpable worry that the current rise in consumer inflation (which is close to 8 percent in India and slightly higher in China) has the potential to reverse dramatically the gains in poverty reduction in both countries. This is a particularly worrisome concern for India because one in every four Indians lives on less than $1 a day, and three in four earn $2 or less.[1] This is because food price inflation is the most regressive of all taxes – it hurts the poor the most because food accounts for a relatively high proportion of their expenses.[2] As Nobel laureate Amartya Sen in his classic *Poverty and Famines* demonstrated, there has never been an acute shortage of food in India – not even during the infamous famine in Bengal in 1943 in which an estimated 1.5 million people died of starvation. Rather, the problem then – and now – is "entitlement," or access to food at affordable prices. Poor households living on a few dollars a day can experience dramatic

---

[1] The first reported rioting occurred in Mexico in December 2007 following a sharp hike in tortilla prices, which quadrupled in some parts of the country. In January 2008, thousands in Indonesia took to the streets to protest high soybean prices. In February 2008, protesters in Burkina Faso, angry about the rising cost of food, attacked government offices and shops. Since then, protests over rising food prices have become commonplace.

[2] Economists know that inflation hurts the poor disproportionately. Thus, inflation is like a tax on the poor because they are least able to hedge against the effects of rising prices.

declines in their purchasing power because even a small increase in food prices contributes to a sharp fall in real incomes and consumption.

Although the current food crisis has multiple roots, the concurrent rise of China and India is often seen as the leading cause. No doubt, growing incomes in developing countries – in particular, China and India – has led to a growing demand for grains, including high-value, protein-rich foods such as dairy, meat, fish, and eggs. Although income growth in both counties will continue to exert pressure on food prices, contrary to the popular view, rising demand from China and India is not the only reason behind the meteoric rise in food prices. Rather, if demand from India and China were the decisive factor, food prices should have risen slowly, not skyrocketed, because the demand for grain in both countries has not varied appreciably over the past decade. Nevertheless, a sharp rise in demand can lead to price volatility of food grains, including high-value foods. For example, the per capita consumption of meat and eggs in China and India has more than doubled over the past decade. This has increased consumption of grain for feed. It has been estimated that to produce a single kilogram of beef or poultry, it may take as much as seven kilograms of grain. Hence, as caloric intake shifts to more protein, more and more grain is demanded for the same number of calories for human consumption.

Demand for food grain and fiber has increased faster than supply primarily because of biofuel policies in industrialized countries, especially the United States, but also in Brazil. Specifically, generous biofuel subsidies have encouraged farmers to divert huge volumes of crops such as corn (or maize), soybean, sugar, and vegetable oil from traditional export markets (both as food and feed) to the production of ethanol and biodiesel.[3] For example, the United States, which produced a record maize harvest in 2007, diverted roughly one-third of it to ethanol production. With petroleum prices at an all-time high, there is every reason to believe that farmers in rich countries will continue to divert more of their acreage to crops that produce the highly profitable biofuel. Of course, this will only make food shortages more acute. Ironically, although the biofuel program is primarily designed to reduce U.S. (and rich-country) dependence on imported oil, it is estimated that even if the United States devoted its entire corn acreage to ethanol production, it would only slightly reduce this dependence. Moreover, the oft-touted claim that biofuels are environmentally friendly is problematic; given the high volume of hydrocarbon fuel used in biofuel production, it is not clear whether there are any tangible reductions in carbon emissions, including any net gain in overall energy production.

---

[3] According to a World Bank estimate, it takes about 450 pounds of maize to produce enough ethanol to fill the twenty-five-gallon tank of an SUV. This same amount can provide enough calories to feed one person for a year.

Compounding this problem are international prices that are denominated in U.S. dollars. Because a single-currency system lowers transaction costs for commodities that trade globally, oil has long traded in U.S. dollars. In recent years, however, while oil prices have been rising on supply-and-demand fundamentals, the dollar has weakened against the currencies of its major trading partners. Thus, as most regional currencies have appreciated against the dollar during 2007–2008 it has reduced people's purchasing power. However, the precipitous decline in the value of the U.S. dollar is only part of the story. Given the strong correlations between commodity prices and the exchange rate for the dollar, every time the dollar has weakened, hedge funds have bought commodities – because commodities are priced in dollars. As a result, when the dollar falls, producers outside the United States raise prices to compensate. This has inevitably led to speculation and even more volatile commodity prices because every time the dollar falls, traders rush to buy commodities, and the subsequent wave of buying only pushes up the prices (the fact that global crop inventories have dropped to record lows is not lost on speculators). The United States seems quite content at the moment to let the dollar fall because a depreciating currency makes exports cheaper. On the other hand, the other major player, the European Central Bank, sees a rising euro as a bulwark against the inflationary pressures caused by higher commodity prices – because a stronger currency makes imports cheaper.[4]

The sharp rise in oil and natural gas prices has also had a negative impact on food prices because fertilizer and pesticide prices are highly dependent on petroleum and natural gas prices and often move in tandem with energy prices. Thus, high energy prices have made agricultural production more expensive by raising the cost of inputs such as fertilizers and pesticides. Adding to the price is the cost of trucking food from farms to local markets and shipping it abroad. Moreover, some major grain-supplying countries have recently introduced export restrictions, if not outright bans, in an effort to reduce domestic food price inflation. For example, food-exporting countries as diverse as Argentina, China, India, Russia, Ukraine, Kazakhstan, and Vietnam have drastically reduced supplies available for world commerce by placing additional taxes or restrictions on exports of grains, rice, oilseeds, and other essential food products, thereby exacerbating the surge in global commodity prices. Erratic weather, trade policies, and seasonal lags have slowed producers' responses to the higher prices. For example, drought in Australia's grain belt

---

[4] For example, the dollar has fallen by about 46 percent from its mid-2001 peak against the euro and 21 percent since 2004. A declining dollar makes oil cheaper for Europeans and other foreign consumers, propping up demand. A weakening U.S. currency also reduces the dollar-denominated supply from foreign producers. How much has the weakening dollar added to oil prices? If the U.S. currency had held its 2001 value against the euro, oil would have traded at about $80 a barrel in early 2008. Therefore, exchange rate movements accounted for roughly a third of the increase in oil prices from 2003 to 2007.

has reduced the country's historically large volumes of wheat and rice exports. No doubt, climate change will pose growing challenges to agricultural production. Although a modest recovery in production was expected for 2008, overall productivity growth in agriculture is simply too low to cope with the increase in global demand. The seasonal nature of agriculture inevitably leads to a lagged supply response. Because demand has outpaced supply, prices have inevitably increased. Finally, after decades of growth in agricultural production and productivity and falling food costs, neglect and complacency set in, and investment in agricultural research and development has fallen. New technologies, especially biotechnology, were set aside for mostly political reasons. The world's poor are now paying the tragic price for this irresponsibility.

Finally, in the case of both China and India, the current food crisis has paradoxical roots. In India it has been exacerbated by poor farm output. As noted earlier, this is due in part to the neglect of investment in agricultural technology, infrastructure, and extension programs. Although the Indian economy has been growing rapidly, this growth has been confined mainly to the manufacturing and services sectors. Agriculture, in contrast, has grown by barely 2.5 percent over the past five years, and the rate of growth is even lower if the past decade and a half is considered. Consequently, per capita output of cereals (wheat and rice) at present is about the level that prevailed in the 1970s. In the case of China, the huge demand is simply outstripping domestic supply. What is similar in both countries is that their increased demand for meat and dairy products to feed the appetites of the growing middle classes has put intense pressure on food supply and prices.

No doubt, the immediate task is to feed the growing ranks of the hungry. Therefore, in the short term, rich countries should provide the necessary food aid to the hard-hit nations to prevent mass starvation and malnutrition. Donor countries and international agencies must closely monitor the distribution process to ensure that recipient-country governments actually distribute the aid supplies to those in need. As noted, several countries have already put in place a series of measures such as export restrictions and price controls to try to minimize the effects of higher food prices on their citizens.[5] For example, as of April 2008, fifteen countries, including China and India, have imposed export restrictions on agricultural commodities. China has banned rice and maize exports, and India has banned exports of rice and pulses. Although these measures may provide some immediate relief, over time they can aggravate the problem because measures such as export bans or high export tariffs may reduce risks of food shortages in the short term but can also make the international market in food supplies smaller and more volatile,

---

[5] Ironically, although tariff barriers on food imports have come down sharply (in India, tariffs on food are below 1 percent), in response to growing food shortages, several countries, including China and India, have imposed export restrictions.

with the unintended consequence of further increasing world food prices. Export restrictions are particularly negative consequences for food-importing countries, of which there are many, including poor countries. Cumulatively, export bans can result in the formation of cartels and revive protectionism, which in turn can lead to further increases in food prices and overall inflation.

Because World Trade Organization rules allow export restrictions for food on food security grounds, countries must work cooperatively to limit the negative effects. If there is a silver lining, it is that higher food prices present an opportunity for farmers to increase food production and benefit from the high prices. To help farmers meet this challenge, governments must expand investment in the agricultural sector, including improving rural infrastructure and domestic and foreign market access to farm products – and in the case of China, secure property rights for peasants. However, over the longer term, the Organisation for Economic Co-operation and Development (OECD) nations must take the lead in implementing policies to rejuvenate global agricultural growth. Specifically, they must eliminate the generous biofuel subsidies that have contributed to this manmade crisis. In fact, the large-scale subsidization of agriculture in OECD countries has prevented developing countries – in particular, the least-developed countries – from further expanding their agricultural sectors. By subsidizing producers and frequently dumping excess supply on international markets, the OECD countries have gravely undermined millions of producers in poor countries. It is essential to eliminate these agricultural trade barriers. Rich countries and emerging economies like China and India have a particular responsibility to reduce the trade barriers that harm poor farmers in developing countries. Ironically, the high commodity prices provide a unique opportunity to conclude the protracted Doha Round negotiations because it makes the protectionist arguments for trade-distorting policies such as domestic support, export subsidies, and high tariffs less compelling. A successful Doha Round will mean less distortion in world food markets and increased international trade.

Skyrocketing Energy Demands

Given their voracious appetite for energy and raw commodities to feed their growing economies, both China and India will continue to put enormous pressure on a variety of global markets. China is the world's leading consumer of coal, steel, and copper and is second only to the United States in oil and electricity consumption. The sharp increase in oil and gas imports by China and India (and the United States) since 2000 has been a major factor behind the sharp increase in oil and commodity prices. Because only about one-third of India's total oil consumption is produced domestically, it is India's largest import by value. India's energy requirements have doubled over the past decade, and economic expansion will add further pressure on demand.

India currently imports 70 percent of its oil and 50 percent of its gas. It is projected to import 80 percent of its energy needs by 2025, if not sooner.

In the case of China, its huge coal reserves (China is the world's leading coal producer and consumer) are the mainstay of its power industry. Coal supplies two-thirds of its total energy needs and fuels 80 percent of its electric power generation. On the basis of current estimates, coal consumption is set to double over the next decade – a trend that will further exacerbate already serious health and environment problems because China is currently responsible for one-quarter of the world's carbon emissions (Chu, Fesharaki, and Wu 2006). Although coal currently fuels about 70 percent of China's energy use, oil and petroleum use are growing exponentially, and China is now second largest consumer of oil after the United States. In the mid-1980s, China was Asia's largest oil exporter, but by 1993, it became a net oil importer. In 2003, it became the second largest consumer of petroleum products behind the United States. According to the U.S. Energy Information Administration (EIA), China accounts for approximately 40 percent of world oil-demand growth since 2004 and consumes approximately 5.6 million barrels of oil per day (bbl/d). The EIA forecasts rapid growth in oil demand by China, reaching 12.8 million bbl/d by 2025 with net imports of 9.4 million bbl/d. This means China's oil demand will double in the next twenty years. India has also increased its oil consumption. In 1995, India's oil consumption was roughly 1.6 million bbl/d. The EIA predicts that India's consumption will grow from 2.2 million bbl/d in 2003 to 2.8 million bbl/d by 2010. This represents a 75 percent increase in fifteen years. India's net oil imports are also increasing rapidly. Since 2000, India's net oil imports increased by 27 percent, from 1.1 million bbl/d to 1.4 million bbl/d in 2003 (Anderson and Buol 2005; Kambara and Howe 2007).

To meet growing demand, China has made energy security through strategic oil stockpiling, development and expansion of petrochemical industries, and promotion of overseas energy investments a top priority (Zweig and Jianhai 2005). China's National Offshore Oil Corporation's (CNOOC) aggressive efforts to secure oil and natural gas supplies around the world (including its bid on U.S.-owned Unocal in 2005) reflect just how strong China's thirst for fossil fuels has become. The United States has been concerned about aggressive Chinese and, more recently, Indian efforts to "lock up" long-term energy deals with nations ranging from Iran to Venezuela. Indeed, growing Chinese and Indian energy investments in "problem states" such as Iran, Venezuela, Myanmar, Sudan, and Syria are adding to U.S. concerns over the impact of China's and India's outward reach for energy resources.

Most troubling is what Kreft (2006) refers to as China's zero-sum "neomercantilist strategy" to lock up foreign oil supplies. The basic thrust of the strategy is to acquire direct control over overseas oil and gas reserves through the purchase of foreign oil and gas fields by the three major Chinese oil companies, the Chinese National Petroleum Company, Sinopec, and CNOOC, and through pipeline agreements with neighboring countries to pipe oil and gas directly to China. By end-2006, Beijing had concluded such "strategic energy alliances" with at least eight countries. As Kreft (2006, 30) notes, most ominous is Beijing's attempt through its oil companies to gain direct control of oil production in major oil-exporting countries. "The aim is to ensure that the output of oilfields under Beijing's control is exported directly to China and not sold on the world oil market as the output of most oil multinationals is. If China succeeds in the attempt to meet its energy needs by turning certain countries into its own exclusive suppliers, the capacity of the world oil market to respond flexibly to sudden shortages or increased demand will be significantly reduced." Suffice it to note that such a strategy has the potential to escalate regional and global tensions. Similarly, since the early 1990s, India and Iran have been discussing the building of a 2,600-mile natural gas pipeline between the two countries. The exact details of this project have varied, with some calling for an onshore pipeline through Pakistan and others for an offshore pipeline. Some have even suggested that in addition to providing energy, the pipeline could also contribute to confidence-building between India and Pakistan. However, the successive U.S. administrations are opposed to both the onshore and offshore pipeline between India and Iran – even warning New Delhi that the Iran and Libya Sanctions Act of 1996 might require the United States to apply economic sanctions against Indian companies doing business with Iran. Finally, in their efforts to enhance their energy security and to reduce their vulnerability to fuel shortages or price shocks, there is a strong possibility that both China and India may revert back to using more coal. Although coal is probably the most polluting source of energy, it is abundant in both India and China (China has the largest reserves of coal in the world, and India has the fourth largest). Also, compared with fossil fuel, coal is relatively cheap. However, the impact on global climate change would be hugely negative.[6]

Growing Environmental Stresses

The push for rapid economic growth in both China and India has come at a price: it has resulted in tremendous environmental stress. Environmental degradation, including polluted water and air, deforestation, soil erosion, and loss of biodiversity and habitat pose a grave threat to economic development and sustainability in both countries. Currently, China and India are the second and third largest polluters or emitters of carbon (behind the United States) in the world, and two-thirds of the world's fifty most polluted mega-cities are in

---

[6] In July 2008, during the G8 meeting, China and India both refused to support halving carbon emissions by 2050. Whereas Australia, South Korea, and Indonesia had expressed support for the 50-percent cuts agreed by the G8, China, India, Brazil, Mexico, and South Africa issued a statement saying that the G8 countries needed to slash carbon emission levels by 80 to 95 percent from 1990 levels.

either China or India. This problem is hard to miss because most of these cities are often wrapped in a perpetual toxic gray fog that literally blocks out the sun for weeks at a time. Pollution in all its deadly manifestations (unhealthy air, unsafe water and food supplies, and severe land degradation) is already responsible for hundreds of thousands of deaths each year in both countries – from respiratory and pulmonary diseases as well as cancer. China's vehicle fleet is projected to rise from about 30 million to some 120 to 150 million by 2020, and India, which produces its own fleet of vehicles, is expected to see similar growth. This will put additional pressure on energy demands and exacerbate pollution problems.

Heavy reliance on coal in both countries has exacerbated pollution levels because the coal used has very high sulfur content. Elizabeth Economy (2007, 39–40; see also World Bank 2007a) provides a vivid and frightening description: "The coal that has powered China's economic growth, for example, is also choking its people. Coal provides about 70 percent of China's energy needs: the country consumed some 2.4 billion tons in 2006 – more than the United States, Japan, and the United Kingdom combined. In 2000, China anticipated doubling its coal consumption by 2020; it is now expected to have done so by the end of this year . . . as much as 90 percent of China's sulfur dioxide emissions and 50 percent of its particulate emissions are the result of coal use. Particulates are responsible for respiratory problems among the population, and acid rain, which is caused by sulfur dioxide emissions, falls on one-quarter of China's territory and on one-third of its agricultural land, diminishing agricultural output and eroding buildings." Similarly, coal is the backbone of India's energy base. Currently, it meets more than two-thirds of the nation's energy needs. Moreover, as more Chinese and Indian citizens use automobiles, the pollution problem will only get worse because neither have effective in-place national standards for carbon emissions or fuel efficiency standards for vehicles. Acid rain (the result of sulfur dioxide emissions from coal) falls on vast swaths of land, damaging, sometimes irretrievably, fragile agricultural ecosystems and polluting crops and waterways.

Seriously compounding this problem is unsustainable water use. In both China and India the growing demand and overuse of groundwater for both personal and agricultural use have stretched these finite resources to near exhaustion. Agricultural runoff from pesticides and fertilizer and the widespread use of waterways such as rivers and lakes as a dumping ground for industrial waste and sewage have severely contaminated fresh water supplies. This in turn has led to serious water shortages, especially during the summer months. In fact, water pollution is such a serious problem that millions of people in both countries have no recourse but to drink contaminated water. Economy (2007, 42–44) notes that "pollution is also endangering China's water supplies. China's ground water, which provides 70 percent of the country's total drinking water, is under threat from a variety of sources, such as polluted surface water, hazardous waste sites, and pesticides and fertilizers . . . the aquifers in 90 percent of Chinese cities are polluted. More than 75 percent of the river water flowing through China's urban areas is considered unsuitable for drinking or fishing, and the Chinese government itself deems about 30 percent of the river water in the country to be unfit for use in agriculture or industry. As a result, nearly 700 million people drink water contaminated with animal and human waste."

Similarly, in India, the Yamuna River, which flows through the capital of New Delhi, is so polluted that its level of fecal bacteria is 10,000 times higher than what is deemed safe for bathing and drinking. Recent World Bank studies (World Bank 2008, also Mertha 2008; Winters and Yusuf 2007, 23–25) note that water shortage in China and India has become a grave threat to human security. The report found that in China alone, well over half the major lakes are severely polluted, only 38 percent of river water is drinkable, only 20 percent of the population has access to unpolluted drinking water, and that almost a quarter of the people regularly drink water that is heavily polluted. The World Bank's impact study on the physical and economic costs of air and water pollution in China as reflected in the burden of mortality and morbidity associated with environmental pollution, pollution-exacerbated water scarcity, wastewater irrigation, fisheries loss, crop loss, and material damage are unprecedented. Specifically, it finds that the health costs of air and water pollution are equivalent to about 4 percent of GDP in China. However, once the non-health impacts of pollution are added, the total cost of air and water pollution in China is equivalent to more than 5 percent of GDP. The situation in India is hardly any better (World Bank 2007).

China: Between Democratization and Trapped Transition

There is truism in the oft-noted observation that although economic reforms in China have proceeded rapidly, meaningful political reforms have moved at a snail's pace. Nevertheless, whether one sees the glass half-full or half-empty, there is no denying that state-society relations have greatly improved in post-Mao China. The draconian controls and the puritanical regimentation of the Mao era have all but disappeared. Citizens now enjoy greater personal freedoms, and daily life has been liberalized or, more aptly, "depoliticized," allowing for participation in a range of activities (e.g., cultural and religious practices and openness to artistic expression, including access to Western pop culture) that were once frowned on and often prohibited. In recent years, the Chinese Communist Party (CCP) has even introduced semicompetitive elections at the village level and sponsored the establishment of numerous civic and professional associations, giving them greater space in the formulation of public policy. Merle Goldman (2007), in *From Comrade to Citizen,* explores these "seeds of democracy" in contemporary China. She lucidly documents how the country's growing civil society is gradually supplanting comradeship with democratic citizenship.[7] To Goldman, a Communist society is characterized by comradeship, whereas a democratic society is characterized by citizenship. A comrade is a loyal follower of Communism who unquestioningly obeys party rules and ideology. A citizen, in contrast, is politically independent, asserts his or her rights, participates freely in public life, and may espouse views at variance with official ideology. According to Goldman, over the past two decades growing numbers of people have begun to abandon their roles as comrades and demand rights that are congruent with democratic citizenship. Although the struggle for individual rights and political pluralism was initiated by pro-democracy "disestablished intellectuals" (as opposed to "establishment intellectuals"), growing numbers of workers, peasants, middle-class professionals, and human rights activists, including environmentalists, pensioners, feminists, and religious rights advocates, have since joined the struggle. These individuals and groups are now demanding not only the rights that are theoretically enshrined in the Chinese Constitution but also the rights and freedoms associated with democratic citizenship, including the right to hold political leaders accountable for their actions. Although Goldman is well aware of the limitations that a Leninist party-state can impose on civil society, she also documents the many creative strategies that activists are using, including "citizenship extending into cyberspace," to organize and mobilize their constituents. Despite the fact the threat of state repression is always present, Goldman nevertheless notes that popular political awareness and the new "citizenship consciousness" is too widely spread to be easily suppressed. Moreover there is no going back on the demands by groups in civil society for a larger public space. Even those calling for an end to Communist Party rule and for the establishment of a democratic political order have become emboldened.

Yet despite such changes, China continues to be ruled by an authoritarian regime dominated by a Leninist party. There have been no substantive changes to the CCP's constitutional monopoly of political power, no creation of effective checks and balances at the institutional level to limit executive power, and no measures to make the political leadership truly accountable to the popular will. China remains a one-party state in which formal authority is highly centralized and no organized political opposition is tolerated. As in the past, the CCP, through its vast and secretive web of party cells in the government, the military, and society, carefully monitor compliance with party policies. An independent civil society (or the existence of a social arena independent of the state) does not exist in contemporary China. All organizations, interest groups, and professional associations such as labor unions; student organizations;

---

[7] According to Saich (2006), as of 2006, there were more than 360,000 registered civil society organizations in China, including trade associations, professional groups and clubs, social welfare organizations, legal aid groups, environmental groups, and research and charitable foundations – double the number in 1996.

professional, cultural, and peasant associations; and religious groups must be sanctioned by the government and their leadership subject to official approval. Only these officially recognized groups can engage in political activity, and then provided that they do not adopt an adversarial posture or directly challenge the authority of the party-state. Given such tight controls, it is not surprising that some two decades since the authorities brutally suppressed the short-lived pro-democracy movement, the CCP is firmly in control.

China's political trajectory challenges the conventional assumption of a linear relationship between per capita income and democratic survival. It has been claimed that if the average income is below US$1,000 a year, democracy is unlikely to last a decade. However, once the average income exceeds US$6,000 a year, democracy is irreversible (Przeworski 1991, 1995). It also refutes the claim that sustained economic growth (rather than the level of income) is most conducive to democratization. Similarly, those who assumed the rise of an assertive civil society and popular demand for "bourgeois liberalization" would lead to the collapse of the CCP and usher in democracy have been sorely disappointed (Gilley 2004; Hu 2000; Inden and Welzel 2005; White, Howell, and Shang 1996), as have those who hoped that the rapid expansion of the private sector and the spectacular growth in the ranks of the middle or professional classes augurs well for democratization (Zheng 2004). China's middle and business classes have hardly championed democracy, let alone ended the hegemonic rule of the Communist Party.

What explains this anomaly? There are several interrelated explanations. According to Shambaugh (2008), the resilience and durability of the CCP is due to its remarkable adaptability, especially it ability to wean itself away from "a protracted state of atrophy." Drawing on a large corpus of inner-party documents and interviews with top party members, he finds that the CCP can be quite objective in assessing its own strengths and weaknesses and learning from the mistakes of other Communist countries as well as from the successes of single-party system such as the People's Action Party in Singapore. In being "proactive," the CCP has not only reinvented itself but also strengthened its grip on power. Given its ability of reinvention, Shambaugh argues that the claims regarding the CCP demise is premature. Others have argued that by successfully blending authoritarian rule with pro-market economic policies, China's party-state has enhanced its legitimacy in the eyes of the masses. Like the "developmental states" of East Asia, China's so-called authoritarian-developmental state has refurbished its image and earned that elusive "mandate from heaven," or the right to rule, by generating robust growth (J. Chen 2004; W. Tang 2005). A number of analysts have suggested that "elite cohesion" – in particular, the post-Tiananmen purge of political liberals – has allowed the "hard-line" conservative technocrats to consolidate power and end the divisive factional and ideological struggles (which spilled into society) that typified the bitter rivalry between the "reformers" and the "conservatives" in the 1980s.

As a result, the party-state has been able to present a unified face, carry out a relatively smooth transition, and maintain order in its ranks and in society. Several analysts have noted that the CCP is hardly a passive actor but one that zealously monitors and manages socioeconomic and political trends in its midst. The party has taken extreme measures to prevent organized demands for political change by selectively accommodating some interests while suppressing others. For example, M. Pei (2006) compellingly argues that the party's entrenched monopoly over key economic assets gives its tremendous leverage – especially in its ability to secure the loyalty of key constituents as well as buy off potential dissidents. He points out that in the post-Tiananmen period, the party has successfully co-opted large sections of the country's economic and social elites (including many leaders of the pro-democracy movement), thereby turning former and potential adversaries into allies of the regime. In similar vein, Dickson (2003) suggests that allowing private entrepreneurs into the party was a strategic decision. It was designed to incorporate a growing and increasingly influential sector of Chinese society, thereby preempting calls for an autonomous political organization by the private sector. Bueno de Mesquita and Downs (2005) note that "democratic convergence" has yet to result from market reforms in China because the CCP shrewdly welcomes wealthy business leaders into its ranks, and the middle classes in China (as in Russia) have not pushed for democratic reforms because they are willing to forgo free expression in exchange for opportunities to get rich and to consume.

Gallagher (2005) provides a novel explanation as to why economic reforms may not lead to political liberalization in China. By focusing on the contradictory role of foreign direct investment (FDI), she argues that FDI liberalization has served to strengthen the Chinese state while simultaneously weakening civil society, especially labor. Specifically, FDI liberalization has placed competitive pressure on Chinese state-owned firms to become more efficient by adopting foreign labor practices and technology. Foreign firms also provided a laboratory in which politically sensitive labor reforms were tried out and then extended to state-owned enterprises. Third, foreign firms, with their economic successes and novel labor practices, helped to establish a new paradigm of successful national industry with the effect of depoliticizing the distinction between private and public industry. As a result, Chinese labor came to accept that there are no viable alternatives to capitalist labor practices. This also explains why labor has shown little antagonism toward the party. Therefore, FDI has served to strengthen the regime because by fundamentally restructuring labor relations, it has fragmented workers' ability to resist reform and thereby delay political liberalization.

Comparative research has also shed some intriguing insights onto the relationship between the middle and business classes and democracy, especially in the developing world. Bellin (2000), for example, argues that these classes' enthusiasm for democracy is largely a function of two factors: state dependence and fear. Bellin defines state dependence as "the degree to which private sector profitability is subject to the discretionary support of the state," while fear refers to the private sector's concern for the protection of private property rights and "securing the long-term profitability of its investments through the guarantee of order" (pp. 180–81). Thus, capitalists and the middle class are "contingent democrats" because their support for democracy is a function of both their level of dependence on the state and their fear of political instability. Dickson's (2003, 19) original research on China's "private entrepreneurs" confirms Bellin's findings. Dickson argues that economic reforms may not lead to political reforms because private entrepreneurs "do not seek autonomy but rather closer embeddedness with the state" because "they recognize that to be autonomous is to be 'outside the system' (*tizhiwai*), and therefore powerless. Instead they seek to be part of the system (*tizhimei*) in order to better pursue their interests and maximize their leverage and wealth." Thus, China's business leaders and the middle classes "see themselves as partners, not adversaries of the state" not to mention that "Party membership gives easier access to loans and protection" (p. 110).

K. Tsai (2007) also provides an interesting perspective. In her aptly titled book *Capitalism without Democracy: The Private Sector in Contemporary China*, she argues that private entrepreneurs in China do not comprise a single coherent class or share similar identities and interests. Rather, divided by region, background, and locality and facing very different economic conditions and concerns, private entrepreneurs have developed a repertoire of adaptive strategies vis-à-vis the central and local governments. Because most are dependent on the state, they are hardly expected to support regime change. To Tsai, if a key prerequisite of class formation is class identity and a prerequisite of class identity is shared values and interests, than China's entrepreneurial classes lack both. This also explains why private business interests adopt a mostly nonconfrontational approach to dispute resolution. Tsai argues that when China's private entrepreneurs are disgruntled with policy issues, they are more likely to use informal channels for resolving their concerns than the legal system or engage in political activities. She finds that although most entrepreneurs agree that there is a need to strengthen rule of law in China, few associate legal reform with democratization. Instead of aspiring for a more liberal political system, most entrepreneurs fear that democratic reforms could lead to instability – which, in turn, could jeopardize economic growth and their prosperity.[8]

Minxin Pei (2006) has aptly called China's economic reforms without political reforms paradoxical, a "trapped transition" that has its own Achilles' heel.

---

[8] Of course, such claims are not new. For example, research on the business communities in Latin America demonstrated that the middle classes can have conflicting interests. The "bureaucratic–authoritarian" and "dependent development" scholarship characterized the

Pei points out that although at first glance the PRC has all the attributes of a "developmental state," it is in fact not one. Rather, Pei's examination of the sustainability of the CCP's developmental strategy – that of pursuing pro-market economic policies under dictatorial one-party rule – leads him to a number of novel conclusions. Most provocatively, he refutes the conventional view that sees the Chinese model as reminiscent of the high-performing East Asian states. To the contrary, unlike East Asia's strong "developmental" states, the Chinese state has become systematically more predatory, especially following the post-1990 reforms. Specifically, as property rights and administrative power were decentralized, local party bosses gained absolute discretion in appropriating or, more appropriately, stripping state assets for themselves and their cronies at the expense of the state. As the reach of the central state further declined and power and "autonomy" of local party bosses and the provincial and regional elites increased, they began to engage in an orgy of self-aggrandizement. As more and more "exit options" became available, especially business opportunities (both legal and illicit), it further reduced their stake in the system and increased their incentive to maximize their incomes and rents as quickly as possible. Thus, rather than a developmental state, China's party-state has increasingly morphed into a "decentralized predatory state." Given these ominous trends, Pei casts doubt on conventional explanations regarding the viability of the Chinese model: that sustained economic expansion will lead to political liberalization and democratization or that a "neo-authoritarian developmental state" is essential to economic takeoff. He compellingly points out that the lack of democratic reforms in China has led to pervasive corruption and a breakdown in political accountability. Ironically, China's decentralized predatory state under the strength of its economic fundamentals hides more than it reveals. Pei warns that only when the economic growth rate begins to taper off will the real extent of predation, including the serious human, environmental, and welfare costs, become evident. However, if in East Asia, correcting the harsh legacies of authoritarianism fell to incipient democratic regimes, in China, Pei fears that "illiberal adaptation" – in which elites limit political liberalization and democratization – is the most likely outcome. The problem of political transition underscores that China still lacks the institutional foundations of a market economy. After all, there are limits to the expedient management of the economy under the conditions of "trapped transition." The informal mechanisms may be sufficient in the early phases of economic development, but they are unlikely to sustain growth and promote democratization if the formal institutions of a market economy are not strengthened.

middle classes and business communities in Latin America as implicit backers of authoritarianism. Both argued that the desire for political stability was instrumental for the support of authoritarian over democratic regimes (Cardoso and Faletto 1978; O'Donnell 1978).

India's Democratic Paradox

Barely a decade after India gained independence, Selig Harrison (1960) expressed grave doubts about the survival of constitutional democracy in India – indeed, the survival of India as a unified nation. In his popular *India: The Most Dangerous Decades,* he pessimistically noted that "odds are almost wholly against the survival of freedom and . . . the issue is, in fact, whether any Indian state can survive at all" (p. 338). Suffice it to note, the anticipation regarding India's descent into anarchy and collapse have proved to be premature. After six decades of democratic rule (and fourteen national elections), democracy is now well established and an indelible part of India's political culture. For all its limitations, India remains the world's largest constitutional democracy with a functioning parliament, a political regime of laws and institutions, civilian control of the military, a free press, and numerous political parties and free elections for which millions of voters turn out to vote. Furthermore, democracy has served India well because it has provided the glue that holds together the polyglot nation with a population of 1 billion, twenty major languages, and an impenetrable checkerboard of identities. Although in many developing countries the issues revolve around democratic transition and consolidation, in India, the dominant issue on the political agenda is no longer whether democracy can survive but whether it can become a meaningful way for diverse sectors of society to exercise collective influence over public decisions that affect their lives.

Yet there is gnawing concern about the "quality" of India's democracy. Fareed Zakaria's (2003, 3) pessimistic (and counterintuitive) assessment that "while democracy is flourishing; liberty is not" is widely shared. What explains this paradox? According to Zakaria, although the idea of democracy (in the sense of devolution of power to the masses) has spread rapidly, it is less clear the extent to which democratic consolidation or the institutionalization and routinization of democratic norms and values within the political system is taking place. Rather, in India (and elsewhere), the trend has been toward "illiberal democracy" – a form of governance that deliberately combines the rhetoric of liberal democracy with illiberal rule. For example, although regular and competitive multiparty elections are held, qualifying the country as an "electoral democracy," the everyday practices of the state are marked by arbitrariness and abuses. Similarly, political freedoms and civil rights may be formally recognized but are hardly observed in practice. The judiciary may officially be deemed independent but is easily compromised, and the free press is harassed in numerous ways to make it compliant. Zakaria argues that in India, democratization has meant "opening up its politics to a much broader group of people who were previously marginalized," and creating new political parties that have made India "more democratic," but "less liberal." Thus, illiberal democracy (that is, nominally democratic government shorn of constitutional liberalism and institutional checks) is potentially dangerous because it brings with it the erosion of liberty, abuse of power, ethnic divisions, and conflict; further, "illiberal democracy has not proved to be an effective path to liberal democracy" (pp. 7–9).[9]

A chilling manifestation of this illiberalism is vividly portrayed in Nussbaum's (2007) *The Clash Within*. She explores the threat posed to India's democracy and its secular institutions by the rise of militant Hindu nationalism and the distortion of Hinduism tolerant ecclesiastical principles by religious chauvinists. With illustrations from violent communal riots over the past decade, especially in the state of Gujarat in 2002 (where a bloody pogrom against Muslims was orchestrated by elected politicians and bureaucrats), she offers a sharp critique of the Indian state, arguing that its "civilized veneer" of secularism and tolerance can easily break out into the worst forms of tribalism. Nussbaum correctly notes that the criminal justice system in India, including in prosperous states like Gujarat, has become increasingly compromised. In fact, it not only fails to protect religious minorities, it is also incapable of bringing ordinary criminals, let alone those allied with the powerful and the well connected, to justice. Das (2006, 12) lucidly sums up the appalling nature of everyday governance in India by noting that "the Indian state no longer generates public goods. Instead, it creates private benefits for those who control it. Consequently, the Indian state has become so riddled with perverse incentives ... that accountability is almost impossible." The problem is even more acute in a number of Indian states that have witnessed sharp increases in violent crimes, including armed insurgency. In some states like Bihar, the delivery of essential public services, especially in health, education, and transport, has long ceased to function, and lawlessness and criminality are pervasive.

Many see the flagrant violations of law and order as fundamentally rooted in the problem of institutional decline because the weakening of representative institutions has made it more difficult to contain and mediate particularistic demands. A number of analysts have highlighted the fragmentation of India's party system to explain the "growing crisis of governance" (Kohli 1990, 2001). The basic argument is that the break up in India's party system after decades of relatively stable one-party rule by the Congress has created deep challenges to efficacious governance. Specifically, since 1989, national elections have resulted in "hung parliaments" in which no party has won a majority.

---

[9] Zakaria provocatively argues that the most effective way to turn developing or traditional societies into liberal democracies is by first fostering constitutional liberty rather than democracy. This is because if electoral democracy is established before a society has achieved constitutional liberty, it is likely to end up as an illiberal democracy or degenerate into authoritarianism. To Zakaria, liberty leads to democracy and democracy ends up undermining liberty. As an illustration, he argues that if free elections were held in Islamic countries, most fundamentalist parties would win and then proceed to destroy liberty: "it would be one man, one vote, one time."

This marked the beginning of a multiparty system and the era of coalition governments, as well as the transition from a relatively inclusive broad-based system dominated by Congress to a more fragmented and "cleavage-based" system dominated by parties with constituencies that include one or several caste, regional, and ethnoreligious groups. The resultant rise of identity politics and political fragmentation with more than thirty political parties represented in the national Parliament has spawned electoral volatility and cumbersome and ineffective governing coalitions composed of at least ten parties such as the Bharatiya Janata Party (BJP)-led National Democratic Alliance and the Congress-led United Progressive Alliance. This has made stable governance exceedingly difficult.

Institutional decline has also negatively affected economic growth, especially the redistributive efforts. In such an unpropitious environment, the poor have little organized "voice," and elections provide, at best, a periodic and ineffective instrument for keeping public officials accountable. As unapologetic personalist leaders fill the void left by eroding representative institutions, macroeconomic decisions have become heavily influenced by political considerations, especially meeting partisan loyalties and the imperatives of the next electoral round. In this environment, incumbents of all hues engage in every manner of populist pork-barrel politics, which places partisan interests above the public good. At both the Center and the states, politically expedient but fiscally irresponsible policies are routinely adopted. Some analysts underscore the distinction between the "procedural" and "substantive" aspects of democracy to explain the limitations of India's democracy in mitigating the problems of poverty and inequality (P. Bardhan 1998). Procedural or formal democracy focuses on democratic institutions, parties, and the structures and procedures, whereas substantive democracy centers on actual democratic conditions and how effectively the polity is achieving the substantive goals of democracy such as liberty, economic equality, and redistributive justice. The fact that persistent economic inequalities coupled with caste and religious exclusion mock the formal political equality of democratic citizenship has led some to conclude that India's seemingly participatory democracy is in fact "elitist" – dominated and controlled by powerful classes and interests.[10] For example, Jalal (1994) refers to India's democracy as "democratic authoritarianism" because, according to her, for democracy to function in a *real* and not *formal* sense, there has to be greater prior economic and political equality among its citizens.

Yet for all its challenges, India's democratic order also has significant strengths. Despite the fact that caste and communal loyalties are significant determinants of electoral outcomes, the proliferation of political parties has

[10] Pranab Bardhan's (1998) influential *The Political Economy of Development in India* presents a devastating indictment of India's democracy, arguing that it conveniently serves the interests of the "dominant proprietary classes" made up of industrial capitalists, rich farmers, and professional bureaucrats.

also given the Indian voter a wide menu of choices. The Indian electorate (despite being largely illiterate) is also relatively informed and actively participates in the political process, and, as the Mahatma predicted, has learned the art of democracy by demonstrating an uncanny wisdom and sophistication. Voter turnout in India has stabilized at around 60 percent, which by international standards is quite impressive. More important, the electorate takes its responsibilities seriously. Since 1947, only a quarter of incumbents have been returned to power. In elections (at least since 1987) for state-level governments, less than 15 percent of incumbent administrations have returned to power. It seems that the Indian electorate is increasingly splitting its vote among different parties in both state and national elections as if to show its preference for deadlocked parliaments. If this trends hold, the message is clear: (a) the volatile voter with a strong bias against incumbents has a low threshold for ineffective or bad governments; (b) no one party can take its rule for granted; (c) multi-caste, multiclass, multireligious, and multilinguistic platforms are essential to win; and (d) ideologically polarized parties must shed their extremism if they are to be successful. As electoral success depends on a party's ability to reach out to individuals and groups in diverse social settings while conveying a political agenda with generalized rather than narrow sectoral appeal, the fears of a "takeover" by right-wing Hindu fanatics or left-wing fanatics (Maoist-inspired Naxalism) is exaggerated. Specifically, because the fragmentation and "diversity" of parties means that no one party or political tendency holds a monopoly on power, the fears about emergence of a Hindu *rashtra* (state) are overblown. Less than a quarter of the electorate voted for the BJP in 2004. In fact, the BJP received a smaller share of the vote than it did in the 1999 elections. Not surprisingly, the BJP has significantly softened its narrow ideological stance and moved toward the political center – the safe traditional mainstream of Indian politics.

Although Indians bemoan the recurring instability associated with coalition governments, it is important to recognize that India's mind-boggling diversity can be effectively reflected in a broad-based coalition government. Indeed, it is the very deepening of democracy that has made the national Parliament and state assemblies more representative of India's society. Arguably, the coalition governments have not necessarily worsened governability. Rather, by facilitating a measure of the much-needed decentralization of power away from New Delhi to subnational units, the various coalition configurations have restored a measure of vitality to regional grassroots democratic institutions. Moreover, under today's coalition governments, politics remains highly pluralistic. Because the prime minister and cabinet are chosen by multiple political actors, their power is also constrained by multiple constituencies. In this regard, Nussbaum's claim that the rise of Hindu nationalism is the result of the collapse of one-party rule under the Congress and the passing of great stalwarts of tolerance – individuals such as Mahatma Gandhi and Jawaharlal Nehru – smacks of elitism. The reality is that India was never the paragon of genteel secularism and cosmopolitanism its champions, the "chattering classes" (the English-speaking elites), have claimed it to be. India's religiosity, social cleavages and sectarian feuds based on faith, caste, and locality have always been real, volatile, and often nonnegotiable. The problem, it seems, is that secularists have come to believe their own myths. Benedict Anderson (1983) has taught that all states create founding myths and traditions that become part of their collective memories. The Indian nationalists – in particular, Gandhi and Nehru – developed a distinctive narrative of India's past that privileged commemorative histories of religious tolerance, sociocultural accommodation and assimilation, and pluralistic syncretism of faith and belief, while devaluing the more authentic and intimate folk traditions based on the vicissitudes of kith, creed, and caste. The "little traditions" spoke of recurrent partitions and pathological conflicts between Hindus and Muslims, high castes and low castes, and the uneasy coexistence between the mélange of peoples and communities that made the subcontinent their home. In India, where civic-based participation remains poorly developed (resulting in what Chhibber (1999) has aptly described as "democracy without associations"), the democratic revolution, by empowering the unlettered masses, has like never before brought to the surface the seemingly latent hostilities and precarious tensions between the multitudes. The neatly compartmentalized privatized religious faith and a secularized public realm is today another mythos. The battle for the soul of India will continue – mostly at the ballot box and occasionally in the streets – for the foreseeable future.

More positively, the self-correcting and regenerating aspects of democracy are also at work in India. In recent years, India's judiciary, including the Supreme Court and the high courts in a number of states; the Election Commission; and the office of the president have reasserted their authority. The courts have sought to weed out corruption at all levels, pursuing civil and criminal cases involving several former ministers in the central government and in the states (including former Prime Minister Narasimha Rao and the former chief minister of Bihar, Lalu Prasad Yadav). Equally impressive, India's once compliant Election Commission has undertaken an energetic and unprecedented campaign to make political parties and their leaders accountable. In addition to demanding that political parties must file returns of their expenditures, both for parties and for individual candidates, the commission has also clamped down on the flagrant use of money to influence voters. In the process, many of the country's once invincible rulers have been humbled. The fact that the Election Commission has used its power to deploy large numbers of security forces to polling stations has helped to prevent violence and voter fraud.

Finally, as Victor Hugo once noted, "there is one thing stronger than all the armies in the world, and that is an idea whose time has come." The idea of market reforms that swept the world some two decades ago is now an accepted part of India's developmental idiom. Although not long ago it was considered politically incorrect to support market reforms, every major political party now recognizes the need for deepening market reforms. Differences that occasionally arise are about the pace of reforms and which should be introduced first. As Prime Minister Manmohan Singh often quips, "the question now is not whether the reforms will be reversed, but how rapidly they will be extended." In fact, when the pro-market, reform-oriented BJP-led National Democratic Alliance was defeated by the Congress-led United Progressive Alliance (supported from the outside by India's Communist parties), many felt that the pendulum would swing back to economic populism and the scuttling of the reforms. Yet in a sign of the broad consensus on the necessity of economic liberalization, the Congress-led government reaffirmed its commitment to reforms, albeit with the caveat that, unlike its predecessor, it would implement reforms with a "human face" – meaning greater attention to redistributing the fruits of reforms to all sectors of society. It seems that such a strong consensus exists on the necessity of reforms that regime transitions do did not presage a different set of policy choices. Nevertheless, unless some of the more glaring contradictions of neoliberalism are mitigated, it can lead to a retreat from market liberalism and return to the irresponsible populist and protectionist policies of the past. In particular, one such contradiction is the tension between democratic citizenship and socioeconomic exclusion and the still-widespread perception that technocratic management of the economy has disproportionately benefited the already well-off. The rise of the parochial personalist leaders such as Mayawati or Lalu Prasad Yadav, who place partisan interests above the public good, underscore that the gains from market reforms can quickly erode.

The Wild Card: India's Dangerous Neighborhood

Finally, although China has greatly improved relations with her neighbors and now enjoys a relatively benign external environment conducive to the pursuit of economic development, India still remains surrounded by an embittered and envious neighbor: Pakistan. India and Pakistan have remained in a constant state of hostility since independence. In fact, even periods of peace between these neighbors have been uneasy, with deeply felt anxiety on both sides – leading one observer to describe the periods of peace as "ugly stability" (Tellis 2001). Despite recent effort at de-escalation of tensions and the tenuous transition to democracy in Pakistan, the danger of conflict, including an all-out war, remains high. This is because of several interrelated factors: low levels of intraregional economic interdependence, weak diplomatic and security institutionalization, contentious territorial disputes, and, perhaps most important, the Pakistani military's penchant for clumsy adventurism. Indeed, the military establishment in Pakistan remains *primus inter pares,* and any meaningful peace with India means questioning its pervasive raison d'être – in particular, questioning India's irredentist claim over Kashmir (Nawaz 2008). Compounding this, India's homegrown Islamists or *jihadi* terrorists, increasingly in cohorts with other extremist and criminal organizations, especially the various Marxist/Maoist-inspired terror groups within and outside India, have the potential and the reasons (their visceral hatred of India) to reignite tensions between New Delhi and Islamabad.[11] The successive Pakistani governments (both civilian and military), by creating and supporting atavistic terrorists groups, including Lashkar-e-Toiba, Jaish-e-Muhammed, Harkat-ul-Mujahideen, Markazdawa, Dawat-ul-Irshad, the Taliban, Al-Qaeda's International Islamic Front, and several other shadowy *jihadi* groups, have literally unleashed the "dogs of war" to wage proxy wars against India (Rashid 2002). Although the gruesome terror wrought by these groups has bought Pakistan international opprobrium, instead of the hoped-for "strategic depth" against India, these groups know very well that provocation (if it is outrageous enough) has the potential to ratchet up tensions and bring both countries into armed conflict – and, from their perspective, a long overdue apocalyptic war with the Hindu infidels. The fact that India has now appropriated Bush's doctrine of preemption means that there is greater compulsion to retaliate. Thus, the militarization and nuclearization of the subcontinent remains a grave threat to peace and stability in a region long characterized by mutual misunderstandings, misperceptions, miscalculations, and brinkmanship.

Counterintuitively, some analysts, drawing on what the strategic analyst Glenn Snyder (1965) termed the "stability/instability paradox," argue that although there may be no breakthroughs in Indian-Pakistani relations, war is unlikely because the deterrence based on nuclear weapons will inhibit escalation to a large-scale nuclear war – although it makes conventional conflict more likely. For example, the fact that neither the 1999 Kargil conflict nor the post-September 11 military standoff escalated beyond a limited conventional engagement was because of the threat of nuclear war. Ganguly (2001, 122–23) sums up this position well, noting that the 1999 Indo-Pakistani border war at Kargil "conformed closely to the expectations of the 'stability/instability paradox.' This proposition holds that nuclear weapons do contribute to stability at one level – for fear of nuclear escalation. Simultaneously, however, they create incentives for conventional conflicts in peripheral areas as long as either side does not breach certain shared thresholds." To Ganguly, barring India's acquisition and deployment of viable antiballistic missile capabilities,

---

[11] Cross-border terrorism, which is responsible for many of the brutal attacks on major cities, is not the only threat to India's internal security. The country also faces an armed Maoist insurgency that afflicts vast swaths of sixteen of its twenty-eight states. Hence, Prime Minister Manmohan Singh has called this insurgency the country's "single biggest challenge to internal security."

nuclear deterrence in South Asia should remain robust. In a similar vein, Basrur (2006) argues that nuclear weapons deterred India from crossing the Line of Control during the Kargil conflict, thereby ensuring that the dispute was resolved without resort to a full-scale war. Indeed, if Basrur is any guide, as long as India's "nuclear-strategic culture" is generally in accord with the principle of minimum deterrence, a full-scale war between India and Pakistan is unlikely.[12]

Although the "existential deterrence" based on nuclear weapons promoted caution and inhibited escalation to nuclear war between the superpowers during the Cold War, such restraint is by no means assured in the subcontinent. Krepon (2005) claims that the overt nuclearization of the subcontinent has made the region more susceptible to war because the history of distrust and absence of robust risk-reduction measures creates a high probability that both may stumble unwittingly into a full-scale war. On a similar vein, S. P. Kapur (2007) argues that although the "stability/instability paradox" explains U.S.-Soviet behavior during the Cold War, it does not explain the ongoing hostilities between India and Pakistan. That is, if "strategic stability" means a low probability that conventional war will escalate into a nuclear one, it also reduces the danger of a conventional war. Therefore, in lowering the potential costs of a conventional war, strategic stability also makes the outbreak of such conflict more likely. This, Kapur argues, is precisely what is happening in South Asia. Even as Pakistan (a revisionist power) and its proxies launch cross-border attacks inside Indian territory, India (a status quo power) has been relatively restrained and refused to retaliate in kind – a behavior that contradicts the stability/instability thesis. Kapur argues that, contrary to the expectations of the stability/instability paradox, a small probability of low-level conventional conflict escalating into a nuclear one would not encourage such behavior because it would reduce the ability of Pakistan's nuclear weapons to deter an Indian conventional attack. Because Pakistan's military is conventionally much weaker than India's, this would discourage Pakistani aggression and encourage robust Indian conventional retaliation against repeated Pakistani provocations. Instead, Pakistani risk-taking and Indian restraint have actually resulted from instability in the strategic environment. A full-scale Indo-Pakistani conventional conflict would create a heightened risk of nuclear escalation. This danger enables Pakistan to launch limited attacks on India while deterring all-out Indian conventional retaliation. Thus, unlike during

---

[12] According to Basrur (2006), "minimum deterrence" is based on the concept that possession of just a handful nuclear weapons is sufficient to deter aggression. He contends that for India, minimum deterrence is not only the most cost-effective strategy but also an "optimal posture" because such a doctrine minimizes the threat to democratic processes inherent in the possession of a nuclear arsenal and offers the fewest vulnerabilities to states threatened by nonstate actors. Thus, it is not in India's strategic interest to adopt a more "maximalist posture."

the Cold War, in contemporary South Asia, nuclear danger facilitates, rather than impedes, conventional conflict.

Furthermore, miscalculation, not to mention Clausewitz's prescient warnings about the "fog of war," can have catastrophic consequences. Unlike the Cold War, which was an ideological struggle, the India-Pakistan conflict is religious and historically rooted and more difficult to resolve. Unlike the superpowers, Pakistan has weak command-and-control arrangements and as the illegal "nuclear bazaar" run by the "father" of Pakistan's nuclear program, A. Q. Khan, revealed, the control of Pakistan's nuclear assets by all manner of *jihadi* and extremist groups both within and outside government can occur with only the slightest disequilibrium in Pakistan's internal politics. Adding to the uncertainty is both countries' rather broad interpretation regarding the use of nuclear weapons. Although India has adopted a "no first-use" doctrine (arguably given its superiority in conventional forces), in January 2000, the Defense Ministry issued its "doctrine of limited war" under the nuclear umbrella. It chillingly noted that war could be waged in the "strategic space" between "low-intensity conflict" and full-scale nuclear war. Not to be outdone, Islamabad announced its own strategy a month later, making it clear that nuclear weapons were not simply for deterrence but an integral part of Pakistan's "overall military instrument." Clearly, the specter of a catastrophic war hangs over the subcontinent like the sword of Damocles.

Yet the integrative forces of globalization have the potential to change India-Pakistan relations for the better, which decades of diplomacy and negotiations have not. Specifically, greater openness and intraregional trade and integration can help ameliorate the security dilemma that currently plagues the region. India's vibrant growing economy (compared with a stagnating Pakistani economy) can serve as a regional economic hub and pull the faltering economies around it. Rapid economic growth has allowed India not only to improve dramatically its power position vis-à-vis Pakistan but also to arrest its economic decline relative to China. This has enhanced its power and prestige – and arguably, it has allowed India, at least since early 2004, to engage in sustained negotiations on all contentious issues with Pakistan from a position of strength. Further, globalization by breaking barriers through information flows, ever expanding people-to-people contacts, and trade linkages has the potential to break down further the old stereotypes and hatreds.

Coming Full Circle: China and India in the Globalization Age

In this era of globalization, no country can be an island. The volume of international capital flows have surged from just under US$2 trillion in 2000 to US$6.4 trillion in 2006. These funds now cross national borders, often at will, despite attempts by governments to control and regulate their movement. The inexorable forces of economic globalization, coupled with China's and

India's embrace of openness, has meant that their economies are now deeply interwoven into the fabric of the global economy as never before. Consequently, as the current subprime-induced financial crisis illustrates, both are subject to the vagaries of economic globalization.

Yet as this book has shown, globalization is hardly a linear or seamless process. Rather, it is characterized by contradictions and paradoxes. The cases of China and India in the midst of the current global economic downturn (if not recession) are illustrative. Both have found it difficult to insulate their economies from the crisis despite the fact their economies are not heavily exposed to the U.S. subprime mortgage securities. None of the major Indian banks have much exposure to U.S. subprime debt. The State Bank of India, ICICI Bank (the country's largest private bank), Bank of Baroda, and Bank of India have exposure to international securitized debt in the form of collateralized debt obligations for around US$3 billion. This is tiny compared with ICICI's US$100 billion balance sheet. In the case of China, the Bank of China has confirmed that it is holding about US$9.7 billion of securities backed by U.S. subprime loans, whereas the Industrial and Commercial Bank of China and China Construction Bank have reported exposure of about US$1 billion each. Of course, in the larger scheme of things, these are extremely small debts. Even if the three Chinese banks have a total US$12 billion exposure to subprime, it is still just 6 percent of the US$199 billion in private foreign securities they hold. More important, the Chinese authorities have made public that none of its massive US$1.5 trillion foreign reserves (the largest in the world) is invested in subprime debt. Although India's total reserve assets declined about 7 percent from August 2008 to US$274 billion in the second week of October 2008, its foreign currency reserves are more than adequate to cover its debt obligations.

What explains this paradox – that China and India are both integrated into the global economy and yet seemingly not fully integrated? This is because both countries are still minor players in the global financial system. For example, Chinese and Indian banks, some of which are large by global standards on the basis of market capitalization and the size of their balance sheets, have only modest international presence. The rupee is hardly used outside India, and the renminbi is hardly used outside China (except for a modest amount in Hong Kong), and Chinese capital markets are not a major source of financing for foreign borrowers. In fact, capital markets in both countries are small relative to the size of the domestic economy, and both rely heavily on foreign direct investment rather than securities investment and other forms of capital flows to access international capital markets. Indeed, although there has been gradual liberalization, both China and India subject portfolio capital flows to various restrictions. As noted earlier, in China, portfolio flows are still largely channeled through large institutional investors through the Qualified Foreign Institutional Investors (QFII) and Qualified Domestic Institutional Investors

(QDII) programs, established in 2002. The QFII program is restricted to funds management and securities companies with at least US$10 billion in assets, including the world's top one hundred commercial banks. In addition, the securities regulator of the QFII's home country must sign a "Memorandum of Understanding" and have a track record of good relations with the China Securities Regulatory Commission (CSRC), and the QDIIs must have assets of more than 5 billion RMB.

Given these buffers, what explains China's and India's vulnerabilities? The answer: economic globalization creates not only deep and entwining linkages between economies but also convergence among them. As such, troubles in one part, especially the largest part (the United States), will inevitably send waves that may become ripples in some places (China and India) and a tsunami in others (Iceland). In the case of both China and India, what were minor ripples when the subprime crisis broke in mid-2007 have become more significant waves. In both countries, because external trade in merchandise and services accounts for a significant portion of their economies, a global slowdown in demand is beginning to have a negative impact on them. Specifically, with continuing declines in consumer spending and the rise of unemployment in the United States, China and India are feeling the effects in their export markets. This is particularly the case in China, which is more export-dependent than India – the economic performance of which is also driven by domestic consumption. However, India's outsourcing industry and export-dependent information technology (IT) sector is already feeling the pain of declining revenues – due not only to a slowdown in global demand but also to the rise in the value of the rupee against the U.S. dollar. In fact, tightening credit and the declining value of dollar have hit India's IT companies rather hard because the industry derives more than 60 percent of its revenues from the United States. Also, because some 30 percent of business coming to Indian outsourcers includes projects from U.S. banking, insurance, and the financial services sector, a sharp slowdown has already affected these businesses. Infosys and Satyam, two well-known outsourcing companies, have laid off workers and expect weaker earnings as their customers in the United States and Europe pull back.

For China, the challenges are more complex. The exponential growth of its massive foreign exchange reserves has been the result of trying to sustain a stable exchange rate between the renminbi and the dollar even in the face of strong economic pressures for appreciation (given China's strong productivity growth, it is natural for the renminbi to appreciate). To prevent this appreciation and to avoid loss of export competitiveness, the People's Bank of China has been aggressively buying dollars and selling renminbi. However, this strategy has not been without costs for China. Besides making domestic macroeconomic management difficult (China's controls on private exchanges of renminbi for other currencies are not always effective), concentration on exchange rate stabilization has meant that Beijing has largely ceded the ability to use monetary policy to target domestic objectives such as controlling inflation. Consequently, the continuous depreciation of the U.S. dollar has increased uncertainties associated with capital movement; by driving up commodities prices in dollar terms, the weaker dollar is also exerting the pressure of imported inflation on China. This poses a real threat because global external shocks can generate runaway inflation. (For example, a sharp hike in food prices can quickly erode the gains made in economic development, especially poverty reduction.) Moreover, in both China and India the subprime-induced tightening of global credit markets and the resulting "credit crunch" has reduced capital flows. Over the short term, this may not be a serious problem because both countries have a fair amount of liquidity in the domestic economy. However, if the problem persists over time, the credit crunch could have a negative impact on both economies. For example, an impact on the business sector's ability to raise funds from international sources can impede investment growth because these businesses would have to rely more on costlier domestic sources of financing, including bank credit. This could, in turn, put upward pressure on domestic interest rates.

Of course, confirming that economic globalization can also be contradictory and paradoxical, there is a silver lining for both countries. A slowdown or a recession in the United States and Western Europe will moderate oil and other commodity prices. This will have a favorable effect because China and India are net importers of many basic commodities. Finally, China's massive trade surplus and foreign reserves give Beijing significant leverage, especially in times of a global credit crunch. Since 2007, Beijing has allocated some US$200 billion into a "sovereign wealth fund" under the management of the government-sponsored China Investment Corporation (CIC) to be used for investment abroad. It is the largest state-owned fund in the world. This financial power provides China a unique opportunity to extend its reach globally, especially the ability to purchase or gain major ownership stakes in businesses, financial institutions, resources, and technology. One of the first announced investments of the CIC was a 10 percent stake in the U.S.-based private equity firm, Blackstone Group. Although the prospect of Chinese influence on U.S. corporate operations through the stock market raised concern on Wall Street, little could be done to stop it. As a large investor in U.S. Treasuries for many years, China claimed that it was simply trying to earn a higher return on its foreign investments by dividing its assets into stocks and bonds as well as commodities such as oil and gold.

Nevertheless, the fact that both China and India seems to have dodged the subprime crisis does not mean that all is well with their banking and financial sectors. As this and previous chapters has shown, significant challenges remain because in both countries, the mainly state-owned banks are saddled with multiple inefficiencies, including dangerously large volumes of nonperforming loans and large sectors of society with no access to formal financial intermediation. Yet, China and India have so far fared better than most during the current financial crisis. Both Chinese President Hu Jintao and Indian Prime Minister Manmohan Singh pledged that their countries will do everything in their powers to help stabilize the global economy. Specifically, both agreed that they could make a positive contribution by maintaining stable growth and resisting the rising protectionism in the United States and Europe. Both countries have also called for the creation of a "global monitoring authority" to better supervise the global financial system, including the creation of a "supervisory mechanism" for credit rating agencies. There is great expectation for China (and to a lesser extent, India) to play a more significant role in the emerging international economic order. Indeed, many world leaders have already publicly stated that they want China to go beyond the role of just a "stabilizer" and do more to kick-start the global economy, for example, by transferring some of its reserves to the IMF to help countries with balance-of-payment problems. The European Commission has urged Beijing to support new financial rules, while Thailand has asked China to ease its currency-conversion restrictions to facilitate pooling of reserves to create a $350 billion fund to protect the region's currencies. No doubt, such requests will continue to mount on China (and to a much lesser extent India), as the world's largest holder of foreign currency (and as the World's largest creditor) to play a more pro-active role in combating the global financial crisis. To date, Beijing has demonstrated its commitment to help stabilize the international financial system by continuing to hold and even buy more U.S. Treasury notes and other assets. China has also worked in good faith with a number of central banks to cut interest rates on three successive occasions, including its massive stimulus package. Clearly, for China (and to a lesser extent India), enhanced economic clout also means enhanced global responsibilities.

In his thoughtful book, *Common Wealth: Economics for a Crowded Planet* (2008), Jeffrey Sachs optimistically notes that this era of globalization, or "convergence" as he calls it, offers a realistic possibility of ending extreme poverty and narrowing the vast inequalities within and between countries. Indeed, the dramatic "catching up of China and India" and their success in rapidly reducing entrenched poverty underscore globalization's promise of shared prosperity. Nevertheless, as this book has shown, despite their achievements, both countries face significant challenges in the years and decades ahead. Perhaps the greatest challenge is making economic growth sustainable and inclusive. With impressive growth behind them, it is time that both India and China rethink how growth itself is conceived. Most fundamentally, each country must come to terms with the fact that growth is not just a matter of increasing GDP. Rather, growth must be sustainable. This means that growth based on a consumption binge by the few, environmental degradation, dependence on hydrocarbons, and the exploitation of scarce natural resources, without reinvesting the proceeds, is not sustainable. Second, growth must be inclusive. Contrary to the "trickle-down theory," there is no trade-off between inequality and growth. Because a country's most valuable resource is its people, it is imperative that policy makers promote strategies that allow the fruits of economic development to be shared equitably by all citizens. Finally, if the rising tide of globalization is to "lift all boats," it will require an unprecedented degree of national and global cooperation. For China and India, despite all their accomplishments, it remains to be seen if they can finally rise above the burdens of history.

Bibliography

Acharya, Shankar. 2006. *Essays on Macroeconomic Policy and Growth in India.* New Delhi: Oxford University Press.

Ahluwalia, Isher Judge. 1998. *India's Economic Reforms and Development: Essays for Manmohan Singh.* New Delhi: Oxford University Press.

_____. 1985. *Industrial Growth in India: Stagnation since the Mid-Sixties.* Delhi: Oxford University Press.

Ahluwalia, Montek. 2002. "Economic Reforms in India Since 1991: Has Gradualism Worked?" *Journal of Economic Perspectives,* **16**, no. 3 (Summer): pp. 67–88.

_____. 2002a. "State-level Performance under Economic Reforms in India," in Anne Krueger and Sajjid Chinoy, eds., *Economic Policy Reforms and the Indian Economy.* Chicago: University of Chicago Press.

Aiyar, Shekhar. 2001. "Growth Theory and Convergence across Indian States: A Panel Study," in Tim Callen, Patricia Reynolds, and Christopher Towe, eds., *India at the Crossroads: Sustaining Growth and Reducing Poverty.* Washington, DC: International Monetary Fund.

Alagappa, Muthiah, ed. 2001. *Coercion and Governance: The Declining Political Role of the Military in Asia.* Stanford, CA: Stanford University Press.

Alford, William. 1995. *To Steal a Book Is an Elegant Offense: Intellectual Property Law in Chinese Civilization.* Stanford, CA: Stanford University Press.

Ananthakrishnan, P., and S. Jain-Chandra. 2005, November. "The Impact on India of Trade Liberalization in the Textiles and Clothing Sector," IMF Working Paper No. WP/05/214. Washington, DC: International Monetary Fund.

Anderson, Benedict. 1983. *Imagined Communities: Reflections on the Origin and Spread of Nationalism.* London: Verso.

Anderson, Richard, and Jason Buol. 2005, January. "What Is Driving Oil Prices?" *The Regional Economist.* St. Louis, MO: Federal Reserve Bank.

Appleby, Paul. 1953. *Pubic Administration in India: Report of a Survey.* New Delhi: Government of India, Cabinet Secretariat.

Ashton, Basil, Kenneth Hill, Alan Piazza, and Robin Zeitz. 1984. "Famine in China, 1958–61." *Population and Development Review,* **10** (December): pp. 613–45.

Aslund, Anders. 2007. *Russia's Capitalist Revolution: Why Market Reform Succeeded and Democracy Failed.* Washington, DC: Institute for International Economics.

———. 1995. *How Russia Became a Market Economy.* Washington, DC: Brookings Institution Press.

———. 1989. "Soviet and Chinese Reforms: Why They Must Be Different." *The World Today,* **45**, no. 11 (November): pp. 188–91.

Athukorala, Prema-Chandra, ed. 2002. *The Economic Development of South Asia.* Northampton, MA: Edward Elgar.

Aubert, C., and Li, X. 2002. "Peasant Burden: Taxes and Levies Imposed on Chinese Farmers," in *China in the Global Economy: Agricultural Policies in China after WTO Accession.* Paris: Organisation for Economic Co-operation and Development.

Austin, Granville. 2003. *Working a Democratic Constitution: A History of the Indian Experience.* New York: Oxford University Press.

———. 1966. *The Indian Constitution: Cornerstone of a Nation.* Oxford: Clarendon Press.

Aziz, Jahangir, Steven Vincent Dunaway, and Eswar Prasad. 2006. *China and India Learning from Each Other: Reforms and Policies for Sustained Growth.* Washington, DC: International Monetary Fund.

Bachman, David. 1991. *Bureaucracy, Economy and Leadership in China: Institutional Origins of the Great Leap Forward.* New York: Cambridge University Press.

Bagchi, Amiya K. 1982. *The Political Economy of Underdevelopment.* London: Cambridge University Press.

Bain, Morris. 2005. *The Making of the State Enterprise System in Modern China: The Dynamics of Institutional Change.* Cambridge, MA: Harvard University Press.

Bajpai, Nirupam, and Jeffrey Sachs. 1997. "India's Economic Reforms: Lessons from East Asia." *The Journal of International Trade and Economic Development,* **6**, no. 2.

Balasubramanyam, V. N. 1984. *The Economy of India.* London: Weidenfeld and Nicolson.

Bandyopadhyaya, Jayant. 1970. *The Making of India's Foreign Policy.* New Delhi: Allied.

Banerjee, Abhijit, Shawn Cole, and Esther Duflo. 2004. "Banking Reform in India." *India Policy Forum,* **1**, pp. 277–332.

Bardhan, Ashok, and Cynthia Kroll. 2003. "The New Wave of Outsourcing." Fisher Center for Real Estate and Urban Economics, paper no. 1103. Berkeley: University of California.

Bardhan, Pranab. 2002. "Decentralization of Governance and Development." *Journal of Economic Perspectives,* **16**, no. 4 (Fall): pp. 185–205.

———. 1998. *The Political Economy of Development in India,* 2nd ed. New Delhi: Oxford University Press.

———. 1984. *The Political Economy of Development in India.* New Delhi: Oxford University Press.

Barnett, Doak, A. 1993. *China's Far West: Four Decades of Change.* Boulder, CO: Westview Press.

———. 1981. *China's Economy in Global Perspective.* Washington, DC: Brookings Institution.

———. 1967. *Cadres, Bureaucracy, and Political Power in Communist China.* New York: Columbia University Press.

———. 1964. *Communist China: The Early Years,* 1949–55. New York: Praeger.

Basrur, Rajesh M. 2006. *Minimum Deterrence and Indian Nuclear Security.* Stanford, CA: Stanford University Press.

Basu, Durga Das. 1993. *Introduction to the Constitution of India*. New Delhi: Prentice-Hall.

Basu, Priya, and Pradeep Srivastava. 2005, June. "Scaling-up Microfinance for India's Rural Poor," World Bank Policy Research Working Paper No. 3646. Washington, DC: World Bank.

Bauer, Peter. 1961. *Indian Economic Policy and Development*. London: George Allen & Unwin.

Baum, Richard. 1994. *Burying Mao: Chinese Politics in the Age of Deng Xiaoping*. Princeton, NJ: Princeton University Press.

————, ed. 1991. *Reform and Reaction in Post-Mao China: The Road to Tiananmen*. New York: Routledge.

————. 1975. *Prelude to Revolution: Mao, the Party and the Peasant Question*. New York: Columbia University Press.

Baxi, Upendra. 1980. *The Indian Supreme Court and Politics*. Lucknow: Eastern Book Company.

Bayly, Christopher A. 1988. *Indian Society and the Making of the British Empire*. London: Cambridge University Press.

Becker, Jasper. 1996. *Hungry Ghosts: Mao's Secret Famine*. New York: Free Press.

Behera, Navnita Chadha. 2007. *Demystifying Kashmir*. Washington, DC: Brookings Institution Press.

Bell, Daniel. 2006. *Beyond Liberal Democracy: Political Thinking for an East Asian Context*. Princeton, NJ: Princeton University Press.

Bellin, Eva. 2000. "Contingent Democrats: Industrialists, Labor, and Democratization in late Developing Countries." *World Politics*, **52**, no. 2 (April): pp. 175–205.

Bergsten, Fred C., Bates Gill, Nicholas R. Lardy, and Derek J. Mitchell. 2006. *China: The Balance Sheet*. Washington, DC: Institute for International Economics.

Bernstein, Richard, and Ross Munro. 1997. *The Coming Conflict with China*. New York: Alfred A. Knopf.

Bernstein, Thomas, and Xiaobo Lu. 2002. *Taxation without Representation in Rural China*. New York: Cambridge University Press.

Bernstein, William. 2008. *A Splendid Exchange: How Trade Shaped the World*. New York: Atlantic Monthly.

Bertsch, Gary, Seema Gahlaut, and Anupam Srivastava, eds. 1999. *Engaging India: U.S. Strategic Relations with the World's Largest Democracy*. New York: Routledge.

Beteille, Andre. 1974. *Studies in Agrarian Social Structure*. Delhi: Oxford University Press.

Bettelheim, Charles. 1968. *India Independent*. New York: Monthly Review Press.

Betts, Richard. 1993. "Wealth, Power and Instability: East Asia and the United States after the Cold-War." *International Security*, **18**, no. 3 (Winter): pp. 34–77.

Bhagwati, Jagdish. 2004. *In Defense of Globalization*. New York: Oxford University Press.

————. 1993. *India in Transition: Freeing the Economy*. London: Clarendon Press.

————, and T. N. Srinivasan. 1975. *Foreign Trade Regimes and Economic Development: India*. New York: Columbia University Press.

————, and Padma Desai. 1970. *India, Planning for Industrialization*. London: Oxford University Press.

Bhalla, Surjit. 2002. *Imagine There's No Country: Poverty, Inequality, and Growth in the Era of Globalization*. Washington, DC: Institute for International Economics.

Bianco, Lucien. 1971. *Origins of the Chinese Revolution, 1915–1959*. Stanford, CA: Stanford University Press.

Bijian, Zheng. 2005. *Peaceful Rise – China's New Road to Development*. Beijing: Central Party School Publishing House.

Blasko, Dennis. 2006. *The Chinese Army Today: Tradition and Transformation for the 21st Century*. New York: Routledge.

Blecher, Marc. 1986. *China: Politics, Economics, and Society: Iconoclasm and Innovation in a Revolutionary Socialist Country*. London: Pinter.

Blinder, Alan S. 2006. "Offshoring: The Next Industrial Revolution?" *Foreign Affairs*, **85**, no. 2, (March/April): pp. 113–28.

Blyn, George. 1966. *Agricultural Trends in India 1891–1947: Output, Availability and Productivity*. Philadelphia: University of Pennsylvania Press.

Bose, Sugata, and Ayesha Jalal. 1997. *Modern South Asia: History, Culture, Political Economy*. New Delhi: Oxford University Press.

Bose, Sumantra. 2003. *Kashmir: Roots of Conflict, Paths to Peace*. Cambridge, MA: Harvard University Press.

Bosworth, Barry, Susan Collins, and Arvind Virmani. 2006. "Sources of Growth in the Indian Economy," in Suman Bery, Barry Bosworth, and Arvind Panagariya, eds., *India Policy Forum*, Vol. 3. New Delhi: Sage, pp. 1–50.

Bowie, Robert R., and John K. Fairbank, eds. 1962. *Communist China 1955–1959: Policy Documents*. Cambridge, MA: Harvard University Press.

Brands, H. W. 1990. *India and the United States: The Cold Peace*. Boston: Twayne.

Brass, Paul. 1990. *The Politics of India since Independence*. New York: Cambridge University Press.

———. 1966. *Factional Politics in an Indian State: The Congress Party in Uttar Pradesh*. Berkeley: University of California Press.

Brecher, Michael. 1959. *Nehru: A Political Biography*. London: Oxford University Press.

Breman, Jan. 1996. *Footloose Labor: Working in India's Informal Economy*. New York: Cambridge University Press.

Breslin, Shaun. 1996. *China in the 1980s: Centre-Province Relations in a Reforming Socialist State*. New York: St. Martin's Press.

Brines, Russell. 1968. *The Indo-Pakistani Conflict*. New York: Pall Mall.

Broadman, Harry. 2007. *Africa's Silk Road: China and India's New Economic Frontier*. Washington, DC: World Bank.

———. 1999. "The Chinese State as Corporate Shareholder." *Finance and Development*, **36**, no. 3, pp. 52–55.

Brooks, Stephen, and William C. Wohlforth. 2008. *World Out of Balance: International Relations and the Challenge of American Primacy*. Princeton, NJ: Princeton University Press.

Brown, Judith. 2003. *Nehru: A Political Life*. New Haven, CT: Yale University Press.

———. 1985. *Modern India: The Origins of an Asian Democracy*. Oxford: Oxford University Press.

Brown, Norman. 1963. *The United States and India and Pakistan*. Cambridge, MA: Harvard University Press.

Brugger, Bill, and Stephen Reglar. 1994. *Politics, Economy and Society in Contemporary China*. Stanford, CA: Stanford University Press.

Bruton, Henry. 1989. "Import Substitution," in Hollis Chenery and T. N. Srinivasan, eds., *Handbook of Development Economics: Volume 2*. Amsterdam: North Holland.

Bueno de Mesquita, Bruce, and George Downs. 2005. "Development and Democracy." *Foreign Affairs*, **84**, no. 5 (September/October): pp. 77–86.

Burns, John. 1988. *Political Participation in Rural China*. Berkeley: University of California Press.

Burns, Nicholas. 2007. "America's Strategic Opportunity with India." *Foreign Affairs*, **86**, no. 6 (November/December): pp. 131–46.

Bush, Richard, and Michael E. O'Hanlon. 2007. *A War Like No Other: The Truth about China's Challenge to America*. New York: John Wiley.

Byres, Terence, ed., 1998. *The Indian Economy: Major Debates since Independence*. New Delhi: Oxford University Press.

Cai, Yongshun. 2006. *State and Laid-Off Workers in Reform China: The Silence and Collective Action of the Retrenched*. New York: Routledge.

Calder, Ken, and Francis Fukuyama, eds. 2008. *East Asian Multilateralism: Prospects for Regional Stability*. Baltimore: Johns Hopkins University Press.

Calomiris, Charles, ed., 2007. *China's Financial Transition at a Crossroads*. New York: Columbia University Press.

Cardoso, Fernando Henrique, and Enzo Faletto. 1979. *Dependency and Development in Latin America*. Berkeley: University of California Press.

Carlson, Allen. 2005. *Unifying China, Integrating with the World: Securing Sovereignty in the Reform Era*. Stanford, CA: Stanford University Press.

Carras, Mary. 1979. *Indira Gandhi: In the Crucible of Leadership*. Boston: Beacon Press.

Cerra, Valerie, Sandra A. Rivera, and Sweta Chaman Saxena. 2004. "Crouching Tiger, Hidden Dragon: What Are the Consequences of China's WTO Entry for India's Trade?" IMF Working Paper. Washington, DC: International Monetary Fund.

Chadda, Maya. 1997. *Ethnicity, Security and Separatism in India*. New York: Columbia University Press.

Chakravarty, Sukhamoy. 1984. *Development Planning: The Indian Experience*. London: Oxford University Press.

Chan, Kam, Hung-Gay Fung, and Qingfeng "Wilson" Liu, eds. 2007. *China's Capital Markets: Challenges from WTO Membership*. Northhampton, MA: Edward Elgar.

Chan, Kam Wing, and Will Buckingham. 2008. "Is China Abolishing the Hukou System?" *China Quarterly*, no. 195 (September): pp. 582–606.

Chanda, Nayan. 2007. *Bound Together: How Traders, Preachers, Adventurers and Warriors Shaped Globalization*. New Haven, CT: Yale University Press.

Chanda, Rupa. 2002. *Globalization of Services: India's Opportunities and Constraints*. New Delhi: Oxford University Press.

Chang, Gordon. 2001. *The Coming Collapse of China*. New York: Random House.

Chang, Maria Hsia. 2001. *Return of the Dragon: China's Wounded Nationalism*. Boulder, CO: Westview Press.

Chaudhuri, Pramit, ed. 1971. *Aspects of Indian Economic Development*. London: George Allen & Unwin.

Chellaney, Brahma. 1998–99. "After the Tests: India's Option." *Survival*, **40**, no. 4 (Winter): pp. 93–111.

Chen, Feng. 1995. *Economic Transition and Political Legitimacy in Post-Mao China: Ideology and Reform.* Albany: University of New York Press.

Chen, Jie. 2004. *Popular Political Support in Urban China.* Stanford, CA: Stanford University Press.

Chen, John-ren. 2005. "China's Way of Economic Transition." *Transition Studies Review,* 12, no. 2, pp. 315–33.

Chen, Shaohua, and Yan Wang. 2001. *China's Growth and Poverty Reduction: Trends between 1990 and 1999.* Washington, DC: World Bank.

Chengappa, Raj. 2000. *Weapons of Peace: The Secret Story of India's Quest to Be a Nuclear Power.* New Delhi: HarperCollins India.

Chhibber, Pradeep. 1999. *Democracy without Associations: Transformation of the Party System and Social Cleavages in India.* Ann Arbor: University of Michigan Press.

———, and Ken Kollman. 2004. *The Formation of National Party Systems: Federalism and Party Competition in Britain, Canada, India and the United States.* Princeton, NJ: Princeton University Press.

China Institute for Reform and Development. 1999. *History of Changes and Innovations of China's Rural Land System.* Haikou: China Institute for Reform and Development.

China National Bureau of Statistics. 2004. *China Statistical Yearbook 2004.* Beijing: China Statistical Publishing House.

Chiu, Becky, and Mervyn Lewis, eds. 2006. *Reforming China's State-Owned Enterprises and Banks.* Northhampton, MA: Edward Elgar.

Choudhury, Golam W. 1975. *The Last Days of United Pakistan.* Bloomington: University of Indiana Press.

Christensen, Thomas. 1996. *Useful Adversaries: Grand Strategy, Domestic Mobilization and Sino-American Conflict, 1947–1958.* Princeton, NJ: Princeton University Press.

Chu Tianshu, Fereidun Fesharaki, and Kang Wu. 2006. "China's Energy in Transition: Regional and Global Implications." *Asian Economic Policy Review,* no. 1, pp. 134–52.

Chun, Li. 2006. *Transformation of Chinese Socialism.* Durham, NC: Duke University Press.

Chung, Chien-peng. 2004. *Domestic Politics, International Bargaining and China's Territorial Disputes.* London: Routledge-Curzon.

Chung, Jae Ho. 2000. *Central Control and Local Discretion in China: Leadership and Implementation during Post-Mao Decollectivization.* London: Oxford University Press.

Cohen, Stephen. 2004. *The Idea of Pakistan.* Washington, DC: Brookings Institution.

———. 2001. *India: Emerging Power.* Washington, DC: Brookings Institution.

Cordesman, Anthony, and Martin Kleiber. 2007. *Chinese Military Modernization: Force Development and Strategic Capabilities.* Washington, DC: Center for Strategic and International Studies.

Cousin, Violaine. 2007. *Banking in China.* New York: Palgrave Macmillan.

Das, Gurcharan. 2006. "The India Model." *Foreign Affairs,* 85, no. 4 (July/August): pp. 2–16.

———. 2000. *India Unbound: A Personal Account of a Social and Political Revolution.* New York: Alfred A. Knopf.

Dasgupta, Bilap. 1977. *Agrarian Change and the New Technology in India.* Geneva: United Nations Research Institute for Social Development.

Datt, Gaurav, and Martin Ravallion. 2002. "Is India's Economic Growth Leaving the Poor Behind?" *Journal of Economic Perspectives*, **16**, no. 3 (Summer): pp. 89–108.

Datta-Ray, Sunanda K. 2002. *Waiting for America: India and the United States in the New Millennium.* New Delhi: HarperCollins.

Deardorff, Alan, and Robert M. Stern. 2002. "What You Should Know about Globalization and the World Trade Organization." *Review of International Economics*, **10**, no. 3, pp. 404–23.

Deng, Yong, and Fei-Ling Wang, eds. 2005. *China Rising: Power and Motivation in Chinese Foreign Policy.* New York: Rowman & Littlefield.

Devarajan, Shantayanan, and Ijaz Nabi. 2006, June. "Economic Growth in South Asia: Promising, Un-equalizing . . . Sustainable?" Washington, DC: World Bank.

Dickson, Bruce J. 2003. *Red Capitalists in China: The Party, Private Entrepreneurs and the Prospects for Political Change.* New York: Cambridge University Press.

Dirlik, Arif. 1989. *The Origins of Chinese Communism.* New York: Oxford University Press.

Dittmer, Lowell, and Guoli Liu, eds., 2006. *China's Deep Reforms: Domestic Politics in Transition.* New York: Rowman & Littlefield.

Dobson, Wendy, and Anil Kashyap. 2006, September. "The Contradiction of China's Gradualist Banking Reform." Paper presented at the Brookings Panel on Economic Activity. Washington, DC: Brookings Institution.

Dollar, David, and Bert Hofman. 2007. "Intergovernmental Fiscal Reforms, Expenditure Assignment and Governance," in Jiwei Lou and Shuilin Wang, eds., *Public Finance in China: Reform and Growth for a Harmonious Society.* Washington, DC: World Bank.

Dollar, David, and Shang-Jin Wei. 2007. "Underutilized Capital." *Finance and Development*, **44**, no. 2, pp. 30–34.

Dong, Xiao-Yuan, and I. C. Xu. 2008. "The Impact of China's Millennium Labor Restructuring Program." *Economics of Transition*, **16**, no. 2, pp. 223–45.

Dreyer, June Teufel. 1993. *China's Political System: Modernization and Tradition.* New York: Paragon House.

Dreze, Jean, and Amartya Sen. 1996. *India: Economic Development and Social Opportunity.* New Delhi: Oxford University Press.

Drezner. Daniel. 2006. *All Politics Is Global.* Princeton, NJ: Princeton University Press.

Dua, Bhagwan. 1979. *Presidential Rule in India.* New Delhi: S. Chand.

Duara, Prasenjit. 1988. *Culture, Power and the State.* Stanford, CA: Stanford University Press.

Eckstein, Alexander. 1966. *Communist China's Economic Growth and Foreign Trade Implications for U.S. Policy.* New York: McGraw-Hill.

Economy, Elizabeth. 2007. "The Great Leap Backwards: The Costs of China's Environmental Crisis." *Foreign Affairs*, **86**, no. 5 (September/October): pp. 38–60.

———. 2004. *The River Runs Black: The Environmental Challenge to China's Future.* Ithaca, NY: Cornell University Press.

———, and Michel Oksenberg. 1999. *China Joins the World: Progress and Prospects.* New York: Council on Foreign Relations Press.

Emmott, Bill. 2008. *Rivals: How the Power Struggle Between China, India and Japan Will Shape Our Next Decade.* London: Allen Lane.

Ernst and Young. 2006. *Doing Business in India.* New Delhi: Ernst and Young.

Evans, Richard. 1994. *Deng Xiaoping and the Making of Modern China.* New York: Viking.

Fairbank, John King, and Merle Goldman. 1999. *China: A New History.* Cambridge, MA: Harvard University Press.

Fan, Shenggen, Linxiu Zhang, and Xiaobo Zhang. 2004. "Reform, Investment and Poverty in Rural China." *Economic Development and Cultural Change,* **52**, no. 2, pp. 395–421.

Farrell, Diana. 2005. "Offshoring: Value Creation through Economic Change." *Journal of Management Studies,* **42**, no. 3 (May): pp. 675–83.

———, and Andrew Grant. 2005, 7 December. "China's Looming Talent Shortage." *The McKinsey Quarterly.* Available at http://www.mckinseyquarterly.com/article_page.aspx.

Feigenbaum, Evan. 2003. *China's Techno-Warriors: National Security and Strategic Competition from the Nuclear to the Information Age.* Stanford, CA: Stanford University Press.

Fewsmith, Joseph. 2001. *China since Tiananmen: The Politics of Transition.* New York: Cambridge University Press.

———. 1994. *Dilemmas of Reform in China: Political Conflict and Economic Debate.* Armonk, NY: M. E. Sharpe.

Findlay, Ronald, and Kevin H. O'Rourke. 2007. *Power and Plenty: Trade, War and the World Economy in the Second Millennium.* Princeton, NJ: Princeton University Press.

Fishman, Ted C. 2005. *China, Inc.: How the Rise of the Next Superpower Challenges America and the World.* New York: Scribner.

Foot, Rosemary. 1995. *The Practice of Power: U.S. Relations with China since 1945.* London: Oxford University Press.

Frank, Katherine. 2002. *Indira: The Life of Indira Nehru Gandhi.* New York: Houghton Mifflin.

Frankel, Francine. 1978. *India's Political Economy, 1947–1977: The Gradual Revolution.* Princeton NJ: Princeton University Press.

———. 1971. *India's Green Revolution: Economic Gains and Political Costs.* Princeton NJ: Princeton University Press.

———, and Harry Harding, eds. 2004. *The India-China Relationship: What the United States Needs to Know.* Washington, DC: Woodrow Wilson Center Press.

Fravel, M. Taylor. 2005. "Regime Insecurity and International Cooperation: Explaining China's Compromises in Territorial Disputes." *International Security,* **30**, no. 2 (Fall): pp. 46–83.

Friedberg, Aaron. 1993–94. "Ripe for Rivalry: Prospects for Peace in Multipolar Asia." *International Security,* **18**, no. 3 (Winter): pp. 5–33.

Friedman, Edward, Paul G. Pickowicz, and Mark Selden. *Revolution, Resistance and Reform in Village China.* New Haven, CT: Yale University Press.

Friedman, Thomas. 2005. *The World Is Flat: A Brief History of the Twenty-First Century.* New York: Farrar, Straus & Giroux.

———. 1999. *The Lexus and the Olive Tree.* New York: Farrar, Straus & Giroux.

Gaddis, John Lewis. 2005. *Strategies of Containment: A Critical Appraisal of American National Security Policy during the Cold War.* Oxford: Oxford University Press.

Gallagher, Mary. 2005. *Contagious Capitalism: Globalization and the Politics of Labor in China.* Princeton: Princeton University Press.

Ganguly, Sumit. 2008. "India in 2007: A Year of Opportunities and Disappointments." *Asian Survey*, **48**, No. 1 (January/February): pp. 164–76.

_____. 2000. "Nuclear Proliferation in South Asia: Origins, Consequences and Prospects," in Shalendra D. Sharma, ed., *The Asia-Pacific in the New Millennium: Geopolitics, Security and Foreign Policy*, Berkeley: Institute of East Asian Studies, University of California, pp. 239–54.

_____. 2001. *Conflict Unending: India-Pakistan Tensions since 1947*. New York: Columbia University Press.

_____. 1999. *The Crisis in Kashmir: Portents of War, Hopes of Peace*. New York: Cambridge University Press.

_____. 1986. *The Origins of War in South Asia*. Boulder, CO: Westview Press.

_____, and Neil DeVotta, eds. 2003. *Understanding Contemporary India*. Boulder, CO: Lynne Rienner.

_____, Larry Diamond, and Marc F. Plattner, eds. 2007. *The State of India's Democracy*. Baltimore: Johns Hopkins University Press.

_____, and Devin T. Hagerty. 2005. *Fearful Symmetry: India-Pakistan Crises in Shadow of Nuclear Weapons*. Seattle: University of Washington Press.

_____, Brian Shoup, and Andrew Scobell, eds. 2006. *US-Indian Strategic Cooperation into the 21st Century*. New York: Routledge.

Gao, Yuan. 1987. *Born Red: Chronicle of the Cultural Revolution*. Stanford, CA: Stanford University Press.

Garnaut, Ross, Ligang Song, and Yang Yao. 2006. "Impact and Significance of State-Owned Enterprise Restructuring." *The China Journal*, no. 55 (January): pp. 35–66.

_____, Fang Cai, and Yiping Huang, eds., 1996. *The Third Revolution in the Chinese Countryside*. New York: Cambridge University Press.

Garver, John W. 2005. "China's Influence in Central and South Asia: Is It Increasing?" in David Shambaugh, ed., *Power Shift: China and Asia's New Dynamics*. Berkeley: University of California Press, pp. 205–27.

_____. 2001. *Protracted Contest: Sino-Indian Rivalry in the Twentieth Century*. Seattle: University of Washington Press.

Gensheng, Zhang. 2001. *Rural Reform in China*. Shenzhen: Haitian.

Gifford, Rob. 2007. *China Road: A Journey into the Future of a Rising Power*. New York: Random House.

Gill, Bates. 2007. *Rising Star: China's New Security Diplomacy*. Washington, DC: Brookings Institution Press.

_____. 1992. *Chinese Arms Transfers: Purposes, Patterns, and Prospects in the New World Order*. Westport, CT: Praeger.

Gilley, Bruce. 2004. *China's Democratic Future*. New York: Columbia University Press.

Gilpin, Robert. 2000. *The Challenge of Global Capitalism: The World Economy and Its Discontents*. Princeton, NJ: Princeton University Press.

Gittings, John. 2005. *The Changing Face of China: From Mao to Market*. New York: Oxford University Press.

_____. 1989. *China Changes Face: The Road from Revolution – 1949–1989*. New York: Oxford University Press.

Goldman, Merle. 2007. *From Comrade to Citizen: The Struggle for Political Rights in China*. Cambridge, MA: Harvard University Press.

———. 1994. *Sowing the Seeds of Democracy in China: Political Reform in the Deng Xiaoping Era.* Cambridge, MA: Harvard University Press.

———, and Roderick MacFarquhar, eds. 1999. *The Paradox of China's Post-Mao Reforms.* Cambridge, MA: Harvard University Press.

Goldman-Sachs. 2003, September 19. *Offshoring: Where Have All the Jobs Gone?* New York: U.S. Economics Analyst.

Goldstein, Avery. 2005. *Rising to the Challenge: China's Grand Strategy and International Security.* Stanford, CA: Stanford University Press.

Goldstein, Morris, and Nicholas Lardy, eds. 2008. *Debating China's Exchange Rate Policy.* Washington, DC: Institute for International Economics.

Goodfriend, Marvin, and Eswar Prasad. 2006, May. "A Framework for Independent Monetary Policy in China," IMF Working Paper No. WP/06/111. Washington, DC: International Monetary Fund.

Gore, Lance. 1998. *Market Communism: The Institutional Foundation of China's Post-Mao Hyper-Growth.* Hong Kong: Oxford University Press.

Gough, Kathleen, and Hari P. Sharma, eds. 1973. *Imperialism and Revolution in South Asia.* New York: Monthly Review Press.

Government of China 2002. *The Monitoring of Rural Poverty in China.* National Bureau of Statistics. Beijing: China Statistics Press.

Government of India. 2007. *Economic Survey: 2005–06.* New Delhi: Ministry of Finance.

———. 2006. *Economic Survey: 2004–05.* New Delhi: Ministry of Finance.

———. 2006a. *Towards Faster and More Inclusive Growth: An Approach to the 11th Five Year Plan.* New Delhi: Government of India.

———. 2002. *Tenth Five Year Plan, 2002–07* (in three volumes). New Delhi: Planning Commission.

———. 1998. *Economic Survey 1997–98.* New Delhi: Government of India Press.

———. 1997. *Report of the Tarapore Committee on Capital Account Convertibility.* New Delhi: Government of India.

———. 1991. *Report of the Narasimham Committee on Financial System.* Mumbai: Government of India.

———. 1992. Ministry of Agriculture. *Indian Agriculture in Brief,* 25th edition. New Delhi: Directorate of Economics and Statistics.

———. 1988. Ministry of Agriculture. *Indian Agriculture in Brief,* 22nd edition. New Delhi: Directorate of Economics and Statistics.

———. 1987. *Economic Survey: 1986–87.* New Delhi: Ministry of Finance.

———. 1970. *Fourth Five Year Plan, 1969–74.* Planning Commission. New Delhi: Government of India Press.

———. 1963. *Progress of Land Reforms.* Planning Commission. New Delhi: Government of India Press.

———. 1961. *Third Five Year Plan, 1961–66.* Planning Commission. New Delhi: Government of India Press.

———. 1959. *Report on India's Food Crisis and the Steps to Meet It.* New Delhi: Ministry of Food and Agriculture and Ministry of Community Development and Cooperation.

———. 1956. *Second Five Year Plan, 1956–61.* Planning Commission. New Delhi: Government of India Press.

————. 1952. *First Five Year Plan, 1951–56.* Planning Commission. New Delhi: Government of India Press.

————. 1950. *Constituent Assembly Debates, Vol. 12.* New Delhi: Government of India Press.

————. 1949. *Report of the Congress Agrarian Reforms Committee.* New Delhi: Government of India Press.

Granick, David. 1990. *Chinese State Enterprise: A Regional Property Rights Analysis.* Chicago: University of Chicago Press.

Gries, Peter Hays. 2004. *China's New Nationalism: Pride, Politics and Diplomacy.* Berkeley: University of California Press.

Griffin, Keith. 2003. "Economic Globalization and Institutions of Global Governance." *Development and Change,* **34**, no. 5, pp. 789–807.

Guha, Ramachandra. 2007. *India after Gandhi: The History of the World's Largest Democracy.* New York: HarperCollins.

Gulati, Ashok, and Shenggen Fan, eds. 2007. *The Dragon and the Elephant: Agricultural and Rural Reforms in China and India.* Baltimore: Johns Hopkins University Press.

————, and S. Narayanan. 2003. *The Subsidy Syndrome in Indian Agriculture.* New Delhi: Oxford University Press.

Gupta, S. P. 1989. *Planning and Development of India: A Critique.* New Delhi: Allied.

Gupta, Sisir. 1966. *Kashmir: A Study in India-Pakistan Relations.* New Delhi: Asia Publishing House.

Gurley, John. 1976. *China's Economy and the Maoist Strategy.* New York: Monthly Review Press.

Hagerty, Devin T. 1998. *The Consequences of Nuclear Proliferation: Lessons from South Asia.* Cambridge, MA: MIT Press.

Hale, David, and Lyric Hughes Hale. 2008. "Reconsidering Revaluation." *Foreign Affairs,* **87**, no. 1 (January/February): pp. 57–67.

Hansen, Thomas Blom. 1999. *The Saffron Wave: Democracy and Hindu Nationalism in India.* Princeton, NJ: Princeton University Press.

Hanson, A. H. 1966. *The Process of Planning: A Study of India's Five-Year Plans, 1950–1964.* London: Oxford University Press.

Hanson, James, and Sanjay Kathuria. 1999. *India: A Financial Sector for the Twenty-First Century.* New Delhi: Oxford University Press.

Hardgrave, Robert. 1984. *India Under Pressure: Prospects for Political Stability.* Boulder: Westview Press.

————, and Stanley Kochanek. 2000. *India: Government and Politics in a Developing Nation,* 6th ed. New York: Harcourt Brace Jovanovich.

Harding, Harry. 1980. *Organizing China: The Problem of Bureaucracy, 1949–1976.* Stanford, CA: Stanford University Press.

Harrison, Selig. 1960. *India: The Most Dangerous Decades.* Princeton, NJ: Princeton University Press.

Hart, Henry, ed., 1976. *Indira Gandhi's India: A Political System Reappraised.* Boulder, CO: Westview Press.

Hasan, Zoya, ed., 2002. *Parties and Party Politics in India.* New Delhi: Oxford University Press.

He, Xin. 2007. "The Recent Decline in Economic Caseloads in Chinese Courts: Exploration of a Surprising Puzzle." *The China Quarterly*, no. 190 (June): pp. 352–74.

Held, David, and Anthony McGrew, eds. 2000. *The Global Transformations Reader*. Oxford: Polity Press.

Heller, Peter, and M. Govinda Rao, eds. 2006. *A Sustainable Fiscal Policy for India: An International Perspective*. New Delhi: Oxford University Press.

Herberg, Mikkal E. 2007, December. *Energy Security Survey 2007: The Rise of Asia's National Oil Companies*, NBR Special Report, No. 14. Seattle, WA: National Bureau of Asian Research.

Herring, Ronald. 1983. *Land to the Tiller: The Political Economy of Agrarian Reform in South Asia*. New Haven, CT: Yale University Press.

Heytens, Paul, and Cem Karacadag. 2001. "An Attempt to Profile the Finances of China's Enterprise Sector," IMF Working Paper No. WP/01/182. Washington, DC: International Monetary Fund.

————, and Harm Zebregs. 2003. "How Fast Can China Grow?" in Wanda Tseng and Markus Rodlauer, eds., *China: Competing in the Global Economy*. Washington, DC: International Monetary Fund.

Hinton, Harold. 1966. *Communist China in World Politics*. New York: Houghton Mifflin.

Hinton, William. 1991. *The Privatization of China: The Great Reversal*. London: Earthscan.

————. 1984. *Shenfan*. New York: Vintage Books.

————. 1966. *Fanshen: A Documentary of Revolution in a Chinese Village*. New York: Vintage Books.

Ho, Peter. 2005. *Land Ownership, Property Rights and Social Conflict in China*. London: Oxford University Press.

Hoda, Anwarul, and Ashok Gulati. 2007. *WTO Negotiations on Agriculture and Developing Countries*. Baltimore: Johns Hopkins University Press.

Hofman, Bert, Yoichiro Ishihara, and Min Zhao. 2007. "Asian Development Strategies: China and Indonesia Compared." *Bulletin of Indonesia Economic Statistics*, **43**, no. 2 (August).

Hoffmann, Steven A. 1990. *India and the China Crisis*. New Delhi: Oxford University Press.

Hope, Nicholas, Dennis Tao Yang, and Mu Yang Li, eds. 2003. *How Far across the River? Chinese Policy Reform at the Millennium*. Stanford, CA: Stanford University Press.

Horn, Robert. 1982. *Soviet-Indian Relations: Issues and Influence*. New York: Praeger.

Houn, Franklin. 1967. *A Short History of Chinese Communism*. Englewood Cliffs, NJ: Prentice-Hall.

Hsu, Immanuel C. Y. 1995. *The Rise of Modern China*, 5th ed. London: Oxford University Press.

Hsu, John C. 1992. *China's Foreign Trade Reforms*. New York: Cambridge University Press.

Hu, Shaohua. 2000. *Explaining Chinese Democratization*. Westport, CT: Praeger.

Huang, Jing. 2000. *Factionalism in Chinese Communist Politics*. New York: Cambridge University Press.

Huang, Yasheng. 2003. *Selling China: Foreign Direct Investment during the Reform Era*. New York: Cambridge University Press.

———. 1996. *Inflation and Investment Controls in China: The Political Economy of Central-Local Relations during the Reform Era.* New York: Cambridge University Press.

———, and Tarun Khanna. 2003. "Can India Overtake China?" *Foreign Policy*, no. 137 (July/August): pp. 74–81.

Hufbauer, Gary Clyde, and Yee Wong. 2004. "China Bashing," International Economics Policy Briefs, no. PB04–5. Washington, DC: Institute for International Economics.

Hughes, Christopher. 2006. *Chinese Nationalism in the Global Era.* London: Routledge.

Hundt, Reed. 2007. *In China's Shadow: The Crisis of American Entrepreneurship.* New Haven, CT: Yale University Press.

Hunt, Michael. 1996. *The Genesis of Chinese Communist Foreign Policy.* New York: Columbia University Press.

Huntington, Samuel. 1968. *Political Order in Changing Societies.* New Haven, CT: Yale University Press.

Hutchings, Graham. 2001. *Modern China: A Guide to a Country.* Cambridge: Harvard University Press.

Hutton, Will. 2006. *The Writing on the Wall: Why We Must Embrace China as a Partner or Face It as an Enemy.* New York: Simon & Schuster.

IISS Strategic Comments. 2007, December. *Chinese Defense Expenditure: Calculating Its True Extent.* Strategic Comments, 13, no. 10. London: International Institute for Strategic Studies.

Ikenberry, John G. 2008. "The Rise of China and the Future of the West." *Foreign Affairs*, **87**, no. 1 (January/February): pp. 23–37.

Inden, Ronald. 1990. *Imagining India.* Oxford: Blackwell.

Inden, Ronald, and Christian Welzel. 2005. *Modernization, Cultural Change, and Democracy: The Human Development Sequence.* Cambridge, England: Cambridge University Press.

International Monetary Fund. 2007. *World Economic Outlook 2007*, Washington, DC: International Monetary Fund.

———. 2005. *Asia-Pacific Regional Outlook: September 2005.* Washington, DC: International Monetary Fund.

Iriye, Akira. 1965. *After Imperialism: The Search for a New Order in the Far East.* Cambridge, MA: Harvard University Press.

Jalal, Ayesha. 1994. *Democracy and Authoritarianism in South Asia.* Cambridge, England: Cambridge University Press.

Jalan, Bimal. 1992. *India's Economic Crisis: The Way Ahead.* New Delhi: Oxford University Press.

Jannuzi, F. Tomasson. 1994. *India's Persistent Dilemma: The Political Economy of Agrarian Reform.* Boulder, CO: Westview Press.

———. 1974. *Agrarian Crisis in India: The Case of Bihar.* Austin: University of Texas Press.

Jayal, Niraja Gopal, ed., 2001. *Democracy in India.* New Delhi: Oxford University Press.

Jefferson, Gary, and Thomas Rawski. 1994. "Enterprise Reform in Chinese Industry." *Journal of Economic Perspectives*, **8**, no. 2 (Spring): pp. 47–70.

Jenkins, Rob. 1999. *Democratic Politics and Economic Reform in India.* New York: Cambridge University Press.

Jensen, John B., and Lori G. Kletzer. 2005. "Tradable Services: Understanding the Scope and Impact of Services Offshoring," in Susan M. Collins and Lee Brainard, eds., *Brookings Trade Forum 2005: Offshoring White-Collar Work.* Washington, DC: Brookings Institution.

Jha, Prem Shankar. 1980. *India: A Political Economy of Stagnation.* Bombay: Oxford University Press.

Jha, S. C. 1971. *A Critical Analysis of Indian Land Reform Studies.* Bombay: Asian Studies Press.

Jian, Chen. 2001. *Mao's China and the Cold War.* Chapel Hill: University of North Carolina Press.

Jingping, Ding. 1995. *China's Domestic Economy in Regional Context.* Washington, DC: The Center for International and Strategic Studies.

Johnson, Chalmers. 1962. *Peasant Nationalism and Communist Power.* Stanford, CA: Stanford University Press.

Johnston, Alastair Iain. 2007. *Social States: China in International Institutions, 1980–2000.* Princeton, NJ: Princeton University Press.

———, and Robert S. Ross, eds., 2006. *New Directions in Chinese Foreign Policy.* Stanford, CA: Stanford University Press.

Joshi, P. C. [1973]. 1975. *Land Reforms in India.* New Delhi: Institute of Economic Growth.

——— 1982. "Poverty, Land Hunger and Emerging Class Conflict in Rural India," in S. Jones et al., eds., *Rural Poverty and Agrarian Reform.* New Delhi: Allied.

Joshi, Vijay, and I. M. D. Little. 1996. *India's Economic Reforms, 1991–2001.* Oxford: Clarendon Press.

———. 1994. *India: Macroeconomics and Political Economy, 1964–1991.* Washington, DC: World Bank.

Kahn, Joseph, and David E. Sanger. 2005, November 20. "Bush in Beijing, Faces a Partner Now on the Rise," *New York Times.* Available at http://www.nytimes.com/2005/11/20/international/asia/20prexy.html?.

Kambara, Tatsu, and Christopher Howe. 2007. *China and the Global Energy Crisis: Development and Prospects for China's Oil and Natural Gas.* Northampton, MA: Edward Elgar.

Kamdar, Mira. 2007. *Planet India: How the Fastest-Growing Democracy is Transforming America and the World.* New York: Scribner.

Kapur, Ashok. 1976. *India's Nuclear Option: Atomic Diplomacy and Decision Making.* New York: Praeger.

Kapur, Devesh, and Pratap Mehta, eds. 2005. *Public Institutions in India: Performance and Design.* New Delhi: Oxford University Press.

Kapur, S. Paul. 2007. *Dangerous Deterrent: Nuclear Weapons Proliferation and Conflict in South Asia.* Stanford, CA: Stanford University Press.

Kashyap, Subhas. 1989. *Our Parliament.* Delhi: National Book Trust of India.

Kaufmann, Daniel, Aart Kraay, and Massimo Mastruzzi. 2005, June. "Governance Matters IV: Governance Indicators for 1996–2004," World Bank Policy Research Working Paper No. 3630. Washington, DC: World Bank.

Keck, Margaret, and Kathryn Sikkink. 1998. *Activists Beyond Borders.* Ithaca, NY: Cornell University Press.

Keliang, Zhu, and Roy Prosterman. 2007, October 15. "Securing Land Rights for Chinese Farmers," *Development Policy Analysis*, no. 3. Washington, DC: Cato Institute, pp. 1–17.

Keller, William, and Thomas G. Rawski, eds. 2007. *China's Rise and the Balance of Influence in Asia*. Pittsburgh: University of Pittsburgh Press.

Kelliher, Daniel. 1986. "The Political Consequences of China's Reforms." *Comparative Politics*, **18**, no. 4, pp. 479–93.

Kelly, David, Ramkishen S. Rajan, and Gillian Goh, eds. 2006. *Managing Globalization: Lessons from China and India*. Singapore: World Scientific.

Kennedy, Scott. 2005. *The Business of Lobbying in China*. Cambridge, MA: Harvard University Press.

Kent, Ann. 2007. *Beyond Compliance: China, International Organizations and Global Security*. Stanford, CA: Stanford University Press.

Keohane, Robert. 2002. *Power and Governance in a Partially Globalized World*. New York: Routledge.

Khanna, Parag. 2008. *The Second World: Empires and Influence in the New Global Order*. New York: Random House.

Khanna, Tarun and Yasheng Huang. 2003. "Can India Overtake China?" *Foreign Policy*, **137**, July-August: pp. 74–83.

Khanna, Tarun. 2008. *Billions of Entrepreneurs: How China and India Are Reshaping Their Futures – and Yours*. Cambridge, MA: Harvard University Press.

Khilnani, Sunil. 1997. *The Idea of India*. New York: Farrar, Strauss & Giroux.

Kidron, Michael. 1965. *Foreign Investments in India*. London: Oxford University Press.

Kirby, William, Robert S. Ross, and Gong Li, eds., 2007. *Normalization of U.S.-China Relations: An International History*. Cambridge, MA: Harvard University Press.

Kleine-Ahlbrandt, Stephanie, and Andrew Small. 2008. "China's New Dictatorship Diplomacy." *Foreign Affairs*, **87**, no. 1 (January/February): pp. 38–56.

Kletzer, Lori. 2001. *Job Loss from Imports: Measuring the Costs*. Washington, DC: Institute for International Economics.

Kochanek, Stanley. 1968. *The Congress Party of India: The Dynamics of One-Party Democracy*. Princeton, NJ: Princeton University Press.

Kochhar, Kalpana. 2006. "India: Macroeconomic Implications of the Fiscal Imbalances," in Peter Heller and M. Govinda Rao, eds., *A Sustainable Fiscal Policy for India: An International Perspective*. New Delhi: Oxford University Press, pp. 44–85.

———, Utsav Kumar, Raghuram Rajan, Arvind Subramanian, and Ioannis Tokatlidis. 2007. "India's Pattern of Development: What Happened, What Follows?" IMF Working Paper. Washington, DC: International Monetary Fund.

Kohli, Atul. 2006. "Politics of Economic Growth in India, 1980–2000," Parts 1 and 2. *Economic and Political Weekly* (1 April and 8 April): pp. 1251–59; 1361–70.

———. 2004. *State-Directed Development: Political Power and Industrialization in the Global Periphery*. New York: Cambridge University Press.

———, ed., 2001. *The Success of India's Democracy*. Cambridge, England: University of Cambridge Press.

———. 1990. *Democracy and Discontent: India's Growing Crisis of Governability*. New York: Cambridge University Press.

————. 1989. "Politics of Economic Liberalization in India." *World Development*, **17**, no. 3, pp. 305–28.

————. ed., 1988. *India's Democracy: An Analysis of Changing State-Society Relations.* Princeton, NJ: Princeton University Press.

————. 1987. *The State and Poverty in India: The Politics of Reform.* New York: Cambridge University Press.

Kohli, Renu. 2005. *Liberalizing Capital Flows: India's Experiences and Policy Issues.* New Delhi: Oxford University Press.

Kornai, Janos. 1992. *The Socialist System: The Political Economy of Socialism.* Princeton, NJ: Princeton University Press.

Kothari, Rajni. 1970. *Politics in India.* Boston: Little, Brown.

Krasner, Stephen. 1999. *Sovereignty: Organized Hypocrisy.* Princeton, NJ: Princeton University Press.

Kreft, Heinrich. 2006. "China's Quest for Energy." *Policy Review*, no. 139 (October/November): pp. 27–34.

Krepon, Michael. 2005. "The Stability-Instability Paradox, Misperception, and Escalation-Control in South Asia," in Rafiq Dossani and Henry S. Rowen, eds., *Prospects for Peace in South Asia.* Stanford, CA: Stanford University Press.

Krugman, Paul. 1994. "The Myth of Asia's Miracle." *Foreign Affairs*, **73**, no. 6 (November/December): pp. 62–78.

Kurlantzick, Joshua. 2007. *Charm Offensive: How China's Soft Power Is Transforming the World.* New Haven, CT: Yale University Press.

Kuroda, Haruhiko. 2007. "The Development of the People's Republic of China and India: Prospects and Challenges." Manila, Philippines: Asian Development Bank. Available at http://www.adb.org/Documents/Speeches/2007/ms2007006.asp.

Kux, Dennis. 2001. *Disenchanted Allies: The United States and Pakistan, 1947–2000.* Baltimore: Johns Hopkins University Press.

————. 1992. *India and the United States: Estranged Democracies.* Washington, DC: National Defense University Press.

Ladejinsky, Wolf. 1977. *Agrarian Reforms as Unfinished Business,* L. J. Walinsky, ed. London: Oxford University Press.

Lam, Willy Wo-Lap. 2006. *Chinese Politics in the Hu Jintao Era: New Leaders, New Challenges.* Armonk, NY: M. E. Sharpe.

Lamb, Alastair. 1973. *The Sino-Indian Border in Ladakh.* Canberra: Australian National University Press.

Lampton, David. 2001. *Same Bed, Different Dreams: Managing U.S.-China Relations, 1989–2000.* Berkeley: University of California Press.

————, ed. 2001a. *The Making of Chinese Foreign and Security Policy in the Era of Reform.* Stanford, CA: Stanford University Press.

Lardy, Nicholas R. 2006, October. "China: Toward a Consumption-Driven Growth Path," Policy Briefs in International Economics, no. PBO6-6. Washington, DC: Institute for International Economics.

————. 2005. "China: The Great New Economic Challenge," in C. Fred Bergsten ed., *The United States and the World Economy: Foreign Economic Policy for the Next Decade.* Washington, DC: Institute for International Economics.

————. 2002. *Integrating China into the Global Economy.* Washington, DC: Brookings Institution Press.

———. 1998. *China's Unfinished Economic Revolution.* Washington, DC: Brookings Institution Press.

———. 1994. *China in the World Economy.* Washington, DC: Institute for International Economics.

———. 1991. *Foreign Trade and Economic Reform in China, 1978–1990.* New York: Cambridge University Press.

———. 1983. *Agriculture in China's Modern Economic Development.* London: Cambridge University Press.

Lau, Lawrence, Yingyi Qian, and Gerard Roland. 2000. "Reform without Losers: An Interpretation of China's Dual-Track Approach to Transition." *Journal of Political Economy*, **108**, no. 1 (February): pp. 120–43.

Layne, Christopher. 2006. *The Peace of Illusions: American Grand Strategy from 1940 to the Present.* Ithaca, NY: Cornell University Press.

Lee, Chae-Jin. 1996. *China and Korea: Dynamic Relations.* Stanford, CA: Hoover Institution Press.

Lee, Ching Kwan. 2007. *Against the Law: Labor Protests in China's Rustbelt and Sunbelt.* Berkeley: University of California Press.

Lee, Hong Yung. 1991. *From Revolutionary Cadres to Party Technocrats in Socialist China.* Berkeley: University of California Press.

Levy, Jonah D., ed. 2006. *The State after Statism: New State Activities in the Age of Liberalization.* Cambridge, MA: Harvard University Press.

Lewis, John P. 1995. *India's Political Economy: Governance and Reform.* New Delhi: Oxford University Press.

———. 1964. *Quiet Crisis in India.* New York: Doubleday.

Li, Cheng. 2001. *China's Leaders: The New Generation.* Lanham, MD: Rowman & Littlefield.

Li, Conghua, and Pat Loconto. 1998. *China: The Consumer Revolution.* New York: John Wiley.

Li, D. D. 2006. "A Survey of the Economics Literature on China's Nonstate Enterprises," in A. Tsui, Y. Bian, L. Cheng, eds., *China's Domestic Private Firms.* New York: M. E. Sharpe, pp. 25–39.

Li, Hua-Yu. 2006. *Mao and the Economic Stabilization of China.* New York: Rowman & Littlefield.

Li, Jingjie. 1994. "The Characteristics of Chinese and Russian Economic Reform." *Journal of Comparative Economics*, **18** (June): pp. 309–13.

Lieber, Robert. 2007. *The American Era: Power and Strategy for the 21st Century.* New York: Cambridge University Press.

Lieberthal, Kenneth. 1995. *Governing China: From Revolution through Reform.* New York: W.W. Norton.

Liew, Leong. 1997. *The Chinese Economy in Transition: from Plan to Market.* Northampton, MA: Edward Elgar.

Limaye, Satu. 1992. *U.S.-Indian Relations: The Pursuit of Accommodation.* Boulder, CO: Westview Press.

Lin, Justin Yifu. 1994. "Chinese Agriculture: Institutional Changes and Performance," in T. N. Srinivasan, ed., *Agriculture and Trade in China and India: Policies and Performance Since 1950.* San Francisco: International Center for Economic Growth Publications, pp. 23–72.

————. 1992. "Rural Reforms and Agricultural Growth in China." *American Economic Review*, **82**, no. 1 (March): pp. 34–51.

————. 1990. "Collectivization and China's Agricultural Crisis in 1959–61." *Journal of Political Economy*, **98**, no. 6 (December): pp. 1228–52.

————, Fang Cai, and Zhou Li. 2003. *The China Miracle: Development Strategy and Economic Reform.* Hong Kong: The Chinese University Press.

Lipset, Seymour Martin, and Jason Lakin. 2004. *The Democratic Century.* Norman: University of Oklahoma Press.

Lipton, Michael. 1977. *Why Poor People Stay Poor: Urban Bias in World Development.* New York: Cambridge University Press.

Liu, Guoli, ed. 2004. *Chinese Foreign Policy in Transition.* Hawthrone: Aldine de Gruyter.

Lubman, Stanley. 1999. *Bird in the Cage: Legal Reform in China after Mao.* Stanford, CA: Stanford University Press.

Luthi, Lorenz M. 2008. *The Sino-Soviet Split: Cold War in the Communist World.* Princeton, NJ: Princeton University Press.

MacFarquhar, Roderick, ed. 1997. *The Politics of China: The Eras of Mao and Deng.* New York: Cambridge University Press.

————, and Michael Schoenhals. 2006. *Mao's Last Revolution.* Cambridge, MA: Harvard University Press.

Macmillan, Margaret. 2007. *Nixon and Mao: The Week That Changed the World.* New York: Random House.

Maddison, Angus. 2003. *The World Economy: Historical Statistics.* Paris: Organisation for Economic Co-operation and Development.

————. 2001. *The World Economy: A Millennial Perspective.* Paris: Organisation for Economic Co-operation and Development.

————. 1998. *Chinese Economic Performance in the Long-Run.* Paris: Organization for Economic Cooperation and Development.

————. 1971. *Class Structure and Economic Growth: India and Pakistan since the Moghuls.* London: Allen & Unwin.

Madsen, Richard. 1995. *China and the American Dream: A Moral Inquiry.* Berkeley: University of California Press.

Majumdar, R. C. 1962. *History of the Freedom Movement in India.* 3 vols. Calcutta: Firma K.L. Mukhopadhyay.

Malaviya, H. D. 1954. *Land Reforms in India.* New Delhi: All-India Congress Committee.

Malenbaum, Wilfred. 1962. *Prospects for Indian Development.* London: George Allen & Unwin.

Malik, Mohan. 2004, October. "India-China Relations: Giants Stir, Cooperate and Compete" (special assessment). Honolulu, HI: Asia-Pacific Center for Security Studies.

————. 2003, December. "Eyeing the Dragon: India's China Debate" (special assessment). Honolulu, HI: Asia-Pacific Center for Security Studies.

————. 2003a. "The China Factor in the India-Pakistan Conflict." *Parameters: U.S. Army War Quarterly*, **33**, no. 1, (Spring): pp. 35–50.

————. 2003b. "The Proliferation Axis: Beijing-Islamabad-Pyongyang." *The Korean Journal of Defense Analysis*, **XV**, no. 1 (Spring): pp. 57–100.

————. 2002, November. "The China Factor in India-Pakistan Conflict," Occasional Paper Series. Honolulu, HI: Asia-Pacific Center for Security Studies.

Malik, Yogendra. 1993. "India," in Craig Baxter, Yogendra Malik, Charles Kennedy, and Robert Oberst, eds., *Government and Politics in South Asia.* Boulder, CO: Westview Press.

Manion, Melanie. 1993. *Retirement of Revolutionaries in China: Public Policies, Social Norms, Private Interests.* Princeton, NJ: Princeton University Press.

Mann, Catherine. 2005. "Breaking Up Is Hard to Do: Global Co-Dependency, Collective Action and the Challenges of Global Adjustment." *CESifo Forum,* **6**, no. 1 (Spring): pp. 16–23.

_____. 2003, December. "Globalization of IT Services and White Collar Jobs: The Next Wave of Productivity Growth," International Economics Policy Briefs, no. PB03-11. Washington, DC: Institute for International Economics.

Mann, James. 2007. *The China Fantasy: How Our Leaders Explain Away Chinese Repression.* New York: Viking.

Manor, James, ed., 1994. *Nehru to the 1990s: The Changing Office of the Prime Minister in India.* London: C. Hurst.

Mansingh, Surjit, ed. 1998. *Indian and Chinese Foreign Policies in Comparative Perspective.* New Delhi: Radiant.

Marathe, S. S. 1989. *Regulation and Development.* New Delhi: Sage.

Martin, Michael F., and K. Alan Kronstadt. 2007, August 31. *India-U.S. Economic and Trade Relations,* Congressional Research Service Report for Congress, Washington, DC.

Maxwell, Neville. 1970. *India's China War.* Dehra Dun: Natraj.

Mayer, Jorg, and Adrian Wood. 2001. "South Asia's Exports in a Comparative Perspective." *Oxford Development Studies,* **29**, no. 1, pp. 5–29.

McKinnon, Ronald. 2005. *Exchange Rates under the East Asian Dollar Standard: Living with Conflicted Virtue.* Cambridge, MA: MIT Press.

_____. 1998. "Monetary Regimes, Government Borrowing Constraints and Market-Preserving Federalism: Implications for the EMU," in Thomas J. Courchene, ed., *The Nation State in a Global/Information Era: Policy Challenges.* Kingston, Ontario: The John Deutsch Institute for the Study of Economic Policy, Queen's University, pp. 101–42.

_____. 1973. *Money and Capital in Economic Development.* Washington, DC: Brookings Institution.

McKinsey Global Institute. 2003, August. *Offshoring: Is It a Win-Win Game?* New York: McKinsey and Company.

McMahon, Robert. 1994. *The Cold War on the Periphery: The United States, India and Pakistan.* New York: Columbia University Press.

Mearsheimer, John. 2001. *The Tragedy of Great Power Politics.* New York: W. W. Norton.

Medeiros, Evan. 2007. *Reluctant Restraint: The Evolution of China's Nonproliferation Policies and Practices, 1980–2004.* Stanford, CA: Stanford University Press.

Mehta, Pratap Bhanu. 2003. *The Burden of Democracy.* New Delhi: Penguin Books.

Meisner, Maurice. 1996. *The Deng Xiaoping Era: An Inquiry into the Fate of Chinese Socialism, 1978–1994.* New York: Hill and Wang.

_____. 1986. *Mao's China and After: A History of the People's Republic.* New York: Free Press.

Mellor, John. 1976. *The New Economics of Growth: A Strategy for India and the Developing World.* Ithaca, NY: Cornell University Press.

Menon, Rajan. 2007. *The End of Alliances*. New York: Oxford University Press.

Mertha, Andrew C. 2008. *China's Water Warriors: Citizen Action and Policy Change*. Ithaca, NY: Cornell University Press.

Mishkin, Federic. 2006. *The Next Globalization: How Disadvantaged Nations Can Harness Their Financial Systems to Get Rich*. Princeton, NJ: Princeton University Press.

Misra, B. B. 1986. *Government and Bureaucracy in India: 1947–1976*. New Delhi: Oxford University Press.

Misra, Kalpana. 1998. *From Post-Maoism to Post-Marxism: The Erosion of Official Ideology in Deng's China*. New York: Routledge.

Misra, Maria. 2008. *Vishnu's Crowded Temple: India since the Great Rebellion*. New Haven, CT: Yale University Press.

Mitter, Rana. 2004. *A Bitter Revolution: China's Struggle with the Modern World*. New York: Oxford University Press.

Mohan, Raja C. 2007. "Balancing Interests and Values: India's Struggle with Democracy Promotion." *The Washington Quarterly*, **30**, no. 3 (Summer): pp. 99–115.

————. 2006. *Impossible Allies: Nuclear India, United States and the Global Order*. New Delhi: India Research Press.

————. 2004. *Crossing the Rubicon: The Shaping of India's New Foreign Policy*. New York: Palgrave Macmillan.

Mohan, Ram. 2005. *Privatization in India: Challenging the Economic Orthodoxy*. New Delhi: Routledge-Curzon.

Montinola, Gabriella, Yingyi Qian, and Barry R. Weingast. 1995. "Federalism, Chinese Style: The Political Basis for Economic Success in China." *World Politics*, **48**, no. 1, October: pp. 50–81.

Moore, Barrington. 1966. *Social Origins of Dictatorship and Democracy: Lord and Peasant in the Making of the Modern World*. Boston: Beacon Press.

Moore, Thomas. 2002. *China in the World Market: Chinese Industry and International Sources of Reform in the Post-Mao Era*. New York: Cambridge University Press.

Morris-Jones, W. H. 1971. *The Government and Politics in India*, 3rd ed., London: Hutchinson.

Moshaver, Ziba. 1991. *Nuclear Weapons Proliferation in the Indian Subcontinent*. New York: St. Martin's Press.

Mukherji, Joydeep. 2006, March. "Economic Growth and India's Future," Occasional Paper No. 26. Philadelphia: Center for the Advanced Study of India, University of Pennsylvania.

Mullik, B. N. 1971. *My Years with Nehru: The Chinese Betrayal*. New Delhi: Allied.

Murphy, Rachel. 2002. *How Migrant Labor Is Changing Rural China*. New York: Cambridge University Press.

Myers, Ramon. 1980. *The Chinese Economy: Past and Present*. Belmont, CA: Wadsworth.

Myrdal, Gunnar. 1968. *Asian Drama: An Enquiry into the Poverty of Nations*. 3 Vols. New York: Pantheon.

Naipaul, V. S. 1990. *India: A Million Mutinies Now*. London: Heinemann.

Nathan, Andrew, and Robert Ross. 1997. *Great Wall, Empty Fortress: China's Search for Security*. New York: W. W. Norton.

Nathan, Andrew. 1990. *China's Crisis: Dilemmas of Reform and Prospects for Democracy*. New York: Columbia University Press.

National Bureau of Statistics of China. 2004. *2004 China Statistical Yearbook*. Beijing: National Bureau of Statistics of China.

_____. 2005. *2005 Statistic Gazette on National Economy and Social Development of China*. Beijing: National Bureau of Statistics of China.

_____. 2006. *2006 China Statistical Yearbook*. Beijing: National Bureau of Statistics of China.

Naughton, Barry. 2007. *The Chinese Economy: Transitions and Growth*. Cambridge, MA: MIT Press.

_____, ed. 1997. *The China Circle: Economics and Technology in the PRC, Taiwan and Hong Kong*. Washington, DC: Brookings Institution.

_____. 1996. *Growing Out of the Plan: Chinese Economic Reform, 1978–1993*. New York: Cambridge University Press.

Nayar, Baldev Raj. 1976. *American Geopolitics and India*. New Delhi: Manohar.

Nayar, Kuldip. 1977. *The Judgment: Inside Story of Emergency in India*. New Delhi: Vikas.

Nawaz, Shuja. 2008. *Crossed Swords: Pakistan, Its Army and the Wars Within*. New York: Oxford University Press.

Neale, Walter. 1962. *Economic Change in Rural India: Land Tenure and Reform in Uttar Pradesh, 1800–1955*. New Haven, CT: Yale University Press.

Nehru, Jawaharlal. 1958. *Jawaharlal Nehru's Speeches, Vol. 1: 1946–1949*. New Delhi: Government of India Press.

_____. 1948. *The Unity of India*. London: Lindsay Drummond.

Noorani, A. G. 1990. *The Presidential System: The Indian Debate*. New Delhi: Sage.

North, Douglass C. 2005. *Understanding the Process of Economic Change*. Princeton, NJ: Princeton University Press.

Nussbaum, Martha. 2007. *The Clash Within: Democracy, Religious Violence and India's Future*. Cambridge, MA: Harvard University Press.

O'Brien, Kevin. 1990. *Reform without Liberalization: China's National People's Congress and the Politics of Institutional Change*. New York: Cambridge University Press.

O'Donnell, Guillermo. 1973. *Modernization and Bureaucratic Authoritarianism: Studies in South American Politics*. Berkeley CA: Institute of International Studies.

Ohmae, Kenichi. 1995. *The End of the Nation State*. New York: Free Press.

Oi, Jean. 1999. *Rural China Takes Off: Institutional Foundations of Economic Reform*. Berkeley: University of California Press.

_____. 1989. *State and Peasant in Contemporary China: The Political Economy of Village Government*. Berkeley: University of California Press.

_____, and Andrew Walder, eds., 1999. *Property Rights and Economic Reform in China*. Stanford, CA: Stanford University Press.

Ollapally, Deepa. 2001. "Mixed Motives in India's Search for Nuclear Status." *Asian Survey*, **XLI**, no. 6 (November/December): pp. 925–42.

Organisation for Economic Co-operation and Development. 2007, October. *OECD Economic Survey: India*. Paris: OECD.

Organisation for Economic Co-operation and Development. 2005, September. *OECD Economic Survey: China*. Paris: OECD.

Overholt, William. 2007. *Asia, America and the Transformation of Geopolitics*. New York: Cambridge University Press.

_____. 1993. *The Rise of China: How Economic Reform is Creating a New Superpower*. New York: W. W. Norton.

Paarlberg, Robert. 1985. *Food Trade and Foreign Policy: India, the Soviet Union and the United States.* Ithaca, NY: Cornell University Press.

Palmer, Norman. 1966. *South Asia and United States Policy.* Boston: Houghton Mifflin.

————. 1961. *The Indian Political System.* Boston: Houghton Mifflin.

Panagariya, Arvind. 2008. *India: The Emerging Giant.* New York: Oxford University Press.

————. 2005, November 7. "The Triumph of India's Market Reforms: The Record of the 1980s and 1990s," Policy Analysis, no. 554. Washington, DC: CATO Institute.

Parish, William L. 1985. *Chinese Rural Development: The Great Transformation.* Armonk, NY: M. E. Sharpe.

————, and Martin King Whyte. 1978. *Village and Family in Contemporary China.* Chicago: University of Chicago Press.

Park, Richard. 1967. *India's Political System.* NJ: Prentice-Hall.

————, and Irene Tinker. 1959. *Leadership and Political Institutions in India.* Princeton, NJ: Princeton University Press.

Paul, T. V. 2005. *The India-Pakistan Conflict: An Enduring Rivalry.* New York: Cambridge University Press.

———— 2000. *Power versus Prudence: Why Nations Forgo Nuclear Weapons.* Montreal: McGill-Queen's University Press.

————, and Baldev Raj Nayar. 2002. *India in the World Order: Searching for Major Power Status.* New York: Cambridge University Press.

Pearson, Margaret. 2000. *China's New Business Elite: The Political Consequences of Economic Reform.* Berkeley: University of California Press.

————. 1991. *Joint Ventures in the People's Republic of China: The Control of Foreign Direct Investment under Socialism.* Princeton, NJ: Princeton University Press.

Peebles, Gavin. 1991. *Money in the People's Republic of China.* Boston: Allen & Unwin.

Peerenboom, Randall. 2002. *China's Long March Toward Rule of Law.* New York: Cambridge University Press.

Pei, Changhong, and Lei Peng. 2007. "Responsibilities of China after Accession to the WTO." *China and World Economy* 15, no. 4, pp. 89–101.

Pei, Minxin. 2006. *China's Trapped Transition: The Limits of Developmental Autocracy.* Cambridge, MA: Harvard University Press.

————. 1994. *From Reform to Revolution: The Demise of Communism in China and the Soviet Union.* Cambridge, MA: Harvard University Press.

Pepper, Suzanne. 1978. *Civil War in China: The Political Struggle.* Berkeley: University of California Press.

Perkins, Dwight. 2006. "China's Recent Economic Performance and Future Prospects." *Asian Economic Policy Review,* no. 1, pp. 15–40.

————. 1994. "Completing China's Move to the Market." *Journal of Economic Perspectives,* 8, no. 2 (Spring): pp. 23–46.

————. 1969. *Agricultural Development in China 1368–1968.* Chicago: Aldine.

————, and Shahid Yusuf. 1984. *Rural Development in China.* Baltimore: John Hopkins University Press.

Perkovich, George. 1999. *India's Nuclear Bomb: The Impact on Global Proliferation.* Berkeley: University of California Press.

Perry, Elizabeth, and Merle Goldman, eds. 2007. *Grassroots Political Reform in Contemporary China.* Cambridge, MA: Harvard University Press.

Pipes, Richard. 1990. *The Russian Revolution.* New York: Alfred A. Knopf.

Podpiera, Richard. 2006, March. "Progress in China's Banking Sector Reform: Has Bank Behavior Changed?" IMF Working Paper No. WP/06/71. Washington, DC: International Monetary Fund.

Polyani, Karl. 1944. *The Great Transformation: The Political and Economic Origins of Our Time.* Boston: Beacon Press.

Potter, David C. 1986. *India's Political Administrators: 1919–1983.* Oxford: Clarendon Press.

Prasad, Eswar. 2005. "Next Steps for China." *Finance and Development,* **42**, no. 3, September: pp. 44–47.

———, Thomas Rumbaugh, and Qing Wang. 2005. "Putting the Cart before the Horse? Capital Account Liberalization and Exchange Rate Flexibility in China," IMF Policy Discussion Paper 05/1. Washington, DC: International Monetary Fund.

Prebisch, Raul. 1950. The *Economic Development of Latin America and its Principal Problems.* New York: UN Economic Commission for Latin America.

Prestowitz, Clyde V. 2005. *Three Billion New Capitalists: The Great Shift of Wealth and Power to the East.* New York: Basic Books.

Prybyla, Jan. 1970. *The Political Economy of Communist China.* Scranton, PA: International Textbook Company.

Przeworski, Adam. 1995. *Sustainable Democracy.* New York: Cambridge University Press.

———. 1991. *Democracy and the Market: Political and Economic Reforms in Eastern Europe and Latin America.* New York: Cambridge University Press.

Purfield, Catriona. 2006. "Is Economic Growth Leaving Some States Behind," in Catriona Purfield and Jerald Schiff, eds., *India Goes Global: Its Expanding Role in the World Economy.* Washington, DC: International Monetary Fund, pp. 12–36.

———. 2006a. "Maintaining Competitiveness in the Global Economy," in Catriona Purfield and Jerald Schiff, eds., *India Goes Global: Its Expanding Role in the World Economy.* Washington, DC: International Monetary Fund, pp. 56–72.

———, and Mark Flanagan. 2006. "Reining in State Deficits," in Catriona Purfield and Jerald Schiff, eds., *India Goes Global: Its Expanding Role in the World Economy.* Washington, DC: International Monetary Fund, pp. 109–27.

———, and Jerald Schiff, eds., 2006. *India Goes Global: Its Expanding Role in the World Economy.* Washington, DC: International Monetary Fund.

Putterman, Louis. 1993. *Continuity and Change in China's Rural Development: Collective and Reform Eras in Perspective.* New York: Oxford University Press.

Pye, Lucian. 1988. *The Mandarin and the Cadre: China's Political Cultures.* Ann Arbor: Centre for Chinese Studies, University of Michigan.

———. 1981. *The Dynamics of Chinese Politics.* Cambridge, MA: Oelgeschlager, Gunn and Hain.

Pyle, Kenneth. 2007. *Japan Rising: The Resurgence of Japanese Power and Purpose.* New York: Public Affairs.

Pylee, M. V. 1992. *India's Constitution.* New Delhi: S. Chand.

Qian, Yingyi, and Jinglian Wu. 2003. "China's Transition to a Market Economy: How Far across the River?" in Nicholas Hope, Dennis Tao Yang, and Mu Yang Li, eds., *How Far across the River? Chinese Policy Reform at the Millennium.* Stanford, CA: Stanford University Press, pp. 31–63.

————, and Chenggang Xu. 1993. "Why China's Economic Reforms Differ: The M-Form Hierarchy and Entry/Expansion of the Non-State Sector." *Economics of Transition*, **1**, (June).

Qing, Simei. 2007. *From Allies to Enemies: Visions of Modernity, Identity and U.S.-China Diplomacy, 1945–1960*. Cambridge, MA: Harvard University Press.

Radhakrishna, R. 2008. *India Development Report: 2008*. New Delhi: Oxford University Press.

————, and K. Subbarao. 1997. "India's Public Distribution System: A National and International Perspective," World Bank Discussion Paper No. 380. Washington, DC: World Bank.

Rajagopalan, Rajesh. 2005. *Second Strike: Arguments about Nuclear War in South Asia*. New Delhi: Penguin Books.

Rajain, Arpit. 2005. *Nuclear Deterrence in Southern Asia*. New Delhi: Sage.

Rajan, Raghuram. 2006. "India: The Past and Its Future." *Asian Development Review*, **23**, no. 2, pp. 36–52.

————, and Luigi Zingales. 2003. "The Great Reversals: The Politics of Financial Development in the Twentieth Century." *Journal of Financial Economics*, **69**, no. 1 (July): pp. 5–50.

Ramesh, Jairam. 2005. *Making Sense of CHINDIA: Reflections on China and India*. New Delhi: India Research Press.

Rao, Govinda M., and Nirvikar Singh. 2006. "The Political Economy of India's Fiscal Federal System and Its Reform." *Publius: The Journal of Federalism*, **37**, no. 1, pp. 26–44.

————. 2005. *The Political Economy of Federalism in India*. New Delhi: Oxford University Press.

Rashid, Ahmed. 2002. *Taliban, Oil and the New Great Game in Central Asia*. New York: I. B. Tauris.

Ravallion, Martin, and Shaohua Chen. 2007. "China's (Uneven) Progress against Poverty." *Journal of Development Economics*, **82**, no. 1, pp. 1–42.

————. 2004. "Learning from Success." *Finance and Development*, **41**, no. 4 (December): pp. 16–19.

Rawski, Thomas. 2001. "What Is Happening to China's GDP Statistics?" *China Economic Review*, **12**, no. 4, pp. 347–54.

————. 1989. *Economic Growth in Prewar China*. Berkeley: University of California Press.

————. 1979. *Economic Growth and Employment in China*. New York: Oxford University Press.

Reserve Bank of India. 2008. *Weekly Statistical Supplement*. New Delhi: Reserve Bank of India.

Rice, Condoleezza. 2008. "Rethinking the National Interest: American Realism for a New World." *Foreign Affairs*, **87**, no. 4 (July/August): pp. 2–27.

————. 2000. "Campaign 2000: Promoting the National Interest." *Foreign Affairs*, **79**, no. 1 (January/February).

Richardson, Philip. 1999. *Economic Change in China, c. 1800–1950*. New York: Cambridge University Press.

Riedel, James, Jing Jin, and Jian Gao. 2007. *How China Grows: Investment, Finance and Reform*. Princeton, NJ: Princeton University Press.

Riskin, Carl. 1987. *China's Political Economy: The Quest for Development since 1949.* New York: Oxford University Press.

Rodden, Jonathan. 2002. "The Dilemma of Fiscal Federalism: Grants and Fiscal Performance around the World." *American Journal of Political Science,* **46**, no. 3, pp. 670–87.

Rodrik, Dani, and Arvind Subramanian. 2005. "From Hindu Growth to Productivity Surge: The Mystery of the Indian Growth Transition." *IMF Staff Papers,* **52**, no. 2, pp. 193–228.

_____. 2004. "Why India Can Grow at 7 Percent a Year or More: Projections and Reflections." *Economic and Political Weekly,* **39**, no. 16, pp. 1591–96.

Rosecrance, Richard. 1999. *The Rise of the Virtual State.* New York: Basic Books.

Rosen, Daniel. 1999. *Behind the Open Door: Foreign Enterprises in the Chinese Marketplace.* Washington, DC: Institute for International Economics.

Rosen, George. 1992. *Contrasting Styles of Industrial Reforms: China and India in the 1980s.* Chicago: University of Chicago Press.

_____. 1985. *Western Economists and Eastern Societies: Agents of Change in South Asia, 1950–1970.* Baltimore: Johns Hopkins University Press.

_____. 1966. *Democracy and Economic Change in India.* Berkeley: University of California Press.

Rosen, Stephen. 1996. *Societies and Military Power: India and Its Armies.* Ithaca, NY: Cornell University Press.

Rothermund, Dietmar. 1988. *An Economic History of India: From Pre-Colonial Times to 1986.* London: Croom Helm.

Rotter, Andrew. 2000. *Comrades at Odds: The United States and India, 1947–1964.* Ithaca, NY: Cornell University Press.

Rowan, Roy. 2004. *Chasing the Dragon: A Veteran Journalist's Firsthand Account of the 1949 Chinese Revolution.* Guilford: Lyons Press.

Roy, Denny. 2003. *Taiwan: A Political History.* Ithaca, NY: Cornell University Press.

Roy, Tirtankar. 2005. *Rethinking Economic Change in India: Labor and Livelihood.* London: Routledge.

Rozhkov, Dmitriy. 2006. "On the Way to a World-Class Banking Sector," in Catriona Purfield and Jerald Schiff, eds., *India Goes Global: Its Expanding Role in the World Economy.* Washington, DC: International Monetary Fund, pp. 88–108.

Rozman, Gilbert. 1987. *The Chinese Debate about Soviet Socialism, 1978–1985.* Princeton, NJ: Princeton University Press.

Rudolph, Lloyd, and Susanne Hoeber Rudolph. 1987. *In Pursuit of Lakshmi: The Political Economy of the Indian State.* Chicago: University of Chicago Press.

Sachs, Jeffrey. 2008. *Common Wealth: Economics for a Crowded Planet.* New York: Penguin.

_____. 2005. *The End of Poverty: Economic Possibilities of Our Time.* New York: Penguin.

_____, Nirupam Bajpai, and Ananthi Ramiah. 2002. "Understanding Regional Economic Growth in India." *Asian Economic Papers,* **1**, no. 3 (Summer): pp. 32–62.

Saez, Lawrence. 2002. *Federalism without a Centre: The Impact of Political and Economic Reform on India's Federal System.* New Delhi: Sage.

Saich, Tony. 2006. "Negotiating the State: The Development of Social Organizations in China," in Lowell Dittmer and Guli Liu, eds., *China's Deep Reform: Domestic Politics in Transition.* New York: Rowman & Littlefield, pp. 285–310.

————. 2001. *Governance and Politics of China.* New York: Palgrave.

Sainath, P. 1996. *Everybody Loves a Good Drought: Stories from India's Poorest Districts.* New Delhi: Penguin.

Samuels, Richard. 2007. *Securing Japan: Tokyo's Grand Strategy and the Future of East Asia.* Ithaca, NY: Cornell University Press.

Schofeld, Victoria. 2003. *Kashmir in Conflict: India, Pakistan, and the Unending War* London: I. B. Tauris.

Schram, Stuart. 1989. *The Thought of Mao Tse-Tung.* London: Cambridge University Press.

————. 1969. *The Political Thought of Mao Tse-Tung.* New York: Praeger.

Schurmann, Franz. 1968. *Ideology and Organization in Communist China.* Berkeley: University of California Press.

Schwartz, Benjamin. 1951. *Chinese Communism and the Rise of Mao.* Cambridge, MA: Harvard University Press.

Schweller, Randall L. 1999. "Managing the Rise of Great Powers: Theory and History," in Alastair Iain Johnston and Robert S. Ross, eds., *Engaging China: The Management of an Emerging Power.* New York: Routledge, pp. 7–17.

Scobell, Andrew. 2003. *China's Use of Military Force: Beyond the Great Wall and the Long March.* New York: Cambridge University Press.

Scott, David. 2007. *China Stands Up: The PRC and the International System.* London: Routledge.

Scott, James. 1998. *Seeing Like a State: How Certain Schemes to Improve the Human Condition Have Failed.* New Haven, CT: Yale University Press.

Scott, Robert E. 2007. "Costly Trade with China: Millions of U.S. Jobs Displaced with Net Job Loss in Every State," EPI Briefing Paper 188. Washington, DC: Economic Policy Institute.

Selden, Mark. 1988. *The Political Economy of Chinese Socialism.* Armonk, NY: M. E. Sharpe.

————. 1971. *The Yenan Way in Revolutionary China.* Cambridge, MA: Harvard University Press.

Sen, Amartya. 2001, "Democracy as a Universal Value," in Larry Diamond and Marc F. Plattner, eds., *The Global Divergence of Democracies.* Baltimore: Johns Hopkins University Press.

————. 1999. *Development as Freedom.* New York: Oxford University Press.

————. 1982. *Poverty and Famines: An Essay on Entitlement and Deprivation.* Oxford: Clarendon Press.

Sen, Bhowani. 1962. *The Evolution of Agrarian Relations in India.* New Delhi: Peoples Publishing House.

Service, Robert. 2007. *Comrades: A History of World Communism.* Cambridge, MA: Harvard University Press.

Shambaugh, David. 2008. *China's Communist Party: Atrophy and Adaptation.* Berkeley: University of California Press.

————, ed. 2005. *Power Shift: China and Asia's New Dynamics.* Berkeley: University of California Press.

————. 2002. *Modernizing China's Military: Progress, Problems, and Prospects.* Berkeley: University of California Press.

_____, ed. 1995. *Deng Xiaoping: Portrait of a Chinese Statesman*. New York: Oxford University Press.

Shane, Mathew, and Fred Gale. 2004, October. "China: A Study of Dynamic Growth," U.S. Department of Agriculture, WRS-04–08. Accessed under Electronic Outlook Report from USDA Economic Research Service.

Sharma, Shalendra D. 2007. *Achieving Economic Development in the Era of Globalization*. London: Routledge.

_____. 2003. *The Asian Financial Crisis: Crisis, Reform and Recovery*. Manchester, England: Manchester University Press.

_____. 2003a. "Is India's Poverty Falling? The Debate Surrounding the 55th NSS Round." *Indian Journal of Social Development*, **3**, no. 1 (June): pp. 33–43.

_____. 2002. "Politics and Governance in Contemporary India: The Paradox of Democratic Deepening." *Journal of International and Area Studies*, **9**, no. 1 (June): pp. 77–101.

_____, ed., 2000. *The Asia-Pacific in the New Millennium: Geopolitics, Security and Foreign Policy*. Berkeley: Institute of East Asian Studies, University of California.

_____. 1999. *Development and Democracy in India*. Boulder, CO: Lynne Rienner.

Shirk, Susan. 2007. *China: Fragile Superpower. How China's Internal Politics Could Derail Its Peaceful Rise*. New York: Oxford University Press.

_____. 1993. *The Political Logic of Economic Reform in China*. Berkeley: University of California Press.

Shixiong, Ni. 2000. "Sino-U.S. Relations: A Chinese Perspective," in Shalendra D. Sharma, ed., *The Asia-Pacific in the New Millennium: Geopolitics, Security and Foreign Policy*. Berkeley: Institute of East Asian Studies, University of California, pp. 52–82.

Shue, Vivienne. 1988. *The Reach of the State: Sketches of the Chinese Body Politic*. Stanford, CA: Stanford University Press.

_____. 1980. *Peasant China in Transition: The Dynamics of Development Toward Socialism, 1949–56*. Berkeley: University of California Press.

_____, and Christine Wong, eds. 2007. *Paying for Progress in China: Public Finance, Human Welfare and Changing Patterns of Inequality*. New York: Routledge.

Sicular, Terry. 1995. "Redefining State, Plan and Market: China's Reforms in Agricultural Commerce." *China Quarterly*, no. **144**, pp. 1020–46.

_____. 1988. "Agricultural Planning and Pricing in the Post-Mao Period." *China Quarterly*, no. **116**, pp. 671–703.

_____, Ximing Yue, Bjorn Gustafsson, and Li Shi. 2007. "The Urban-Rural Income Gap and Inequality in China." *Review of Income and Wealth*, **53**, no. 1, pp. 93–126.

Sidhu, Waheguru Pal Singh, and Jing-dong Yuan. 2003. *China and India: Cooperation or Conflict?* Boulder, CO: Lynne Reiner.

Singh, Baljit, and Shri Dhar Mishra. 1965. *A Study of Land Reforms in Uttar Pradesh*. Honolulu: University of Hawaii Press.

Singh, Jaswant. 2007. *In Service of Emergent India: A Call to Honor*. Bloomington: Indiana University Press.

_____. 1998. "Against Nuclear Apartheid." *Foreign Affairs*, **77**, no. 5 (September/October): pp. 41–52.

Singh, Manmohan. 1964. *India's Export Trends and Prospects for Self-Contained Growth*. Oxford: Clarendon Press.

Singh, Nihal. 1986. *The Yogi and the Bear: Story of Indo-Soviet Relations.* New Delhi: Allied.

Sinha, Aseema. 2005. *The Regional Roots of Developmental Politics in India: A Divided Leviathan.* Bloomington: Indiana University Press.

Sisson, Richard, and Leo E. Rose. 1990. *War and Secession: Pakistan, India and the Creation of Bangladesh.* Berkeley: University of California Press.

Siu, Helen. 1989. *Agents and Victims in South China: Accomplices and Victims in Rural Revolution.* New Haven, CT: Yale University Press.

Skocpol, Theda. 1995. *Social Policy in the United States.* Princeton, NJ: Princeton University Press.

———. 1979. *States and Social Revolutions: A Comparative Analysis of France, Russia and China.* New York: Cambridge University Press.

Slaughter, Anne-Marie. 1999. "Governing the Global Economy through Government Networks," in Michael Byers, ed., *The Role of Law in International Politics.* New York: Oxford University Press.

Smith, Donald. 1966. *South Asian Politics and Religion.* Princeton, NJ: Princeton University Press.

———. 1963. *India as a Secular State.* Princeton, NJ: Princeton University Press.

Snow, Edgar. 1961. *Red Star over China.* New York: Grove Press.

Snyder, Glenn H. 1965. "The Balance of Power and the Balance of Terror," in Paul Seabury, ed., *The Balance of Power.* San Francisco: Chandler.

So, Alvin. 2007. "Peasant Conflict and the Local Predatory State in the Chinese Countryside." *The Journal of Peasant Studies,* vol. **34**, nos. 3–4 (July/October): pp. 560–81.

Solinger, Dorothy. 1999. *Contesting Citizenship in Urban China: Peasant Migrants, the State, and the Logic of the Market.* Berkeley: University of California Press.

———. 1993. *China's Transition from Socialism: Statist Legacies and Market Reform.* Stanford: Stanford University Press.

Solomon, Richard. 1971. *Mao's Revolution and the Chinese Political Culture.* Berkeley: University of California Press.

Spear, Percival. 1961. *India: A Modern History.* Ann Arbor: University of Michigan Press.

Spence, Jonathan. 1990. *The Search for Modern China.* New York. W. W. Norton.

Sridharan, Eswaran. 2005. "Coalition Strategies and the BJP's Expansion: 1989–2004." *Commonwealth and Comparative Politics,* **43** (July): pp. 194–221.

Srinivasan, T. N., ed. 1994. *Agriculture and Trade in China and India: Policies and Performance since 1950.* San Francisco: International Center for Economic Growth.

———, and Suresh Tendulkar. 2003. *Reintegrating India with the World Economy.* Washington, DC: Institute for International Economics.

Starr, John Bryan. 1979. *Continuing the Revolution: The Political Thought of Mao.* Princeton, NJ: Princeton University Press.

Stavis, Benedict. 1978. *The Politics of Agricultural Modernization in China.* Ithaca, NY: Cornell University Press.

Stein, Arthur. 1969. *India and the Soviet Union: The Nehru Era.* Chicago: University of Chicago Press.

Steinfeld, Edward S. 1998. *Forging Reform in China: The Fate of State-Owned Industry.* New York: Cambridge University Press.

Stern, Robert W. 1993. *Changing India: Bourgeois Revolution on the Subcontinent.* London: Cambridge University Press.

Strange, Susan. 1996. *The Retreat of the State: The Diffusion of Power in the World Economy*. New York: Cambridge University Press.

Sun, Yan. 2004. *Corruption and Market in Contemporary China*. Ithaca, NY: Cornell University Press.

———. 1995. *The Chinese Reassessment of Socialism, 1976–1992*. Princeton, NJ: Princeton University Press.

Sundrum, R. M. 1987. *Growth and Income Distribution in India: Policy Performance Since Independence*. New Delhi: Sage.

Suri, K. C. 2006. *Parties under Pressure: Political Parties in India since Independence*. New Delhi: Centre for the Study of Developing Societies.

———. 2004. "Democracy, Economic Reforms and Election Results in India." *Economic and Political Weekly*, **39**, no. 51, pp. 5404–11.

Sutter, Robert. 2005. *China's Rise in Asia: Promises and Perils*. New York: Rowman & Littlefield.

Suzuki, Yasushi, Md. Dulal Miah, and Jinyi Yuan. 2008. "China's Non-Performing Bank Loan Crisis: The Role of Economic Rents." *Asian-Pacific Economic Literature*, **22**, no. 1 (May): pp. 57–70.

Swaine, Michael D., and Ashley J. Tellis. 2000. *Interpreting China's Grand Strategy: Past, Present, and Future*. Santa Monica, CA: Rand Corporation.

Tai, H. C. 1974. *Land Reform and Politics: A Comparative Analysis*. Berkeley: University of California Press.

Talbott, Strobe. 2004. *Engaging India: Diplomacy, Democracy, and the Bomb*. Washington, DC: Brookings Institution Press.

Tandon, Ajay, Juzhong Zhuang, and Somnath Chatterji. 2006. "Inclusiveness of Economic Growth in the People's Republic of China: What Do Population Health Outcomes Tell Us?" *Asian Development Review*, **23**, no. 2, pp. 53–69.

Tandon, Prakash. 1989. *Banking Century: A Short History of Banking in India*. New Delhi: Viking.

Tang, Tsou. 1986. *The Cultural Revolution and Post Mao Reforms*. Chicago: University of Chicago Press.

Tang, Wenfang. 2005. *Public Opinion and Political Change in China*. Stanford, CA: Stanford University Press.

Tannan, Mohan. 2001. *Banking Law and Practice in India*. New Delhi: India Law House.

Tanner, Murray Scot. 1999. *The Politics of Lawmaking in Post-Mao China: Institutions, Processes and Democratic Prospects*. New York: Oxford University Press.

Tanzi, Vito. 2000, November 20. "On Fiscal Federalism: Issues to Worry About." Paper presented at Fiscal Decentralization conference, International Monetary Fund, Washington, DC.

Taylor, Ian. 2006. *China and Africa: Engagement and Compromise*. London: Routledge.

Teiwes, Frederick. 1979. *Politics and Purges in China: Rectification and the Decline of Party Norms, 1950–1965*. Armonk, NY: M. E. Sharpe.

Tellis, Ashley J. 2007. "China's Military Space Strategy." *Survival*, **49**, no. 3 (Autumn): pp. 41–72.

———. 2006. *India as a New Global Power: An Agenda for the United States*. Washington, DC: Carnegie Endowment for International Peace.

———. 2001. *India's Emerging Nuclear Posture: Between Recessed Deterrent and Ready Arsenal*. Santa Monica, CA: Rand Corporation.

————, and Michael Wills, eds., 2007. *Domestic Political Change and Grand Strategy.* Seattle, WA: The National Bureau of Asian Research.

Terrill, Ross. 1992. *China in Our Time: The Epic Saga of the People's Republic from the Communist Victory to Tiananmen Square and Beyond.* New York: Simon & Schuster.

Thakur, Ramesh. 1995. *The Government and Politics of India.* New York: St. Martin's Press.

Tharoor, Sashi. 1997. *From Midnight to the Millennium.* New York: Harper Perennial.

Thaxton, Ralph E. 1999. *China Turned Right Side Up: Revolutionary Legitimacy in the Peasant World.* New Haven, CT: Yale University Press.

Thorner, Daniel. 1976. *The Agrarian Prospect in India.* Bombay: Allied.

Thornton, Patricia. 2007. *Disciplining the State: Virtue, Violence and State-Making in Modern China.* Cambridge, MA: Harvard University Asia Center Press.

Thurston, Anne. 1988. *Enemies of the People: The Ordeal of the Intellectuals in China's Great Cultural Revolution.* Cambridge, MA: Harvard University Press.

Tian, Weiming. 1998. *Dynamics of Development in an Opening Economy: China since 1978.* Commack, NY: Nova Science.

Tinker, Hugh. 1962. *India and Pakistan: A Political Analysis.* New York: Praeger.

Townsend, James. 1967. *Political Participation in Communist China.* Berkeley: University of California Press.

Transparency International. 2007. *Global Corruption Report: 2007.* New York: Cambridge University Press.

Trevaskes, Susan. 2007. *Courts and Criminal Justice in Contemporary China.* Lanham, MD: Rowman & Littlefield.

Tsai, Kellee. 2007. *Capitalism without Democracy: The Private Sector in Contemporary China.* Ithaca, NY: Cornell University Press.

————. 2002. *Back-Alley Banking: Private Entrepreneurs in China.* Ithaca, NY: Cornell University Press.

Tsai, Lily L. 2007. *Accountability Without Democracy: How Solidarity Groups Provide Public Goods in Rural China.* Cambridge, England: Cambridge University Press.

Tucker, Nancy Bernkopf, ed. 2005. *Dangerous Straits: The U.S.-Taiwan-China Crisis.* New York: Columbia University Press.

Tucker, Robert C. 1969. *The Marxian Revolutionary Idea.* New York: W.W. Norton.

Tzou, Byron N. 1990. *China and International Law: The Boundary Disputes.* New York: Praeger.

United Nations Development Program. 1999. *The China Human Development Report.* New York: Oxford University Press.

Uppal, J. S. 1983. "Agrarian Structure and Land Reforms in India," in J. S. Uppal, ed., *India's Economic Problems: An Analytical Approach.* New Delhi: Tata-McGraw Hill.

U.S. Congressional Research Service. 2008, March 7. *CRS Report for Congress: China-U.S. Trade Issues.* Prepared by Wayne M. Morrison, International Trade and Finance Foreign Affairs, Defense, and Trade Division, Washington, DC.

U.S. Department of Defense. 2006. *Quadrennial Defense Review Report.* Washington, DC: Office of the Secretary of Defense.

Van Welsum, Desirée, and Graham Vickery. 2005. "Potential Offshoring of ICT Intensive Using Occupations," DSTI Information Economy Paper, DSTI/ICCP/IE (2004)19/FINAL. Paris: Organisation for Economic Co-operation and Development.

Varshney, Ashutosh. 1999. "Mass Politics or Elite Politics? India's Economic Reforms in Comparative Perspective," in Jeffrey Sachs, Ashutosh Varshney, and Nirupam Bajpai, eds., *India in the Era of Economic Reforms*, New Delhi: Oxford University Press.

Vertzberger, Yaakov. 1984. *Misperceptions in Foreign Policymaking: The Sino-Indian Conflict, 1959–1962*. Boulder, CO: Westview Press.

Visvesvaraya, M. 1934. *A Planned Economy for India*. Bangalore: Bangalore Press.

Vogel, Ezra, Yuan Ming, and Tanaka Akihiko, eds. 2002. *The Golden Age of the US-China-Japan Triangle, 1972–1989*. Cambridge, MA: Harvard University Press.

Wachman, Alan. 2007. *Why Taiwan? Geostrategic Rationales for China's Territorial Integrity*. Stanford, CA: Stanford University Press.

Wade, Robert. 1990. *Governing the Market: Economic Theory and the Role of Government in East Asian Industrialization*. Princeton, NJ: Princeton University Press.

_____. 1987. *Village Republics: Economic Conditions for Collective Action in South India*. New York: Cambridge University Press.

Wadhwa, Charan. 1994. *Economic Reforms in India and the Market Economy*. New Delhi: Allied.

_____. 1977. *Some Problems of India's Economic Policy*. New Delhi: Tata McGraw-Hill.

Walinsksy, Louis, ed. 1977. *Agrarian Reforms as Unfinished Business: Selected Papers of Wolf Ladejinsky*. London: Oxford University Press.

Walker, Kenneth. 1984. *Food Grain Procurement and Consumption in China*. London: Cambridge University Press.

Wan, Guanghua, ed., 2008. *Inequality and Growth in Modern China*. New York: Oxford University Press.

Wang, James C. F. 1995. *Contemporary Chinese Politics*, 5th ed. Englewood Cliffs, NJ: Prentice-Hall.

Wank, David. 1999. *Commodifying Communism*. New York: Cambridge University Press.

Warriner, Doreen. 1969. *Land Reform in Principle and Practice*. Oxford: Clarendon Press.

Wasserstrom, Jeffrey N. 2007. *China's Brave New World – and Other Tales for Global Times*. Bloomington: Indiana University Press.

Waterbury, John. 1993. *Exposed to Innumerable Delusions*. New York: Cambridge University Press.

Wedeman, Andrew. 2003. *From Mao to Market: Rent-Seeking, Local Protectionism and Marketization in China*. New York: Cambridge University Press.

Weiner, Myron. 1962. *The Politics of Scarcity: Public Pressure and Political Response*. Chicago: Chicago University Press.

_____. 1963. "India's Two Political Cultures," in Myron Weiner, ed., *Political Change in South Asia*. Calcutta: Firma K. L. Mukhapadhyay.

_____. 1967. *Party Building in a New Nation: The Indian National Congress*. Chicago: University of Chicago Press.

_____. 1968. "Political Development in the Indian States," in Myron Weiner, ed., *State Politics in India*. Princeton, NJ: Princeton University Press.

_____. 1983. *India at the Polls, 1980*. Washington, DC: American Enterprise Institute for Public Policy Research.

_____. 1986. "The Political Economy of Industrial Growth in India." *World Politics*, **xxxviii**, no. 4, pp. 596–610.

————. 1992. *The Child and the State in India*. Princeton, NJ: Princeton University Press.

Weingast, Barry. 1995. "The Economic Role of Political Institutions: Market-Preserving Federalism and Economic Development." *Journal of Law, Economics and Organization*, 11, no. 1, pp. 1–31.

Weiss, Linda, ed., 2003. *States in the Global Economy: Bringing Democratic Institutions Back In*. New York: Cambridge University Press.

————. 1998. *The Myth of the Powerless State: Governing the Economy in a Global Era*. Ithaca, NY: Cornell University Press.

Wen, Dale Jiajun. 2007. "Too Much Growth, Too Little Development: The Reality behind China's Economic Miracle." *Development*, **50**, no. 3, pp. 30–35.

White, Gordon. 1993. *Riding the Tiger: The Politics of Economic Reform in Post-Mao China*. Stanford, CA: Stanford University Press.

————, Jude Howell, and Xiaoyuan Shang. 1996. *In Search of Civil Society: Market Reform and Social Change in Contemporary China*. New York: Oxford University Press.

Whiting, Allen. 1975. *The Chinese Calculus of Deterrence: India and Indochina*. Ann Arbor: University of Michigan Press.

Whiting, Susan. 2001. *Power and Wealth in Rural China: The Political Economy of Institutional Change*. New York: Cambridge University Press.

Wilson, Dick, ed., 1977. *Mao Tse-Tung in the Scales of History: A Preliminary Assessment*. London: Cambridge University Press.

Winters, Alan, and Shahid Yusuf, eds., 2007. *Dancing with Giants: China, India, and the Global Economy*. Washington, DC: World Bank.

Wirsing, Robert. 1994. *India, Pakistan and the Kashmir Dispute*. New York: St. Martin's Press.

Wolf, Martin. 2005. "Why Is China Growing So Slowly?" *Foreign Policy*, no. 146 (January–February): pp. 49–50.

Wolpert, Stanley. 2006. *Shameful Flight: The Last Years of the British Empire in India*. New York: Oxford University Press.

————. 2000. *A New History of India*. New York: Oxford University Press.

————. 1996. *Nehru: A Tryst with Destiny*. New York: Oxford University Press.

Womack, Brantly. 1991. *Contemporary Chinese Politics in Historical Perspective*. New York: Cambridge University Press.

————. 1987. "The Party and the People: Revolutionary and Post-Revolutionary Politics in China and Vietnam." *World Politics*, **39**, no. 4 (July): pp. 479–507.

Wong, Christine, Christopher Heady, and Wing Thye Woo. 1995. *Fiscal Management and Economic Reform in the People's Republic of China*. Hong Kong: Oxford University Press.

Wong, John. 2006. "China's Economy in 2005: At a New Turning Point and Need to Fix Its Development Problems." *China and World Economy*, **14**, no. 2, pp. 1–15.

World Bank. 2008. *Cost of Pollution in China: Estimates of Economic and Physical Damage*. Washington, DC: World Bank.

————. 2007. *World Development Indicators* (CD-ROM). Washington, DC: World Bank.

————. 2007a. *Strengthening Institutions for Sustainable Growth: Country Environmental Analysis for India*. Washington, DC: World Bank.

_____. 2006. "On-Line China Country Profile." *World Development Indicators*. Available at www.devdata.worldbank.org/wdi2006/contents/home.htm.

_____. 2006a. *World Development Report: 2006*. New York: Oxford University Press.

_____. 2005. *World Development Indicators 2005*. Washington, DC: World Bank.

_____. 2004. *Improving the Investment Climate in India*. Washington, DC: World Bank.

_____. 2003. *India: Sustaining Reform, Reducing Poverty*. Washington, DC: World Bank.

_____. 2003a. *Improving the Investment Climate in India*. Washington, DC: World Bank.

_____. 2002. *Globalization, Growth and Poverty: Building an Inclusive World Economy*. New York: Oxford University Press.

_____. 2000, January. *India: Policies to Reduce Poverty and Accelerate Sustainable Development*, Report No. 19471-IN. Washington, DC: World Bank.

_____. 2000a. *China: Overcoming Rural Poverty*. Washington, DC: World Bank.

_____. 1997. *China 2020: Development Challenges in the New Century*. Washington, DC: World Bank.

_____. 1983. *China: Socialistic Economic Development. Vol. 1*, Washington, DC: World Bank.

_____. 1997. *China Engaged: Integration with the Global Economy*. Washington, DC: World Bank.

_____. 1996. *World Bank Development Report, 1996*. New York: Oxford University Press.

Wu, Harry. 2007. "The Chinese GDP Growth Rate Puzzle: How Fast Has the Chinese Economy Grown?" *Asian Economic Papers*, **6**, no. 1, pp. 1–23.

Xiaoping, Deng. 1994. "Reform Is China's Second Revolution," in *Selected Works of Deng Xiaoping: 1982–1992*. Beijing: Foreign Language Press.

Xu, Chenggang, and Juzhong Zhuang. 1998. "Why China Grew: The Role of Decentralization," in Peter Boone, Stanislaw Gomulka and Richard Layard, eds., *Emerging from Communism: Lessons from Russia, China and Eastern Europe*. Cambridge, MA: MIT Press.

Yabuki, Susumu, and Stephen Harner. 1998. *China's New Political Economy*. Boulder, CO: Westview Press.

Yang, Dali. 1997. *Beyond Beijing: Liberalization and the Regions in China*. New York: Routledge.

_____. 1996. *Calamity and Reform in China: State, Rural Society, and Institutional Change since the Great Leap Famine*. Stanford, CA: Stanford University Press.

Young, Alwyn. 2003. "Gold into Base Metals: Productivity Growth in the People's Republic of China during the Reform Period." *Journal of Political Economy*, **111** (December): pp. 1220–61.

_____. 2000. "The Razor's Edge: Distortions and Incremental Reform in the People's Republic of China." *Quarterly Journal of Economics*, **115**, no. 4 (November): pp. 1091–135.

Yusuf, Shahid, Dwight Perkins, and Kaoru Nabeshima. 2006. *Under New Ownership: Privatizing China's Enterprises*. Stanford, CA: Stanford University Press.

Zakaria, Fareed. 2003. *The Future of Freedom: Illiberal Democracy at Home and Abroad*. New York: W.W. Norton.

Zebregs, Harm. 2003. "Foreign Direct Investment and Output Growth," in Wanda Tseng and Markus Rodlauer, eds., *China: Competing in the Global Economy.* Washington, DC: Interational Monetary Fund.

Zhang, Kevin Honglin, ed., 2006. *China as the World Factory.* London: Routledge.

Zhang, Li. 2001. *Strangers in the City: Reconfigurations of Space, Power and Social Networks within China's Floating Population.* Stanford, CA: Stanford University Press.

Zhao, Suisheng, ed. 2007. *China-U.S. Relations: Perspectives and Strategic Interactions.* London: Routledge.

————. 2004. *A Nation-State by Construction: Dynamics of Modern Chinese Nationalism.* Stanford, CA: Stanford University Press.

Zhao, Zhongwei, and Fei Guo, eds. 2007. *Transition and Challenge: China's Population at the Beginning of the 21st Century.* London: Oxford University Press.

Zheng, Yongnian. 2004. *Will China Become Democratic? Elite, Class and Regime Transition.* Singapore: Eastern Universities Press.

Zhengzheng, Gong. 2006, March 3. "Steel Sector to Produce Slim Profits This Year." *China Daily,* p. 9.

Zhou, Kate Xiao. 1996. *How the Farmers Changed China: Power of the People.* Boulder, CO: Westview Press.

Zweig, David. 2002. *Internationalizing China: Domestic Interests and Global Linkages.* Ithaca, NY: Cornell University Press.

————. 1997. *Freeing China's Farmers: Rural Restructuring in the Reform Era.* Armonk, NY: M. E. Sharpe.

————, and Bi Jianhai. 2005. "China's Global Hunt for Energy." *Foreign Affairs,* **84,** no. 5 (September/October): pp. 25–38.

————, and Chen Zhimin, eds. 2007. *China's Reforms and International Political Economy.* London: Routledge.

Index

economic globalization
  capital flows, 270–271
  convergence, 272
  exchange rate stabilization, 272–273
  global financial system participation,
    271–272
  poverty reduction, 274–275
  sovereign wealth fund, 273–274
  subprime debt exposure, 271
economic reforms (China)
  fiscal/administrative decentralization,
    64–65
  industrial sector, 61–64
  investment and banking sectors, 66–69
  to modern market economy, 69–73
  rural sector, 56–60
  special economic zone (SEZ) creation,
    65–66
  township and village enterprises (TVEs),
    60, 61, 70
economic reforms (India)
  economic foundations (pre-1991), 75–76
  economic liberalization program, 77
  macroeconomic reforms, 77–79
  political economy of reforms, 87–90
  structural reforms
    FDI regime, 83–84
    financial sector, 84–87
    fiscal federalism, 79–82
    industrial policy, 82–83
    outcomes, 87
electorate participation, 264–265
emergency rule (India), 15, 17, 38, 39
energy consumption/demands, 168–169,
  252–254
Energy Information Administration (EIA),
  253
Engaging India (Talbott), 190
environmental stresses, 254–256
Essential Commodities Act (1955), 151
ETDZ (Economic and Technological Zones),
  66
export processing zones (EPZs), 84, 146, 147

Factories Act (1948), 151
family farming, 58, 59
federalism
  fiscal, 18–19, 154–158
  forms of, distinction between, 80
  quasi-federalism, 111–112
fenshuizhi (tax sharing system), 71–72
Fernandes, George, 176–177
fertilizer prices/subsidies, 150–151, 250
Finance Commission, 79

financial/banking sector modernization
  (China)
  commercial banking activities, 122–123
  financial system, 116–117
  foreign investment, 125–126
  governance/infrastructure requirements,
    126–127
  lending decisions, 117–118
  money supply growth, 118–119
  nonperforming loans (NPLs), 120–121
  policy lending, 117
  reform measures, 119–120
  regulatory/oversight role, 121–122
  WTO rules/obligations, 123–125
Findlay, Ronald, 132–133
FIPB (Foreign Investment Promotion Board),
  84
fiscal contracting system (*caizheng chengbao
  zhi*), 64
fiscal deficit (India)
  economic liberalization, 156–157
  government transfers, 155–156
  interjurisdictional competition, 157–158
  size of problem, 154–155, 158
fiscal federalism, 79–82
Fiscal Responsibility and Budget Management
  Act (FRBMA), 82, 154
Fissile Material Cut-off Treaty (FMCT), 192
"Five Principles of Peaceful Coexistence"
  (*Panchsheel*), 169–170
Five-Year Plans
  China, 44, 46–47
  India, 30–31
fixed-tenure system (China), 75
food crisis, global
  agriculture subsidization, 252
  biofuel policies, 249
  export restrictions, 250
  farm output/productivity, 251
  fertilizer/pesticide prices, 250
  food-aid, 251–252
  foodgrain demand, 249
  global prices, 248–249
  single-currency system, 249–250
  supply response, 250–251
foodgrain production, 35–36, 249
foreign direct investment (FDI), 67, 259
foreign exchange markets (China), 70–71, 226
Foreign Exchange Regulation Act (FERA), 37,
  83
Foreign Investment Promotion Board (FIPB),
  84
foreign trade reforms (China), 66–69
Frankel, Francine, 33